Periodical Famines

Periodical FAMINES

Irish Memories
in Transatlantic News Media,
1845–1919

Lindsay Janssen

Indiana University Press

This book is a publication of

Indiana University Press
Office of Scholarly Publishing
Herman B Wells Library 350
1320 East 10th Street
Bloomington, Indiana 47405 USA

iupress.org

First Printing 2025

Cataloging information is available from the Library of Congress.

ISBN 978-0-253-07189-7 (hardback)
ISBN 978-0-253-07190-3 (paperback)
ISBN 978-0-253-07191-0 (web PDF)

CONTENTS

ACKNOWLEDGMENTS

This project was made possible by the financial support of the Irish Research Council (IRC); through one of its individual two-year Government of Ireland Postdoctoral (GOIPD) research grants (Project ID: GOIPD/2017/1133), I was able to do most of the research and part of the writing for *Periodical Famines*.

The corpus of periodical materials at the heart of this book was partially collected online. With the help of individual and institutional subscriptions, I made use of the Irish Newspaper Archive and the British Newspaper Archive. I am grateful for great open access resources such as the Library of Congress's Chronicling America project, Canadiana, the Bibliothèque et Archives nationales du Québec (BAnQ), the Boston College Newspapers collection, the HathiTrust digital collection, and the Internet Archive.[1] I also visited several research libraries and archives: Library and Archives Canada (Ottawa), Concordia University Library (Montreal), the Hesburgh Libraries at Notre Dame (South Bend), Boston Public Library (BPL), the Library of Congress (Washington, DC), the British Library (London), the Dublin City Library, and the National Library of Ireland (NLI; Dublin). Many thanks to the kind staff at these libraries and archives for their assistance. Images and texts included in this book are part of the collections of the BAnQ, NLI, BPL, and Hesburgh Libraries; thanks to these libraries and archives for the permissions granted to use their materials.

Parts of this book were published earlier and in a different form. Chapter 4 is an adapted and expanded version of the article "From Silence to Plenty: The Famine in Early Twentieth-Century Periodical Fiction." I want to thank *Éire-Ireland* and editor Vera Kreilkamp for permission to republish the piece. Some of the contextual information on Margaret Dixon McDougall and the Montreal *Witness* newspaper included in chapter 3 appeared in my chapter "From Special Correspondence to Fiction: Veracity and Verisimilitude in Margaret Dixon McDougall's Writings on Ireland," published in *Irish Women's Writing at the Turn of the Twentieth Century: Alternative Histories, New Narratives* (Brighton: Edward Everett Root, 2020). Thanks to the book's editors Kathryn Laing and Sinéad Mooney are in order.

Two anonymous reviewers and Chris Morash provided detailed feedback on earlier versions of this book. Many thanks to all three reviewers for their invaluable contributions to refining and deepening the book's argument and their support for its publication.

I am not going to provide a list of family members, friends, and colleagues who deserve thanks for their support throughout my longer academic journey; rather, I will limit myself to mentioning four people because of what they have meant for *Periodical Famines* specifically. Chris Cusack has been a great colleague and friend. He not only read and commented on parts of *Periodical Famines* and helped me reconsider arguments when I felt stuck but was also one of the book's biggest cheerleaders. Chris, many thanks for your friendship, collaboration, help, and infectious sense of humor. For my IRC fellowship, I was affiliated to University College Dublin (UCD). Living in Dublin is expensive, and I truly could not have done the project without Brian Dolan. Brian, thanks a million for your kindness and opening your Dublin home to me.

Margaret Kelleher was crucial to the project and to my development as an academic starting well before my time at UCD: we met when I did a research internship with Margaret at the research institute An Foras Feasa (Maynooth University) in 2010. We kept in touch, and in 2016, Margaret encouraged me to submit a GOIPD application. As my mentor, she was always available for feedback or a chat, going beyond scholarly input for the project. Margaret, my heartfelt thanks for your advice on the book, work in academia, and life. Even more importantly, thank you for the great conversations and your enthusiasm, kindness, and friendship.

Last but certainly not least, my biggest thanks go to Marc. Thank you for not being an academic and letting me be something else as well. Thank you for giving me the freedom to do this research project and for putting up with a wife who works in what can be a crazy field. Thank you for listening to my rants and countering my doubts. Most of all, thank you for your never-ending support. I could not have done this without you by my side.

Note

1. Chronicling America: https://chroniclingamerica.loc.gov/; Canadiana: https://www.canadiana.ca/; Bibliothèque et Archives nationales du Québec: https://www.banq.qc.ca/; Boston College Newspapers: https://newspapers.bc.edu/; HathiTrust: https://www.hathitrust.org/; Internet Archive: https://archive.org/.

Periodical Famines

INTRODUCTION

On May 25, 1901, the New York *Irish-American* published an illustration of an Irish eviction rendered as a battle scene complete with armed English troops, gun smoke, ominous overhanging clouds, and Irish peasants communally defending their homes. The illustration also contained a miniature with overtones of religious iconography of an elderly victim being cared for by an Irishwoman (fig. 0.1). The caption of the illustration read: "An Irish Eviction Scene under English Misrule." Two years later, the Wyndham Land Act, a key land reform introduced by the British government in Ireland, was passed. It "fundamentally transformed the nature of landholding in Ireland" and was a crucial step toward peasant proprietorship.[1] While the act was welcomed by some Irish commentators, others criticized it, including those writing for the *Irish-American*. In the run-up to the passing of the act, the highly popular newspaper reused the eviction illustration (fig. 0.2); again it featured prominently on the newspaper's first page. This time, the caption read: "What the New Land Bill Must End. From a Parliamentary return just issued, it appears that ten thousand tenants have been evicted in Ireland during the past twenty-five years, none of whom have been reinstated."

The reuse of the eviction illustration in the *Irish-American* provides a connection between 1901 and 1903; the caption draws the image back further, some "twenty-five years." If one revisits the 1901 illustration and takes

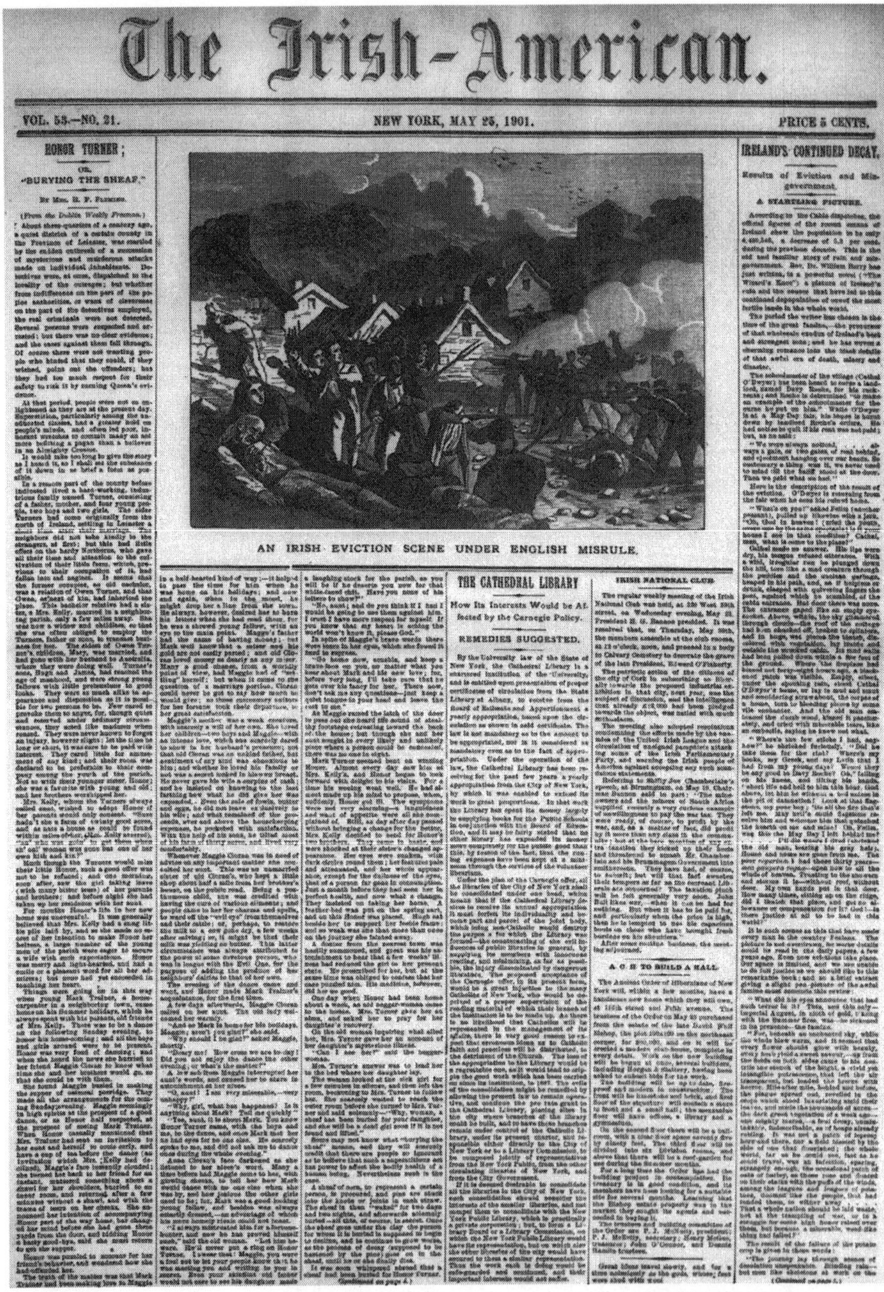

Figure 0.1. *Irish-American*, May 25, 1901, 1. Page including illustration "An Irish Eviction Scene under English Misrule." Source: Library of Congress.

Figure 0.2. *Irish-American*, May 23, 1903, 1. Illustration "What the New Land Bill Must End." Source: Library of Congress.

into account what else was included on the first page, the connection is extended even further into the past. Under the title "Ireland's Continued Decay: Results of Eviction and Misgovernment; A Startling Picture," the *Irish-American* placed a review with a lengthy excerpt from William Barry's *The Wizard's Knot* (1901) that included the novel's depictions of the Great Irish Famine of 1845–52. The review specifically pointed out the topicality of Barry's famine novel in relation to England's supposed misgovernment and concomitant present evictions. "An Irish Eviction Scene," "What the New Land Bill Must End," the latter's caption, and the excerpt from Barry's novel together establish a transhistorical cotextual effect: conjunctly, they establish a framework of suffering and evictions caused by English mismanagement of Ireland spanning from the mid-nineteenth to the early twentieth centuries. The newspaper used transhistorical combinations more often to provide commentary on different episodes in Ireland's recent history and its present condition.[2]

This example demonstrates key combinatory processes at the heart of *Periodical Famines*. This book investigates how recollections of the Great Famine, the biggest demographic disaster to hit Ireland in recent history, traveled in transatlantic Irish periodical culture and how recollections operated in comparative constellations. Analyzing newspapers and magazines published between the Famine and the early twentieth century, the book moreover examines how periodical elements paired cotextually on the same page or in a periodical issue inflect each other and collaboratively establish meaning. In so doing, *Periodical Famines* considers not only transhistorical links like the connection provided by the *Irish-American* but also links forged to other communities. Investigating how Irish famine memory becomes reinvested with new transhistorical and transnational meanings, the book explores the effects of appropriating existing memories and interpretations in later times and in different locations and periodical outlets.

During the period covered in this book, communication technologies, transport, and periodical publishing and reading underwent substantial transformations, and the British and American presses became increasingly transatlantic. By the turn of the twentieth century, within networks of newspapers and magazines, information was flowing more easily than ever. These changes affected Ireland too, as Irish port towns became important hubs within expanding networks of communication and transportation.[3] By 1900, the country had become "part of a globalized mass media industry and market." Because of the collapse of "physical boundaries of time and space" in the sharing of information, some scholars consider this era a Victorian precursor to the internet.[4]

This book focuses specifically on Irish, Irish American, and Irish Canadian newspapers and magazines, adding to existing scholarship on these sources by investigating transatlantic connections between Irish periodical cultures in Ireland, the US, and Canada. While a significant amount of research has been done on the British and American publication markets (examples include scholarship by Laurel Brake and Marysa Demoor, David E. Sumner, Joel Wiener, and Alan and Barbara Nourie) and the Irish American press (see scholarship by Matthew Frye Jacobson and the volume edited by Debra Reddin van Tuyll, Mark O'Brien, and Marcel Broersma), the Irish aspect of the transatlantic periodical market has remained understudied, with the exception of Cian T. McMahon's work.[5]

While previous scholarship in periodical studies has often focused on either newspapers or magazines, *Periodical Famines* considers both because of their shared audiences, contributors, and materials.[6] Doing so demonstrates hitherto underexplored connections across these types of print media. The book comparatively considers creative works (prose fiction and poetry) and nonfiction (news articles, opinion pieces, historical treatises, letters to the editor, editorials, and special correspondence) and the interplay between modes of writing in magazines and newspapers. Putting equal weight on creative works and nonfiction, the book crucially stresses the need to consider the former and literary magazines when exploring social, political, and economic debates.

Periodicals rose to the status of mass medium during the second half of the nineteenth century. Functioning as carriers and shapers of social, cultural, and political ties and identities, they helped establish "imagined communities"; for the Irish, scholars like McMahon speak of a "Greater Ireland," a global Irish community connected through periodicals.[7] The collective spirit established through periodicals also has a temporal dimension; tying the medium's orientation on the present to the establishment of communities, Margaret Beetham points out that by reading periodicals, "people imagined others reading the same words in the same dated publications but also in the same timeframe."[8]

Periodicals especially held community-building capacity for communities that experienced pressure on their collective identity, for instance through colonial oppression, emigration, and concomitant tensions and hostilities in receiving societies. In periodicals geared to Irish communities specifically, editors, journalists, literary authors, and correspondents in Ireland, Canada, and the US instructed readers on how to remain good Irishmen and Irishwomen while living in the New World, suggesting what sides to take in international events such as the US takeover of Cuba or the Boer Wars. They also suggested how to interpret and respond to events unfolding in Ireland, such as the Land War of the 1880s and the passing of the Wyndham Act. Historical pieces on both sides of the Atlantic honored the feats of rebels from Ireland's heroic past and more recent acts of rebellion by heroes of the developing Irish nationalist canon. Works of fiction such as Richard Baptist O'Brien's *The D'Altons of Crag: An Irish Story of '48 & '49* (1879) or Mary Anne Sadlier's *Bessy Conway; or, The Irish Girl in America* (1861) circulated in the transatlantic periodical market: these works contained heroic Irish ideal types to be emulated. In short, while these mass media functioned as outlets for entertainment and the news, they also functioned as instruction guides on Irishness and the Irish community's placement in a global context. As such, periodicals are valuable indicators of how Irish and Irish-diasporic communities fashioned collective memory and identity and of what enmities and affiliations they forged to other cultural groups.[9]

Through an approach that combines memory studies, Irish studies, and periodical studies, *Periodical Famines* contributes to existing scholarship. Analyzing how famine memory functions as a node in transatlantic periodical culture, the study makes three major claims. First, it argues for the vital significance of periodicals in the study of transhistorical and transnational patterns of how famine memory traveled. *Periodical Famines* innovatively adopts both quantitative and qualitative ways to substantiate circulation patterns in transatlantic periodical culture, exhibiting that the Irish at home and in diaspora engaged with that fund of memory in sustained ways from the crisis itself until the early twentieth century. Through its focus on the periodical, the book moreover makes the case for the combined analysis of creative writing and nonfiction.

Second, the periodical corpus at the heart of this study shows the simultaneous existence of normative and divergent temporalities tied to famine memory, showcasing the subversive power of nonnormative Irish temporality. Through comparisons in which Irish famine memory is embedded to give meaning to later events, memory receives transhistorical critical potential, for example, clarifying debates concerning Irish land reforms from the 1870s to the early twentieth century. Transhistorical constellations place the Famine in historical trajectories that diverge from normative British notions of temporality and progress; in so doing, they conflate different periods of famine. Studying how famine memory travels within Irish transatlantic periodical culture elucidates alternative temporalities that swing from acknowledging stasis as dominant in nineteenth-century Ireland to advocating for and imagining different futures, typically in an anticolonial context.

Third, in transnational and diasporic comparisons, memories of the Famine are used in both competitive and noncompetitive or "multidirectional" ways (this term is discussed in more detail below).[10] Ranging from incorporation in US land reform debates in the late nineteenth century to inclusion in reports on famine and human suffering in India and South Africa around the turn of the twentieth century, transnational modes of memory comparison reinforce anticolonial opposition and economic criticism in a global context. These comparative acts also inspire transnational solidarity. Crucially, both the transnational and transhistorical comparisons central to this book show that in transatlantic periodical culture, Irish famine memory resists unilateral interpretations concerning the catastrophe's historical placement and meaning for the global Irish community.

This introduction ends with an explanation of the book's structure; first, it provides the theoretical framework for major claims made in the book.

RECOLLECTIONS OF THE IRISH FAMINE AS *NŒUDS DE MÉMOIRE*

As a portable fund of memory, famine memory has long been key to Irish cultural memory and identity formation. The examples from the *Irish-American* that open this chapter signify but two instances of how this fund was kept alive through periodical circulation. The Great Irish Famine formed the culmination point of dogmatic policymaking and inadequate administrative responses in British colonial practice and vulnerabilities within Irish society and economy. These factors included shortcomings of the colonial government's laissez-faire economic and political approach, poor land management, an outmoded system of landownership, and over-reliance on a single crop. In 1841, the Irish population had reached its highest point to date and counted about 8.1 million people; by the 1851 census, this number had fallen to about 6.5 million. Estimates vary, but about one million Irish died because of the potato failures. The demographic decline was caused by not only a loss of lives but also a strong rise in emigration; while substantial waves had occurred in earlier periods, emigration levels peaked due to the Famine, and some 1.8 million Irish moved to North America in the famine decade alone. Many continued to leave long after the Famine, and by 1890, four out of ten persons born in Ireland still decided to emigrate. Ireland's population would continue to decrease well into the next century.[11]

The Famine is considered a watershed in Irish history, and many scholars have noted its influence on Irish culture, politics, and society even today and across national borders. In recent decades, and especially since the sesquicentenary of the Famine in the mid-1990s, famine scholarship has witnessed a steady rise, leading to the establishment of the subdiscipline of Famine studies within Irish studies. The period has inspired many creative products; these include popular novels by Emma Donoghue (*The Wonder*, 2016), Paul Lynch (*Grace*, 2017), Joseph O'Connor (*The Star of the Sea* from 2002 and *Redemption Falls* from 2007), Peter Behrens (*The Law of Dreams*, 2006), and Marita Conlon-McKenna (including her children's fiction *Under the Hawthorn Tree* from 1990 and her adult novel *The Hungry Road* from 2020), a graphic novel by Damien Goodfellow (*Black '47*, 2019) and films by Lance Daly (*Black '47*, 2018) and Tomás Ó Súilleabháin (the Irish-language drama *Arracht*, 2019). In music, works by Sinéad O'Connor and

Declan O'Rourke can be included: O'Connor released her song "Famine" in 1994, and O'Rourke released his concept album *Chronicles of the Irish Famine* in 2017 (the latter was followed by the novel *The Pawnbroker's Reward* in 2021). Examples from poetry include Máighréad Medbh's *Tenant* (1999) and Cherry Smith's *Famished* (2019). In dance, the famine eviction scene in Michael Flatley's *Celtic Tiger* (2005–6) comes to mind.

In his widely criticized bestseller *The Famine Plot: England's Role in Ireland's Greatest Tragedy* (2012), Tim Pat Coogan draws skewed analogies between the impact of the recent financial crisis on Ireland and Irish–British relations during the Famine. In stark contrast to Coogan's polemic argument, Ireland's President Michael D. Higgins stated in 2016 that Europeans should learn from the Famine in their (rhetorical) approach to the ongoing European refugee crisis. Additionally, during the Famine Commemoration of 2020, Ireland's Minister for Culture, Heritage and the Gaeltacht Josepha Madigan drew parallels between the COVID-19 pandemic and the Great Famine, praising caretakers during the Famine and seeing "the same qualities of courage and commitment to others in our healthcare staff today."[12] The bases for these contemporary appropriations of famine memory vary widely, but they all demonstrate the continuation of combinatory processes examined in this study and the ongoing importance of famine memory for the global Irish community.

These present-day examples and the reuse of the eviction image and famine memory in the *Irish-American* underscore the oft-quoted dictum by Richard Terdiman that memory is the past made present. In similar vein, this book investigates how famine memory as a node informs broader political and cultural discourses. In so doing, it seeks to not only demonstrate how the Irish used Irish history in their own sociopolitical discourse and constructions of self but also further our understanding of how the Irish rhetorically reached out to other communities to give shape to their identity and political goals.[13]

MEDIUM AND MEMORY: TRANSATLANTIC IRISH
PERIODICALS THROUGH A CULTURAL MEMORY LENS

Transatlantic Irish periodical culture constituted a dynamic network for the circulation of famine memories. Highly responsive to the concerns and interests of its audiences, this periodical network testified to the continued topicality of famine memory for Irish and Irish-diasporic editors, authors, contributors, and audiences between the mid-nineteenth and early twentieth centuries. Cultural memory studies offers a particularly useful theoretical framework for studying how famine recollections in periodicals travel across time and space and provide later events with new meaning while, in turn, being inflected by these new connections. This book engages with the field's theorizations of narrativization and comparative uses of memory.

In transnational and transhistorical combinations of memory, different historic events are brought together to form stories about a community's past that carry meaning for its current identity and projected future, a process commonly termed "narrativization." Indeed, Astrid Erll writes of a "narratology of cultural memory," thereby referring to the close interconnections between narrative, individual and/or cultural memory and identity, and sociocultural context.[14] Narrativization often happens through the use of existing imagery and plotlines, and, as Ann Rigney contends, cultural memory is "by definition a matter of vicarious recollection."[15] Specifically, the process in which "existent media . . . provide schemata for new experience and its representation" is known as "premediation" in memory studies.[16] In line with this insight, famine scholar Jenny Edkins posits not only that "existing discourses on famine" "produce [the object of study] in a particular way" but also that premediation happens in transnational constellations.[17]

The periodical format has its own forms of time representation and management predicated on both sameness and change, known and unknown. It also has a premediating function, as it offers a material framework in which formal features help readers structure and interpret new knowledge. The periodical format's capability of presenting the new—such as a news item or a story or poem—as the known, making use of characteristics such as existing sections, departments, and columns, helps categorize the world. As James Mussell explains, through this embedding, the new is not presented as a "disruptive symptom of an unknowable reality" but is rather turned into a "variation within a known system."[18]

In periodicals, narrativization of a past event into larger contexts can be informed by connections across texts and images. The interplay between different items on a page, within a periodical, or across issues of the same title has been a central consideration in periodical studies. Other texts included in a periodical, so-called cotexts, help to place texts within larger contexts of meaning, sometimes affording them "with unanticipated resonances."[19] Advocating cotextuality as a methodological approach, Linda K. Hughes suggests "moving and thinking sideways," as doing so can "make legible an array of temporal and material cruxes in print culture" and help scholars "explore, identify, and assess the convergences in printed text" in both their "original and remediated format."[20] When a magazine or newspaper is analyzed through a cotextual lens, it becomes clear how not only different texts but also different genres and modes of writing can interact and reinforce a specific message, rhetoric, or reading of an event. Additionally, the cotextual approach adopted by periodical editors and authors suggests a strategic, intentional practice that goes beyond simply combining elements on a page. Cotextuality can be considered a material manifestation of and support to the combinatory processes of recollection investigated in this book. To explore the transhistorical and transnational contexts in which famine memory functions, it is therefore crucial to read "laterally."[21]

Cotextuality demonstrates that meaning is constructed through reading both the "linguistic code" (the semantics or meaning of the text) and its "bibliographic code"—or more specifically, "periodical codes" (matters such as typefaces and layout)—at play in a magazine or newspaper.[22] The approach adopted in this book constitutes a dual consideration of the periodical medium and a methodological focus on cotextuality. This approach, which is novel in the context of Famine studies, allows us to study the narrativization of famine memory across texts and to analyze meaning-making processes between different funds of memory not included in the same text but on the same page or in the same issue.

The Famine as a Transhistorical Node

In 1846, the London *Times*, displaying famine fatigue, labeled Ireland's grievances "anomalous" and spoke of a "circulation of cause and effect" in Ireland.[23] In 1851, the American philanthropist Asenath Nicholson noted that her writings about the Famine appeared "out of common course, and out of the order of even nature itself."[24] These examples demonstrate that already during the crisis, commentators were noticing the diverging effect of the Famine on Irish temporality.

This temporal effect continued to feature in later considerations of the period and its aftereffects. On January 14, 1899, the New York *Irish World and American Industrial Liberator* reused an interview previously published in the *Pall Mall Gazette* in which Irish Home Rule politician John Dillon (1851–1927) spoke of "periodical famines" plaguing Ireland.[25] Dillon's phrase provides the title of the current study for three reasons. First, it obviously refers to the medium central to this book. Second, "periodical famines" serves as an apt label for the combinatory mnemonic processes related to famine memory found in Irish and Irish North American periodicals. Finally, the term neatly identifies the existence of a repetitive temporality in relation to famine memory, in which famines are a recurring feature of Irish life. Such understandings of history manifest frequently in the periodicals analyzed for this study, ranging from acknowledging the existence of stasis to imagining different futures. *Periodical Famines* seeks to demonstrate which underlying causes, present circumstances, and future possibilities are linked to alternative temporalities.

The concept of temporal divergence is central to postcolonial studies. Traditional Western historical consciousness has been predicated on linearity and a concomitant sense of progress. Traditional hegemonic views of development, aligned with what Jean François Lyotard terms the "grand récits" of history, not only ignore the plurality of temporalities but also see other temporalities as somehow deviant or lesser. Keya Ganguly explores the conceptualization of time in postcolonial studies; taking her cue from Ernst Bloch, she describes "non-synchronousness" (*Ungleichzeitigkeit*) as the "presence of distempered world views and modes of existence" within a present.[26]

Writing about the history of the novel in Ireland, Joe Cleary includes that in nineteenth-century Ireland, "different perceptions of the temporality of history" "were critical to various social tensions and conflicts."[27] Similarly, in his exploration of history, memory, and identity in Ireland, Ian McBride writes that different political orientations (loyalist vs. republican, separatist vs. unionist) informed diverging views on Irish temporality and could "not merely reveal rival accounts of the same events, but alternative cultural codes which give rise to different ways of structuring historical experience."[28] While McBride and Cleary focus on the national context, in *Periodical Famines* I show that the argument can be extended to the Irish-diasporic context. Moreover, my argument elucidates the interaction between such ideas and the temporal properties of the periodical medium.

For the purposes of this book, temporality is understood as describing a meaningful connection between past and present paired with a specific understanding of future prospects. Temporalities are often considered tied to a specific collective or collective experience—a post-Enlightenment understanding of progress, the British temporality of progress, or a nationalist rhetoric concerning the transition from colonial subservience to independence, to name a few. The definition adopted here is first and foremost meant to underline plurality and equality. In the British discourse of progress, Ireland was seen as backward and economically, agriculturally, and industrially out of step with the imperial center. In fact, as David Lloyd comments, Irish temporalities were not archaic or backward; they were adaptable forms "recalcitrant to capitalist logic" that continued to create rifts in the dominant discourse.[29] For example, the alternative understanding of progress as articulated in the cultural nationalism of Young Ireland caused a rift and reinstated temporal plurality by reinscribing the suffering and deaths of Famine victims, which otherwise were "effectively erased" in the "British narrative of progress."[30]

Some of the most telling examples of the coexistence of disparate world views are the different interpretations of the role and temporal placement of the Famine, which as "a topos of modernity" is "marked by conflicting temporalities and historical teleologies," as Christopher Cusack writes.[31] These temporalities show that the Famine can be considered a "memory crux." Memory cruxes, to quote Oona Frawley, "mark spaces that are not yet agreed upon" and offer "conflicting, oppositional, and sometimes intensely problematic answers about the way that a culture considers its past."[32] Because of this interpretative space, the Famine can become "something greater than itself" and not only takes on different meanings but crucially demonstrates "the failure of dominant systems to manage complex pluralities," as Anelise Hanson Shrout writes in her book on transnational famine philanthropy and its political discourses.[33] Some commentators—most famously Charles Trevelyan, assistant secretary to the treasury during the Famine—saw the crisis as "a transient evil" that in posterity would be seen as the "commencement of a salutary revolution in the habits of a nation long singularly unfortunate." In other words, the Famine was seen as a necessary evil that helped accelerate the modernization of Irish society, agriculture, and industry, thus fitting Ireland into a dominant teleology premised on the discourse of Political Economy. In this providentialist rhetoric, the Famine constitutes a turning point in history, the end point to supposed national deficiency or sinfulness and the starting point of a new era in which Ireland would modernize and adjust to the rest of the United Kingdom.[34]

At the same time, longitudinal views informed nineteenth-century millenarianism and were incorporated into Irish nationalist viewpoints during and shortly after the Famine. This view demonstrates a consideration of Irish temporality as continuous yet premised on an inescapable endpoint, with connotations of apocalyptic prophecy. As these examples show, the endpoint looked radically different depending on whether millenarian ideas were voiced by Irish nationalist or British commentators. Many Irish separatists interpreted the Famine as part of a continuum and, using the period as ultimate justification for the need for self-rule, hoped its excess of suffering heralded the end of foreign dominance; their views rejected the legitimacy of continued British rule in Ireland.[35]

When the periodical materials consulted for this study imply a divergence or irregularity to Irish temporality, they typically consider this temporality static or repetitive. An especially apt illustration can be found in "The Shadow of Death; or, The Story of the Old Larch Tree," published in the *Irish-American* on May 5, 1888. The story details the prolonged suffering of a poor Irish family between the smaller famine of 1879 and the Plan of Campaign of 1886–91, when renewed rural agitation and rent strikes took place. A dystopic dream sequence shows what would happen if the colonizer's path is taken (all family members except one son perish) and if the route of the oppressed is chosen (the son, mother, and a sister survive through resistance and allegiance to the Plan of Campaign). The story demonstrates that in facing the threat of repetition, the past can be used in subversive ways, providing alternative possibilities for the future. The very different uptakes on the meaning of famine included above demonstrate how different temporalities carry their own future possibilities.[36]

The terms "stasis" and "repetition" suggest a connection to cultural trauma studies, a connection far from uncommon in the context of the Famine. Jeffrey C. Alexander writes that "cultural trauma occurs when members of a collectivity feel that they have been subjected to a horrendous event that leaves indelible marks upon their group consciousness, marking their memories forever and changing their future identity in fundamental and irrevocable ways."[37] Cathy Caruth, one of the key scholars of cultural trauma theory's psychoanalytic branch, provides us with an influential definition that shifts symptoms from the individual to the collective sphere and ties in the notion of temporal deferral. According to Caruth, cultural trauma is "an overwhelming experience of sudden, or catastrophic events, in which the response to the event occurs in often delayed, and uncontrolled repetitive occurrence of hallucinations and other intrusive phenomena."[38] This Freudian-inspired explanation has become leading in public discourse on the Famine as a cultural trauma and is often tied to concepts of silence and absence. To make sense of how divergent Irish temporalities are represented in transatlantic periodical culture, *Periodical Famines* at points engages with the concepts of individual and cultural trauma. In so doing, it problematizes the applicability of the latter, for the periodical corpus resists notions of collective silence and absence as well as the blanketing effects associated with the term.[39]

While interpretations of the Famine's place in history and aftereffects differ, representations of the period share a reliance on a limited storehouse of imagery. Many of these elements are offered collectively in the illustration with which this book opens, visually supporting the transhistorical connection between the turn of the twentieth century and the Famine established through cotextuality.[40] The repertoire of imagery in fact partly predates the 1840s but quickly became emphatically linked to the Famine. Indeed, as Christopher Morash argues, "in the living skeletons and specters who materialise again and again in the pages of Famine writing, we see a discourse of Famine taking shape, with its own particular vocabulary."[41] As *Periodical Famines* demonstrates, during the postfamine nineteenth and early twentieth centuries, authors writing about other periods of famine also frequently used this repertoire.[42] In popular and cultural expressions of famine memory, some aspects of memory gained prominence over others. This form of narrativization through premediation demonstrates what cultural memory scholar Rigney has termed "differential memorability," a principal positing that "not all events are equally memorable because they do not equally lend themselves to the scarce number of cultural forms we have for talking about them." Differential memorability thus suggests that existing structures not only shape representations of newer events but also delimit their expression.[43]

The use of tropes and images from an established cultural storehouse led at times to the representational fusing together of different periods of famine predating and succeeding the mid-nineteenth century. Historical commentators did not always clearly differentiate between periods of famine and the Great Famine in their references—Margaret Dixon McDougall's journalistic and novelistic work, discussed in chapter 3, and William Carleton's novel *The Black Prophet*, discussed in chapter 1, are cases in point. Through premediation and referential unclarity, representations of the past become conflated.[44] Rather than seeing this as a narrative inconsistency, *Periodical Famines* argues that temporal conflation is a vital element of an Irish temporality that distinguishes itself from then-dominant British senses of time and progress. Regardless of whether such temporal unclarity is intentional or not, it impacts the ways the Great Irish Famine is embedded in larger narratives and discourses, inflecting potential interpretations of the effects of the crisis. This temporally ambiguous political dimension foregrounds premediation and how later famines are haunted by the memory of the Famine. Crucially, then, this study demonstrates the discursive political power of a divergent Irish temporality and its conflation of famine periods, exploring temporality's key role in political arguments for land reform and self-rule and against imperialism.

With regard to the publication of literary works in periodicals, Katherine Bode remarks that these works do not exist in isolation but rather "accrue meaning in the multiple contexts in which they are produced and received."[45] This remark is also valid for the circulation of memory in a periodical culture. At each instance of famine memory featuring in a periodical, its context and meaning are affected. Cotextuality is key in this process of accruing meaning; for this reason, the current study considers it a textual manifestation of the accumulation of historical periods.

The formal qualities of the periodical medium connect to the conceptual framework regarding temporality *Periodical Famines* borrows from memory studies. Therefore, periodicals are especially suited to investigate the different takes on the impact and temporality of the Famine that circulated in the societies that read and produced them. Considering temporality as a core theoretical concept and formal characteristic of the medium, *Periodical Famines* works toward a synthesis between memory studies and periodical studies. In other words, the book takes temporality as a common denominator, analyzing the translation of that shared characteristic to the pages of Irish and Irish North American periodicals and the interpretations of the Famine as a constituent element of Irish cultural memory in these outlets.

The Famine as a Transnational Node: Memory Comparisons

Discussing famine fiction written by the Irish in Ireland, Canada, and the US between 1847 and the early 1880s, Marguérite Corporaal speaks of "a shared transcultural memory with regard to the Famine."[46] Margaret Kelleher and Sourit Bhattacharya have studied representations of famine in India and Ireland, while scholars including Michael Silvestri, Kate O'Malley, and Amy Martin have analyzed the connections between the two locations on the basis of their nationalist movements during the nineteenth and twentieth centuries. This book examines such links as well, showing how famine memory is used in service of transnational, economic, nationalist, anti-British, and anti-imperialist rhetoric. Demonstrating the versatility and transportability of famine memory, as well as the jagged edges of cultural memories and identities, a study of transnational comparative uses reveals how Irish famine memory informs global paradigms concerning the consequences of British imperialism and reinforces anticolonial opposition in Ireland, the US, and Canada. My comparative approach demonstrates the political power of famine memory beyond the Irish context and shows how that memory inspired cross-community solidarity in multiethnic labor reform movements in late nineteenth-century America.[47]

Erll points out that across the humanities, different terms have been used to describe border-crossing acts of recollection and how we study them: "transnational, diasporic, hybrid, syncretistic, postcolonial, translocal, creolized, global, or cosmopolitan."[48] For the purposes of this book, two forms of spatial orientation are distinguished: diasporic and transnational. Diasporic subjects find their bearings by establishing relations to the home (or the concept of home), the diasporic space, and the receiving community. The diaspora is a space in which different consciousnesses meet, clash, influence each other, and overlap; as Avtar Brah explains, it provides room for the "confluence of narratives."[49] Additionally, I understand the diasporic orientation as reasoned from the perspective of the diasporic community and how that community stands vis-à-vis its receiving community. For example, for the Irish American community, the diasporic consciousness demonstrates concern with the home (Ireland), the community in diaspora, and that community's cultural survival in the US.

In contrast to a diasporic orientation, a transnational consciousness shows concern for others beyond one's own community; through such concern, what Edward Said calls "affiliation" can occur.[50] Of the different terms that memory studies scholarship offers for border-crossing acts of comparison, this study adopts the term "transnational." Memory studies acknowledges that the nation-state is no longer the natural container and goal of collective formations of memory. This does not mean, however, that our assumptions concerning the nation are no longer of importance when it comes to how we mentally delimit memory cultures. Memory studies has offered the crucial awareness that the concept of the nation exists alongside other frameworks of cultural production.[51] Consequently, nations are "imagined differently," to quote Aleida Assmann, "as inherently and externally relational, embedded and contextualised, always implicated in and partaking of larger processes and changes."[52] The processes described in the following chapters are best seen as acts of memory in which "scales of remembrance . . . intersect in the crossing of *geo-political* borders" and are, as such, transnational in nature. While the term "transcultural" also covers the processes investigated in *Periodical Famines* to an extent, it is less suitable than "transnational." This study considers how the Irish reached out to other cultures and used famine memories to give meaning to the plights of others; in that sense, the hybridization inherent to transcultural acts of memory does not take place.[53]

The views of newspaper editor Patrick Ford serve as an apt illustration of the difference between diasporic and transnational orientations. Ford's concern for famine victims in Ireland and his consideration of the representation of the Irish in the US can be seen as a diasporic orientation. However, in his combination of the plight of Irish laborers at home and of American workers—not just Irish American workers, as supported by the double orientation of his paper and its title, *Irish World and American Industrial Liberator*—Ford displayed a transnational consciousness. Through his concern for the well-being of those downtrodden by industrialization and the workings of the free market, Ford was oriented toward Irish, American Irish, Americans, and beyond, emphasizing their common plight.

When focusing on transnational connections, memory studies scholarship also takes into consideration potential ethical or moral implications. The "moral politics" of memory can be ambiguous, as comparison can offer "a conduit to recognition and empowerment" but can also stimulate "discrimination and exclusion."[54] When, for example, memories of famine in India and Ireland are brought into contact, are links established on the basis of similarity (a shared victimhood at the hands of an oppressor) or on the basis of difference and perhaps even competition (with respect to the degree and causes of suffering and distress)? Moreover, comparative use of memory often happens on an unequal basis. A substantial part of Irish studies scholarship and the Irish (diasporic) general public subscribes to notions of exceptionality concerning the Famine, which have given the period a prominent position in a global hierarchy of suffering. When recollections of the hardships of one cultural group weigh more heavily than those of others or are claimed to be unique, an empathic approach is made more difficult.[55]

Michael Rothberg explores mnemonic comparisons and overlaps between different memory cultures, acknowledging that such comparisons are often established on a competitive basis.[56] Rothberg explains that this competitive approach takes the guise of a "zero-sum struggle for pre-eminence" in which the public sphere is seen as a discursive space with limited room for the expression of cultural memories. However, he argues that we may adopt a more egalitarian approach that sees the public sphere not as confined but as a malleable space where various cultural memories come into contact, overlap, and help shape each other. He labels this stance a "multidirectional" ethics to memory. He describes multidirectional memory as "subject to ongoing negotiation, cross-referencing, and borrowing" and as "productive and not privative."[57]

In line with McMahon's work, *Periodical Famines* views the transatlantic periodical market as a discursive public sphere. In it, collective memories and identities are expressed, combined, and overlapped. I adopt a slightly modified understanding of Rothberg's multidirectionality to study these processes: while Rothberg considers the interaction between memories and the adoption of Holocaust memory by subjects from other cultural groups, in this study I do not analyze how other groups incorporate Irish famine memory (although it does sometimes feature). Rather, I focus on how the Irish send memory outward, establishing transnational constellations of memory to make sense of events happening elsewhere. Despite this difference, "multidirectionality" remains an applicable analytic term because the outward processes of comparison done by the Irish at home and in diaspora establish similar connections between cultural memories and identities of different groups.[58]

The periodical medium supports the diasporic and transnational dimension to memory comparison, as transnational links are created not only within the rhetoric of the text but also through the cotextual pairing of different periodical elements on the page. While a focus on the transnational is known in Irish studies, the current study moves beyond this existing paradigm. By demonstrating international publication patterns of creative works on famine (chap. 1) and analyzing in which transnational, often anti-imperialist, contexts famine memory was utilized, *Periodical Famines* demonstrates that Irish famine memories were of global relevance; it accordingly advocates for their further study in this spatial context.

The application of a memory studies methodology that focuses on comparative uses of memory demonstrates that in historical periodicals, recollections of the Great Famine were not just used in contests over who suffered most but were also incorporated in multidirectional ways.[59] Added value in the exploration lies in analyzing when this memory was used as a tool for the former and the latter. By adopting a cultural memory studies lens, *Periodical Famines* reveals that in periodicals, contrasting interpretations of the catastrophe circulated from early on and, crucially, existed simultaneously. Irish studies scholarship needs to be open to both these ways of considering the impact of the Famine to avoid confirmation bias and exclusionary corpus definition and to do full justice to the polyphonic character of a rich primary corpus.

The introduction and chapter 1, respectively, set up the theoretical and infrastructural parameters of this study; chapters 2 to 7 provide a series of case studies that demonstrate the processes of narrativization and diasporic, transnational, and transhistorical comparison described above. Morash, Corporaal, Fegan, and Kelleher have investigated the direct post-famine decades in detail for popular poetry and prose fiction, also within the periodical medium. In this book, I am especially interested in how famine memory is narrativized and appropriated in new processes of meaning making, processes at a temporal remove from the period itself. For these reasons, my case studies start in the mid-1870s. That does not mean that earlier decades do not feature in *Periodical Famines*; they are part of the overarching analysis of publication networks provided in chapter 1. Additionally, when chronological patterns are drawn in the subsequent case study chapters, earlier decades are included as well.

By necessity, the case studies included in this book do not provide an exhaustive representation of the vast primary corpus. Rather, they were chosen because collectively, they show the various ways in which memories of the Irish Famine are used as connecting nodes. The case studies contribute to existing scholarship on famine memory by focusing on unknown or little-known dimensions of familiar writings and figures and underresearched but fascinating materials that merit further scholarly attention. The latter include disparate genre forms and neglected journalism by editors and authors largely unknown outside of nineteenth-century Irish studies scholarship.[60]

The chapters are divided into two sections, "Transhistorical Connections" and "Diasporic and Transnational Connections." Since its occurrence, the Famine has been represented in various novels, short stories, poems, plays, books, and periodicals; this collective body of creative work is the focus of chapter 1. First analyzing a few extended publication histories of (once) popular and widely circulated works of fiction and nonfiction and then providing larger overviews of dissemination patterns for creative works including famine in the transatlantic publication market, chapter 1 offers an infrastructural contextualization for the case studies to follow. In periodical cultures of the time, using existing copy from other sources was common practice. Reprinting patterns have recently received more sustained scholarly attention; in the context of Irish periodicals, little has been done yet in this direction. Suggesting that reuse patterns—which include

not only reprinting but also adaptation and translation—can be considered
a material manifestation of comparative memory usage, chapter 1 considers both the longitudinal and geographical dimensions of the use and reuse
of famine memory, demonstrating the enduring topicality of this fund of
memory for the Irish at home and in diaspora. The chapter shows that the
Famine is never absent from creative writings between the 1840s and the
early twentieth century. Moreover, it quantitatively proves that in periods
of similar or related hardships, distress, and resistance, famine memories
feature more frequently in creative writings. This trend demonstrates a direct correlation between the increased presence of famine memory and sociopolitical relevance in later decades.

Covering materials published during the 1870s and 1880s, chapter 2
discusses the relevance of famine memory during a tumultuous period of
global economic downturn and renewed famine and the Land War in Ireland. It analyzes a selection of works of famine prose fiction and poetry
published or republished in *Young Ireland: An Illustrated Magazine of Entertainment and Instruction*. The chapter considers these texts in light of
how they engage with Irish sociopolitical issues of their time of publication,
as well as how they represent Irish temporality between the Famine and
the 1870s and 1880s. Although the works of fiction discussed in the chapter
can be seen to represent Irish temporality as static, that does not mean that
they all suggest or advocate for the same future directions. Indeed, proposed future trajectories vary from sanitized reimaginings of feudalism to
progressive adherence to Land League ideals of landownership for tenants
and the end of the landlord system. By extension, the chapter hypothesizes
that the variety of futures offered in *Young Ireland*'s creative works are the
result of literary genre parameters, temporal qualities of the medium, and
the period's transitional nature with regard to Ireland's rural class system
and land legislation.

In 1881, Belfast-born Canadian author and journalist Margaret Dixon
McDougall was commissioned by the Montreal *Witness* newspaper to act
as special correspondent in Ireland. While special correspondence by male
journalists has been studied in detail, this female correspondence has received only limited scholarly attention. Her letters for the *Witness* can be
considered early examples of literary journalism. Considering McDougall's
works within the context of insights offered by Paul Ricoeur and Hayden
White on the overlap between historical and fictional modes of writing in
the formation of narrative, I investigate the crossover between journalistic
and literary writing visible in McDougall's letters. To give shape to current

developments in Ireland, McDougall made use of established referential cultural repertoires. Moreover, her letters were published alongside famine fiction—Annie Keary's successful *Castle Daly; The Story of an Irish Home Thirty Years Ago* (1874–75)—that cotextually supported McDougall's use of famine memory as well as her political message. McDougall considered Ireland to be characterized by a temporality of repetition, which becomes visible in her use of memories of the Great Famine to describe contemporary famine conditions. In McDougall's correspondence for the *Witness*, recent events are narrativized through the narrative mold of famine memory in service of the author's overall call to abolish land monopoly and improve Irish tenants' legislative positions and property rights. Her work illustrates the discursive power of temporal conflation.

In the years following the passing of the Wyndham Land Act (1903), a substantial number of rural fictions and specifically famine fictions were published in the Dublin-based literary magazine the *Irish Packet*; these works of fiction are at the heart of chapter 4. In the early years of the twentieth century, firsthand memory of the Great Famine was becoming rare. In lieu of direct recollection, *Irish Packet* authors relied on shared narrative techniques and imagery to enhance and underscore the ostensible veracity and affective potential of their narratives. Building on the previous chapter's theorization regarding the interdependency of modes of writing, chapter 4 focuses on tension between fiction and historicity. Moreover, the narratives included in the magazine provide ways to remember the Famine ethically for those who did not experience it themselves, who belonged to "the generation after."[61]

Chapter 5 is the first chapter of the diasporic and transnational section. It returns to the 1870s and early 1880s, when several Irish American newspapers posited themselves as key advocates for workers' rights in the US. The chapter directs our focus to *McGee's Illustrated Weekly*, demonstrating how this New York magazine used famine memory to argue for better conditions for Irish laborers in the US and advocate support for their relocation to the US interior through the Catholic colonization scheme. The magazine strove to teach the Irish how to be good Americans, and in its creative works and nonfiction, it repurposed memories of famine to advocate a turn to rural life and work. Transcending temporal and geographical boundaries in the pages of *McGee's*, recollections of Irish hunger become tropes for radical uses of memory in a diasporic context. Back in Ireland, the Land League also sought to improve the rights of the rural population. Catholic colonization and the Land League were considered rival initiatives by some; as such, chapter 5 investigates the transatlantic debate about both in the pages of various Irish and Irish American periodicals. Finally, by exploring the transfer of connotations from Irish famine memory to US labor issues, the chapter demonstrates the cotextual effect of transnational and transmodal (between modes of writing) cross-pollination, two key dimensions of the book.

Chapter 6 moves to the turn of the nineteenth century and discusses Maud Gonne's periodical writings. This chapter contributes to existing scholarship on Gonne by exploring the combined discourse of Irish hunger and gender-based inequality in her nationalist and anti-imperialist writings, largely focusing on her contributions to the Dublin *United Irishman*. In her explorations of the injustices caused by imperial aggressor Britain, Gonne utilized Irish famines as examples of what nationalists saw as the British Empire's willful, destructive policies and argued that starving the colonized female constituted a symbolic political act of humiliating the subjected nation. This chapter explores transnational connections Gonne and the *United Irishman* drew between the colonial oppression of Ireland and the two Boer Republics around the second Boer War (1899–1902). In so doing, it explores unresolved tensions between traditionalist and progressive orientations in Gonne's gender politics.

Over several decades, comparisons were made between famines in India and Ireland in Irish and Irish North American periodicals; the New York *Irish World and American Industrial Liberator* frequently served as an outlet for criticism of imperialist practices. Economist and sociologist Robert Ellis Thompson was a regular contributor to the newspaper during the late 1890s, and his writings aligned with *Irish World* editor Patrick Ford's concerns for the downtrodden around the globe. As chapter 7 shows, Thompson contextualized representations of the Great Famine in a transnational framework by using his own childhood memories to represent the dire situation in contemporary India. Moreover, he placed Irish famine memories in service of a global economic and anti-imperialist argument in favor of self-rule, protective trade tariffs, and stimulation and diversification of home industries. Thompson considered his anti-imperialist and economic approach the only way that India, Ireland, and any country in a similar situation could stop being a "famine country."[62] His egalitarian approach to recollections of the Irish Famine functions in a multidirectional fashion and thus resists competitive memory and hierarchy formation.

The conclusion collectively considers the plurality of views on Irish temporality and the meanings of the Great Famine offered in Irish transatlantic periodical culture between the Famine and the early twentieth century, arguing that this plurality resists homogenization. Consequently, the conclusion proposes a critical reconsideration of the applicability of a traditional trauma paradigm to recollections of the Great Famine. Moreover, in reflecting on transnational acts of comparative recollection, the chapter applies Emilie Pine's concept of "anti-nostalgia" to famine memory; this concept suggests a future-centric perspective and is in my argument combined with Rothberg's multidirectionality.[63] *Periodical Famines* innovatively demonstrates that Irish famine memory had radical, transformative potential for the Irish at home and in diaspora—and that they envisioned this potential going beyond their own communities. The chapter stresses the added value of a synthesis between Irish studies, memory studies, and periodical studies when investigating the Famine's legacies. Specifically, it drives home the point that without the adoption of cotextuality as an analytic approach, the full breadth and depth of transnational and transhistorical uses of memories of the Great Irish Famine would not be visible.

Notes

1. Campbell, "Irish Popular Politics," 755.

2. "Ireland's Continued Decay," 1, 5. Cotextuality is discussed in more detail later in the chapter.

3. Wiener, *Americanization of the British Press*; Nicholson, "Transatlantic Connections," 164, 169; Morash, *History of the Media*, 84.

4. Rains, "City Streets," 143–44. Also see Morash, "Ghosts and Wires."

5. Brake and Demoor, *Dictionary of Nineteenth-Century Journalism*; Sumner, *Magazine Century*; Wiener, *Americanization of the British Press*; Nourie and Nourie, *American Mass-Market Magazines*; Jacobson, *Special Sorrows*; Tuyll, O'Brien, and Broersma, *Politics, Culture, and the Irish-American Press*. In *Global Dimensions of Irish Identity*, McMahon focuses on both the US and Australian Irish diaspora, exploring how members of the Young Ireland movement and their fellow Irish used newspapers to construct and express an international identity.

6. King, Easley, and Morton, "Introduction."

7. Benedict Anderson coined the term "imagined communities" in relation to the periodical press (*Imagined Communities*); see McMahon, *Global Dimensions of Irish Identity*. Janis also explains the validity of the term "Greater Ireland" in relation to the Land League and transatlantic Irish nationalism (see *Greater Ireland*). In her exploration of reactions to the Irish Famine and displays of solidarity for the Irish in the Canadian press, Pauline Collombier-Lakeman suggests that "the Famine may also be regarded as an imperial and even global issue." She adds that communication networks from the mid-nineteenth century onward were vital to this development (Collombier-Lakeman, "Canadian Press," paragraphs 1 and 43).

8. Beetham, "Periodicals and the Time of the Now," 332.

9. These works of fiction were also published in book form. R. B. O'Brien's *D'Altons of Crag* was first published in Montreal's *Harp: A Magazine of General Literature* in 1879–80 and republished in Dublin by James Duffy in 1882. Sadlier's *Bessy Conway* was first published in

the New York *Tablet* and by D. and J. Sadlier in Boston, New York, and Montreal in 1861. On affiliation, see Said, *The World, the Text, and the Critic.*

10. Rothberg, *Multidirectional Memory.*

11. Cronin, *History of Ireland*, 145; Ó Gráda, *Black '47 and Beyond*, 4, 9–10, 15–16. Ó Gráda refers to restraints imposed on official government aid during the Famine. Rejecting the interpretation of the Famine as a British act of genocide, he states that "if policy failure resulted in deaths," these deaths "were largely the by-product of a dogmatic version of political economy, not the deliberate outcome of anti-Irish racism" (9–10). Ó Gráda also discusses the matter of Ireland's heavy reliance on the potato, which made the blight a far greater demographic disaster there than in other European countries also hit by *phytophthora infestans* (15–16). Daly, *Social and Economic History*, 89. Kenny, *American Irish*, 89–90. Daly refers to a famine "decade" in a different way when she stresses that "in the worst-affected areas it lasted for more than ten years" ("Something Old and Something New," 75). Akenson, *Ireland, Sweden*, 171. Fanning, *Irish Voice*, 74.

12. Higgins in "Irish Famine," *BBC News*, September 12, 2016. Madigan, "Minister Josepha Madigan's Full Address," n.p. The commemoration was held on May 17, 2021. In his speech during the annual Famine Commemoration, President Higgins referred to O'Connor's song (Higgins, "Speech at the National Famine Commemoration").

13. Terdiman, *Present Past*. I am borrowing the term "node" from Michael Rothberg, who speaks of *"noeuds de mémoire"* (nodes of memory) when discussing multidirectional engagement with Germany's WWII history by immigrants. See Rothberg, "Multidirectional Memory in Migratory Settings," 128.

14. Erll, "Narratology and Cultural Memory Studies," 215.

15. Rigney, "Plenitude, Scarcity," 15.

16. Erll, "Remembering across Time," 111; See also Beiner, "Probing the Boundaries," and Bond, "Types of Transculturality," 62.

17. Edkins, *Whose Hunger*, 18.

18. Mussell, "Cohering Knowledge," 97, 101.

19. D'hoker, "Introduction to Special Section," paragraphs 3 and 7. D'hoker discusses short stories in magazines, but her comment can be drawn out to other periodical materials as well.

20. Hughes, "SIDEWAYS!," 21.

21. McCormack, "Never Put Your Name," 115.

22. Brooker and Thacker, "General Introduction," 5–6. See also Huculak, "Reading Forensically," 165. The terms "linguistic code" and "bibliographic code" come from McGann, *Textual Condition*.

23. *Times* quoted in Fegan, *Literature and the Irish Famine*, 41.

24. Nicholson, *Annals of the Famine*, preface.

25. "People of Ireland Demand Unity," *Irish World*, January 14, 1899, 1.

26. Ganguly, "Temporality and Postcolonial Critique," 174.

27. Cleary furthermore explains that unionists "largely subscribed to a Whig view of history that saw the Williamite Wars as securing a decisive expansion of modern liberties over absolutist despotism and 'old corruption,'" while nationalists "were more inclined to view these wars as a consolidation of a deeply oppressive process of domination." Cleary, *Outrageous Fortune*, 52–53.

28. McBride, "Introduction," 27.

29. Lloyd, *Irish Times*, 4.

30. Morash, *Writing the Irish Famine*, 102.

31. Cusack, "Memory, History, and Identity," 55.

32. Frawley, "Introduction," 2.

33. Shrout, *Aiding Ireland*, 10.

34. Trevelyan, *Irish Crisis*, 1. Political Economy is discussed in more detail in chapter 6.

35. Morash demonstrates that the poem "Foreshadowings" by Jane Elgee ("Speranza") considers the Famine as existing outside of linear time (*Writing the Irish Famine*, 111); he also discusses millenarianism in detail (ibid., chaps. 4 and 5).

36. 5; the story was published under the pseudonym Murty Mullowney.

37. Alexander, *Trauma: A Social Theory*, 6.

38. Caruth, "Unclaimed Experience," 181.

39. Ó Gráda firmly rejects the term "cultural trauma" for its homogenizing effects ("Famine, Trauma, and Memory," 14); See also Ó Ciosáin, "Was There Silence about the Famine?," 10; Frawley, "Introduction," 10. In the context of commemoration and monuments, Emily Mark-FitzGerald problematizes the idea of a "'cohesive' cultural memory of the Famine" and a supposed silence or absence of famine memory (*Commemorating the Irish Famine*, 7, 82–83). See also Corporaal, *Relocated Memories*, 8.

40. On visual representations of the Famine in nineteenth-century periodicals, see Mark-FitzGerald, *Commemorating the Irish Famine*, chapter 2.

41. Morash, "Spectres of the Famine," 76.

42. In a similar vein, Morash comments that by the 1870s and 1880s, images of famine suffering had become transferrable to other contexts and pointed to a "seemingly timeless rural suffering that, in the world of telegraph and steam travel, should have been banished" (Morash, "Ghosts and Wires," 26).

43. Rigney, "Remembering Hope," 371.

44. In my dissertation, I point out this dimension in fiction specifically (see "Famine Traces").

45. Bode, *World of Fiction*, 40.

46. Corporaal shows this shared transcultural famine memory in her book *Relocated Memories*, which covers the period 1847–70. The quote is taken from "Black Patches," in which she explores various works of fiction written between the late 1850s and early 1880s (251). In our PhD dissertations, Cusack and I explore such connections in popular prose fiction as well; see "Memory, History, and Identity" and "Famine Traces," respectively.

47. In chapter 4 of *Feminization of Famine*, Kelleher discusses literature of the Bengal famine. Bhattacharya writes comparatively about the Great Famine and the Bengal famine to contextualize readings of Liam O'Flaherty's *Famine* (1937) and Bhabani Bhattacharya's *So Many Hungers!* (1947); see "Writing Famine." Silvestri and O'Malley focus on the twentieth century in *Ireland and India* and *Ireland, India and Empire*, respectively. Martin discusses Irish representations of the Indian Rebellion; see "Representing the 'Indian Revolution.'" In *Multidirectional Memory*, Rothberg argues that cultural memories are not neatly separated entities but have jagged edges.

48. Erll, "Travelling Memory," 9, 10.

49. Brah, *Cartographies of Diasporas*, 183.

50. Said describes affiliation as a sort of "compensatory order" in the absence or failure of "filiation" or natural connection. Through affiliation, new allegiances are acquired by "social and political conviction, economic and historical circumstances, voluntary effort and willed deliberation" (*The World, the Text, and the Critic*, 20, 24–25).

51. De Cesari and Rigney, "Introduction," 1, 4.

52. Assmann, "Transnational Memories," 547.

53. Rothberg, "Multidirectional Memory in Migratory Settings," 129–30.

54. De Cesari and Rigney, "Introduction," 11.

55. Rothberg acknowledges that hierarchies are frequent effects of memory encounters ("From Gaza to Warsaw"); Ó Gráda argues that in collective memory, all famines produce a "hierarchy of suffering" ("Famine, Trauma, and Memory," 123). On hierarchy formation in the Irish context, see Kennedy, *Unhappy the Land*. For a broader consideration of hierarchy, see De Cesari and Rigney, "Introduction," 10; Craps and Rothberg, "Introduction," 518.

56. Rothberg in Moses and Rothberg, "Dialogue on the Ethics," 32.

57. Rothberg, *Multidirectional Memory*, 3.

58. McMahon, *Global Dimensions of Irish Identity*, 4.

59. Notions of exceptionalism also fed into considerations of the Famine as a cultural trauma (Ó Gráda, "Famine, Trauma, and Memory," 14).

60. Any acknowledgment of a canonical or core selection of periodicals would be a presentist interpretation of the historical corpus; indeed, with regard to the "enormity" of this corpus, Turner denies the existence of such a core ("Unruliness of Serials," 14).

61. Hirsch labels the descendants of those who experienced a highly disruptive event the "generation after" ("Surviving Images").

62. As chapter 7 shows, Thompson used this phrase more frequently.

63. Pine, *Politics of Irish Memory*, 8.

Section I
Transhistorical Connections

1

FAMINE PRINT PATTERNS

On April 7, 1900, just before Queen Victoria's visit to Ireland, the *United Irishman* published famous nationalist Maud Gonne's "The Famine Queen," an article that denounced the Queen for her role in causing "sixty years of organised famine" and evictions in Ireland.[1] The British government was less than pleased with Gonne's article. Alleging libel, the authorities confiscated all available copies of the *United Irishman* and suppressed the paper. This was not the end of the story, however: the article traveled far and wide. Just a day later, on April 8, the *Indianapolis Journal* reprinted excerpts from Gonne's article, accompanied by criticism regarding the suppression of the *United Irishman* lifted from the pages of Irish papers. Two days later, the *Wichita Daily Eagle* also included a substantial excerpt from Gonne's essay.[2] On May 12, the *Kentucky Irish American* reported that the article had been read aloud at a "meeting of the [Hibernians'] Ladies' Auxiliary Division 1 of Baltimore" and had led to the initiation of eleven new members.[3] Using information provided by the Dublin correspondent of the *Chicago Chronicle*, both the Minneapolis *Irish Standard* and the *Kentucky Irish American* included a denunciatory article about the suppression of the *United Irishman* because of "The Famine Queen."[4]

The article continued to receive extensive coverage. News about the storm caused by Gonne's article reached across the world, ending up in the pages of a Dutch East Indies newspaper. On May 1, 1900, less than a month after the article's publication in the *United Irishman*, the *Soerabaiasch*

Handelsblad: Staat- en Letterkundig Dagblad van Nederlands-Indië (*Surabayan Trade Journal: Political and Literary Daily Newspaper of the Dutch East Indies*) wrote about the suppression of the paper and took from a motion accepted by the Dublin City Council that "the majority of the Irish people would never be able to give its full and loyal support to the British government, and would never be satisfied until a National Parliament would be restored."[5] The dates above are indicative of the speed at which news could travel around the turn of the twentieth century. Moreover, the publication journey of Gonne's article demonstrates a pattern of Famine memory spreading not just across the Atlantic but also to other geographic contexts.

Visualizing patterns, the current chapter concerns itself with the geographical and temporal spread of famine memory in the transatlantic publication market. It considers the publication and republication of writings that include famine, looking at both periodicals and books. The chapter starts by exploring the publication journeys of three (once) best-selling book-length texts. Then, it analyzes patterns in the spread of creative writings on famine.

Additionally, textual representations of Irish famine circulated through reuse, a practice that not only shows connections between editors but also is indicative of and can enhance the popularity of certain subject matter.[6] Throughout the period this book covers, reuse practices were common in periodical production. They went beyond the covers of the medium, as materials published in book form in one place were integrated into periodicals in another (and vice versa). Reuse refers not only to practices of reprinting but also to revision, subversion, and translation; it refers, for example, to the translation from French to English of Gonne's "The Famine Queen" and the incorporation of an excerpt from a literary work in a printed speech.

The process of syndication through agencies like Tillotson's Fiction Bureau further facilitated the dissemination of texts in different periodicals. By the 1870s, syndication had become "highly systematic and nationwide in scope." Syndicators offered various materials, including fiction, advertising, intelligence, and material geared to specific target audiences, and delivered these on plates such as stereotypes.[7] This meant that materials could be set in combination before they reached a publisher. However, as my exploration of cotextual effects suggests, publishers consciously decided to reprint or combine materials. Editors thought about how to pair new and existing materials, how different texts could match and fortify each other's messages, and how historical/existing materials could be utilized to interpret and provide viewpoints on current developments.

This chapter is the qualitative backbone to this study. Crucially, it, for the first time, qualitatively and quantitatively endorses that in periods of related distress, famine memories feature more frequently in creative works (prose fiction and poetry). While a correlation between societal and political developments and creative engagement with famine memory demonstrates itself, the chapter shows that this fund of memory has a continued presence in the Irish transatlantic publication market between the Great Famine and the early twentieth century. Consequently, it shows that the publication of creative materials on famine operates within two temporal patterns: one indicating the continued presence of famine memory and the other suggesting its repeated resurgence.

Printing and Reprinting William Carleton, John Mitchel, and Annie Keary

Before the International Copyright Act of 1891 (also known as the Chace Act), transatlantic reprinting was common, though not embraced by all.[8] Borrowings were sometimes acknowledged; frequently they were not. In 1877, New York–based magazine *McGee's Illustrated Weekly: Devoted to Catholic Art, Literature and Education* discovered that the London *Universe* had copied installments of Margaret Anna Cusack's popular novel *From Killarney to New York; or, How Thade Became a Banker* shortly after they had appeared as original fiction in *McGee's*. Seeing this reuse as indicative of a larger problem, *McGee's* grumbled that "in the absence of all copyright legislation between us and Great Britain, foreign editors have the power to take up any American publication, book, magazine, or newspaper, and use it in what way they please, without the consent of the publisher or author." The magazine wanted to protect the "interest of the writers who have been kind enough to contribute to our columns, and who naturally expect proper recognition for their meritorious efforts to afford amusement and instruction to the public."[9] This was a two-way issue, as the rights of the works of foreign authors were not protected in the US either, and many British works were cheaply reproduced across the Atlantic. Reuse practices not only pertained to works of poetry and prose fiction; partially due to the unclear status of newspapers under the British Copyright Act of 1842, "the time-honoured practice of 'lifting' articles wholesale from other periodicals with acknowledgement but without authorization continued well after the mid-century."[10] When discussing the reprinting of nonfiction, newspaper editors of the time spoke of "scissors and paste journalism."[11]

With the help of digital humanities (DH) techniques, reprinting practices have recently received more sustained scholarly attention; in the context of Irish periodicals, little has yet been done in this direction.[12] At the time of writing *Periodical Famines*, the digital corpus of Irish, Irish American, and Irish Canadian periodicals is still relatively limited and not easily accessible for large-scale data-mining techniques. To find new and recycled periodical texts about the Famine, the current study has relied on traditional archival research, benefiting greatly from several digitized periodicals that can be accessed online (some through a subscription and others freely).

When considering reuse practices, it is important not to limit one's vision to periodical culture, as it did not exist in isolation but frequently and vitally interacted with the book publication market. The inclusion of (lengthy) excerpts from literature in newspaper articles such as the excerpt from William Barry's *The Wizard's Knot* (1901) mentioned in the introduction and the publication of Margaret Dixon McDougall's special correspondence in different formats (see chap. 3) are cases in point. Irish author Charles Kickham's works are another, as they were popular material for republication. His *Sally Cavanagh; or, The Untenanted Graves: A Tale of Tipperary* (1869) and *Knocknagow; or, The Homes of Tipperary* (1870) were frequently included in periodicals such as the *Hibernian Magazine*, the Dublin *Shamrock*, and the *Gaelic American* and were published in book form by James Duffy, J. J. Lalor, and W. B. Kelly in Dublin; Simpkin, Marshall and Co. in London; and Patrick Donahoe in Boston.

To illustrate the ways in which many (once) famous works traveled, this section explores the publication journeys of three key works that engage with the Great Famine: William Carleton's *The Black Prophet: A Tale of Irish Famine* (1846–47), John Mitchel's *Jail Journal* (1854), and Annie Keary's *Castle Daly* (1875). The journeys of these bestsellers speak to their long lives and transnational circulation as well as the enduring engagement with the Famine in transatlantic periodical culture. It should be noted that my research into republications that informs the publication journeys of Keary's, Mitchel's, and Carleton's books as well as the figures included in the section "Patterns of Creative Writing on Famine in Books and Periodicals" predominantly deals with known and attributed copies; as such, this study is preconditioned and influenced by contemporary parameters. While I have been able to locate a few anonymous or retitled reprints, many of these types of reprinting have gone unnoticed. Especially before the 1891 Copyright Act, untitled and uncredited reprinting of full works and excerpts was more common. The journeys of Keary's, Carleton's, and Mitchel's works therefore are not complete, but they certainly indicate the temporal and geographic spread of these works.[13]

While Carleton's *The Emigrants of Ahadarra*, a novel dealing with famine, was reprinted on both sides of the Atlantic, his *The Black Prophet* was most-wanted reprint material.[14] As figure 1.1 shows, *The Black Prophet* was first published as a serial in the *Dublin University Magazine* in 1846 and 1847 and was published in book form by Simms and M'Intyre in London and Belfast in the latter year. The narrative was published in periodical format in Ireland. Carleton's tale of famine suffering and prophecy, with its dark Gothic atmosphere, is set in 1817, but its lengthy and ghastly descriptions of famine suffering were undoubtedly very recognizable for reading audiences during the Great Famine. In representing famine conditions predating the 1840s but connected to the 1840s, *The Black Prophet* aligns with several other early works of famine fiction, as Marguérite Corporaal explains.[15]

Carleton drove home the transhistorical connection in *The Black Prophet*'s concluding chapter, stating: "'Time, the consoler,' passes not in vain even over the abodes of wretchedness and misery. The sufferings of that year of famine we have endeavoured to bring before those who may have the power in their hands of assuaging the similar horrors which have revisited our country in this. The pictures we give are not exaggerated, but drawn from memory and the terrible realities of 1817."[16] Because of the novel's continued popularity and because much of the imagery used by Carleton to describe an earlier period of famine would come to serve as the representational storehouse of imagery related to the Great Famine, *The Black Prophet* demonstrates the transhistorical nature of that storehouse and shows a temporal repetition reaching back to the prefamine nineteenth century. In this sense, the novel is an early example of the temporally diffuse representation of famine.

Carleton's work was highly anticipated; periodicals such as the *Belfast Newsletter* and the *Nation* announced its publication in ads and commented on the story as it unfolded. The *Leinster Express* of November 14, 1846, praised the author for displaying in *The Black Prophet* "his usual vigorous and truthful style."[17] These comments are indicative of the novel's

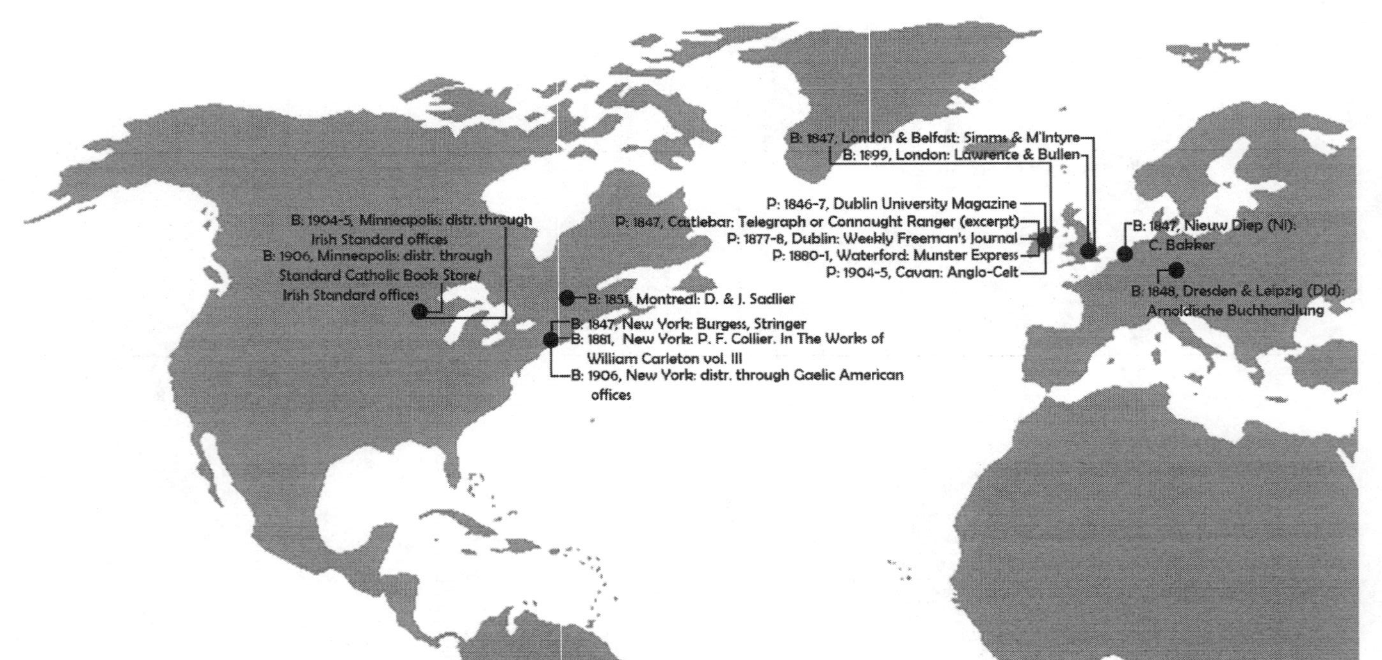

Figure 1.1. Publications of Carleton's *The Black Prophet*. *B* stands for book publication; *P* stands for periodical publication. Source for base map: Wikimedia Commons (public domain). Image created by the author.

coming success; it circulated extensively (see fig. 1.1). Shortly after its first publication, it was published in London, Belfast, New York, and Montreal. The London and Belfast editions of 1847 were included in the famous Parlour Library. While most publication venues were located within the transatlantic Irish community, Burgess, Stringer and Co. also published the novel. This publishing house was not specifically Irish (American) in orientation, suggesting a broader interest in Carleton's work from early on. Moreover, the book was translated to German and Dutch. Although in less devastating degree than Ireland, the Netherlands, Flanders, and central Europe were also affected by the potato blight; Carleton's novel was therefore of transnational relevance.[18]

Throughout the period *Periodical Famines* covers, *The Black Prophet* was republished repeatedly in book and serial form on both sides of the Atlantic. Newspapers placed regular ads to alert readers of new publications of the novel. The Montreal *True Witness and Catholic Chronicle* included ads for the D. and J. Sadlier edition of the novel in 1851, and in 1877 and 1878, the recurring "Notes for the Week" included in the *Freeman's Journal* made frequent mention of *The Black Prophet*'s republication on its own pages.

The *Freeman's Journal* of June 4, 1846, stated that Carleton's narrative "bids fair equal to the greatest of his works, he never displayed more knowledge of the Irish character, or human nature in general."[19] In 1890, William Butler Yeats praised Carleton in similar terms: in his letter to the *Nation* titled "Carleton as an Irish Historian," he described *The Black Prophet* as full of "impassioned scenes of entirely Catholic life" and called Carleton "this one great peasant writer of [the] country, the man who remained ever a peasant, one of themselves, full of all their passion, all their feelings."[20] The 1899 edition was illustrated by Yeats's brother, Jack B. Yeats, a successful artist and illustrator, further attesting to the status and appreciation of the book as a cultural product over fifty years after its first publication.[21]

Periodicals functioned as significant publication avenues from a didactic perspective, and their educational purposes were an important factor behind the continued circulation of Carleton's and many other texts. The novel was a regular feature on lists of suggested books, which often were sold postage free to readers. Indeed, the novel was included on these lists for its educational merit, as it supposedly aided Irish readers at home and in diaspora in knowing their history. On December 22, 1906, the New York *Gaelic American* argued that the Irish should read more and praised the Gaelic League for its efforts in this regard. In response to the titular question of the recurring item "Are the Irish a Reading People?" the newspaper reflected:

> If Not They Are at a Considerable Disadvantage. Every Nationalist Should Know the History of Ireland and Have Some Knowledge of her Literature and Poetry. . . . A new spirit has come into Ireland and is steadily spreading to the race abroad. They want to know more of the history and literature of the land of their fathers and to let their children know what a noble part the race has played in the world. . . . Every Nationalist family should have a supply of books that will give the rising generation the requisite knowledge and foster the race pride that is necessary to enable the Irish-Americans to hold their own. Without mental food they are at the mercy of the Anglo-Saxon propaganda.[22]

Carleton's novel was considered not only suitable to educate new generations on shared cultural identity but also beneficial to stimulate "race pride." The Minneapolis *Irish Standard* included *The Black Prophet* on its suggested reading lists as a "sensible holiday present" and, when not in the festive season, as one of the "Good Books for the Home and Fireside"; the book also featured on the Standard Catholic Bookstore's list. Both inclusions imply the novel's suitability for the act of communal reading within the home.[23]

In the 1870s, there was a global economic depression, and in the late 1870s and early 1880s, Ireland experienced an agricultural depression, a smaller famine, and a period of heightened tension and violence known as the Land War. Some two decades later, the 1903 Wyndham Act expanded tenant rights and tenants' possibilities to purchase land with state support. As such, it heralded the end of landlordism in Ireland. The republications of Carleton's *The Black Prophet* in 1877, 1878, 1880, 1881, 1904, and 1905 suggest that current hardships and issues provided this famine novel with a specific topicality.

Ardent nationalist, journalist, and popular historian John Mitchel wrote for various outlets on both sides of the Atlantic. Debra Reddin van Tuyll lists that Mitchel edited at least seven newspapers in two countries and corresponded for six newspapers from three continents. During his career, Mitchel became a contested figure, "a transnational symbol of what was both right and wrong about nationalism."[24] From first publication onward, his writings were republished often—in part or whole, in book or serial format. One example is his *Last Conquest of Ireland (Perhaps)* of 1861, which places the Famine in a historical context and sets out the argument that the Famine was but the latest British attempt to quell Irish resistance.

Figure 1.2. Publications of Mitchel's *Jail Journal*. Source for base map: Wikimedia Commons (public domain). Image created by the author.

The Famine featured frequently in Mitchel's writings, and his *Ireland since '98* delivered the oft-quoted slogan "The Almighty, indeed, sent the potato blight, but the English created the famine."[25] As Bryan P. McGovern explains, the advanced nationalist came to the conclusion that the Famine constituted an act of genocide. *Jail Journal* "proved to be Mitchel's most widely read and influential work," and it had great impact on subsequent nationalists.[26] In 1884, a "survey on the reading habits of the Catholic Young Men's Society" of County Cork listed *Jail Journal* as one of the most popular works; in 1915, the New York *Gaelic American* quoted a speech in which *Jail Journal* was labeled a "literary masterpiece." Intentionally or not, this appellation indicates *Jail Journal*'s generic position between history, personal memoir, and work of literature. The journal had significant formal impact: "it helped establish the prison memoir as one of the central works in the Irish nationalist canon."[27]

Jail Journal details Mitchel's response to being transported and imprisoned. It combines memory with history, affect with interpretation of fact. Mitchel's personal narrative is prefaced by a historical overview of Irish history that "imaginatively explor[es] the boundaries between personal and national history."[28] The preface is meant to demonstrate that this history "impelled a few Irishmen to brave . . . risks" against "their cruel and cunning enemy"; it furthermore defends the individual "contumacy and inveterably rebellious spirit" of *Jail Journal* as a whole. On the first page of that introductory chapter, Mitchel acridly exposes the "sanctimonious tale" of Britain's benevolence toward the Irish, ironically stating that Britain stretches "forth its open hand to relieve those same turbulent and now starving wretches, when Heaven smote the land with Famine—the anxieties, the cares, the expenses, that an unthrift island cost her more prosperous sister, who would not, for all that, desert her in her extremity, but would ameliorate her to the last."[29] If the biting tone of *Jail Journal* does not already drive home the deep sarcasm intended through this statement, Mitchel's continued attacks on British policy in Ireland—famously focusing on food exports while the Irish starved and the purportedly willful ousting, neglect, and extermination of the Irish—do. The historical overview furthermore includes the issues of free trade and British Political Economy, as well as Irish subjection to an "alien and hostile class of landlords" that together ensured the Irish were reduced to "starved skeletons."[30] Mitchel contends that the condition of famine is inherent to British domination, as "for twenty years after the Union the country was as absolutely prostrated in means and spirit as she seems to be now; and as a matter of course she had her cruel famine every year. Without a famine in Ireland, England could not live as she had a right to expect; and the exact complement of a comfortable family dinner in England, is a coroner's inquest in Ireland: verdict, *starvation*."[31]

With its polemic style, *Jail Journal* is a forceful indictment against British imperial rule. It was very popular within the transatlantic Irish community but offended more moderate Irish nationalists. Indeed, *Jail Journal* not only was very critical of Daniel O'Connell and his constitutional approach—stating that O'Connell had led the Irish "all wrong for forty years"—but also criticized some of Mitchel's former fellow Young Irelanders and their support for constitutional nationalism; the latter dimension of Mitchel's argument appealed to later Fenian sympathizers.[32]

Jail Journal (fig. 1.2) was first published in New York in 1854 at the offices of the *Citizen*, Mitchel's own newspaper. That same year, P. M. Haverty published it in New York; while most larger Catholic publishing houses in the US avoided printing nationalists' accounts of their own experiences or of court proceedings of their trials, the smaller Haverty was an exception. Haverty regularly produced its *Irish-American Illustrated Almanac*, and excerpts of *Jail Journal* were included in the 1886 edition of this publication "brimful of good things especially interesting to Irish readers."[33] *Jail Journal* and *The Last Conquest* had an important effect on the shape of Irish history, as Morash argues: in both readings, "Irish history after 1848 enters a state of suspended animation—suspended in the midst of famine." This interpretation of the impact of the Famine as heralding a period of stasis, abruptly halting Irish history, matched the experiences of members of Mitchel's readership who were part of the tide of famine emigration, suddenly forced to leave their lives in Ireland behind.[34] It also had a political purpose that came to be used often: the temporal stasis following the Famine served to stress the need to end British rule in Ireland.

In 1863, *Jail Journal* was published by James Corrigan in Dublin; the Dublin *Freeman's Journal* lauded Mitchel's book as "[a] work that should be read by all classes of Irishmen."[35] The *Nation* later republished parts of *Jail Journal*. The book received a sequel, and in 1869, the *Nation* serialized "a continuation of his *Jail Journal*" in the form of "John Mitchel's Journal" taken from Mitchel's *Citizen* newspaper. Alexander M. Sullivan became the sole proprietor of the *Nation* in 1858. He was a constitutional nationalist who in the 1840s had affiliated with the conservative faction in Young Ireland, not with Mitchel's radical brand of nationalism. Under his leadership, "the paper moved towards equating nationalism with Catholicism."[36]

Thus, while Sullivan's and Mitchel's nationalisms did not align in terms of conservatism versus radicalism and Catholic versus ecumenical approach, the *Nation* continued to publish Mitchel's work, testifying to the work's popularity as well as proprietor Sullivan's business acumen. In 1875, Cameron and Ferguson in Glasgow and London reprinted the book; in 1892, the *Nation* indicated that this publisher was to put out a new edition. *Jail Journal*'s fame lasted. In 1907, it was serialized by the *Kerryman*, and in 1913 Gill and Son published a new version, edited and prefaced by Arthur Griffith and accompanied by "the brilliant and terrible article in June in the famine year which appeared in the 'Nation' in 1847" and reprints of the *Illustrated London News* of 1848.[37] It was stressed that this was the journal as it had originally appeared in the New York *Citizen*.[38] In 1910, it was translated by Eóghan Ó Neachtain into the Irish *Irisleabhar Príosúin Sheáin Mhistéil* and published by M. H. Mac Goill (Gill) in Dublin.

Advertisements for the book were frequently included in periodicals. Throughout 1864 and 1865, the Dublin *Irish People* placed weekly ads; in 1916 and 1920, the *Gaelic American* and Philadelphia *Irish Press* advertised the book for $2.50 and $3.50, respectively. As was the case for *The Black Prophet*, didactic merit stimulated continued circulation, and *Jail Journal* was often included on suggested reading lists. The Chicago-based *Irish Republic: A Journal of Liberty, Literature, and Social Progress* frequently included Mitchel's book on its lists in 1868. In 1886, the Dublin *Irish Fireside* compiled a list of "the best fifty Irish books suitable for Irish homes" that contained *Jail Journal*. The book was included on a similar list by the Brooklyn *Gael* in 1900. Earlier, in 1877 and 1878, the *Nation* had repeatedly included it in the "Irish National Library," a catalog of "Standard Works" "no Irish Household should be without."[39] The book's inclusion on reading lists continued the original didactic ideals of Young Ireland, which its members had attempted to realize through nationalist reading rooms and the *Nation* in the 1840s. On January 17, 1891, the newspaper again mentioned *Jail Journal*, now among a list of "National Works" that could be ordered postage free from the offices of the *Nation*. The book, along with Mitchel's *Last Conquest of Ireland (Perhaps)*, was given as a prize to students who correctly answered questions about Mitchel's *History of Ireland*, again attesting to *Jail Journal*'s perceived educational strengths.[40]

As figure 1.2 shows, *Jail Journal* was frequently published in periodicals and books. Reprintings and advertisements demonstrate that the text was republished not only during times of renewed hardship and tension, such as the economic depression, failed harvests, smaller famine, and Land Wars of the period between 1875 and 1886 and the run-up to the Home Rule Act of 1914, but also outside periods of heightened turmoil. As such, continued publication of *Jail Journal* on both sides of the Atlantic shows sustained engagement with Mitchel's nationalist rhetoric by both Irish and Irish American sympathizers.

Annie Keary's *Castle Daly* (for an analysis of its plot, see chap. 3) was republished on a regular basis between the start of its serialization in 1874 and 1881, the height of the Irish Land War (see fig. 1.3). The novel was very popular, and its concentrated republications suggest that its popularity was due not only to the quality of the work and esteem for the author but also to its relevance in the late 1870s and early 1880s. *Castle Daly* tells of the sufferings of a kindhearted Catholic landlord family—the titular Dalys—and their tenantry during the Great Famine. It furthermore deals with the failed Young Ireland rebellion of 1848 and the protracted aftereffects of the Famine. Its preference for nonviolence can be considered a countervoice to Irish nationalist violence in a transatlantic context, as the rise of the Clan-na-Gael in the US throughout the 1870s made the threat of Irish American nationalist violence in the UK very real. Exploring effects such as emigration and the human desolation of the Irish rural landscape, the novel foregrounds the human cost of the Famine and praises Young Ireland's patriotic spirit while rejecting physical-force nationalism.[41]

This mitigated message partially explains the novel's broad appeal outside of Irish and specifically Irish nationalist publication outlets. *Castle Daly* was published in book form in London by Macmillan, in Philadelphia by Porter and Coates, in Dublin by M. H. Gill and Son, and in New York by G. Munro. Besides London-based magazine *Macmillan's*, *Young Ireland* (Dublin) and the Montreal *Witness* serialized the novel, the latter in daily and weekly editions. The *Witness* was a Protestant outlet, geared to a Canadian rather than Irish Canadian audience (see chap. 3 for a discussion of the *Witness*). In 1875, the *Nation* included excerpts in its review of the novel and repeatedly endorsed its serialization in its sister magazine, *Young Ireland*. It considered *Castle Daly* of great interest for Irish nationalists. According to the newspaper, *Castle Daly* was "the best novel of the season," despite some faults.[42] Keary's novel was also published in Leipzig, Germany, by Bernard Tauchnitz in 1875; unlike the German and Dutch editions of *The Black Prophet* in 1847 and 1848, Keary's novel was not translated but published in English as volumes 1547 and 1548 of Tauchnitz's substantial collection of British authors that was launched in 1841 and lasted over a

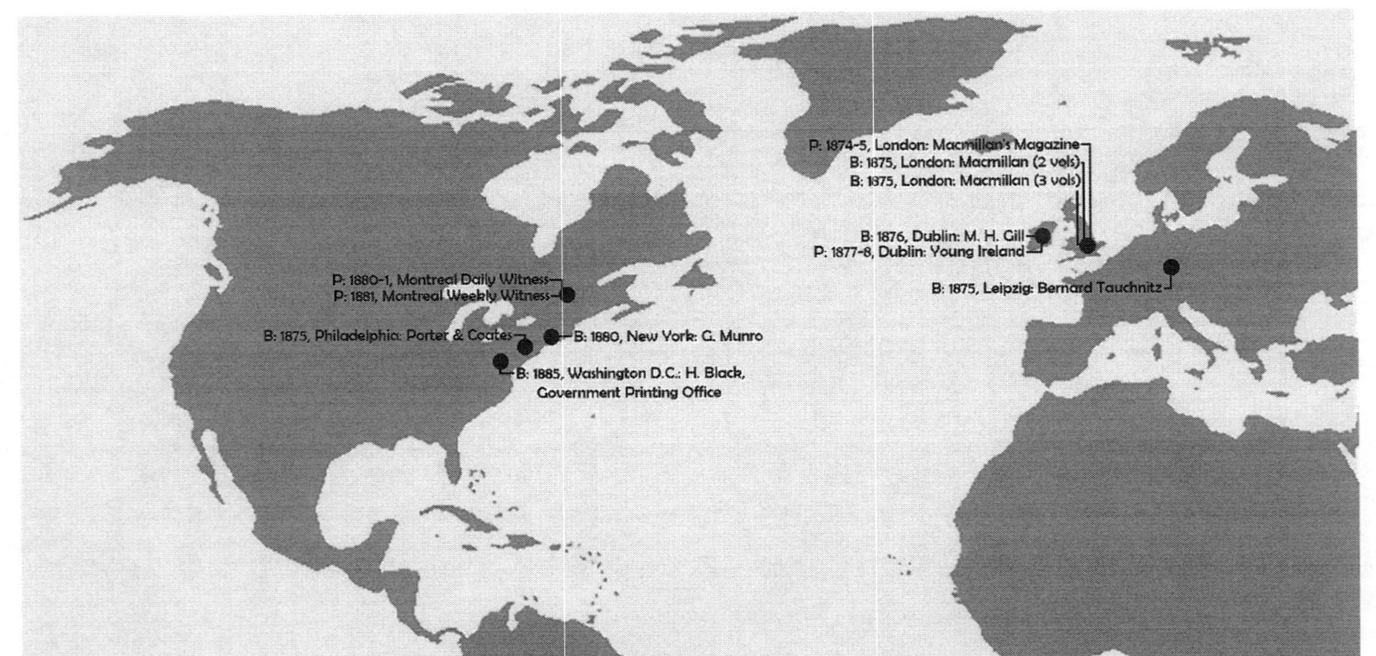

Figure 1.3. Publications of Anne Keary's *Castle Daly*. Source for base map: Wikimedia Commons (public domain). Image created by the author.

hundred years. As part of this series, it was also disseminated to Paris and made widely available through "all Booksellers and Railway Libraries on the Continent."[43] German and broader European interest for Keary's novel in 1875 does not seem to have been inspired by local developments as was arguably the case for the Dutch and German editions of *The Black Prophet*, instead suggesting international interest for the author as a prime example of British authorship.

Castle Daly's concentrated publication history does not reveal much about how existing copies of the novel continued to circulate or about their full geographic dissemination. A more substantial reading history is implied through suggested reading lists and essays. The novel was picked up on the Hawaiian Islands, as the *Hawaiian Gazette* of May 6, 1885, included it on its list "English Novels for English Ladies." In so doing, the *Gazette* directed female readers to a copy published by J. H. Black at the GPO (Government Printing Office).[44] On March 19, 1890, the *Charlottetown Herald* (Charlottetown, Prince Edward Island) included the essay "Recent Irish Novelists," in which well-known author Rosa Mulholland wrote that "the best Irish story written in later years is Miss Keary's 'Castle Daly.'" She lamented that Keary, because of her early death, was unable to produce more works like *Castle Daly*.[45] In November 1900, the Brooklyn-based *Gael* listed Keary's novel as one of seventy books that should be in every Irish Library.[46] And last but not least, European interest for the novel seems to have spanned multiple decades, as the Tauchnitz edition was republished in 1905.

The three publication journeys explored above demonstrate ongoing interest for these (once) appreciated authors and the fund of famine memory their books tap into. They show an ongoing engagement extending beyond later periods of hunger, suffering, or struggle. The fact that republications can frequently be connected to later periods of hardship and turmoil is demonstrated by Carleton's and Keary's novels. Crucially, the publication journeys of these novels reveal a correlation between societal and political developments and the use of famine representations in creative writing, a literary-societal connection that is, as other chapters in this book further demonstrate, both transhistorical and transnational. In other words, the republication journeys of *The Black Prophet* and *Castle Daly* are material manifestations of the workings of memory: the reprinting patterns of both novels demonstrate how famine memory served current needs. The publication in translation of Carleton's work in Germany and the Netherlands during the late 1840s extends this argument on topicality beyond the Irish transatlantic community.

This section contributes to existing scholarship by exploring the correlation between societal developments and the inclusion of famine memories in publications of creative works on a substantial quantitative scale. In *A World of Fiction*, Katherine Bode writes that "the meaning derived from a literary-historical dataset—like the interpretation of a literary work—is shaped, profoundly, by the methodology and critical frameworks through which it is approached and by the selections and amplifications those frameworks produce."[47] This comment certainly applies to the current study; I would add the accessibility of corpora to Bode's comment. The partially digital, partially hard copy corpus of Irish, Irish American, and Irish Canadian periodicals analyzed for this study is necessarily inexhaustive. And, although digital repositories have greatly expanded the corpora available off-site to the periodical scholar, combing through them, even in database form, often remains a human enterprise. Perhaps more importantly, these digital sources are but a selection, as the digital corpus is incomplete and uneven. In the Library of Congress's impressive and freely accessible newspaper corpus *Chronicling America*, for example, DH and periodical scholar Ryan Cordell finds that minority papers and papers from specific US states are underrepresented.[48] Additionally, in the case of Irish, Irish American, and Irish Canadian periodicals, magazines tend to be underrepresented at the time of writing this book, as substantial online databases such as the British Newspaper Archive and Irish Newspaper Archive hold only digitized newspapers. And while some research and university libraries and initiatives such as the HathiTrust Digital Library, Canadiana, and the Internet Archive provide digital access to some better-known Irish, Irish American, and Irish Canadian magazines, many periodicals are currently available only in hard copy or microform format and have to be consulted on-site. Despite such caveats, I believe that extensive perusal through hard copy and digital materials yields a representative understanding of how famine memory traveled through the transatlantic Irish periodical market. It is my hope that the insights delivered throughout *Periodical Famines* inspire practices of distant reading and data mining in the future.

This section draws out patterns in the publication of creative works containing famine memories. It focuses specifically on prose fiction and poetry for two reasons. First, tracing the publication history of texts part of the substantial corpus at the heart of this study is painstaking work and of an impractical scale when considering both fiction and nonfiction. For fiction, valuable cataloging exists on which to base further searches through periodicals and thus provide a representative list. The second, and most important, reason concerns the importance of creative writing for Irish and Irish-diasporic identities, which deserves to be emphasized and investigated further.

When we consider the reuse of famine memory in periodicals, we examine how that memory functions as a tool for constructing identity and establishing cultural and political affiliations. As such, we are dealing with the historical programs of those periodicals, which, as Doris Lechner explains, concern "aspects like the ideological, economic, or social intentions, that result in a singular periodical's characteristic mix of material on the past."[49] Lechner's study engages with nonfictional materials; Leslie Howsam's article "Mediated Histories: How Did Victorian Periodicals Parse the Past?" also focuses on nonfictional historical writings. Such scholarship provides valuable insights into the function of nonfictional historical materials in the historic-didactic program of periodicals. The didactic importance of (historical) prose fiction and poetry was acknowledged by authors and readers well before the nineteenth century. Nevertheless, the role of creative works in a periodical's historical and political program—and, by extension, the avenues creative works in periodicals provided for the formation of identities and sociopolitical affiliations—has received limited attention.

During the period this book covers, exchanges between book and periodical markets were substantial; as the case studies of Keary's, Mitchel's, and Carleton's works show, authors and their writings easily crossed the boundaries between these media. To demonstrate the connectivity between books and periodicals and to chart the way famine memories traveled through and between realms, I have compiled a list of publications and republications of creative works, in periodical and book form, that include famine (see app. 4). For reasons explained in the introduction, I have added to the list creative works about Irish famine in general, not only the Great Famine. Not including these works would undermine the point on temporal convergence key to this study, placing an unnatural division between representations of the Famine and of famine in Ireland; it would also create a division made by a scholar writing in the twenty-first century, not necessarily by contemporary commentators. Nevertheless, with this disclaimer in place, it is important to realize that most of the creative works on the list do contain memories of the Great Famine specifically.

My extensive catalog of famine prose fiction and poetry is based on important work done by Charles Fanning (*The Exiles of Erin: Nineteenth-Century Irish-American Fiction* and *The Irish Voice in America: 250 Years of Irish-American Fiction*) and Rolf and Martha Loeber and Ann Mullin Burnham (*A Guide to Irish Fiction 1650–1900*) on Irish and Irish American literature more generally, as well as on scholarship on famine literature more specifically by Christopher Morash (*Writing the Irish Famine* and *The Hungry Voice: The Poetry of the Irish Famine*), Margaret Kelleher (*The Feminization of Famine: Expressions of the Inexpressible?*), Melissa Fegan (*Literature and the Irish Famine 1845–1919*), Marguérite Corporaal, Christopher Cusack, and myself for the project "Recollecting Starvation," and the periodical research I have conducted since 2017, when I started the research that led to this book. The list goes slightly beyond the period this book covers and contains close to 580 creative works; there are certainly more to be found.[50]

Figure 1.4 provides a combined overview of the publication of creative works on famine in book and periodical form. Three publication spikes are especially noticeable: 1847–49 (thirty publications in 1847, twenty-three in 1848, and thirty in 1849), 1869 (twenty publications), and 1880 (thirty-four publications, with a follow-up of sixteen in 1881). While some works of prose fiction, including Carleton's *The Black Prophet* and *The Emigrants of Ahadarra*, were published during the late 1840s, the first peak consists mainly of works of famine poetry by authors including James Clarence Mangan, Richard D'Alton Williams, and Lady Wilde (Jane Francesca Agnes Wilde, née Elgee, who used the famous pen name "Speranza"). These poems were mainly published in Irish periodicals; Morash has anthologized and carefully analyzed them in *The Hungry Voice* and *Writing the Irish Famine*. This poetry shows the importance of periodicals as publishing outlets during the mid-nineteenth century: "With a few notable exceptions, the main poetic activity of those years took place in the periodicals," and the *Nation*, the *United Irishman*, and the *Irishman* were main outlets.[51]

The peak for 1869 likely is a response to the 1867 Fenian Rising, during which members of the Irish Republican Brotherhood rebelled against British rule in Ireland. The connection between famine suffering and nationalist resistance is borne out by the contents of many narratives, for the peak contains, among other works, the simultaneous publications of Fenian Charles Kickham's *Sally Cavanagh* by various book publishers in Ireland and England (and in the US a year later). In Kickham's novel, the titular Sally's famine sufferings later inspire her son to fight for his country's

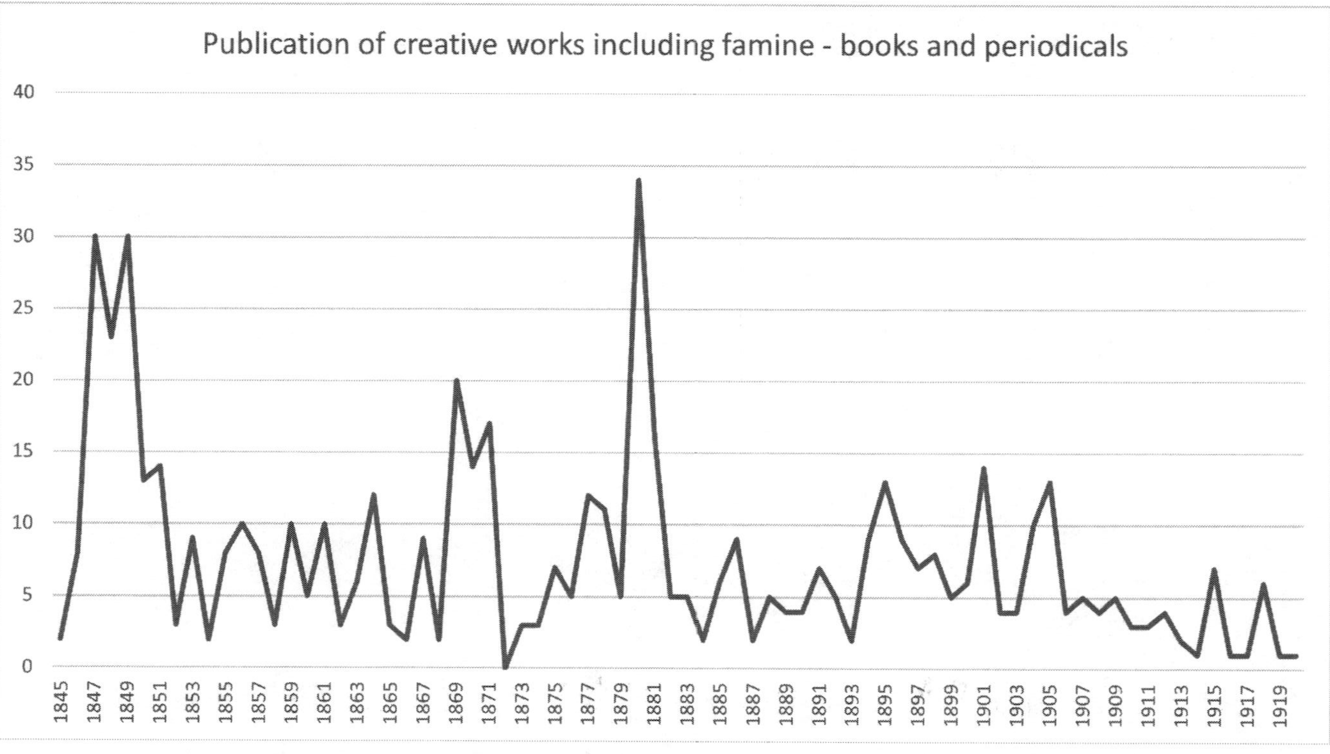

Figure 1.4. Graph of publication of creative works including famine—books and periodicals. Periodicals are both newspapers and magazines. Image created by the author.

liberation. Around the Fenian rebellion, connections between the Famine and earlier resistance featured in, for example, William Gorman Wills's *The Love That Kills* (1867), which combines starvation, land issues, and the Young Ireland rebellion. In Mrs. Lorenzo Nunn's *Heirs of the Soil* (1869), the protagonist experiences the Famine and eviction, then emigrates to the US and joins the American army to return to Ireland and train Fenians. The protagonist of William Anderson Cawthorne's *Tim Doolan: The Irish Emigrant* (1869) also emigrates to the US; from there, he goes to Canada to help repel a Fenian invasion. Last, in 1870, not only was Kickham's *Sally Cavanagh* reissued, but his *Knocknagow*, which combines starvation and the Land Question and supports the Fenian rhetoric that violence is justified if the law serves as the enemy of the people, was also published.[52]

The number of creative works on famine published around the Fenian Rising indicates that literary engagements with famine memory were considered especially relevant during periods of increased physical-force nationalism; the plots of these works suggest that the connection between nationalist resistance and starvation was firmly established in fiction as well. At the same time, the quantity of famine prose fiction and poetry published in 1869 should be nuanced, as it is also caused by the separate listing of three poems by then recently deceased Irish Canadian politician and author Thomas D'Arcy McGee (1825–68) and six poems by Irish poet Aubrey de Vere (1814–1902), published as part of the collected volumes *The Poems of Thomas D'Arcy McGee* and *Irish Odes*, respectively.

The most substantial peak is explained by the occurrence of famine during 1879–80 and the then ongoing Land War (1879–82). It includes the republication of *The Black Prophet, Castle Daly*, and Charlotte Grace O'Brien's *Light and Shade* in the Dublin-based magazine *Young Ireland*, as well as the publication of Edward N. Hoare's *Mike: A Tale of the Great Irish Famine* in London and New York, Richard Baptist O'Brien's *The D'Altons of Crag: An Irish Story of '48 and '49* in the Montreal *Harp*, and several short stories and poems by authors such as John Locke, Rosa Mulholland, and Lady Wilde. This peak consists of twenty-one works of poetry and thirteen works of prose fiction. While this peak seemingly suggests that more famine poetry was published than famine prose fiction, it should be taken into account that serialized works of fiction are counted as one work in these figures unless their protracted publication spans multiple years (in which case they are counted once for each year of publication). Longer works were published as serials in periodicals, and as such, periodical audiences encountered them in many installments and over longer periods of time. The

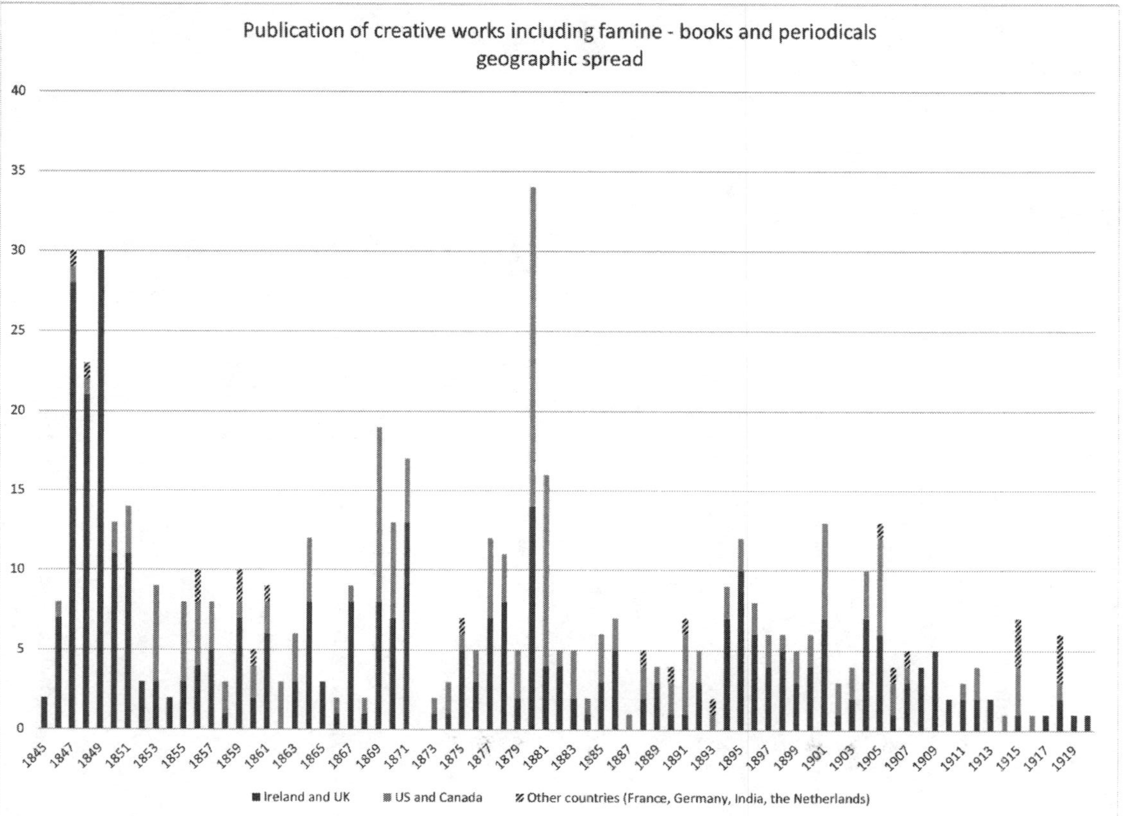

Figure 1.5. Graph of publication of creative works including famine—books and periodicals, geographic spread. Image created by the author.

graph does not do sufficient justice to this vital longitudinal dimension of serial fiction.

Figure 1.5 shows the geographic division of the publication of famine creative works; from this figure, it becomes clear that publications in the UK (especially pertaining to Ireland) are predominant during the Famine and that North American engagement with representations of Irish famine in prose fiction and poetry is at its most frequent during the Land War era. In 1880 and 1881, North American publications outnumber publications from the UK with twenty versus fourteen and twelve versus four works, respectively. The Great Famine had caused a substantial rise in emigration from Ireland to North America, especially to the US; in the early 1880s, this group of Irish immigrants contributed to increased and sustained engagement with the homeland and famine memory specifically.

In relation to the distribution pattern visualized in figure 1.5, it should be noted that throughout the full period this study covers, engagement occurred much more frequently by the Irish community in the US than by its counterpart in Canada. A combination of reasons lies at the heart of this more substantial US-Irish engagement, an important one being the considerable size of the Irish American community and publication market. Moreover, while societal tensions and Protestant anti-Catholicism were present in Canada, Canada seemed more welcoming than the US, as it provided better opportunities for Irish immigrants to work in agriculture and the timber trade. Indeed, in 1877, Irish Canadian historian Nicholas Flood Davin celebrated the Irish presence in Canada and stated: "I am convinced, from what I saw in the States, and from all that I have heard, that the position of the Irishman in Canada is better than in the States."[53] Although Irish American political engagement with Ireland predates the Land War period, Irish Americans became increasingly involved in Irish nationalism and agrarian politics during the 1870s and 1880s. Political engagement with the homeland featured in Canada as well, but it was much more vehement in the US, home to the organization of advanced Irish nationalism.[54] This ardent transatlantic political engagement consequently led to more sustained engagement with famine memory in creative works and nonfiction during periods such as the Land War.

When publications in book and periodical form in the UK and North America are split, the patterns in figures 1.6, 1.7, and 1.8 become visible. These figures tell us that the book publication and periodical publication markets contributed differently to the dissemination patterns of famine prose fiction and poetry. For 1851, thirteen book publications containing

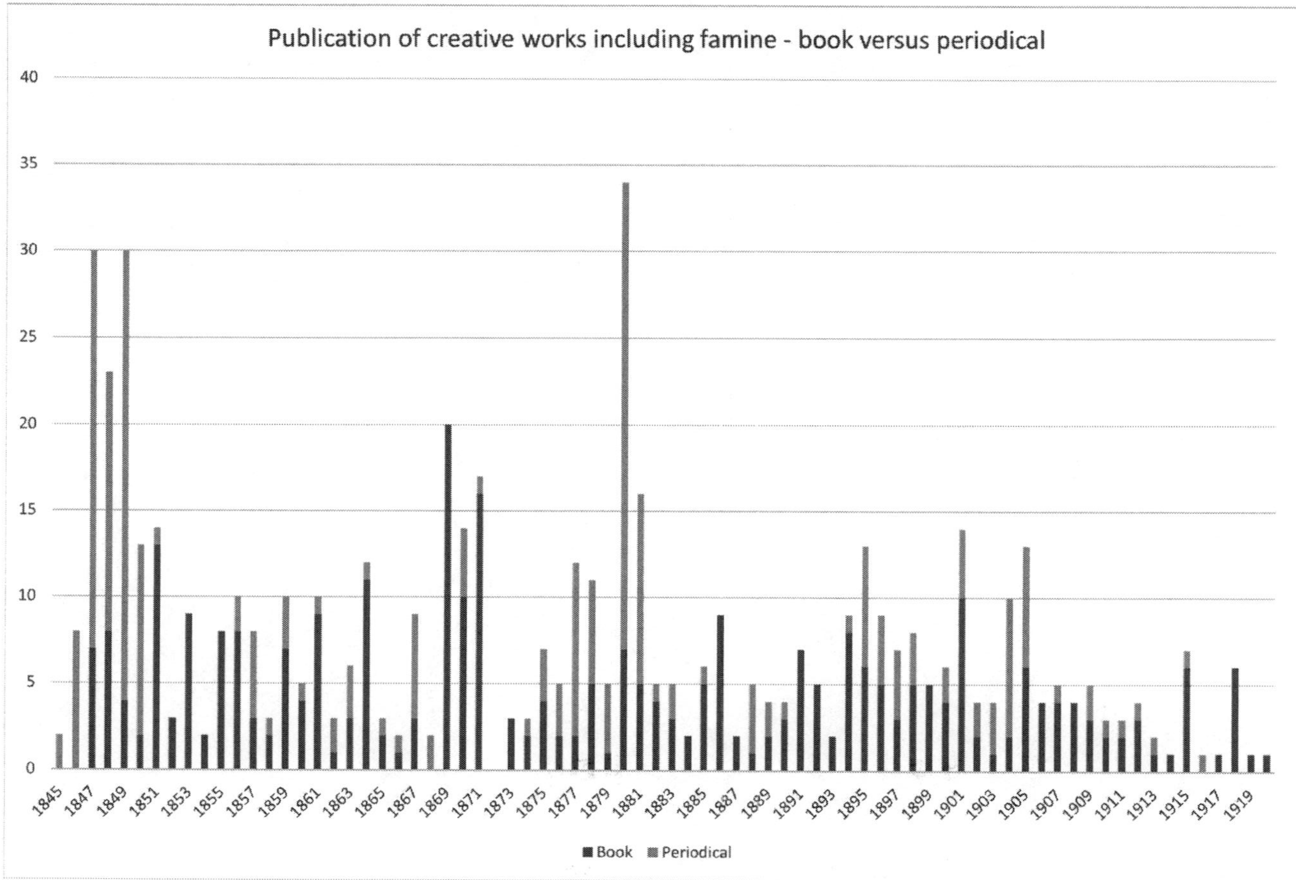

Figure 1.6. Graph of publication of creative works including famine—book versus periodical. Image created by the author.

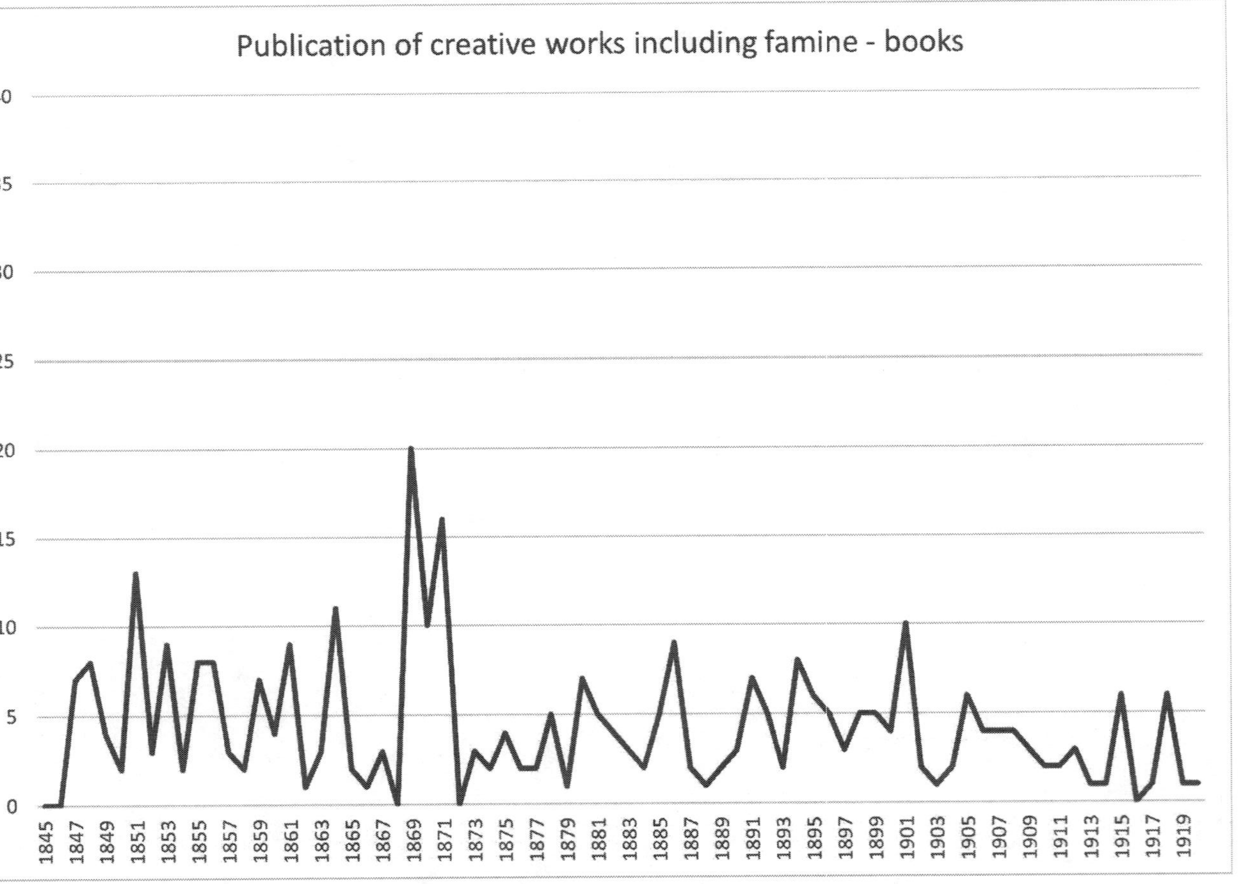

Figure 1.7. Graph of publication of creative works including famine—books. Image created by the author.

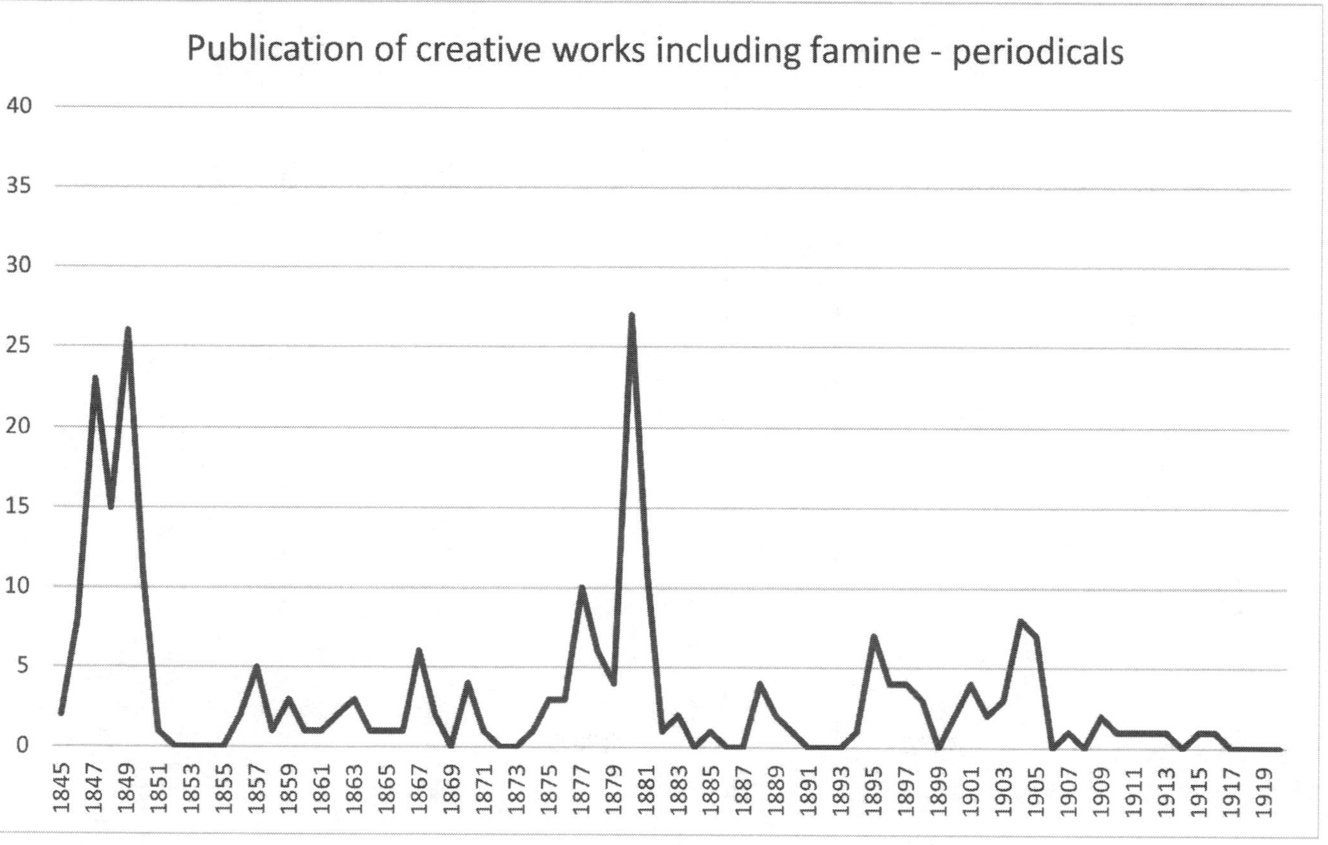

Figure 1.8. Graph of publication of creative works including famine—periodicals. Image created by the author.

representations of famine in Ireland are listed. This number becomes nuanced when considering that it includes the London and Dublin publications of multiple stories on famine included in *Shamrock Leaves; or, Tales and Sketches from Ireland* by Mrs. Mary Anne Hoare. The highest spike for book publications—twenty works in 1869 (with a follow-up of ten in 1870 and sixteen in 1871)—as said, can be associated with the recent occurrence of the Fenian Rising. In any case, high numbers of publications in book form in 1869, 1870, and 1871 can be assigned to the aforementioned multiple publications of Kickham's *Sally Cavanagh* and the publication of various poems by D'Arcy McGee and De Vere in collected volumes. Additionally, the peak contains the multiple publications of Julia and Edmund O'Ryan's novel *In Re Garland: A Tale of Transition Times* (published in London, Derby, Dublin, and New York in 1870), Mrs. Lorenzo Nunn's novel *Heirs of the Soil* (published in Dublin and London in 1869–70), and various poems by Lady Wilde collected in *Poems* (published in Glasgow by Cameron and Ferguson in 1871).

For 1886, nine book publications are listed. This is not a huge rise, but it is worth exploring. Due to continued agricultural distress that year, the Plan of Campaign manifesto—which stated that when landlords refused to lower rents, tenants were legitimized to go on strike—was issued. Subsequently, between 1886 and 1891, Ireland witnessed a second land war. Three of the books responsible for the higher number of publications in 1886 are republished novels set during the Great Famine: Margaret Brew's *The Chronicles of Castle Cloyne; or, Pictures of the Munster People* (first published in 1885), Richard Baptist O'Brien's *The D'Altons of Crag* (first published in 1879), and Hugh Quigley's *The Cross and the Shamrock* (first published in 1853). Because they were reprints, quick publication in response to recent events was possible. The other seven publications can be attributed to multiple publications of Rosa Mulholland's *Marcella Grace* and Emily Lawless's *Hurrish: A Study* in England, Scotland, Ireland, and the US.

In the tumultuous 1880s, the increase in 1886 should not be tied only to events that took place that year. At first glance, it seems that the famine and first Land War of 1879–82 did not spark an at least equal number of book publications and republications (seven for 1880, five for 1881) as in 1886. The narratives by Mulholland and Lawless, responsible for six out of nine book publications in 1886, cover the smaller famine of the late 1870s and the first Land War period; the production of these books was likely spurred by those earlier events. As a result, the increase in 1886 can be considered a delayed effect of the earlier period. In any case, in 1886, creative works provided readers with a transhistorical connection between the Great Famine, the 1879 famine, and the first and second Land War periods. Also useful to note is the continued interest in these works going beyond the Irish and Irish-diasporic communities. *Hurrish* was republished in 1887 and 1888, the latter by Tauchnitz; it was also translated into Dutch in 1890 (*Hurrish: een Ierse Roman*). *Marcella Grace* was republished twice in 1891, by the Vatican Library in New York and Grüneberg in Braunschweig (Germany).[55]

Engagement with representations of famine in creative works during the early 1880s is much more clearly reflected in periodical publications, where we can see twenty-seven items for 1880 and eleven for 1881. The noticeable spikes for 1846–50 in figure 1.8 (eight in 1846, twenty-three in 1847, fifteen in 1848, twenty-six in 1849, and eleven in 1850) were explained earlier in this chapter. Two smaller increases in periodical publishing can be detected in the 1890s and early 1900s. In 1895 and 1896, the Dublin-based literary magazines the *Shamrock* and *Irish Emerald* published several short stories about famine conditions. And in 1904 and 1905, both Irish and Irish American periodicals published multiple pieces about famine. These include the New York *Gaelic American* and *Irish-American* newspapers, the *Rosary Magazine* (Somerset, OH), the Dublin story paper the *Irish Packet* (for a case study on this magazine, see chap. 4), and the Cavan *Anglo-Celt*. The minor increases of the 1890s can be linked to the occurrence of several smaller periods of agricultural distress in Ireland during the decade: in 1890 and 1894, the blight returned, and 1897 brought widespread crop failures.[56] The 1904–5 increase followed the passing of the Wyndham Act of 1903, which was initially met with mixed, critical, and concerned responses, as later chapters demonstrate.

Generally speaking, figures 1.7 and 1.8 show that publications of famine creative works in book form display a less erratic pattern than periodical and book publications combined. This trend can be seen as a result of the natures of both media and their respective speeds of production. Book publications of creative works on famine remain a relatively steady presence throughout the period, suggesting that, when it comes to this specific category of creative writings in book form, the impressive rise of the periodical as a medium after the mid-nineteenth century had a limited negative impact.

The patterns for periodical and book publications of creative works including famine visualized in this chapter show that larger amounts of such works often correlate to events or important periods in (Irish) rural society, such as new periods of agricultural distress and societal and nationalist unrest and resistance. Here, as was the case for the publication journeys of Carleton's *The Black Prophet* and Keary's *Castle Daly*, publication patterns can be considered material manifestations of the workings of cultural memory; indeed, they support the claim that memory is the past made present.

The differences in book versus periodical publication patterns can furthermore be explained by the fact that book production (writing and publishing) is much more time-consuming than periodical production. Indeed, looking at figures 1.6, 1.7, and 1.8, during and shortly after periods of heightened distress or tension—periods responsible for significant increases in publication—periodical publications dominate, while in between such periods, book publications feature more frequently. This might sound like an apparent point, but it is worthwhile to make, for it suggests that during the decades covered in this study, the Famine was considered sufficiently important for both quick and extended production cycles of creative writing.

Crucially, the publication patterns also suggest two ways in which the Famine gave meaning to the Irish past, present, and future—and that these meaning-making processes operated on different timescales. Publication increases during periods of heightened distress or tension demonstrate that the inclusion of famine memory catered to shorter-span contemporary demands. At the same time, publication spikes occurring with a temporal lag and constant publications of creative works on famine together demonstrate that the Famine was of continued interest for Irish audiences in a transatlantic context. This interest can be explained, at least partially, from a political perspective. Periodicals were often politically affiliated; while the *Nation*, for example, was the representative outlet for the Young Irelanders in the 1840s, the New York *Irish World and American Industrial Liberator* and Dublin *Freeman's Journal* aligned with the Land League during the 1870s and 1880s. Therefore, engagement with famine memory in the pages of such periodicals should also be considered products of literary-political ties. Continued interest in the Famine as a rhetorical tool to support political discourses is logical for these outlets, as Ireland remained part of the British Empire throughout the period covered here. However, not every creative work lends itself for such political ends, nor can we claim that every author wrote with a political mindset. Moreover, it is important to add that texts published during earlier times did not just disappear; popular narratives circulated beyond their publication dates and continued to entertain, inform, and influence audiences.

Perhaps most importantly, as this is where *Periodical Famines* contributes to existing scholarly understanding of the spread and appropriation of famine memory, the charts provided in this chapter show that publications containing representations of the Famine and/or famine are never absent. If we consider the Irish transatlantic periodical and book publication cultures as public spheres, as this study does, the Famine was never absent from that sphere between the late 1840s and early twentieth century. Continued engagement with the Famine suggests that the crisis was integrated into Irish cultural memory from early on and further underscores claims against the persistent conviction that the Famine was "forgotten in popular or public discourse" in Ireland and its diaspora.[57]

As said, at a more protracted timescale, book publications assured that recollections of the Famine continued to circulate. The combined publication patterns in periodicals and books crucially suggest that the need for acute responses to ongoing senses of danger, starvation, and unrest was met through the ephemeral and ready medium of the periodical, which had the potential to reach vast audiences because of widespread dissemination and affordable pricing. Periodicals offered authors and editors the opportunity for cotextual linkage to different texts and images. As such, the topicality of (historical) prose fiction and poetry could be emphasized further. The functioning and effects of these combinatory processes are illustrated in detail in the chapters to follow.

The figures provided in this chapter highlight the key role periodicals played as publication outlets for the dissemination of famine memory. The following chapters further elucidate the importance of famine memory for transatlantic processes of identification and affiliation as visible in and stimulated through periodicals. The current chapter has focused on creative works; adding engagements with the Famine in nonfictional periodical writings to these visual patterns—think of works by authors such as Mitchel and other Irish nationalists at home and in diaspora but also by the political and economic commentators and special correspondents discussed throughout this book—would only further demonstrate the frequent publication and continued presence of that fund of memory in transatlantic periodical culture.

NOTES

1. Gonne, "Famine Queen," 5.
2. Steele, *Maud Gonne's Irish Nationalist Writings*, 55, 275n. "Maud Gonne's Famine Queen," 1. The *Indianapolis Journal* was not a specifically Irish publication. "Maud Gonne's Roast," 8.
3. "Hibernians," 4.

4. "Seizure of a Newspaper," *Irish Standard*, June 16, 1900, 1; "Seized by Police," *Kentucky Irish American*, June 16, 1900, 1. The contents of "The Famine Queen" are discussed in chapter 6.

5. The article "De Engelsche Koningin . . ." ("The English Queen . . .") ends with "that the people of this country will never be able to give its loyal support to the current Government, and that the vast majority of the people in this country will never be satisfied nor loyal before our National Parliament is restored." (dat het volk van dit land nimmer aan het Regeeringsstelsel, aldus ingesteld, zijn trouwe steun geven kan, en dat, voor zoover de overgroote meerderheid van het volk betreft, er nimmer tevredenheid noch trouw in dit land zal wezen voor ons Nationale Parlement hersteld zal zijn.) *Soerabaiasch Handelsblad*, May 15, 1900, 1. Seven years earlier, Maud Gonne had also been mentioned in a Dutch East Indies newspaper: the more conservative *Java-Bode, Nieuws, Handels- en Advertentieblad voor Nederlandsch-Indië* (*Java Messenger: News, Trade and Commercial Journal for the Dutch East Indies*) had criticized Gonne's fierce nationalism. The newspaper stated that "from such a sweet appearance people would tolerate a lot and would likely believe what she says. But if this is not the case, a girl like Maud Gonne should get married; then it [her fierceness] will pass." (Van zulks eene lieve verschijning laat men zich veel zeggen en gelooft men allicht wat zij zegt. Maar anders moet een meisje als Maud Gonne trouwen, dan gaat het wel over.) "Haagsch Nieuws," December 11, 1893, 2.

6. Bode, *World of Fiction*, 39; Cordell, "Reprinting," 418.

7. Law and Patten, "Serial Revolution," 157–58.

8. Before 1891, "publishers were free to edit, illustrate, rearrange, and market texts from the other country with little concern for the author's monetary or artistic desires" (DeSpain, *Nineteenth-Century Transatlantic Reprinting*, introduction). Focusing on the antebellum US, Meredith McGill explains that while "American defenders of the reprint trade wielded considerable political power" and managed to hold off "an international copyright agreement" until 1891, there was "substantial domestic opposition to the culture of reprinting" (*American Literature and the Culture of Reprinting*, 3–4).

9. "International Unfairness," September 29, 1877, 290. Cusack's narrative is discussed in chapter 5.

10. Law, "Copyright," 143.

11. Feely, "Scissors and Paste Journalism," 561.

12. With the aid of DH techniques, Ryan Cordell and others investigate reuse practices in the Library of Congress's digitized collection of nineteenth-century US periodicals. See, for example, the project "Viral Texts" (https://viraltexts.org/); Cordell, "Reprinting, Circulation, and the Network Author"; Smith, Cordell, and Maddock Dillon, "Infectious Texts."

13. Bode argues that "studying literature through the lens of authors whose identities are known today preconditions us to view the past through contemporary parameters" (*World of Fiction*, 91).

14. *The Emigrants of Ahadarra* was also published under the title *The Emigrants: A Tale of Irish Life*.

15. Corporaal, *Relocated Memories*, 42–44.

16. Carleton, *Black Prophet*, 452.

17. "Literature," 3.

18. Carleton's novel was translated in Dutch and German as *De zwarte profeet: Een verhaal uit den tijd van den Ierschen hongersnood* and *Der schwarze Prophet: Aus den Zeiten irischer Hungersnoth*, respectively. On famine in Germany, Switzerland, Austria, the Netherlands, and Flanders, see "Germany, Switzerland and Austria" by Collet and Krämer and "Low Countries" by Curtis et al.

19. "University Magazine," 3.

20. Yeats, "Carleton as an Irish Historian," January 11, 1890, 9.

21. The 1899 edition was published in London by Lawrence and Bullen. Arnold, "Yeats, Jack Butler," n.p.

22. "Are the Irish a Reading People?," 7.

23. *The Black Prophet* could be ordered through the *Irish Standard* for $0.90, and the newspaper offered to "pay the postage or express charges on all orders." See, for example, "Good Books for the Holidays," December 17, 1904, 2 and "Good Books for the Home and Fireside," March 11, 1905, 2.

24. Tuyll, "John Mitchel," 118.

25. Quinn, *Young Ireland*, 103–4. The quote comes from Mitchel, *Ireland since '98*, 152.

26. McGovern, *John Mitchel*, 44. Quinn, *Young Ireland*, 103; McGovern, *John Mitchel*, xiv.

27. J. Pope-Hennessy, "What Do the Irish Read?" from the *Nineteenth Century* magazine, quoted in Quinn, *Young Ireland*, 129. "John Mitchel Centenary," *Gaelic American*, December 18, 1915, 2. Quinn, *Young Ireland*, 103.

28. Quinn, *Young Ireland*, 102.

29. Mitchel, *Jail Journal*, 24, 9. Mitchel argued that Ireland produced more than double the foodstuffs needed in the country (McGovern, *John Mitchel*, 38). Revisionist and postrevisionist historians like Cormac Ó Gráda, Peter Gray, and Mary E. Daly have corrected this view; Daly, for example, explains that closing the ports would not have ended the crisis (Daly referenced in McGovern, *John Mitchel*, 38). I discuss this historical revision in more detail in chapter 7.

30. Mitchel argues that while the Irish population continued to increase before the Famine, so did British food exports from Britain (*Jail Journal*, 16). See also *Jail Journal*, 17–18, 29. Mitchel "asserted that the government utilized starvation as a means to kill the Irish people, or, at the very least, to force the emigration of those Irish people who were not loyal to the government" (McGovern, *John Mitchel*, 36). The quote is taken from Mitchel, *Jail Journal*, 12.

31. Mitchel, *Jail Journal*, 14.

32. Ibid., 15. Quinn, *Young Ireland*, 103.

33. Donahoe was also an exception to this exclusion (Sullivan, "Community in Print," 47–48). The quote is taken from "Book Notices," *True Witness*, February 10, 1886, 8.

34. Morash, *Writing the Irish Famine*, 61.

35. "John Mitchel's Jail Journal" (ad), September 10, 1863, 2.

36. For republications, see, for example, Mitchel, "Leaves from John Mitchel's 'Jail Journal,'" *Nation*, September 10, 1863, 6. Maume, "Sullivan, Alexander Martin," n.p.

37. "Books and Bookmen," *Irish Independent*, August 18, 1913, 9.

38. "'Jail Journal' of John Mitchel," *Dublin Evening Herald*, August 23, 1913, 5.

39. "Irish Industries Depot" (ad), *Gaelic American*, July 29, 1916, 5; "Irish Store of New York," *Irish Press*, June 26, 1920, 8. The *Irish Republic* was published in Chicago until April 4, 1868; from that date it was published in New York. "Fireside Gossip," *Irish Fireside*, April 3, 1886, 240. Mitchel's book was part of seventy books "which should be in every Irish library." "Correspondence," *Gael*, November 1900, 325. See, for example, "Irish National Library," *Nation*, February 3, 17.

40. 19.

41. Gantt, *Irish Terrorism*, 132–33, 128. For an analysis of this novel as an Irish *Bildungroman*, see Janssen, "(Re)building Self and Country."

42. "Reviews: Ireland Thirty Years Ago," September 4, 1875, 10.

43. The front matter of the Tauchnitz edition of Keary's novel indicates collaboration with the Librairie C. Reinwald and Galignani Library in Paris. As the back matter to the 1905 republication of the 1875 Tauchnitz edition shows, *Castle Daly* could be bought for one German mark or two French francs per volume. The series was ongoing at the time, eventually reaching its 3834th volume. The British Library has fully cataloged the Tauchnitz collection ("Todd-Bowden Collection of Tauchnitz Editions").

44. "English Novels for English Ladies," supplement.

45. "Recent Irish Novelists," 1.

46. "Correspondence," *Gael*, 325.

47. Bode, *World of Fiction*, 25.

48. Cordell, "Q i-jtb the Raven"; "What Has the Digital Meant," 3.

49. Lechner, *Histories for the Many*, 15.

50. A list also containting nonfiction is available through my website: https://lindsay bjanssen.wordpress.com/. "Recollecting Starvation" was funded by the European Research Council and ran from 2011 until 2016. Output includes Corporaal's *Relocated Memories*, Cusack's dissertation "Memory, History, and Identity," and my dissertation "Famine Traces." My postdoctoral work was funded by an Irish Research Council Government of Ireland Postdoctoral Fellowship (2017–19).

51. Morash, *Hungry Voice*, 26.

52. For a longer discussion of *Sally Cavanagh*, see Corporaal, *Relocated Memories*; in connection to Kickham's novel, Corporaal demonstrates the central role of the ruin in Irish famine fiction as a heterotopic site of suffering and resistance (169–71, 187–88). Fegan discusses *The Love That Kills* (*Literature and the Irish Famine*, 226–27). Loeber, Loeber, and Mullin Burnham also locate an 1869 edition of *Heirs of the Soil* but do not provide full publication details. I have listed the 1870 version in the bibliography (Loeber and Loeber, with Mullin Burnham, *Guide to Irish Fiction*, 984). American Fenians committed several unsuccessful raids in Canada in the late 1860s and early 1870s; these were attempts to pressure Britain for Irish independence. Also see Loeber and Loeber, with Mullin Burnham on *Sally Cavanagh* (*Guide to Irish Fiction*, 700).

53. The project "Relocated Remembrance" has shown that from the Famine until the 1920s, the amount of Irish Canadian publications steadily decreased. MacRaild, *Irish Migrants in Modern Britain*, 155. MacRaild, "Crossing Migrant Frontiers," 46. Davin, *Irishman in Canada*, 8n.

54. For a detailed analysis of Irish American involvement in Irish land politics and nationalism during the period, see Janis, *Greater Ireland*.

55. The Dutch translation was done by Anna Bok for Gouda Quint, a publisher based in Arnhem.

56. Kelleher, *Feminization of Famine*, 114.

57. Emily Mark-FitzGerald discusses the persistence of this erroneous notion in *Commemorating the Irish Famine* (58). See also Geary, *Land War in Ireland*, 127.

2

FAMINE AND TEMPORAL
STASIS IN A STORY PAPER

Young Ireland Magazine, 1875–88

ON MARCH 28, 1875, THE *Irish-American* honored the recently deceased nationalist John Mitchel with several pieces on his life and deeds, the first of which started with the remark that for Irish Americans, the news of Mitchel's death was "the saddest news ever wafted to them across the great ocean since the hour when they were told that, by the machinations of an alien government, their race was enshrouded in the folds of a double calamity—famine and pestilence."[1] A few weeks earlier, that same newspaper had printed a lengthy letter titled "The Great Irish Famine." Its author stressed the longitudinal nature of Irish suffering by stating: "I firmly believe that, at no distant period, after their long night of suffering and sorrow, and exile, they [the Irish] will be finally gathered together in their mother-land, free from English-made famines, to enjoy the independence and liberty for which they have yearned and struggled through so many centuries of darkness and despair."[2] Unfortunately, the period to follow would provide opportunities to draw further parallels to the Great Famine. From 1873 onward, the world experienced a protracted economic depression. In Ireland, conditions for farmers worsened further in 1877–78 due to crop failures, which resulted in a famine the following year.[3] These conditions fueled the Land War, a period of agrarian agitation led by the popular Land League, the land reform movement founded by Michael Davitt (1846–1906).

The period also witnessed the rise to popularity and power of future Irish Parliamentary Party leader and president of the Land League

Charles Stewart Parnell (1846–91). Indeed, with regard to Irish Land and Home Rule politics, the late 1870s and 1880s constituted a highly transformative era.

Again during the early 1880s, the topicality of the 1840s Famine was signaled frequently. Between March and May 1880, *The Celtic Monthly: An Illustrated Irish-American Magazine; Devoted to Literature, Music, the Drama, and the Arts and Current Events* included a serialized historical treatise on the Famine.[4] Various authors of creative works and nonfiction made explicit the placement of the Famine in a longer line of suffering irreconcilable with British notions of progress. After visiting Ireland in 1881 and 1882 and writing letters for the Philadelphia *Press*, American reporter and professor David Bennett King reflected that famine could only have occurred "where great numbers of people were living on the very brink of want and distress . . . and were regularly separated from starvation by only a crop of potatoes"; King spoke of "*chronic* distress."[5] Similar interpretations of Irish suffering were expressed in works of fiction written in the later part of the nineteenth century by authors including Thomas Sherlock, Rosa Mulholland, and William C. Upton.[6] In the latter's novel *Uncle Pat's Cabin; or, Life among the Agricultural Labourers of Ireland* (1882), the continued suffering and eventual downfall of a poor laborer between the 1840s and 1880s provide such historical embedding. The New York–based *Irish-American* included the article "Perpetuating 'Irish Famine'" in 1880.[7] Scottish American journalist James Redpath's special correspondence from Ireland during the Land War circulated in various periodicals and received praise from the Irish in America. As Margaret Dixon McDougall would also do in her special correspondence (see chap. 3), Redpath drew parallels between the 1840s and his contemporary famine. *McGee's Illustrated Weekly: Devoted to Catholic Art, Literature and Education* (discussed in detail in chap. 5) provided a sarcastic take on the (British) tendency to see Irish acquiescence at barely "making both ends meet" as an indication of present "Irish prosperity." It extended this irony to the past, stating that, similarly, "the Famine had been a great thing for the Irish."[8] Chapter 1 has shown the substantial publication numbers of creative works dealing with famine during this time. Together with the examples above, they demonstrate that famine memory resurfaced frequently during the late 1870s and 1880s in creative works and nonfiction.

The manifestation in prose fiction of temporal parallels features prominently in the current chapter. In *Novel Institutions: Anachronisms, Irish Novels and Nineteenth-Century Realism* (2019), Mary L. Mullen explores representations of temporality in Irish and English realist novels. Mullen demonstrates how realist novels represent "the shared time of institutions," or institutional time—in *Periodical Famines*, the time of the British Empire—and its clashes with the "heterogenous times of anachronisms," represented by "out-of-date characters, obsolete practices, untimely chronologies."[9] The temporality of modern institutions orients itself toward the future in a self-serving manner and excludes alternative presents and futures implied by anachronisms. Additionally, David Carr argues that narratives can introduce "the synthesis of the heterogenous." He points out that governing time is applied to synthesize what is originally heterogeneous time. This synthesized narrative is then taken to describe rather than form history, while it effectively does the latter. In so doing, ill-fitting elements are converted into deviations and irregularities. Carr demonstrates the simultaneous normalizing and exclusionary power of this synthesis and consequently states that narratives can "put across a moral view of the world" that is "in the interests of power and manipulation."[10]

In the fiction included on the pages of *Young Ireland: An Irish Magazine of Entertainment and Instruction*, tensions between different times and future trajectories are mapped out. The stories by Irish authors included in *Young Ireland* and discussed in the current chapter show how idiosyncratic Irish temporality clashes with the normalizing power of British state-supported narratives of development and progress. The selection of fiction from *Young Ireland* represents Ireland as "out of common course" since the Famine, caught in stasis.[11] The analyses below consider whether these narratives suggest the possibility of breaking that stasis and, consequently, what solutions they propose—in other words, exploring the future possibilities offered in these creative works. Moreover, the chapter considers works of prose fiction in light of their cotexts in the magazine, demonstrating how the temporality of stasis is strengthened through cotextuality.

In line with the transitory nature of the period, the acknowledgment of a static quality to Ireland's condition in the late 1870s and 1880s on the pages of *Young Ireland* resulted in diverging future directions varying between traditionalist reimaginings and progressive solutions. Reactionary in their resistance, works of fiction such as *Light and Shade* (1878) by Charlotte O'Brien and *Dick O'Dell* (1876–77) by Nannie H. H. acknowledge stasis yet see a way out of this condition through a return to the past.[12] In contrast, works of fiction such as unknown author M. Mackey's "Con Driscoll; or, The Hatchet the Smith Made" (1881) and "His Honour's Word; or, A Victim of 'Painful Duty': A Tale of the Times" (1881) provide progressive views, predicting the downfall of landlordism and the survival of the Irish rural community through the adoption of Land League tactics. By extension, these stories envision a shift in the dominant temporality for Ireland. Finally, Hester Sigerson's *A Ruined Race; or, The Last MacManus of Drumroosk* (1888) holds no such radical nostalgia or clear progressive message; rather, it provides a semisentimental, semirealist depiction of dire circumstances without any distinct suggestion for improvement. In so doing, the narrative demonstrates the impossibility of cotemporaneity in contemporary rural Ireland.

YOUNG IRELAND'S EDITOR T. D. SULLIVAN'S
ENGAGEMENT WITH FAMINE AND LAND

The story paper *Young Ireland* was the popular sister magazine to the *Nation*, the newspaper established by the Young Ireland movement in the 1840s that continued until 1900.[13] An issue of *Young Ireland* typically counted sixteen pages and cost a penny per issue—the magazine had a standard price. Emphasis was placed on literature and poetry, and while the magazine provided commentary on current issues, it did not provide news articles as such. The magazine's range of topics was quite broad; like many Irish magazines of its time, it contained historiographical nonfiction (typically on Irish heroes and significant events in Irish history), historical fiction, poetry, comedy, Gothic and detective stories, and adventure fiction set in mysterious and exotic locations. *Young Ireland* presented its readers with a combination of anonymous, little-known, and well-known writers. The latter included William Carleton, Charles Kickham, and Lady Morgan. For its youngest readers, the magazine included a weekly "Children's Corner" as well as frequent installments of children's adventure and detective stories. Like many later story papers, *Young Ireland* was "designed to appeal to younger male readers," but much of its material suggests that the magazine sought to appeal to adult and female audiences as well.[14] Moreover, the masthead (see fig. 2.1) includes both a female figure reading to children and older readers reading by themselves, implying a broad audience and the communal act of reading, possibly within the family sphere. As such, *Young Ireland* can be classified as a typical family magazine.[15]

Britain had put in place a national school curriculum in Ireland by 1831, and Irish nationalist commentators criticized it for its absence of Irish history. They developed an alternative curriculum in which literary magazines such as *Young Ireland* provided young people with historical knowledge unavailable through the national school system. As *Young Ireland* was

Figure 2.1. On November 13, 1875, *Young Ireland* opened with the first installment of Charles Kickham's "The Home by Slievenamon." This story originally appeared as "Never Give Up" in the *Celt* in 1859 and was republished in the *Shamrock* in 1899. Image courtesy of the National Library of Ireland.

published by the offices of the *Nation*, the brothers Sullivan were its proprietors and editors. The didactic use of cultural products had been fully embraced by the Young Irelanders in the 1840s, and Alexander M. (A. M.) Sullivan (1829–84) considered himself a guardian of that tradition.[16]

When A. M. left Dublin in 1876, his brother Timothy D. (T. D.) Sullivan (1827–1914) took over in the offices of the *Nation*. Like his brother, T. D. was an author and influential politician. The Sullivans hailed from a politically active family and had been involved briefly with the Confederate Club in the early 1840s. However, from the late 1840s, T. D. Sullivan associated only with constitutional nationalism. He was involved with the Home Rule movement, agrarian agitation, obstructionist politics in the early 1880s, the Plan of Campaign (1886–91), and municipal and parliamentary politics.[17] Perhaps his most popular legacy is writing the song "God Save Ireland" in 1867, which served as the unofficial Irish nationalist anthem for quite some time. Before becoming proprietor of the *Nation* and *Young Ireland*, he had contributed pieces to both publications, including a serialized memoir on Thomas Francis Meagher and the serialized treatises "The Friends and Foes of Ireland" and "The Story of England," which provided an Irish nationalist interpretation of the historical relations between Britain and Ireland. Sullivan did not advocate full independence but believed in the "capacity of reform to heal relationships within the context of the empire."[18]

Young Ireland printed several famine narratives besides those already mentioned, including "The Sleeveen" (1880) by the widely published Thomas Sherlock and *Sally Cavanagh; or, The Untenanted Graves: A Tale of Tipperary* (1878) by Kickham. In the short piece "A True Story of Black '47" (1882), author F. G. uses present conditions in Ireland as an opportunity to recollect an episode of the Great Famine, leaving it unclear whether it is fiction or not; in effect, the unclear status of the story—truth or verisimilitude— underscores that this is a moot distinction, that the piece describes a general, atemporal Irish truth.[19]

Both A. M. and T. D. witnessed famine suffering firsthand, and in his autobiography, *Recollections of Troubled Times in Irish Politics* (1905), T. D. describes the scenes he witnessed in Bantry and Skibbereen as "heartrending."[20] He uses the image of the living skeleton, an oft-employed embodiment of famine memory, in his recollection: "To my sorrow, I saw many of them—saw some of the living skeletons at the doors of their cabins, or trying to totter about to beg food—saw also the 'trap-coffins' in which bodies were being carted to the burying ground, there to be slid, coffinless, into the common pit or fosse that had been dug for them. Affairs were even worse in Skibbereen." Sullivan goes on to describe how he witnessed a young boy aiding another with the burial of the latter's mother in a shallow grave, commenting that "the impression made on his mind by that scene was indelible."[21] Although Sullivan describes the formative effect the burial process had on this young boy—and reveals that the boy was, in fact, Jeremiah O'Donovan Rossa—the suggestion is that the event had a similar effect on Sullivan as an observer. By extension, it becomes evident that, for *Young Ireland*, substantial engagement with famine memory directly aligned with the personal history and preoccupations of the editor himself.

To date, *Young Ireland* magazine has received only limited scholarly attention.[22] In his survey work *Irish Literary Magazines: An Outline History and Descriptive Bibliography* (2003), Tom Clyde calculates the average lifespan of a literary magazine published during the period 1870–91 to have "declined to a pitiful ten months." In relation to this average, *Young Ireland* magazine's lifespan of sixteen years (it appeared on a weekly basis between 1875 and 1891) is impressive.[23]

The author Wilkie Collins (1824–99) once lamented the sameness of much serialized fiction in penny magazines. Clyde notes that the era's magazines show little coherence and "few signs of innovation or originality." With regard to *Young Ireland* (not included in Clyde's research), there seems to be some truth to these remarks. Collins's and Clyde's comments suggest that combining familiarity with novelty in a magazine was a delicate balancing act tied to the temporal qualities and selling potential of the periodical: as James Mussell writes, "too much sameness and the periodical might lapse into stasis," an undesired effect in a turbulent market.[24]

Clyde states that although he expected a "strong correlation between the level of political activity in the country, and the level of cultural activity" of literary magazines, this connection seems absent during the period 1870–91. However, when we broaden our lens to a transatlantic perspective and focus on the larger category of periodicals rather than literary magazines alone, the period does not seem to experience a low point or lack of correlation between contemporary events and "cultural activity" at all; rather, the period constitutes a high point. Like other periodicals of the time, *Young Ireland* certainly interacted with contemporary sociopolitical issues, and works of fiction, including those discussed below, engaged with contemporary developments such as famine conditions, the Land War, the Land League, and Catholic colonization. In this context, one has to consider the fact that the narratives included in *Young Ireland* and other periodicals could link to recent developments in seemingly indirect ways, commenting through reappropriation of the past and using events such as the Great Famine and the Fenian Rising to provide lessons for Ireland in the present and future.[25]

Traditionalist Reimaginings

In 1880, *Young Ireland* serialized Charlotte Grace O'Brien's two-decker *Light and Shade*, a novel demonstrating how the combined forces of Anglo-Irish marriage and caring landlordism could save an Irish estate. The novel had been published in book form in 1878 by Kegan Paul (London) and Harper (New York) and serialized in the *Illustrated Celtic Monthly* (New York) in 1879 before making the pages of *Young Ireland*. O'Brien was born in Caher-moyle House (County Limerick) in 1845 and died in Foynes (County Limerick) in 1909. The novelist, children's author, poet, and social activist was the daughter of well-known nationalist politician William Smith O'Brien (1803–64), to whom she dedicated *Light and Shade*. Her father had been a constitutional nationalist until the Famine "drove him to sheer despair."[26] He was sentenced to death for his involvement in the Young Ireland rebellion; this sentence was later commuted to transportation. During her childhood, Charlotte O'Brien spent several years abroad with her father, following him into exile in Tasmania. They came back to Ireland in 1856, when he was allowed to return. As an adult, Charlotte O'Brien was involved in several social causes, including the improvement of conditions for females on board emigrant ships and in boarding houses on both sides of the Atlantic. She contributed to multiple journals, including *United Ireland* and the *Nation*. Supportive of Parnell, O'Brien was a convinced Land Leaguer until her death. She was not a separatist but stood for the right of "the King, Lords, and Commons of Ireland" to "make laws for Ireland"; "that was Grattan's, that is ours."[27]

Light and Shade is set in O'Brien's native province of Munster and describes the tense atmosphere in rural Ireland in the run-up to the Fenian rebellion. O'Brien gathered substantial information from men who had been active in the rebellion, and she was friends with William C. Upton and John Boyle O'Reilly (1844–90). O'Reilly had been a member of the Irish Republican Brotherhood in the 1860s and, after arrest and transportation, had made his way to the US, where he edited the Boston *Pilot*. Little is known about Upton except that he had been "head centre" in the Fenian organization, corresponded with Charlotte O'Brien, and wrote the aforementioned agrarian novel *Uncle Pat's Cabin*.[28]

Light and Shade focuses on young adults Tom and Edith Vanhurst—Anglo-Irish children of a kind landlord who identify with and are loved by their tenantry—and a newly arrived English landlord, Lord Dunallen. The novel contains many descriptions of the bad conditions under which Dunallen's tenants live due to the actions of the previous absentee landlord; it poses the microcosm of the Dunallen estate as representative for larger Ireland. In one of his early conversations with Dunallen, Tom Vanhurst remarks that most likely "the degraded state of the peasantry" at present can be attributed to "the usual story—neglected estates, land let at enormous rents to large farmers, who finding grazing most profitable, have no employment to give to the over-plentiful population, who are therefore forced to emigrate or starve." At various times, Vanhurst refers to the longevity of the suffering of the Irish poor, alleging that Dunallen's estate at present is in "a condition little if anything better than when Dunallen's grandfather had left the country."[29] Consequently, he utilizes the ethical potential of memory and refers to the Great Famine to convince Dunallen of his moral obligation to help his suffering tenantry: "Do you think if your father had lived here, if even he had come here pretty frequently, as he should, that things would have been in this state . . . ? If he had been here in the famine years, would the people have been lying dead, and no one to bury them, about these very fields? You will not back out of your duty because it is painful or even dangerous?"[30] Vanhurst lays bare what, according to the novel, lies at the heart of Ireland's present condition: lack of access to land for the Irish poor combined with absenteeist neglect. Furthermore, he demonstrates that Ireland has been more or less static in this condition since the Famine.

Young Ireland's issue of February 28, 1880, opened with an installment of *Light and Shade* that contains a glimpse into the backstory of Dunallen's agent, Mr. Lloyd, who has largely come to the same conclusions as Tom Vanhurst. According to the kindhearted Lloyd, the estate has long been filled with "the miserable cabins of the poverty-stricken population," and he adds that "there is hardly any part of Ireland where the degradation and misery is so complete as hereabouts."[31] For more than forty years, Mr. Lloyd has overseen the estate in place of the absentee lord and has witnessed the injustice of the Irish land system firsthand. Lloyd cares for the tenantry but also feels the anxiety and limitations inherent to his position. He realizes "that he would certainly be blamed" for the bad condition of the estate, "when in fact the course he had pursued was that which alone had been open to him. Money was what his employer required, and his business was to supply it; and except during the famine years, he had always contrived, often at considerable inconvenience and risk to himself, to have the full tale forthcoming. It was not his work to improve. That could not be done without an immediate expenditure, not likely to be authorised by one who had never set foot in Ireland."[32] Lloyd acknowledges that matters have always been as bad as they are at present because absentee landlords are only interested in their own financial gain, not in any improvements of the tenantry's condition, even during the Famine. The agent serves as a human link between the estate's past and present and as direct witness to the prolonged nature of the dire condition in which the tenantry finds itself in the narrative's present. By extension, he functions as a synecdoche for Ireland's ambiguous position in the union: caught between the desires and demands of his English master and the needs of the Irish poor, Lloyd is stuck in the impossible position of having to cater to both sides.

In the installment of March 27, 1880, Edith Vanhurst reflects on the duties of the new English landlord toward his Irish tenantry. The installment offers further parallels to the Famine: immediately after yet another description of famine-like hardships during the late 1860s, Edith recalls famine emigration by thinking that during the Great Famine, the majority of the Dunallen tenantry were "so poverty-stricken" that they could not avail of "the hope thus held out" by leaving Ireland.[33] Indeed, as Cormac Ó Gráda argues, while emigration worked as a "safety valve," as the death toll of the Famine would have been higher without it, "North America was beyond the reach of the poorest and the weakest."[34] The next installment of O'Brien's narrative points out that the long-existing combination of "religious persecution, famine, misrepresentation, laws bearing hardly on the poor and lightly on the rich, and the administration of law under the word of padded juries" has caused the Irish to lose trust in the British government. Crucially, it is the full weight of this unchanging history that provides the tipping point for Dunallen: after much deliberation, he decides to become a resident and invested landlord in Ireland. O'Brien provides positive closure by returning to the Romantic plot device of the national marriage plot and has Edith Vanhurst marry Dunallen, thereby revamping Irish feudalism. By using this generic convention from the Big House novel, *Light and Shade* attempts to resolve the stasis in which Mr. Lloyd and the Irish tenantry are caught—but not by remedying its root causes.[35]

By clinging to a corrupted societal hierarchy, *Light and Shade* seeks to normalize idealized feudalism in a time when this form of governance and its accompanying hierarchical divisions and interactions were no longer the norm. Nevertheless, *Light and Shade* was not alone in this choice:

such plotlines were widespread, and their presence continued long after such ideals were considered feasible.[36] Further examples of this storyline are Keary's *Castle Daly* and *Dick O'Dell* by Nannie H. H.; beyond the pages of *Young Ireland*, it can be found in Irish author Lalla McDowell's *The Earl of Effingham* (1877), Irish author Rosa Mulholland's *Marcella Grace* (1891), and *Rose O'Connor: A Story of the Day* (1880) by American author Emily Fox, writing under the pseudonym "Toler King."

Genre can be considered a "form," as theorized by Caroline Levine. In *Forms: Whole, Rhythm, Hierarchy, Network* (2015), Levine explores the relationship between form—aesthetic, social, and political—and historical context. Defining forms as "all shapes and configurations, all ordering principles, all patterns of repetition and difference," Levine explains that forms, ordering principles varying from genre conventions to family structures to institutions, bring order to the world; in this sense, both the purportedly unreal form of the novel and real-world forms have real ordering power and, thus, political power in the Foucauldian sense. The possibilities characteristic to specific ordering forms include their imagined futures and are called "affordances."[37]

In an era of great sociopolitical upheaval, *Light and Shade* and similar novels navigate asynchronous, clashing societal hierarchies that cannot coexist. They opt for an imaginative regression, dictated by nostalgia and the formal parameters of the Big House genre, rather than real-world possibilities.[38] In reaching for anachronisms, they try to sanitize existing rural hierarchies. Irish society under imperial rule was marked by nonsynchronousness, and certain classes were kept from constitutive roles in society. By clinging to outdated modes, traditionalist rural novels of the 1870s and 1880s in effect keep this Ungleichzeitigkeit and unequal distribution of societal power in place. The objectives and desires of the excluded classes are not part of the affordances of Big House novels, and, as a perhaps unintended yet inherent consequence, these narratives exclude important future trajectories of governing rural Ireland. Thus, a link between literary genre and the impossibility of alternative temporalities is suggested. A plot type that hinges on nostalgic regression brings social stasis with it; the genre does not readily lend itself to a more progressive temporality.

Light and Shade's emphasis on stasis and the longevity of Irish suffering was cotextually supported through interactions with prose fiction, poetry, articles, and opinion pieces on the pages of *Young Ireland*. In the issue of February 28, 1880, "A Reproach" by "A Clareman" was included. The poem directs its reprimand to England and juxtaposes the wealth and prosperity of England with the poverty and hardships of Ireland, pointing out the unfairness of the situation:

> You reap what we painfully sow;
> . . .
> The fat of the land is your portion—
> The skeleton body is ours.
>
> You have medical men to attend you,
> And treat for your tiniest ache;
> Of famine, exhaustion, and fever
> We die by the ditch and the brake.
> You build loathsome prisons to hold us,
> And call them workhouses—a name
> That, like holy Charity's, covers
> A mountain of sin and of shame.[39]

The contents of the poem are not linked to a specific temporal or geographical location, and the poem is written in the present tense, suggesting that the terrible condition A Clareman describes is transhistorical, timeless. The poem deepens the divergence of Irish temporality at the heart of *Light and Shade*, dehistoricizing protracted famine conditions.

In the issue that contained the first installment of *Light and Shade* (February 7, 1880), the poem "To C. S. Parnell, M. P., on His Visit to the United States" was printed. In the poem, author P. Carpenter welcomes the "Chief" and "Friend of Justice! Friend of Peace!" to the US and emphasizes the dire need for Parnell's fundraising campaign by drawing on historical Irish hardships, including leveled farmhouses, and those "sick and dying on the road" at the hands of "tyrant rulers."[40] In contrast to "A Reproach," "To C. S. Parnell" is explicit in its temporal placement. As cotexts, these poems and O'Brien's narrative cumulatively provide narrative connections between the Famine, the Fenian rebellion, and the Land War era. This line was further extended by the fiction published throughout the 1880s and discussed below.

PROGRESSIVE VIEWS

The Land League had as its purpose to "pressure the British government to reform the Irish landholding system and allow Irish political self-rule."[41] The organization campaigned for the so-called Three Fs: fair rent, freedom of sale, and fixity of tenure. It encouraged tenant farmers of all classes to take control of the distribution of land and strive for individually owned holdings. Consequently, the rural Irish could begin to "envision a future of private ownership" for themselves.[42] The 1880s signified a shift toward more progressive and egalitarian visions of the distribution of land and the potential form of Irish rural society, which resulted in several pieces of land legislation over the next decades, including the 1881 Land Law (Ireland) Act and the 1885 Purchase of Land or Ashbourne Act. The 1881 act and its amendment were designed to address the Three Fs and to lower rents, thereby ending agitation (for the moment). Some people, including Parnell's sister and driving force behind the Ladies' Land League Anna Parnell, were critical of the act. They opined that due to revisions, the act would not be of much help to those for whom it was intended, as leaseholders (one-sixth of the Irish peasantry) and those in rent arrears were excluded and the land courts—installed to carry out the Land Act—were weighted in favor of the landlords. The Ashbourne Act provided loans for tenants to purchase land. The process toward a more egalitarian distribution of land culminated in the Land Act (Ireland) or Wyndham Act of 1903; by the First World War, landlordism had disappeared from Ireland.[43]

In 1880, Thomas O'Brien, who regularly contributed to *Young Ireland* using the pen name "Clontarf," wrote:

> Onward, brothers, now or never,
> > For the land that gave you birth;
> Or, if not, remain for ever
> > Crawling slaves upon the earth.

According to the poem, Irish slavery would prove continuous and the "sireland" would never be free unless the Irish "join the Land and Labour League."[44] In similar vein, while still emphasizing the static nature of Irish temporality at least since the Famine, several narratives included in *Young Ireland* during the late 1870s and early 1880s shift toward progressive outlooks.

M. Mackey's "Con Driscoll; or, The Hatchet the Smith Made" from 1881 is set during the 1860s but deals with hot issues of its time of publication. The narrative does not cover a period of famine but is clearly set in a rural Ireland scarred by the Famine. As such, it draws connections between the 1840s, 1860s, and early 1880s. The story's fictional parish of Bannat has been largely razed when the reader encounters it; in all its silence, the desolate landscape is likened to "the calm face of a beautiful corpse."[45] This ambiguous description, which uncomfortably includes beauty and death in the same breath, is reminiscent of postfamine representations of the Irish rural landscape in fiction and travel narratives. Con Driscoll and his neighbors live under the yoke of their careless, evicting, greedy landlord William Tully, who, as "a distinguished scientific agriculturist," has found it lucrative to replace his tenantry with "cattle, bullocks and sheep." Tully raises the rents until otherwise peaceful tenant Driscoll opines that he will pay as much as he can but that "there is a point at which resistance is a duty." Tully then attempts to sell Driscoll's and a fellow tenant's farms to a Scotsman.[46]

The landlord's actions refer to the postfamine transition from small-scale tillage to large-scale pasture. Several commentators reported on this development, including special correspondent Redpath, who directly linked it to the Famine. Surveying the rural landscape in 1880, Redpath wrote that when poor Irish peasants were starving, "the Landlords of the West answered [their] piteous moans by sending processes of ejectment to turn them out into the roadside or the poorhouse to die, and by hiring crow-bar brigades to pull down the roof that had sheltered the gasping people. As fast as the homeless peasants died or were driven into exile their little farms were rented out to British graziers."[47]

In Mackey's story, Driscoll manages to reverse the odds: through a clever, nonviolent ruse, he gets Tully to sign a 999-year lease on his farm and settle on a fair rent, fulfilling two out of the Three Fs—fair rent and fixity of tenure. When confronting Tully, Driscoll delivers a heartfelt speech on the transhistorical injustices of foreign claims on Irish soil, which have caused him and his ancestors much hardship and date back as far as the days of Cromwell. After thus emphasizing the static nature of Irish history, the narrative fast-forwards and shows a return to happiness for the remaining Bannat tenants: while not all have survived, those who have are doing well and enjoying "peace, pleasure, bright hearths, and happy homes."[48] The narrative's message and transhistorical link to the 1840s are intertextually emphasized in its final lines, as the villagers sing the last stanza of "A Scene in the South" (1846), written by Thomas Davis (1814–45). It details an eviction and, like Mackey does in 1881, calls for the punishment of abusive landlords:

> "God of Mercy" I cried, "send Thy Spirit down
> On these lords so cruel and proud;
> Soften their hearts and relax their frown—
> Or else," I cried aloud,
> "Vouchsafe Thy strength to the peasant's hand
> To drive them at length from off the land."[49]

Although the narrative does not depict the end of landlordism, it does predict the disappearance of landlords from Ireland: Tully has plans to leave the country, and the tenants hope his peers will follow. The narrative is inconclusive regarding short-term future prospects but is progressive in its encouragement of Land League–style tactics of resistance. Driscoll's story of nonviolent resistance is presented as a lesson for "the people of Ireland" and, in fact, "any other people on earth" to obey the "first law of nature"—that of "self-preservation."[50]

Mackey's "His Honour's Word; or, A Victim of 'Painful Duty': A Tale of the Times" (1881) equally emphasizes that current hardships are part of a long-standing condition: protagonist James Burke and his ancestors have always struggled to survive and have been evicted several times. The narrative traces the merciless eviction practices of Irish landlords back to the Great Famine. It is set at the foot of the Galtee Mountains, quite likely referencing William O'Brien's well-known critical special correspondence "Christmas on the Galtees" (1878; I return to O'Brien's correspondence in the following chapter). Mackey describes the contemporary famine as caused by bad weather conditions, government inaction, and lack of economic protectionism: "Seasons were bad—crops failed; foreign competition reduced prices to an undreamt-of standard. . . . Famine stared thousands in the face; the government looked idly on. The governing classes followed the noble example thus set them." Shortly after, the phrase "these bad times" is used, wording often used to describe the midcentury Famine.[51] Discursively connecting both periods, the temporal conflation of Mackey's story serves as a political argument for joining the Land League. In "His Honour's Word," Burke's decision to not join the Land League and instead trust his landlord not only leads to his demise but also puts him out of step with Ireland's projected path; there is no place for him in the vision for a new Ireland suggested by the Land League.

From a British perspective, the 1881 Land Act could be considered a defiance of Political Economy, signifying a departure from laissez-faire principles. In such reasoning, however, the passing of the act could be defended on the grounds of a divergent Irish temporality, the temporality of a country that had not yet reached the stage of contract tenancy and the economic law of supply and demand and still embraced the purportedly primitive concept of possessory right for the tiller of the soil.[52] Opponents of the Land League furthermore argued that the Irish people were "too underdeveloped to become agents in their own right," "too anachronistic." Pro–Land League voices reversed this logic and argued that the League "depicted the system of land tenure and the landowners as anachronistic vestiges of feudalism."[53] The *Harp: A Magazine of General Literature* also stressed the inadequacy of feudalism in the 1880s: "Feudalism, wherever else it existed in Europe, was found long since to have lost its usefulness and has in consequence almost completely disappeared, and it is only in Great Britain and Ireland that the nobility have succeeded in preserving their feudal privileges." The Montreal-based magazine consequently utilized a Shakespearean reference—"there is something rotten in the State"—to point out the static nature of the existing land-tenure system, which "results in poverty to the peasantry in good years and famine in bad ones."[54] It cotextually strengthened the link to 1840s Ireland by following the article with Young Irelander Thomas Francis Meagher's well-known "Sword Speech" from 1846. Two decades later, Isaac Butt also used the term "anachronism" in *The Fall of Feudalism* (1904), writing that the Land League had sought to abolish "anachronism in the control of Irish rural affairs."[55]

The *Young Ireland* stories discussed in this section suggest that the continuation of feudalism not only was anachronistic but also trapped the Irish subject in a static position of (continual threat of) famine conditions, which prohibited the development of the subject. David Lloyd argues that while some considered Irish temporality as outmoded during the period this book covers, it was actually composed of alternative "formations that live on as the altered shape of practices which, rendered unviable by the inroads of colonial capitalist rationalization, find new and resistant ways to persist."[56] For the stories analyzed in this section, it is only with the end of landlordism in sight that the rural lower and middle classes have a future trajectory. Through this realization, the stories imply that a substantial shift might occur in what form of temporality becomes the dominant institutional temporality in Ireland. Seeing the Land League's narrative as the way forward, the stories reject British institutions and their trajectories in favor of a specific Irish path of development.

The periodical format houses a variety of temporal orientations. It is a recursive format tied to the past, as the medium's formal features—repetitive elements such as layout, serialization, and recurring segments—not only project future issues but also firmly tie the periodical to its past iterations.[57] The periodical is characterized by a simultaneous orientation toward the present, new, and future and, through features such as serials, relies on a sense of progress. As an influential mass medium, it can be said to provide "the rhythm[s] of modernity." I am using the plural "rhythms" because, as Mark Turner points out, the format does not provide one rhythm, nor does it necessarily establish "temporal symmetry"; rather, it offers a "cacophonous sense of time."[58] The familiar textual genre of rural fiction, more specifically of famine fiction, and the casting of this fiction in the familiar formatting of the periodical medium root these stories in a historical continuity, in the past. At the same time, their contents gesture toward the future. In so doing, these stories put to use the temporal trajectories offered by the periodical medium as well as the transhistorical potential of famine memory to instigate future change.

While these stories are too few to make any definitive claims, it is worth considering that, in contrast to the novels discussed in this chapter (one reprinted and one first published in *Young Ireland*), these stories provide the most progressive outlook. Elke D'hoker and Chris Mourant explain that short fiction writing really took flight from the 1880s; "far from only resulting in formulaic magazine fiction," there was "a veritable explosion of creativity in which writers across the literary spectrum turned to explore the possibilities of the [short story] form."[59] Arguably, the progressive futures and transformation of temporalities suggested in these stories can be ascribed to the speculative space afforded by the short story form.

No Hope?

Hester Sigerson's novel *A Ruined Race; or, The Last MacManus of Drumroosk* combines injustices committed toward Irish tenants with temperance. It was first published in serial form in *Young Ireland* between September 14 and October 27, 1888, and was revised and republished as a novel by London-based publishers Ward and Downey in 1889. Sigerson (1828–98) was born into the well-to-do Varian family in County Cork; in *The Cabinet of Irish Literature*, the Varians are described as "devoted to literature and music, all thinkers and all thoroughly Irish in feeling."[60] Hester Varian married the physician, author, and Gaelic scholar George Sigerson, a leading figure in the Gaelic Revival who went to Connaught in 1880 to investigate the origins and character of the ongoing epidemic.[61] Described as a periodical author first, Hester Sigerson contributed to various journals and newspapers, including the *Cork Examiner* and the *Irish Monthly*. She primarily wrote poetry and short fiction and was considered a "woman of fine literary talent."[62] Working as editor for the *Irish Fireside Club*, Sigerson used the medium to "urge club members to learn about the ideals and literature of Young Ireland and initiated essays on subjects relating to the movement."[63]

Hester Sigerson wrote only one novel; it maps out the life and downfall of Dan MacManus, an exemplary Irish farmer living in the West of Ireland. Dan marries Mary, and they experience newly wed bliss for a few years. When the weather turns bad, Dan's crops repeatedly fail. The couple's children die, and Dan and Mary are eventually evicted. Dan is arrested and taken to jail for assaulting the evil local process server during the eviction, and Mary, out of her wits, is taken to the poorhouse hospital to die. Having nothing left, Dan goes to Dublin, where he succumbs to the lure of alcohol, falls off the quay inebriated, and dies, happy to join his family in heaven.

The narrative ascribes rural hardships to the combined effects of abusive landlords, bad weather conditions, and prolonged unequal treatment of the poor peasantry. Hardworking and honest Dan is of the "old stock," but while his ancestors used to own the castle overlooking the village of Fortmanus, years of anti-Catholic sentiment and unfair treatment by those out to better themselves at the cost of their poor fellows have diminished the MacManus fortune to Dan's present destitution. The MacManuses are not alone in this, as Dan explains to his daughter: "An' many a fine family in these parts wor robbed the same as we wor in the dark days long ago. But, sure 'tis only the way o' the world—the way o' the people, you know, darlin'."[64]

Sigerson's novel repeatedly emphasizes the long pedigree of Dan MacManus's noble Irish lineage and the extended suffering of his family, which results in a consideration of time as static and of rural Ireland's condition as continually deteriorating. Even those who are doing well at the end of the narrative cannot rest assured. When Dan is about to leave his village, he warns farmer Jim Treacy: "Don't be giving into high rints, Jim; they beggared me. . . . Lave . . . an' go somewhere else—no matter how hard it may be." In response, "Jim felt a chill creep over his heart, as he heard Dan's words. It seemed as though they foreshadowed some hard fate that was to come to him also."[65]

The novel remains temporally undefined until the reader learns Mary's death date: her tombstone reads "August 28, 1857." This date suggests that Dan and Mary's suffering extends well beyond the Famine, and the narrative demonstrates that such hardships pertain to the whole village of Fortmanus. When Dan returns from prison, many of his neighbors have left or have not survived: "many of the cabins had disappeared altogether, and sheep grazed on the little spots of earth which, but a short time ago, had been consecrated to humanity."[66] Earlier, the novel shows that good fortunes were once possible in Ireland: Mary comes from a comfortable family, and Dan and Mary live happily for a few years. However, the underlying, unchanging structure of Irish rural society makes for an unstable and toxic foundation. The novel shows that, when left unchecked, conditions worsen and are eventually the death of the good Irish farmer; it offers no clear path to improvement. As such, while *A Ruined Race* demonstrates the existence of both repetition and stasis in recent Irish history, it leans toward the latter, suggesting a conflation of temporalities.

The fortunes of Dan and the other Fortmanus tenants stand on disastrous footing with the underlying system that governs Irish rural life. Save a few upright, strong farmers, those who survive typically do so by escaping the system altogether through emigration or by committing abuses made possible by a corrupted system, turning on their peers and aligning themselves with the ruling system and the future it offers. Sigerson's narrative paints an atmosphere that sustains inequality and oppression and, as such, shows the great destructive power in the hands of those Michael Rothberg calls "implicated subjects": "implicated subjects occupy positions of power and privilege without being themselves direct agents of harm; they contribute to, inhabit, inherit, or benefit from regimes of domination but do not originate or control such regimes."[67]

As a representative of a disappearing class, Dan MacManus can be read as an anachronism. MacManus and the traditional life he represents—the benevolent, old-stock Catholic living in balance with his fellow countrymen—are representative of a mode of life that has no future in rural Ireland. As such, this character "cannot be easily assimilated into institutions" and "confirms the imperial narrative of 'the vanishing primitive.'"[68] Moreover, *A Ruined Race* shows that at present, there is no room for cotemporaneity: the life Dan stands for is not allowed to coexist within or alongside the governing system's temporal trajectory. The novel does not offer room for the future existence of the life Dan represents and in that sense is bleak but more realistic than rural novels such as O'Brien's *Light and Shade*.

Sigerson's novel was republished a year later with several new sections and even whole new chapters added. In one of these additions, Sigerson provides some hope, in contrast to the serialized first edition. In the 1889 version, after Dan dejectedly declares that he and his peers can be crushed down "as easy as I'd put my fut upon a worm," the narrator interjects: "Thank God there is a new leaf turned over in Ireland's history since poor Dan MacManus spoke those words. And there is now some hope to brighten the path of the Irish peasant if the apparent improvements which have been obtained can be held from degenerating into changes only of form, and not of fact."[69] This progressive streak remains vague, as Sigerson never pinpoints what those "apparent improvements" are. One can assume, however, that Sigerson is referring to recent acts of resistance: Dan's advice to Jim Treacy to sooner leave than pay exorbitant rents (already included in the *Young Ireland* edition) aligns with the tactic of rent strikes adopted during the Plan of Campaign. Other improvements referred to by Sigerson likely entail the acts of 1881 and 1885. In any case, the absence of any positive outlook in the *Young Ireland* version of *A Ruined Race* and the very cautious remark on recent improvements by Sigerson's narrator in the Ward and Downey publication suggest that, at the time of writing, the achieved legislative improvements still seemed precarious and unfinished to Sigerson—for the author, time would have to tell their full implications.

At the same time, a cautious yet more positive interpretation had already arisen in *Young Ireland*. Other works of fiction and poetry included in the magazine around the time *A Ruined Race* was serialized called further attention to the plight of the Irish rural poor and the evils conducted by landlords. The serialized story "The American Letter: A Tale of the Great Famine" by "Olena" shows how benevolent landlords and tenants alike suffer but together survive the Famine, demonstrating that such reactionary approaches could still feature in fiction. The poems "Evicted!" by "Croghan" and "The Exile's Message" by Annie M. Kenny lament evictions and exile. The latter also includes general references to starvation.[70] In the poems "The Evicted Tenant's Ruined Home" by "Isidore" and "To Irish Slavery" by M. J. O'Horahan, the colonial presence and landlords more specifically are labeled "tyrants"; O'Horahan additionally represents them in monsterlike terms.[71] Some creative works include a belief in a better future. A positive tone is found in "To Irish Slavery"—the poem mentions "Brian" (Boru) and "Charles" (Parnell) in the same breath, suggesting a heroic, old-stock parentage to the latter. Additionally, the poem urges the Irish to nobly resist "Slavery."[72] Isidore expresses hope for a time "when landlords shall no more have power / To lay the poor man's homestead low."[73] A further note of promise is found in another poem by the same author. Published simultaneously with an installment of *A Ruined Race*, "Old Times" provides the recollections of an octagenarian. The age of the speaker serves to emphasize the duration of the conditions he describes. His memories include "hard-hearted" landlords, depopulation, and famine suffering:

> There came trials hard and heavy which the
>> Lord can only know,

When the famine and the sickness laid the good
    old neighbours low;
The mountain sides grew lonesome and the
    valleys filled with gloom—
It was a fearful judgment and a sudden, dreadful
    doom.

Yet despite these experiences, the speaker is hopeful, stating that "thank God, there are great changes for the better" and "bright days are comin'."[74]

These stories and poems published around the time same time as *A Ruined Race* are, like Sigerson's novel, largely open ended in their views for the future. However, they do provide careful messages of promise, as Sigerson herself did in the later republication of *A Ruined Race*. In advocating resistance and repeating hope, these texts show the "internal dialogics" of the magazine, cotextually supporting change in the forseeable future and thus providing support for reading the *Young Ireland* edition of Sigerson's novel in a cautiously positive light.[75]

VALIDATING IRISH TEMPORALITY

The prose fiction, poetry, and nonfiction included in *Young Ireland* and discussed in this chapter show that Ireland's temporality could be considered static since at least the Great Famine but even from an earlier point onward, with unfair societal hierarchies and ruling systems seen as predating the 1840s. Some commentators saw the Famine as an exceptional period in terms of lives damaged or lost, but because the root causes and ills plaguing Irish society were frequently considered to predate the Famine and because the period was placed in a longer line of similar events, the Famine did not receive an atemporal quality. Demonstrating stasis, taken together the *Young Ireland* narratives do not suggest a unilateral view on the solution to that temporal condition. This variety in views can be accredited to the different generic parameters discussed above and is inherent to the heterogeneous voice of the collective form that is the magazine. It can also be connected to the uncertain future trajectory regarding land legislation and self-rule for Ireland during the 1870s and 1880s.

The creative works from *Young Ireland* analyzed above show the simultaneous presence of different temporalities. To give room to such coexistence, Daniel Levy argues for reinvigorating the difference between memory and history. Although the difference has been questioned since the advent of memory studies, Levy readopts this juxtaposition by explaining that memory is opposed to history because it gives way to "a co-existence of simultaneous time transcending multitudes of pasts" and the accompanying "cultural validation" of fragmented and diverse memories. As such, Levy's preference for communal memories as an alternative to singular history is connected to the plurality of temporalities. Following Levy, the narratives included in *Young Ireland* can be considered to advocate for the cultural validation of Irish memories and temporal trajectories that diverge from the norm.[76] In so doing, they hold the power to make readers consider Irish temporality as at least equally normative to its British counterpart.

NOTES

1. "John Mitchel: The Dead Patriot," 2.

2. Reville, "Great Irish Famine," March 6, 1875, 5.

3. Clark, *Social Origins of the Land War*, 3; Cronin, *History of Ireland*, 155; Geary, *Land War*, 4.

4. C. P. M., "A Chapter of Irish History," vol. 3, issues 3–5.

5. King, *Irish Question*, preface, 73–74.

6. I discuss various such works in "Famine Traces"; see chapter 3 especially.

7. "Perpetuating 'Irish Famine.'" February 28, 1880. The article was taken from the Liverpool *Catholic Times* of January 31.

8. "All the Correspondents . . . ," February 15, 1879, 194.

9. Mullen, *Novel Institutions*, 5, 2. Levine discusses institutional time in *Forms* as well, explaining that historicist scholars often equate "the beginnings and ends of periods to the working of social institutions," the latter meaning both official organizations and "regulative practices" (Levine, *Forms*, 57).

10. Carr, *Time, Narrative and History*, 15, 16.

11. The quote is from Nicholson, *Annals of the Famine*, preface.

12. Nannie H. H. did not sign her stories; for *Dick O'Dell, Young Ireland* includes that the narrative was written by the author of "Kate O'Donnell's Dream." In "'Young Ireland'—A Retrospect," J. G. reflects on the twelve years *Young Ireland* had been published and identifies the author: "'Nannie H. H.' was her signature. She could write well, whoever she was" ("'Young Ireland'—A Retrospect," February 5, 1887, 88). The *Waterloo Directory* further identifies her as a "Mrs Beazley" who also contributed to the *Nation* ("Nation, The," n.p.).

I discuss *Castle Daly* at greater length in chapter 3. *Castle Daly* and *Dick O'Dell* are not discussed further in the current chapter; also see my forthcoming chapter "(Re)building Self and Country" for further analyses of these narratives.

13. The *Nation* reprinted praise for the patriotic spirit of both the magazine and editor from various Irish newspapers; see, for example, "Christmas Number of 'Young Ireland,'" December 25, 1875, 12. In 1884, the *Wexford People* praised *Young Ireland* as a national magazine and called it a "popular periodical" ("Christmas Number of 'Young Ireland,'" December 20, 2).

14. Rains, "Do You Ring?," 18.

15. In "Young Ireland and *The Nation*," Ríona Nic Congáil classifies the magazine as a children's magazine. Jennifer Phegley writes that family magazines offered an assembly of reading materials meant as shared reading in the parlor or by the fire (Phegley, "Family Magazines," 276). She includes the typical contents of penny family magazines: they "were dominated by adventurous, melodramatic, and sensational fiction. The standard sixteen-page issue also

featured domestic, historical, biographical, and scientific articles as well as poetry." *Young Ireland* is typical of the format (ibid., 279).

16. Walsh, "National System of Education," 8; Quinn, *Young Ireland*, 127, 128.

17. David J. O'Donoghue writes that T. D. became editor after A. M. left and that he held that position until selling "the property a few years ago" (O'Donoghue, *Poets of Ireland*, 239). Confederate Clubs were Young Ireland clubs, established in reaction to Daniel O'Connell's denunciation of violent measures in the struggle for Home Rule (Rynne, "Young Ireland and Irish Revolutions," 113 and 50n on same page). Cronin, "Sullivan, Timothy Daniel," n.p. For Sullivan's discussion of obstructionism, see Sullivan, *Recollections of Troubled Times*, chapter 20 (181–89).

18. Cronin, "Sullivan, Timothy Daniel." "The Friends and Foes of Ireland" and "The Story of England" were published in vol. 1, 1875, and vol. 2, 1876.

19. F. G., "A True Story of Black '47," March 4, 143. Sherlock was also editor of the magazine for some years; it is unclear precisely when (O'Donoghue, *Poets of Ireland*, 229).

20. A. M. Sullivan served as a clerk in the Skibbereen district relief works during the Famine (Maume, "Sullivan, Alexander Martin"). In *New Ireland* (1878), he spends several chapters on Young Ireland, the Famine, and its aftermath, repeatedly emphasizing his own presence as eyewitness.

21. Sullivan, *Recollections of Troubled Times*, 5, 6.

22. A notable exception is Nic Congáil's article "Young Ireland and *The Nation*."

23. Clyde, *Irish Literary Magazines*, 30.

24. Ibid.; Collins quoted in Phegley, "Family Magazines," 280; Mussell, "Repetition," 351.

25. Clyde, *Irish Literary Magazines*, 30. Elizabeth Tilley writes that "political and social crises in Ireland were often accompanied by an increase in titles published" ("Periodicals in Ireland," 209). See chapter 5 of *Periodical Famines* for a detailed discussion of Catholic colonization.

26. Loeber and Loeber, with Mullin Burnham, *Guide to Irish Fiction*, 989. The quote is taken from Gwynn, "Introductory Memoir," 8.

27. Gwynn, "Introductory Memoir," 104; from a letter by O'Brien (ca. 1884), quoted in O'Brien, *Charlotte Grace O'Brien*, 97–98. Loeber and Loeber, with Mullin Burnham, *Guide to Irish Fiction*, 985–86.

28. Loeber and Loeber, with Mullin Burnham, *Guide to Irish Fiction*, 989. Gwynn, "Introductory Memoir," 44, 76. Upton's *Uncle Pat's Cabin* covers the period between the Famine and Land War. After emigrating to the US, Upton self-published a revised edition of his novel in 1914.

29. O'Brien, *Light and Shade, Young Ireland*, February 28, 1880, 130.

30. Ibid., March 6, 1880, 146.

31. Ibid., February 28, 1880, 130.

32. Ibid., 131.

33. Ibid., March 27, 1880, 197.

34. Ó Gráda, "Ireland," 181.

35. For a study on the Big House novel that also discusses the trope of the national marriage plot, see Kreilkamp, *Anglo-Irish Novel*.

36. Such narrative choices involve the sanitization of a system that Joe Cleary aptly describes as "bastardized feudalism." See Cleary, *Outrageous Fortune*, 35. Marguérite Corporaal, Christopher Cusack, and I discuss the recurrence of the trope in the period 1860–95, indicating that its popularity continued until well after the rise and successes of the Land League in the 1880s and, in fact, is found after the "watershed" turning point signaled by James Murphy. See Corporaal, Cusack, and Janssen, "Reimagining Rural Ireland"; Murphy, "Rosa Mulholland, W. P. Ryan," 220. I also discuss this trope in more detail for the period 1871–91 in "Famine Traces"; especially see chapter 3 and table 3.1 (106). From a corpus of eighteen famine

novels from Ireland and the Irish communities in the US and Canada, eleven contain the reinstatement of an idealized, Irish form of feudalism.

37. Levine, *Forms*, 3, 14; see also Foucault, *Discipline and Punish*.

38. Christopher Morash explores this tension between traditional novelistic conventions and societal possibilities in chapter 2 of *Writing the Irish Famine*.

39. A Clareman, "A Reproach," 139.

40. Carpenter, "To C. S. Parnell," 95. The poem was reprinted from the Boston *Pilot*.

41. Janis, *Greater Ireland*, 3.

42. Jordan, "Irish National League," 149.

43. Ward, *Unmanageable Revolutionaries*, 20–21. Special correspondent Margaret Dixon McDougall also had concerns about the 1881 act; see chapter 3 of *Periodical Famines*. McCarthy, *Respectability & Reform*, 90; Dooley, "Big House," 166; Cronin, *History of Ireland*, 170.

44. O'Brien, "Work for Ireland," December 4, 780.

45. Mackey, "Con Driscoll," October 22, 1881, 673.

46. Ibid., October 22, 1881, 674; October 29, 1881, 691.

47. Redpath wrote for the New York *Tribune*, but his popular letters were reprinted in several periodicals, including the New York *Celtic Monthly* and *Irish-American*, the Montreal *Harp*, and Dublin's *United Ireland*. This specific excerpt is taken from "Famine Scenes in Ireland," *Harp*, July 1880, 436–37. In this letter, Redpath also writes that the coming of graziers was a postfamine development.

48. Mackey, "Con Driscoll," November 5, 1881, 706, 708.

49. Ibid., 708. The first line is misquoted, as it starts with "God of Justice" (Davis, *Poems of Thomas Davis*, 191–94).

50. Mackey, "Con Driscoll," October 29, 1881, 692.

51. Mackey, "His Honour's Word," September 10, 1881, 579. As the narrator states, "in no other country under the sun is the performance of 'painful duty' better understood, or more readily, constantly and cheerfully practiced, than in Ireland. It has been carried on briskly and constantly for the past thirty-three or four years by landlords and their henchmen." This passage traces the practice back to the year 1847 (ibid., 577). The story is discussed in more detail in chapter 5.

52. Boylan and Foley, *Political Economy and Colonial Ireland*, 154.

53. Mullen, *Novel Institutions*, 187.

54. Kavanagh, "Is a Change Necessary," March, 214, 216, 215.

55. Mullen, *Novel Institutions*, 187.

56. Lloyd, *Irish Times*, 4.

57. Mussell, "Repetition," 349–51.

58. Turner, "Periodical Time," 184–85, 187–88, 190. See also Allen, "Pause You Who Read This," 34; McCormack, "Never Put Your Name," 115; and Tilley, *Periodical Press*, 86.

59. D'hoker and Mourant, "Introduction," 9.

60. Read and Hinkson, *Cabinet of Irish Literature*, 32.

61. Geary, *Land War*, 30–31.

62. Loeber and Loeber, with Mullin Burnham, *Guide to Irish Fiction*, 1196. O'Toole, *Dictionary of Munster Women Writers*, 227. The quote is taken from Read and Hinkson, *Cabinet of Irish Literature*, 201.

63. Nic Congáil, "Young Ireland and *The Nation*," 58.

64. Sigerson, *Ruined Race*, *Young Ireland* (new series), September 15, 1888, 249.

65. Ibid., October 13, 1888, 308.

66. Ibid., 306. In the revised novel published a year later, Mary's death date is changed to "August 28, 18–"; this adjustment further emphasizes the prolonged or even timeless quality of the MacManuses' suffering (Sigerson, *Ruined Race*, 226).

67. Rothberg, *Implicated Subject*, 1.

68. Mullen, *Novel Institutions*, 4. James Clifford quoted in Mullen, *Novel Institutions*, 88.

69. Sigerson, *Ruined Race*, 226.

70. Olena, "American Letter," February 4 and 18; Croghan, "Evicted!," June 11, 1887, 375; Kenny, "Exile's Message," March 2, 1889, 134.

71. Isidore, "Evicted Tenant's Ruined Home," January 15, 1887, 36; O'Horahan, "To Irish Slavery," September 3, 1887, 564.

72. O'Horahan, "To Irish Slavery," 564.

73. Isidore, "Evicted Tenant's Ruined Home," 36.

74. Isidore, "Old Times," September 15, 1888, 255.

75. Ann Ardis quoted in D'hoker and Mourant, "Introduction," 11.

76. Levy, "Changing Temporalities," 29.

3

SPECIAL CORRESPONDENCE ON IRELAND IN THE EARLY 1880s

Current and Past Famines in Margaret Dixon McDougall's "A Tour through Ireland"

THE LATE NINETEENTH CENTURY SAW transformations in the practice of journalism. Technological developments, such as the laying of telegraph wire across oceans and continents, sped up the delivery of news and made it possible for newspaper authors to travel after the news and be there first. Political developments in Ireland between the mid-nineteenth and early twentieth centuries prompted extensive newspaper coverage, and, as Glenn Hooper demonstrates in his anthology *The Tourist's Gaze: Travellers to Ireland 1800–2000* (2001), many journalists were contracted by newspapers to travel to Ireland. The second half of the nineteenth century also witnessed a change in the public perception of the journalist, as the practice of journalism became a respectable employment. Within this development, the special correspondent enjoyed a relatively high status and could even attain the status of national celebrity. For the British imperial and American contexts, Andrew Griffiths and Tim Lanzendörfer, respectively, argue that these reporters' impact was extensive and that they influenced not only public opinion but also policymaking.[1]

Griffiths and Lanzendörfer focus on war correspondence, but their arguments can be extended to the broader field of special correspondence. During the winter of 1877–78, Irish journalist and later nationalist MP William O'Brien (1852–1928) went to the Buckley estate in the Galtee Mountains to report on hardships for the *Freeman's Journal*. His series of articles, later published as the pamphlet "Christmas on the Galtees," is considered an early example of literary journalism. In 1880, O'Brien repeated the exercise and wrote a series of articles about famine conditions in the West of Ireland.[2] As Christopher Morash argues, these reports constituted a powerful political move: in O'Brien's case, "the act of writing, of bearing witness, becomes a transforming political act in its own right, in that it directs that most potent of forces, public opinion." Indeed, following the Galtees articles, Nathan Buckley was forced to make changes to the management of his estate, and "the campaign for Irish land reform scored a resounding public relations victory."[3]

Besides O'Brien, others reported on hardships and abuses in (rural) Ireland: American philanthropist Asenath Nicholson, English special correspondent Harriet Martineau, Scottish Quaker philanthropist James Hack Tuke, American journalist and political economist Henry George, and Scottish-born American reporter James Redpath traveled the island during the 1840s, early 1850s, late 1870s, and early 1880s. These commentators and their reports have been studied by scholars such as John McKivigan, Christopher Morash, Felix Larkin, Giulia Bruna, Teja Varma Pusapati, and Maureen Murphy. The current chapter investigates writings from Ireland during the Land War by Irish-born Canadian author and journalist Margaret Dixon McDougall (1826/8–99). Taking place at a time when women's rights, women's activism, and female participation in the public and political spheres were much debated issues on both sides of the Atlantic, McDougall's work as a female special correspondent signifies a rare and fascinating case study.[4]

Describing the Irish Land Question as a "burning question" that "it behooves every man and every woman, having Irish blood in their veins, to look into," McDougall used her writing to plead for the betterment of the lot of the poor tenants and laborers of Ireland.[5] Her letters were published in the Montreal *Witness* as "A Tour through Ireland" and received acclaim. Their success is evidenced by readerly responses printed in the *Witness*, the letters' republication in other newspapers, and the fact that the letters were collected in the volume *The Letters of "Norah" on Her Tour through Ireland* (1882), published through the offices of the *Witness* and paid for by public subscription. The following year, McDougall also recast her letters into the novel *The Days of a Life*.

This chapter starts by providing insight into the dynamics between the Montreal *Witness* and McDougall's writings. It moves on to an analysis of the letters, concentrating on a few particularly noteworthy ones, and highlights two vital aspects regarding McDougall's letters: their acknowledgment of the repetitive nature of Irish history and the cotextual support of other works included in the *Witness* that emphasized McDougall's core message.[6] In representing the Land War and famine of 1879–82, McDougall is not always clear on whether she is referring to her contemporary famine or the Great Famine; this lack of temporal specificity does justice to her informants' experiences. McDougall makes use of a broad framework consisting of fictional and nonfictional imagery. She utilizes biblical and literary intertexts and elements from an existing framework of famine memory. The latter features in her work through familiar tropes and witness testimonies by survivors of the Great Famine. Her referential framework transgresses the dividing line between past and present, fact and fiction, modes of journalistic and literary writing, navigating what John Hartsock describes as the "space of complex and dynamic relationships between" "narrative literary journalism" and "conventional fiction," also called the "reality boundary."[7] Moreover, her letters were published alongside Annie Keary's *Castle Daly* (1875). The chapter discusses the narrativization of recent and past events and demonstrates how on the pages of the *Witness*, Keary's fiction cotextually supports McDougall's key points on the importance of the mnemonic legacy of the Famine and the need to improve the Irish tenants' legislative position and property rights to break rural Ireland's repetitive streak.

The Montreal *Witness* and Margaret Dixon McDougall's Tour

The Protestant Montreal *Witness* was published between 1845 and 1938, and its initial editor and proprietor was Scottish-born fervent Protestant Evangelist and journalist John Dougall (1808–86). The newspaper seems to have built up a sizable circulation and by 1876 had "attained a high place among [the] Dominion newspapers."[8] J. G. Snell writes that it "had a sufficiently large circulation in the English-speaking areas around Montreal to ensure moderate financial success."[9] The *Witness* was also read outside of the Montreal area, indicated by the newspaper's inclusion of the US and Britain in its subscription rates and its list of public subscribers in the collected *Letters*; the latter also included subscribers situated in St. Paul (present-day Alberta), Manitoba (Winnipeg), elsewhere in Ontario, and in Paris (France) and Nebraska (US).[10]

The *Daily Witness* typically counted eight pages, and its scope was broad. Dougall wrote that, while the *Witness* would cover news and events "as occur in, or concern Canada," it would also contain "the best works that issue from the Press on both sides of the Atlantic," singling out "important leading articles from the journals of Great Britain and the United States" on a daily basis.[11] The *Witness* had a broad understanding of what information would "concern Canada," as it included news from all over the globe, such as articles on the situation in the Transvaal, the Nihilists in Russia, Chief Sitting Bull in the US, revolt in Tunis, and peace conditions in Basuto (present-day Lesotho). In its early publication days, the newspaper contained many pieces of general interest and relatively few articles discussing news and recent events and, moreover, relegated the news proper to later pages: for example, in the issue of January 4, 1847, the news is not included until the very last page. By contrast, in the early 1880s, news, cable telegrams, articles on recent events, and letters to the editor were staple features of the first three pages of each issue of the *Witness*. A noteworthy feature of the newspaper is the extent to which it included readerly interaction in its pages in the form of letters to the editor.

According to its prospectus, the newspaper was called into existence to fill a lacuna in the Canadian periodical market of the 1840s—that of the "*general* Religious and Literary Newspaper, devoted to the best interests of the people, temporal as well as spiritual." Dougall stated that in this endeavor, he would be assisted by "literary friends of various Evangelical denominations," underscoring the unifying and inclusive thrust of the newspaper.[12] The *Witness* quickly became considered "aggressive and intolerant of Catholics, Irish and French Canadians," an intolerance seemingly based on religious rather than ethnic differences. The paper was perceived as so vehemently anti-Catholic that it sparked the publication of a specifically Catholic counterpart, the *True Witness and Catholic Chronicle*, in 1850. In its first issue, the *True Witness* took issue with the *Witness*'s anti-Catholicism, denouncing Dougall's attacks on Catholic practices and the charity done by Montreal's Grey Nuns on behalf of orphaned children, specifically. Moreover, in 1875, when the paper was edited by Dougall's son John Redpath Dougall, bishop of Montreal Ignace Bourget placed an ecclesiastical ban on the paper.[13]

In the early 1880s, the newspaper devoted much attention to events in Ireland, and the Land War, Land Law (Ireland) Act (1881), Land League, and famine were almost daily features. Engagement with Ireland in Canada, specifically by the non-Irish press, had a long history: several Canadian newspapers had shown much interest in the Famine of the 1840s. Important reasons for this interest included the potato crop failures in North America that preceded those in Ireland and the link forged through migration between Ireland and Canada, which peaked during 1847. The latter made emigration from Ireland a Canadian domestic issue. Research by Pauline Collombier-Lakeman on Canadian press reactions to the Great Famine shows that "there existed a form of deep moral and emotional connection between Ireland and Canada." Compassion and acts of altruism went across denominations, and reports and reactions in the Canadian press show that solidarity for the Irish could be attributed to "pity for fellow human beings" and empathy for fellow Catholics or Christians, Irishmen and women, or "'*brethren*' within the British Empire."[14]

While at the outset, Dougall Sr. had stated that he intended the *Witness* to steer clear of "party politics and sectarian discussions," the paper did show its political colors. For example, under the guidance of John Redpath Dougall, the paper openly denounced the aforementioned James Redpath's (no relation) heated political enunciations about the Irish Question, voiced its opinion on the viability of the Land Bill, and was critical of the Land League and of Charles Stewart Parnell and John Dillon.[15]

In 1881, the paper enlisted the Ulster Scots Canadian author and journalist McDougall to act as special correspondent in Ireland. McDougall, née Margaret Moran Dixon, was born into a prosperous family in Belfast in 1826 or 1828 and came to Canada with her family in 1843. She married lumberman Alexander Dougald McDougall in 1852, and the couple had six children. McDougall was a schoolteacher in her own school, an author of both fiction and nonfiction, and a writer for various Canadian newspapers. In the early 1880s, Alexander and Margaret moved to Croswell (Michigan), where several family members had settled earlier. After the death of her husband, McDougall became active in the Baptist Home Missionary Society in Michigan. She was praised for her lectures in support of the education of freed slaves in the southern states of the US. McDougall died in Seattle in 1899.[16]

On January 27, 1881, McDougall left for her native Ireland. She spent the better part of the year there, starting in the north and traveling all over the island. McDougall's first letter was included in the March 9 issue of the Montreal *Daily Witness*, and over the span of 1881, the newspaper printed almost sixty of her letters, in both its weekly and daily editions. Some thirty years earlier, Harriet Martineau had received substantial criticism for writing about typically male issues such as Political Economy and land tenure and as a result had first published her foreign correspondence for the *Daily News* anonymously and sometimes with a male authorial voice. McDougall did not have to resort to such tactics in 1881. Granted, McDougall's name was not printed with her letters, but this was common for special correspondence. In the issue that carried her first letter, the newspaper immediately identified her as "Mrs. Alexander McDougall, author of 'Life in Glenshie,' and other tales."[17]

In her letters, McDougall repeatedly reflects on the ruined homes and "pitiful desolation" of the landscape.[18] In the letter included in the *Daily Witness* on April 16, 1881—included as an appendix to this book—she reflects on the postfamine transition from small-scale agriculture to large-scale cattle farming and blames the emptying of the landscape on the policies of landlords. She cites as an example landlord Mr. Stewart, who, "when cattle became high-priced, thought that cattle were much preferable to human beings, so he evicted gradually the dwellers who had broken in the hills, and entered into possession, without compensation, of the field, the produce of the other's toil and sweat." McDougall also describes public relief works as features of the Irish landscape and explicitly mentions the practice of "road-making" "in famine time," a policy turned to during the Great Famine and the smaller famine of her present.[19] The resulting "famine roads" were stretches of road frequently left unfinished, functioning as uncanny reminders of the human lives lost alongside them. Famine roads became literary tropes in their own right and have been employed frequently. They feature, for example, in Emily Lawless's "Famine Roads and Famine Memories" (1898) and, more recently, Emma Donoghue's novel *The Wonder* (2016) and Paul Lynch's novel *Grace* (2017). Other imagery reminiscent of famine writings features in the letters: self-sacrificing clergymen, evictions, people dying alongside the road, and special attention for child, female, and elderly victims. Consequently, these images place McDougall's journalism in connection to a larger body of famine writings.[20]

McDougall stresses that the law in Ireland only protects the interests of the wealthy: "The law . . . was only for the rich, and was known to the poor, if they dared to contend with their landlord, as an engine of oppression."[21] In their defense of the rights of the poor, McDougall's views differed markedly from those of her publishing outlet. On the first page of the issue of July 27, 1881, the *Witness* included a telegram and accompanying article about the upcoming third reading of the Irish Land Bill. In it, Lord Randolph Churchill (member for Woodstock and father of Winston Churchill) is quoted; he argued that the original Land Bill was "the result of a revolutionary agitation" and that it "endangered individual liberty and diminished the security of property, and that while it would not increase the prosperity of Ireland it would endanger the unity between Ireland and

England."[22] On page four, the paper reported the return of the infamous Captain Boycott to his residence near Lough Mask, commended his bravery, and condemned any "flagrant acts of injustice" such as those committed against him. The article referred to the "shameful failure of juries to convict murderers and assassins whose guilt the clearest evidence has established," siding with the landlords of Ireland in this case of antilandlord violence.[23] These examples demonstrate that the *Witness* defended economic individualism and the property rights of the prosperous, placing it in opposition to McDougall's support of increased legal and landholding rights for the poor.

In the context of this discrepancy, the choice of McDougall as special correspondent might seem surprising. However, it can be explained in light of several perspectives. The newspaper might not have been aware of how McDougall's views would come to differ from its own ideology—when the first letter was published, it indicated that "Mrs. McDougall has gone on her mission to her native land remarkably free from prejudices on either side of the Irish Question." It added that "her instructions are to state with the strictest impartiality whatever can be learned in favor of either party, and we have full confidence in her faithful and capable fulfilment of this delicate task."[24]

Arguably, sending McDougall, a correspondent "of warm sympathies with the people," sympathies that "know no limit of race or creed," was a strategic move.[25] Reader responses to the Irish Land Question sent to the newspaper differed substantially. Readers "Montreal" and "Three Rivers," for example, were critical of "popery" in Ireland, with Montreal going as far as seeing it as the root cause of an Irish "distaste" for "intellectual and political freedom" and the reason why the Irish were economically backward in contrast to other parts of the empire. Montreal went on to argue that, contrary to their Scottish and English peers, the Irish were not "professional agriculturists" and would not benefit from substituting lease holding for annual tenancy through law. Rather, the Irish tenants themselves needed to be improved.[26] Three Rivers, also critical of Roman Catholicism but to a lesser degree than Montreal, was highly offended by the description of the Irish and critical of the analysis of the Land Question offered by Montreal. Three Rivers saw landlordism and absenteeism in Ireland as the main evils and argued that Ireland wanted "justice" from the British, "her defamers."[27] Aside from their religious orientation, these letter writers were polar opposites in their views on the Irish Land Question. Moreover, as said, the *Witness* newspaper had earlier been accused of anti-Catholic bias, which these letters in varying degrees continued. Publishing letters by a Baptist special correspondent said to be sympathetic and open to all classes and creeds, then, shows a more tolerant streak to the *Witness* newspaper as well as an attempt to meet the different views expressed by its readership.

Perhaps the most important reason for continuing to include McDougall's travel reports was that they were a success. The newspaper praised her work, stating that "Mrs. McDougall's particular gift lies in description and realistic delineation of character, in which departments she has not many equals."[28] That the newspaper considered the letters important material also becomes evident from the fact that in both the daily and weekly editions, the letters appeared on early pages (pages two and three, respectively), printed alongside national and international telegraph messages and news reports. Its US sibling, the New York *Witness*, also published the letters, as did the Ontario-based *Almonte Gazette*. This favorable reception is further underscored by letters to the editor commending McDougall's writing.[29] The different positions taken by the newspaper and McDougall described above, as well as their different stances vis-à-vis Charles Stewart Parnell, did not influence McDougall's position in the paper, as throughout the full publication run of her tour, the letters did not become less substantial nor were they less prominently placed.

The letters have a set format but are generically and stylistically diverse: they alternate between travel narrative, witness account, sociopolitical exposé, and literary writing. While the voice of McDougall as the author is present, the letters pay special respect to the experiences of common subjects in a manner similar to the emerging literary journalism.[30] In her letters, McDougall shares her sentiments and convictions with her readership, gives many facts and figures, and questions several ingrained practices. Emotional language is used sparingly, especially compared to the melodramatic tone that adorns the later novel based on her travels, *The Days of a Life*. The personal and "novelistic" style of reporting of the literary journalism of the day could compromise "impartiality and [threaten] to overwhelm the facts reported with personal responses."[31] However, this need not be the case: for example, in his analysis of O'Brien's "Christmas on the Galtees," Larkin contends that the "combination of precise analysis and passionate advocacy" makes the articles "perfect specimen[s] of the early New Journalism."[32] In other words, the personal dimension fortifies rather than detracts from the facts. McDougall's style, characterized by selective use of emotional observations in favor of more factual information, bears similarities with O'Brien's journalistic social commentary, preventing her letters from the pitfalls of emotional strain.

LITERARY TECHNIQUES AND FAMINE TIMES ON LOOP

When describing Ireland's supposed economic backwardness, reader "Montreal" pointed out Ireland's divergent temporal position, including that "Ireland is behind the age."[33] In her novel *The Days of a Life*, McDougall rather suggests a repetition to Irish temporality, concluding that Irish "history repeats itself."[34] This view of Irish history is present in McDougall's *Witness* letters as well: the author and her informants draw connections between the Great Famine and smaller famine, pointing out lessons to be learned from history in the early 1880s. McDougall's use of the word "famine" can be imprecise, lending itself for the comparison—here through conflation—of the two periods. McDougall learns that memories of the Great Famine are so engrained in the collective psyche of the rural communities she encounters that they easily resurface to give meaning to recent hardships, forecasting that repetition is in store unless significant changes to legislation and the property rights of the tenantry are made.

One of the most memorable letters McDougall wrote during her tour was published in the *Daily Witness* on July 27, 1881 (included as an appendix to this book). The letter opens with McDougall's discussion with her driver, who, looking at the empty landscape surrounding Ballycroy (County Mayo), ironically considers that supposedly Ireland once suffered from overpopulation: "Sure, I do feel my heart afire when gintlemen sit on my car driving through this loneliness an' talk of 'over-population.' 'Over-population' and the country empty!" Immediately after, McDougall expresses her lack of understanding at the cruelty shown by some toward their fellow humans during the Great Famine:

> It is most amazing to think that, when the world at large was sending help to save the Irish alive in the awful visitation, so many were throwing their tenants out on the road to die, and these people had by hard toil won a living here and paid rent. Every road of this land, every cabin had helped to swell the princely revenues, until the finger of God came down in famine and, then, when the revenue stopped, there was no pity, and it seemed to these poor people that there was no one that regarded. I do not ever wish to come to that time of life when I can hear of the scenes that wasted this country without feeling a passion of sorrow and regret.

McDougall is of the opinion that an affective response to such scenes is but a logical human reaction. She points to the rift between the affective reaction and action undertaken by the world at large on the one hand and the relative uncaring displayed toward the suffering Irish poor by the ruling classes of Ireland on the other. She reiterates this point later in the letter, ironically referring to "a worthy gentleman" who, in conversation with McDougall, "brushed away" her remarks about the extortion of and lack of pity for the people during the Famine "as if it were a fly, saying, 'Oh, that is long past, thirty years and more.'"[35]

The remarks about aid during the Great Famine serve as pointers to newspaper readers on how they should remember the human hardships of that period. In giving these pointers, McDougall significantly highlights the moral dimension inherent to processes of memory transfer. For such acts of passing on, Marianne Hirsch's concept of "postmemory" offers a useful if complex framework. Hirsch considers historical collective trauma, memory transfer, and moral responsibility in the context of the Holocaust. My use of the term applies to moral appeals to members of a culture who inherit recollections of highly disruptive events. In borrowing Hirsch's concept, I in no way attempt to offer avenues for comparison between the Holocaust and the Irish Famine. Rather, as Morash explains, while in representations of the suffering, fragmented body, an "unconscious relationship between the Famine and the Holocaust" can be found, comparisons between the Famine and Holocaust cannot be made on the basis of the "intentionality, culpability, or persecution" part of the latter event.[36] In borrowing Hirsch's term "postmemory" to explore the morality of memory transfer, then, I separate it from the specific contexts of the Holocaust and cultural trauma. Moreover, in my reading, moral appeals to descendants of the victim generation do not suggest the transfer of traumatic memory between generations. Rather, such appeals function as moral incentives to share and learn from memories in the present. For McDougall, it seems imperative that she and her peers (potentially also those not of Irish descent, as the *Witness* did not cater to an exclusively Irish audience) remember the Great Famine not only out of a moral responsibility to remember the victims but especially for what that memory means at present: in the letters, the fund of famine memory is used to address and hopefully change similar injustices at present.[37]

The local population McDougall spoke to of course did not need mnemonic incentives. The Great Famine was the last major famine; the famine of 1879–80 was of a significantly smaller scale, marked by severe privation and low excess mortality. Nevertheless, the renewed threat of famine led to panic, especially in poorer districts.[38] Many Irish living in the early 1880s had been alive during the Famine, and this response demonstrates how the 1840s premediated 1879–80. The workings of premediation on the collective level are contemplated later in the letter as well, as McDougall discovers that memories of the Great Famine are very much present among the rural Irish, structuring not only their current interpretations but also their future expectations: "Memory is very strong among people who seem to have little to look forward to—the past seems the principal outlook. Every incident of the French landing here so far back as '98 is told to me with a freshness of detail as if it happened a few years ago; one can imagine, therefore, how the cruel evictions of the famine time fit themselves into the memory of the people, especially as the rush of fresh evictions are awakening all the horrors of the past."[39] This passage is written as a general remark. Our correspondent does not tie it to a specific informant, direct witness, or survivor of the Famine, implying that recollections of the Great Famine have become part of a communal fund of memory among the poor people of the West.

Viewed from a formal perspective, McDougall's letter published on July 27 constitutes a fascinating example of the employment of literary techniques in journalism. Hayden White and Paul Ricoeur have famously explored the similarities between the modes of writing fiction and writing history. In a similar vein, works of literary journalism from the nineteenth century onward have demonstrated the crossover between ostensibly factual journalism and literary styles of writing. As a collective or polytextual form, the historical periodical resists clear divisions between genres and modes of writing; nineteenth-century and early twentieth-century magazines and newspapers were much more fluid in the types of writing and genres they contained than their modern-day counterparts. White points out that modes of literary and history writing are of a similar narrative structure and that "art [literature] can complement, rather than undermine, science [history]."[40] Ricoeur moreover writes that the dividing line between writing history and writing fiction is a questionable one: we use techniques from fiction writing to organize and "refigurate" traces of the past into narratives in the present. Some historians include strategies not commonly associated with (objective) historiography, such as the use of first-person narrative through "integration of victims' voices and experiences" that pierces the historical (master) narrative.[41] Similarly, while more objective journalism tends to obscure the presence of a narrative consciousness, literary journalism foregrounds this presence.

In the letter of July 27, McDougall cites a direct witness of the Great Famine. The informant, "a gentleman connected with the executive of the law for a quarter of a century [who] knows the heart-rending inner history of legal eviction," discusses evictions by an unidentified landlord during "the dark days of famine." In the larger part of the letter, McDougall adopts the role of overtly present first-person narrator who discusses the words spoken by informants in third-person indirect speech—this narrative format, in fact, dominates most of the letters. However, in this particular instance, McDougall alters her narrative approach and, as narrator, takes a step back to let the informant speak from a first-person perspective and in direct speech. His words constitute a substantial part of the text. She also leaves out dialogue tags ("he said," "I asked," etc.), in effect creating a coherent direct monologue. In the following extended excerpt, McDougall begins to speak, but most of the text is voiced by her informant; all text between quotation marks is stated by the latter:

The desire to change the nationality and religion of his tenants was so strong in one landlord that, in the words of my informant, "A scene of ruthless havoc began among his tenantry. To stimulate the slowness of the crowbar brigade he was known to tear down human habitations with his own hands. I remember these poor people standing in the market in

THOSE DARK DAYS OF FAMINE,

having their bits of furniture for sale on the streets and there were none to buy. I have heard the wailing of men, women and children on the coach-top day after day, when these fortunate unfortunates were escaping from their native land forever. I saw those who could not go in the agonies of death in the fever sheds. These scenes happened over thirty years ago, but they will never be forgotten. Four large townlands, on which eighty homes had been, became a wilderness of grass and rank weeds. No Scotch were forthcoming for the wrecked farms. There was a Nemesis in store for him. His day of eviction came about, and in his troubles his tenants saw retribution. As charity kept some of his tenants alive, so he also was indebted to the charity of friends, and passed away to meet his tenants at a bar where high blood or aristocratic connections does not sway the Judge who sits on the throne of justice, nor does party prejudice blind his eyes. When Miss Gardner [Gardiner] came of age it took all the property of her father to pay the money secured to her by her mother's settlement, and she entered into possession in his stead. Like Queen Elizabeth, whom Miss Gardner greatly resembles, she had in her youth known troubles; sympathy for these trials, so well known to the peasantry, made them receive her with open arms and open hearts. In the interval between and her coming under the influence of Miss Pringle she set herself to repair the havoc made by her predecessor, and was the idol of her tenantry. She was near neighbor to the model farm and orphanage presided over by the Scotch ladies. Philanthropy collected the vast sums which bought and stocked the model farm at Ballinglen. When their mode of managing matters there could be no longer hidden from the Presbyterian Church which they misrepresented, the mission came out largely indebted to these ladies. It took all the stock to pay off its indebtedness to one lady, and the farm itself to pay the other. It is the lady who got the farm as her share, that lives with Miss Gardner, and gets the credit of her every unpopular act. She has divided between her and her only friend in the dark days. This Scotch hag found her a kind-hearted woman, and has made her into an ogre." Some of this communication, the hardest of it, I shall reserve. Also several confirmatory anecdotes given me at Westport.

In mercy to the readers, I will only say that Miss Gardner has intense courage and an intellect of masculine strength, and resembles Queen Elizabeth in more ways than one. It is a great pity that she has not Queen Bess's popularity or care for her people.

By foregrounding the informant's message, McDougall heightens its direct impact. She chooses this approach at various key moments in her travel account, breaking her "monophonic" authority as reporter.[42] Scholars working in the field of affect theory suggest that narratological choices can impact the affective reaction of readers to a text. For example, direct discourse representation and "perspectival mobility"—or the potential to shift between different perspectives within a narrative—can influence readerly orientation and engagement.[43] McDougall chooses to switch from overt to covert narration, third-person to first-person perspective, and indirect to direct speech representation. She seems to employ these narratological features typically associated with literary modes of writing to increase the sense of veracity of the passage and heighten the impact of her informant's firsthand memories on the audience, thereby facilitating the potential stimulation of engagement in her readership. As such, these narratological choices complement her journalistic message.

In his monologue, the informant seamlessly transitions from memories of the Famine to his present time, in which Harriet Gardiner (1821–92) ruled as the estate's landlady. Both Gardiner and her companion Susanna Pringle (called the "Scotch hag" by the informant) were notorious figures. Gardiner featured repeatedly in newspapers and was known for many brutal evictions carried out on the Belcarra estate as well as her ongoing strife with her tenantry. On December 11, 1880, the *Nation* reported of a public falling out when Gardiner was struck in the face by a tenant, refused her custom by a shop owner, and hooted down the street by an excited crowd, after which she "drew a large six-chamber revolver, and, turning round, presented it at the crowd, telling them that she would and could use it if necessary."[44] Reporting on April 4, 1885, of a new round of evictions, the *Connaught Telegraph* vehemently spoke of "legalized murder" and called Pringle and Gardiner "a pair of malevolent old wretches" and "feminine Shylocks" with "demon-souled greed for malicious deeds of evil" who "would not be satisfied till they beheld their wretched tenants converted into homeless wayside wanderers."[45]

McDougall's informant functions as an embodiment of memory, linking two famine periods together by his firsthand witness account, a device to which McDougall would later return. As McDougall had left Ireland for Canada in 1843, she did not witness the Famine herself; in absence of personal firsthand memories, her direct witnesses give comparative remarks regarding the Great Famine gravitas, a sense of truth, and an affective dimension that she herself cannot provide.[46]

In the letter included in the *Daily Witness* on April 16, McDougall reflects on her time in County Donegal and writes about "the relief works in famine time." This and similar remarks have a historically imprecise quality. However, rather than seeing this imprecision as cause for confusion, I would argue that in adopting this specific form of temporal narrative emplotment, McDougall aligns with a different conceptualization of time and further underscores the transhistorical character of Irish (famine) suffering. The atemporality makes clear that, in a sense, these periods are uncannily familiar and therefore cannot receive a pinpointed, temporally definite position in people's memories. Her letters can be considered acts of what Daniel Levy calls "realignment of temporalities." Different points or periods in time are brought together, and in this case, recollections of the Great Famine are used to give shape and meaning to Irish suffering during the Land War era.[47] This view more closely aligns with the way in which "social memory integrates various frameworks and rhythms of time" than with typical Western interpretations of time as linear and chronological.[48] Furthermore, a link can be drawn to how famine features in Irish folklore: as Guy Beiner points out, "in folklore the term *Aimsir an Drochshaoil* (the Bad Time) commonly denoted the Great Famine period but could also refer to memories of other famines and even allude to other dark periods remembered in communal history."[49] McDougall's compounded treatment of history can be seen as a form of famine temporality not aimed primarily at historicity but at approximating, at authenticating her informants' experiences.

Much of McDougall's writing about Ireland shows the despair and suffering of the people, but she also makes sure to provide more positive notes for her readers. She frequently mentions the beauty of the landscape and buildings she visits, praises the hospitality of the poor, includes little jokes, provides snippets of local lore, and discusses benevolent landowners.[50] In doing the latter, she not only follows the *Witness*'s assignment to show both sides to the Land Question but also demonstrates that, although hunger and hardship are ever-present threats to the Irish rural poor, the condition of famine is neither enduring nor accreditable to any innate national deficiencies. Although the system of landownership is undeniably corrupt, rural hardships are presented as contingent on the extent to which landlords abuse the system. Irish rural life, according to McDougall, is unpredictable and dependent on unsteady factors such as the weather and the passage of lands between landlords. In that sense, famine conditions are not so much continuous as repetitive.

Referring to an article in the Liverpool *Catholic Times*, the Montreal *Harp: A Magazine of General Literature* equally stressed repetition, claiming that "Ireland is the one country in Europe which has a famine every quarter of a century for upwards of a hundred years past. It is futile to even hint that laws and systems are free from the blame."[51] When revisiting her letters for her 1882 collection *The Letters of "Norah,"* McDougall added statements to flesh out her principal arguments, which align with the comment made in the *Harp*. In a newly added closing chapter, McDougall concisely formulated what she considered the ill at the root of Ireland's current condition: "I blame the system, not the men"; "land tenure is the main cause of Ireland's miseries." McDougall insisted that the landlords of Ireland were not "as a rule, naturally worse than other men, but they have too much power, and when 'self the wavering balance shakes, it's rarely right adjusted.'"[52] Such ills had led to a rural society in which featured starvation and a population of peasants equaled nowhere in Europe in how badly they were fed, clothed, and housed.[53] Agricultural and legal reform, according to our correspondent, were necessary to cure a diseased social system and counter Ireland's repetitive streak. McDougall was concerned that the 1881 Land Bill would prove ineffective. As she stated in the letter of July 27: "If ever the land Bill became law, if there is any relief contained in it which the educated cannot evade when contending with the ignorant, there will be but few left comparatively speaking to receive the benefit of it."[54]

THE INTERTEXTUAL AND COTEXTUAL SUPPORT OF FICTION

Memory formation is characterized by what Chiara De Cesari and Ann Rigney call the "multi-scalarity of socio-cultural processes," as social constructions on personal, local, national, and global scales mutually inflect one another and overlap.[55] Using the Irish Folklore Archive to examine how famine memory is represented and disseminated in Ireland, Niall Ó Ciosáin distinguishes three interacting levels of knowledge, which can be applied more broadly to narratives outside the scope of the archive as well: the global, the popular, and the local. The global consists of "abstract and usually national" information, "which usually derives from written, even academic, accounts." The local "consists of strictly local knowledge, rarely following an extended or elaborated narrative, and very often featuring named individuals." The popular is located between these two ends of the spectrum, and on this level, "informants draw on a repertoire of images, motifs, and short narrative, many of which . . . are part of a wider international narrative repertoire."[56] These scholars suggest that there is a close "proximity" between the construction of personal or "intimate" and global memories.[57]

McDougall resorted to several sources besides direct observation and witness accounts to give shape and meaning to Ireland's condition in 1881. Combining various scales, she adopted a broad frame of reference including nonfiction and creative writings from common repertoires. These include the Bible as well as canonical works by authors such as William Shakespeare, Lord Byron, Charles Dickens, and Washington Irving.[58] These references function as explicit intertextual forms of premediation. Many writers of the time used intertextual references to showcase their own cultural, religious, and/or political knowledge and contextualize events in broader transnational and transhistorical frameworks, allowing their readership to engage in different ways with events. As such, McDougall's writing style follows a common practice.

After discussing with a Leitrim landlord the raising of rents during recent "bad years," which "have stripped the poorer tenants bare," McDougall compared the tenantry's suffering with the biblical suffering of the Israelites.[59] Her intertextual references seem to serve mostly illustrative purposes and do not provide opportunities to draw sustained or in-depth cotextual comparisons. However, coupled with her use of literary devices and techniques, such intertextual references do make the letters into variegated exercises in the combination of fact and fiction. The complex generic nature of the letters was picked up by a loyal reader: in a letter to the editor, "Justitia" referred to the literary and journalistic crossovers in the letters, lauding the letters' high "literary merit" combined with McDougall's talent to provide "the naked truth so pointedly."[60] As such, the fictional mode of writing frequently adopted in the letters fortified the impact of their factual contents.

Interactions between McDougall's letters and fiction manifested in another way, extending beyond McDougall's own references, as her earlier letters were printed alongside the serialized publication of Annie Keary's *Castle Daly*.[61] The first installment of Keary's 1875 novel had been included in the *Witness* on November 17, 1880, demonstrating that the newspaper's engagement with Ireland's historical and present famine conditions preceded McDougall's tour. *Castle Daly* and McDougall's letters share crucial political views, and the former provided cotextual support for the latter. Keary, daughter of an Irish Anglican clergyman, was born in Wetherby (Yorkshire) in 1825. She spent most of her life in England and the South of France and never resided in Ireland, save a two-week sojourn.[62] Like McDougall, Keary wrote from an outsider's perspective—although also an engaged outsider's perspective.

In travel writing of the postfamine nineteenth century, Ireland was often envisioned as picturesque—but ambivalently so, for the island's picturesque beauty was by and large a product of the desolation caused by the disappearance of the people. McDougall admired the beauty of the landscape while repeatedly noticing its desolation. For example, in her letter of April 16, 1881, she speaks of "roofless homes, levelled walls, desolation and silence" on the Derryveagh hamlets. McDougall attributed the desolation of the landscape to the effects of both famines.[63]

Similarly, in her novel, Keary discusses at length the desolation of the landscape and accredits it to the Great Famine. *Castle Daly* contains a pastoral space that functions as a nostalgic reminder of an idealized rural Ireland, Good People's Hollow. As the Famine progresses, the hollow disintegrates. In the latter part of *Castle Daly*, the hollow, along with all the lands of the now destitute Daly estate, has become desolate. As the narrative draws to a close, Ellen Daly, the novel's heroine, remarks how she mourns over "the deserted villages and the silent hill-sides."[64] The empty landscape is paradoxically described in beautiful tones: "The [Hollow] valley had never looked fairer, or showed more like an enchanted region, jewel-paved with emerald, and diamond and azure, than it appeared when Ellen found herself left alone to gaze on the misty outline of its protecting hills, the blue thread of its winding river, its opal-coloured lake, and its green slopes all growing momentarily more distinct in the brightening sunshine. There was something wanting; the old sights were there, but not the old sounds. A strange silence reigned all about the place that fell like an ache on Ellen's heart."[65]

Castle Daly presents the marriage between Ellen Daly and the Dalys' English estate agent John Thornley as a solution to the estate's problems; their nuptials function as a typical national marriage between Ireland and England, a plot device found more often in traditional Big House fiction. The combination of Irish heart and English rationale survives the ordeal of the Famine, but no unambiguous happy ending is provided.

Keary's narrative contains a belief in the righteous and heroic character of Irish nationalism—here in the pan-religious ideology of the Young Irelanders—in the face of societal injustice and great suffering, at the same time critiquing its violent outbursts. By association, on the pages of the *Witness*, this sentiment could influence McDougall's writings concerning rural unrest and civic discontent in the early 1880s, justifying their foundational sentiment without approving of their actions.[66] Keary's novel sympathizes with the Irish, but not unquestioningly. It bemoans the great losses caused by the Famine, wishes to keep the existing rural hierarchy in Ireland, "is sympathetic to Home Rule," and criticizes the coolness of British government policy.[67] However, it also represents some arguments provided by English characters—such as the stimulation of emigration—as inevitable and even desired to prevent another famine. It does not call for Irish independence or the end of British rule in Ireland but rather for increased self-governance through a more balanced and nonviolent approach within the context of the union. Similarly, McDougall did not advocate for Home Rule. She supported the Land League's goals to secure the Three Fs and Charles Stewart Parnell's intentions to improve the property and legal rights of the Irish tenantry. However, she did question how feasible Parnell's aim "at the entire abolition of landlordism" was and "could not help wondering how it could be done."[68]

On the pages of the Montreal *Witness*, *Castle Daly* and McDougall's letters had a joint, cumulative effect. Both authors supported constitutional nationalism and nonviolence and upheld a belief in the power of legislative change within the context of the union. Moreover, both Keary and McDougall used famine memory and the prolonged aftereffects of the Famine as transhistorical support. The final installments of Keary's novel in the *Witness* were published in quick succession; they deal with the aftermath of the failed Young Ireland rebellion, Ellen's brother and rebel leader Connor Daly's forced emigration to the US, and, fast-forwarding several years, the continued aftereffects of the Famine on Ireland.[69] We meet Ellen, Thornley, and Connor on a peaceful and beautiful yet desolate estate, peopled by few inhabitants and marked by famine roads. By extension, the novel's prolepsis allows readers to contemplate the mnemonic legacy of the Great Famine in their own time. *Castle Daly*'s closing chapters in the *Witness* function as condensed premediating support for one of McDougall's key convictions made a month later: the power of famine memory to continue to affect people's views on their present and future conditions.

Effects of the Journey

As Hooper states, "if travel allows for anything it allows for the possible reinvention of the self"; undoubtedly, McDougall's "Tour through Ireland" did not signify just a physical sojourn.[70] As had been the case for Redpath when he went to Ireland, McDougall's "travelling through [her] native country" changed her "sentiments and the convictions forced upon [her]."[71] As Griffiths writes, audiences of the time were just as interested in the correspondent herself as they were in the events reported. Throughout her letters, the self-proclaimed "enthusiastic Irishwoman" gave her readership insight into both the journey and the author and expressed admiration for Irish political figures such as John Dillon, Parnell, and his sister Anna, stating that she felt "honored" to be (repeatedly) mistaken for the latter.[72]

Perhaps due to the different sociopolitical and economic convictions held by the correspondent and her outlet, McDougall did not include her stronger concluding remarks in the *Witness* letters and saved them for the later collection *The Letters of "Norah."* After her tour, McDougall wrote she was shocked by the harsh treatment of the starving poor and baffled by the realization that "public opinion seems to have absolutely no sympathy with the common people when they were behind on their rents, although they were emerging from a period of agricultural distress, culminating in absolute famine." She added that she used to glory "in the British Constitution, its justice, its mercy!" but in 1881 encountered events and opinions she had previously thought "impossible under British law."[73]

McDougall explained her change of heart and convictions due to her journey as follows:

> Brought up in the North of Ireland in a purely Hiberno-Scotch neighbour-
> hood, I drank in with my native air all the ideas which reign in that part
> of Ireland. The people with whom I came in contact were Conservatives of
> the strongest type; from my youth up, therefore, I had the cause of Ireland's
> poverty and misery as an article of belief. I never dreamed that the tenure
> of land had anything to do with it. Landlords were lords and leaders, bene-
> factors and protectors to their tenants in my imagination.
>
> I changed my opinion while in Ireland, and now I believe that the land
> tenure is the main cause of Ireland's miseries.[74]

McDougall rejected any form of monopoly and wrote that "there is no
monopoly . . . which bears such evil fruit as the monopoly of all the land of
a country in the hands of a few." Land monopoly, according to McDougall,
goes against divine laws: "God's law, which is the law of our faith, shows
plainly how the Great Lawgiver regards the monopoly of land by the care
which He took to have a direct interest in the land of Canaan by personal
inheritance for every Jew."[75]

Making a distinction between good and "exterminating" landlords,
McDougall writes: "These things have convinced me that exterminating
landlords are the parties who are guilty of high treason against the com-
monwealth of England. The loyalty of Irish Catholics to a country that had
scant justice to give them has been proven on every battle field from far
India to the Crimea. No history of England's wars in these later times can
be written truly without acknowledging the Irish blood given like water for
England's honor."[76] Not only does McDougall express a strong antipathy
toward abusive landlords, but she also subverts common colonial rhetoric
by arguing that landlords, through their immoral actions, commit high
treason against the British crown and that Irish Catholics, in their loyalty
to a country that has done little to treat them with justice, have proved
themselves more loyal to Britain than their masters. As a final call, McDougall appeals to the authorities in Ireland "to try a little conciliation instead
of such strong doses of coercion."[77]

Combining Famines, Combining Forms of Writing

In her journalistic work, McDougall blends the historical events of the
famines of 1845–52 and 1879 and refers to biblical history and canonical
fiction to create a diverse and broad framework of signification spanning
both creative writing and nonfiction. This framework aptly demonstrates
how narrative journalism is marked by (complex) navigations of the reality
boundary.

For past events that "generate feelings of considerable ethical intensity," like the Irish Famine, the analytic and deindividuated approach inherent to the mode of history writing is insufficient, writes Ricoeur. For such events, techniques from fiction writing can provide a necessary, individuated approach.[78] In other words, to achieve a seemingly truthful "standing-for" the absent famine past, a representation of that past that is individuated but still maintains a critical distance and a more factual claim to truth is necessary. Combining history and memory with religious, journalistic, and fiction writing, McDougall's journalism achieves this standing-for: it is able to assign meaning to current events by adding the gravitas of historical fact, the moral dimension of Christian teachings, and the imaginative and individuating power of fiction. This latter aspect is enhanced by the cotextual support offered by Keary's *Castle Daly.*

David Lloyd argues that "the past and its possibilities are not the goal of the present, but they are the sign of unclosed and unworked possibilities of life . . . whose recalcitrant living on demands that we do justice still to the alternatives they represent." Addressing past injustices should not be understood as "a matter of reverent or therapeutic morning"; rather, I understand Lloyd to mean that our unfinished business in the past, seen as temporalities we never followed, informs us of how to deal with current and future injustices.[79] We cannot belatedly fix the past, but we can preventatively guard ourselves against repetition. In a similar vein, McDougall's exposé on affective responses and moral obligations to the recalcitrant mnemonic traces of the Great Famine deepens the sense of indignation with regard to Ireland's famine past. Rather than dwelling on vindicating past wrongs, McDougall, through her demonstration of the repetitive streak plaguing Ireland, creates urgency to address present injustices and secure a better future for the rural Irish tenantry.

Reader of the Montreal *Witness* "Justitia" suggested that the letters be collected so that as one volume they might influence the Land Act of 1881—which the reader considered "most sweeping in its character." Justitia felt that McDougall's letters could very well become a "more potent" influence on existing land laws than "the statute book" on Ireland had been so far.[80] While no clear indication of such impact exists, arguably McDougall's vivid pictures of the Irish and her explanations of the causes for their distress had the potential to positively influence views on British injustices in Ireland and on Irish identities. Additionally, Collombier-Lakeman argues that through the inclusion of the Famine in the colonial press, the 1840s catastrophe became an imperial, even global matter. This argument can be extended to McDougall's special correspondence on famine and the Land War in the *Witness* in the early 1880s. Because her letters were published in a nonethnic, non-Catholic newspaper, her message went beyond the limits of the (Catholic) Irish-diasporic community itself and reached audiences of a different denomination in and outside of Canada.[81]

NOTES

1. Morash, "Ghosts and Wires," 24–25. Hooper, *Tourist's Gaze*, 115. Griffiths, *New Journalism*, 16, 21–22. Griffiths mentions this celebrity status in the context of Britain specifically (ibid., chap. 1). For the American context, Lanzendörfer speaks of reporters more generally, but the examples he uses pertain to war reportage in the US during the nineteenth century (Lanzendörfer, "Periodicals and Journalism").

2. Larkin, "Green Shoots," 36, 41. O'Brien's new series of articles appeared in the *Freeman's Journal* under the title "Famine in the West." Geary writes that O'Brien's correspondence captured features of the crisis reminiscent of the Great Famine (Geary, *Land War*, 15).

3. Morash, "Ghosts and Wires," 30.

4. The Database of Canada's Early Women Writers (DoCEWW) at Simon Fraser University gives 1828 as McDougall's birthdate (DoCEWW, "MacDougall [or McDougall], Margaret Dixon"), while the Canadian Writing Research Collaboratory (CWRC) gives 1826 (CWRC, "Margaret Dixon McDougall").

George was sent to Ireland by Patrick Ford of the *Irish World and American Industrial Liberator* in 1881 (Murphy, "Ford, Patrick," n.p.). Redpath wrote for the New York *Tribune*; his letters were included in other periodicals as well, including the New York *Celtic Monthly*, Montreal *Harp*, and Dublin-based *United Ireland*. Hooper's anthology contains excerpts from writings of a large number of travelers to Ireland between 1800 and 2000. In 1852, Harriet Martineau went to Ireland to report on the condition of postfamine Ireland for the *London Daily News* (Pusapati, "Going Places").

In *A Happy Holiday: English-Canadians and Transatlantic Tourism, 1870–1930* (2008), Cecilia Morgan devotes part of a chapter to McDougall's *The Letters of "Norah."* My chapter "From Special Correspondence to Fiction" discusses the publication journey of McDougall's special correspondence and analyzes its transformation into an edited collection and novel.

Margaret Ward focuses on the Irish context of the larger development of women's sociopolitical positioning in *Unmanageable Revolutionaries*; Tara M. McCarthy discusses Irish American women's activism specifically in *Respectability & Reform*. Joel H. Wiener explains that opportunities for women in journalism in the US and the UK were limited before the First World War (Wiener, *Americanization of the British Press*, 219, 223–25).

5. McDougall, *Days of a Life*, preface.

6. For more substantial discussions of the novel, please see my "Famine Traces" and "Margaret Dixon McDougall's *The Days of a Life*." In these works, I consider the repetitive nature of history as represented in McDougall's fiction.

7. Hartsock, *Literary Journalism*, 2; Norman Sims discusses the reality boundary in "Problem and the Promise."

8. I include a similar but more concise characterization of the *Witness* in "From Special Correspondence." Some of the contextual and biographical information provided in the current chapter also features in that earlier chapter.

The year 1845 pertains to the weekly edition; the daily edition was added in 1860 (Snell, "Dougall, John"). The *Witness* provided circulation numbers: on April 14, 1881, it stated that daily circulation for April 4–9 had been between 12,520 and 13,100; the weekly number was 28,635 ("Circulation of THE WITNESS . . . ," *Daily Witness*, April 14, 1881, 4). In 1886, these numbers had risen to 14,265 and 39,134, respectively (Butcher, *W. W. Butcher's Canadian Newspaper Directory*, 25). That year, newspapers in Quebec had circulations varying from 400 at the lowest to 24,959 and 120,000, the latter numbers belonging to the daily and weekly Montreal *Family Herald and Star* (ibid., 24). Few other newspapers in the province equaled or surpassed the *Witness*, suggesting that it had a sizable circulation. The quote is taken from Wood, *T. F. Wood & Co's Canadian Newspaper Directory*, 14.

9. Snell, "Dougall, John."

10. McDougall, Letters of "Norah."

11. Dougall, "Prospectus," December 15, 1845, 1. All issues of the *Witness* used in this chapter were consulted through the website of the Bibliothèque et Archives nationales du Québec (http://numerique.banq.qc.ca/).

12. Ibid.

13. Snell, "Dougall, John"; "We Reproduce Today," *True Witness*, August 16, 5–6. John Redpath Dougall ran the newspaper from 1870 until 1934; he was followed by his son Frederick E. Dougall, who ran the newspaper between 1934 and 1938. See additional information on the *Witness* provided by the Bibliothèque et Archives nationales du Québec ("Montreal Witness"). Snell mentions the ecclesiastical ban ("Dougall, John"). N. Merrill Distad and Linda M. Distad note that one of the hurdles to intellectuals operating in the Canadian, and specifically Quebec, periodical market was the "monolithic and occasionally censorious Roman Catholic church in Quebec." They also state that Bourget was responsible for the flourishing Ultramontane movement in Quebec (Distad and Distad, "Canada," 106).

14. Collombier-Lakeman, "Canadian Press," paragraphs 39, 36, 4, 14. Emphasis in original.

15. Quote taken from Dougall, "Prospectus," 1. "Redpath Becomes Again Vituperative," July 27, 1881, 3. "Irish Agitation," April 12, 1881, 2. When discussing the bill, the *Witness* criticized Parnell and Dillon's convictions, stating that

> MR. PARNELL, seeing that the passage of the land Bill may be made subservient to the continued organization of his clientele, is on the whole in favour of it, and believes it "will lead to very remarkable results," among which are "the abolition of landlordism and the prosperity of our country." There are some things in the Bill which need rectification, however, and Mr. Parnell believes that he will be able to have this done. We can hardly see the ground of his hope. . . . Mr Dillon, like all enthusiastic imitators, runs a mile ahead so as to be no whit behind his leader, condemns the land bill out and out, and warns the tenant farmers against "accepting it" (ibid.).

Earlier, commenting on Parnell's intended tour through the US, the newspaper had stated that the tour showed that he "was not content with reducing the freedom of Parliament to a farce and making free speech impossible," furthermore labeling the IPP leader a "demagogue" and "agitator" ("Mr. Parnell, Not Content . . . ," February 12, 1881, 4). For criticism on the Land League and its leadership specifically, see "Land League," February 15, 1881, 4.

16. DoCEWW, "MacDougall (or McDougall), Margaret Dixon"; CWRC, "Margaret Dixon McDougall"; Loeber and Loeber, with Mullin Burnham, *Guide to Irish Fiction*, 814–15.

17. On Martineau, see Pusapati, "Going Places"; Easley, "Authorship, Gender and Power"; "Our Correspondent in Ireland," March 9, 1881, 4.

18. McDougall, "Tour through Ireland," April 16, 1881, 2.

19. McDougall, "Tour through Ireland," April 16, 1881, 2. In the 1870s, livestock counted for as much as 75 percent of the total output of Irish agriculture (Daly, *Social and Economic History*, 27). See also Curtis Jr., *Depiction of Eviction*, 57–58.

20. Lawless's narrative is part of the collection *Traits and Confidences* (142–62). For McDougall's use of well-known imagery, see for example her "Tour through Ireland" letter of April 12, 1881.

21. McDougall, *Letters of "Norah,"* 302, 298.

22. "Today's Telegraphs," 1.

23. "Announcement That Capt. Boycott . . . ," 4.

24. "Our Correspondent in Ireland," 4.

25. Ibid.

26. Montreal, "Irish Land Question," February 9, 1881, 2.

27. Three Rivers, "Irish Land Question," March 5, 1881, 2.

28. "Our Correspondent in Ireland," 4.

29. Loeber and Loeber, with Mullin Burnham, *Guide to Irish Fiction*, 814–15. In the March 25, 1881, issue of the *Almonte Gazette* (1), McDougall's letter subtitled "Belfast—Temperance—'The Eve of a Great Rebellion'—The Poor-House—County Down—Making Ends Meet—Waiting for Something to Turn Up" was published. While this was not the first letter included in the Montreal *Witness* (it was included in the *Daily Witness* on March 15, 1881, 2), it might have been the first installment included in the *Almonte Gazette*. On July 13, 1883, publisher Templeman wrote that the *Gazette* had reprinted more of McDougall's letters a few years earlier ("Misapprehension," 3). Reader J. P. G., for example, commended McDougall's correspondence ("Ireland and 'The Tour in Ireland,'" August 4, 1881, 2).

30. Tulloch and Keeble, "Mind the Gaps," 6. Griffiths, *New Journalism*, 3. Griffiths speaks of "the New Journalism" rather than literary journalism.

31. Griffiths, *New Journalism*, 38.

32. Larkin, "Green Shoots," 38.

33. Montreal, "Irish Land Question," 2.

34. McDougall, *Days of a Life*, 418.

35. McDougall, "Tour through Ireland," April 27, 1881, 2.

36. Morash, "Famine/Holocaust," 146. I explain my distancing from this problematic comparison in more detail in "From Silence to Plenty"; in that article, I also call for a reconsideration of the concept of cultural trauma in relation to the study of the Irish Famine.

37. Hirsch, "Surviving Images." Ernst van Alphen argues against the notion that traumatic memories can be transferred between generations, that there is a "fundamental continuity between first and second generations" ("Second-Generation Testimony," 474).

38. Ó Gráda, "Ireland," 182, 184; Gray, "Irish Social Thought"; Rynne, "Great Famine in Nationalist and Land League Propaganda," paragraph 5; Geary, *Land War*, 7, 37.

39. McDougall, "Tour through Ireland," July 27, 1881, 2.

40. White, *Metahistory*, introduction; quote from White, "History Fiction Divide," 18.

41. Ricoeur, *Time and Narrative*, vol. 3: 186. Discussing the complex relationship between narrative and reality, Ricoeur prefers the term "refiguration" over "representation" to underscore the changes inherent to narrativization (ibid., 100). Goldberg, "Empathy, Ethics, and Politics," 63.

42. James Clifford quoted in Bruna, "Travel Journalism," 351.

43. Keene, "Introduction," 16.

44. "Western Landlady," 12.

45. "Legalised Murder," 4. On Gardiner and Pringle, also see McGreal, "Terrible Reign," *Mayo News*, May 21, 2013. McGreal discusses the book *When Crowbar & Bayonet Ruled: The Land War on the Belcarra Estate of Harriet Gardiner & Susanna Pringle, 1879–1910* (2013) by Michael M. and James R. O'Connor.

46. A clergyman features as embodied memory in *The Days of a Life* as well. The biographical details are provided in DoCEWW, "MacDougall (or McDougall), Margaret Dixon."

47. Levy, "Changing Temporalities," 15.

48. Beiner, *Remembering the Year of the French*, 124.

49. Ibid., 128. As chapter 2 of *Periodical Famines* shows, author M. Mackey also uses the term "these bad times" to denote the Land War era in the story "His Honour's Word" (1881).

50. For example, McDougall discusses the Galgorm estate near Ballymena (County Antrim), which in the Encumbered Estates Court passed from a bad absentee landlord to the possession of a benevolent resident proprietor, writing "the change is something miraculous. The waste pasture-like demesne is reclaimed and planted. The worst cabins have entirely disappeared; the rest are improved till they hardly know themselves" ("Tour through Ireland," March 24, 1881, 2). On April 27, she writes about landlords such as the Marques of Donegal, who "was spoken of as a merciful landlord all through the hard years. He had forgiven them rent which they could not pay, and lowered the rent when they did pay, returning them some of the money, and the poor people spoke of him with warm gratitude" (April 27, 1881, 2).

51. "Distress in Ireland," *Harp*, January 1880, 124.

52. McDougall, *Letters of "Norah,"* 297, 298. The quote is an intertextual reference to Robert Burns's poem "Epistle to a Young Friend" (1786).

53. McDougall, *Letters of "Norah,"* 300–301, 299.

54. McDougall, "Tour through Ireland," July 27, 1881, 2. The 1881 Land Bill would not meet Parnell's or McDougall's hopes and demands. While originally supporting the bill, Parnell in the end criticized it, also for fear that it would weaken the struggle for Home Rule (Cronin, *History of Ireland*, 162).

55. De Cesari and Rigney, "Introduction," 5.

56. Ó Ciosáin, "Famine Memory," 101, 102.

57. De Cesari and Rigney, "Introduction," 5.

58. McDougall, "Tour through Ireland," April 12, 1881, 2.

59. Ibid., June 8, 1881, 2.

60. Justitia, "Ireland and the 'Witness' Correspondent," October 26, 1881, 2.

61. The final installment of Keary's novel was published in the *Daily Witness* on May 17, 1881. I discuss Keary's novel at greater length in "Famine Traces" and as an example of an Irish Bildungsroman in "(Re)building Self and Country."

62. Sutherland, "Keary, Annie [Anna Maria]," 345.

63. Thompson, "Famine Travel," 164. See also Frawley, *Irish Pastoral*, 45. For a contemporary account, see Balch, *Ireland, as I Saw It* (1852). On page 115, Balch accredits desolation to the Famine. McDougall's descriptions of the desolate landscape feature in her letters for the *Daily Witness* of July 27, 1881 (2) and September 29, 1881 (2).

64. Keary, *Castle Daly, Daily Witness*, May 17, 1881, 6.

65. Ibid., May 13, 1881, 6.

66. For example, McDougall shows her understanding of how the Fenian mindset developed. When viewing a depopulated landscape in County Mayo, she states: "To doubt that this fair and desolate Mayo is overpopulated is to show signs of lunacy or worse. Fenianism, Communism or even Nihilism is possible if there is no lunacy to account for such strange ideas" ("Tour through Ireland," July 13, 1881, 2).

67. Sutherland, "Keary, Annie [Anna Maria]," 345.

68. DoCEWW, "MacDougall (or McDougall), Margaret Dixon." McDougall, "Tour through Ireland," October 19, 1881, 2. In an 1879 speech, Parnell called for "the abolition of landlordism through land purchase because this would benefit the greatest number of people and make the country prosperous." If landlords refused, it would lead to "a repetition of 1847–8." Curtis Jr., *Depiction of Eviction in Ireland*, 88–89.

69. Between April 30 and May 17, installments appeared daily.

70. Hooper, *Tourist's Gaze*, xiii.

71. McKivigan states that Redpath became a "convert" to the Irish Land League almost as soon as he arrived in Ireland (*Forgotten Firebrand*, 155). McDougall, *Letters of "Norah,"* 297.

72. Griffiths, *New Journalism*, 30. Griffiths sees interest in the correspondent as one of the "consequences of the more personal style of the New Journalism" (ibid.). McDougall used the

term "enthusiastic Irishwoman" in "Tour through Ireland," May 14, 1881, 2; quote from ibid., May 16, 1881, 2.

73. McDougall, *Letters of "Norah,"* 299–300.

74. Ibid., 297.

75. Ibid.

76. Ibid., 302.

77. Ibid., 303.

78. Ricoeur, *Time and Narrative*, vol. 3, 187–88.

79. Lloyd, *Irish Times*, 8.

80. "Justitia," "Ireland and the 'Witness' Correspondent," 2.

81. Collombier-Lakeman, "Canadian Press," paragraph 43.

4

FAMINE, FICTION, AND HISTORICITY IN THE *IRISH PACKET* DURING THE FIRST YEARS OF THE TWENTIETH CENTURY

> "Do you remember any incidents of the
> famine of forty-seven?" I asked of James Daly, as
> we sat in his comfortable parlour.
> "Yes, certainly," he answered, "and I will tell
> you of the one that most impressed itself on my
> memory."
> The incident I will now relate, word for word.
>
> *Harry Allen, "The Frenzy of Famine"*

THESE LINES OPEN THE SHORT story "The Frenzy of Famine: A Tale of '47," included in the *Irish Packet* on March 12, 1904. Besides this story, the Dublin-based literary magazine printed multiple works of famine fiction over the course of its existence. As such, the *Irish Packet* was part of and informed a larger cultural repertoire of famine memory in the early years of the twentieth century, keeping this repertoire alive and current by disseminating it and emphasizing its prolonged affective potential. Around the turn of the century, more periodical and book publications included rural and famine prose fiction and poetry, as shown in the moderate publication increase at that time (see fig. 1.4 in chap. 1; see also app. 4). Examples in periodicals include "One Hundred Years," a poem detailing the many hardships undergone in Ireland since the Act of Union with Britain, which was included in the Dublin-based story paper the *Irish Emerald* in 1901. It contains stanzas detailing grain exports, hunger, and other famine hardships. In 1902, the New York *Irish-American* reprinted M. M. Armstrong's

"A Friend in Need; or, The Piper's Gift: A Story of the Irish Famine," a narrative originally featured in *McGee's Illustrated Weekly: Devoted to Catholic Art, Literature and Education* in 1877.[1] And between 1903 and 1905, the New York *Gaelic American* posthumously serialized Charles Kickham's *Knocknagow; or, The Homes of Tipperary* (1879). The rural fiction included in the *Irish Packet* is part of this corpus of turn-of-the-century creative writings.

The opening sentences to Harry Allen's "The Frenzy of Famine," a story discussed in more detail below, highlight key characteristics of rural fiction found in the *Irish Packet*: the use of a firsthand witness, a framing narrative, a truth claim, and an emphasis on the Famine's great aftereffects—how the event "impressed itself" on the subject's memory. Connecting to an Irish reader's likely historical knowledge, the story uses common imagery of famine victimhood. Such narrative techniques and devices feature more broadly in famine fiction from the latter quarter of the nineteenth and the early years of the twentieth century. By the end of the nineteenth century—some fifty years after the Famine—firsthand memory of the period was becoming increasingly rare. Thus, in lieu of direct recollection, authors relied on narrative techniques such as the use of firsthand witness figures and stock imagery to enhance and emphasize the veracity of their narratives.[2] Because in this regard the *Irish Packet* is exemplary of a larger development in Irish and Irish-diasporic fiction, it functions as the focal point of this chapter's case study on witnessing and historical authenticity in the early twentieth century.

Chapter 4 does not offer a cotextual analysis; rather, it embeds creative works in the larger context of the magazine spanning several years and within considerations of textual genre. Narrative techniques underscore the historicity of events narrated. They also help "individuate" events and their aftereffects. As mentioned in the previous chapter, the modes of fiction and history writing overlap, and techniques from fiction writing can, as Ricoeur argues, "help to realize" history's "project of standing-for."[3] While the balance in Paul Ricoeur's work on crossovers between history and fiction leans toward the use of the mode of fiction writing in historiography, in this chapter I use his insights to analyze how fiction can stimulate a sense of historicity and truth claim in the form of verisimilitude. Advancing existing scholarly understandings of the use of stock imagery and narrative techniques in the retention and passing on of famine memory in/through creative texts, this chapter investigates how the use of firsthand witnessing, techniques from oral storytelling, and familiar images of victimhood achieve a sense of verisimilitude. For later generation(s), a peril to refiguring the past lies in the vicarious appropriation of the previous generation's disruptive experiences without due distinction between own and inherited memory.[4] The famine narratives included in the *Irish Packet* achieve a standing-for the absent past while averting vicarious appropriation of famine recollections and experiences. In so doing, they display a way in which famine recollections have transhistorical critical potential, elucidating the moral dimension inherent to comparative uses of memory.

THE *IRISH PACKET*, SHORT STORIES, AND RURAL FICTION

The *Irish Packet* was a literary magazine published by the offices of the nationalist *Freeman's Journal* in Dublin. It was one of the main story papers published in Ireland by the early twentieth century and targeted an upper-working- and lower-middle-class audience. Stephanie Rains explains that evidence for circulation figures are "almost non-existent" and unverified at best; nevertheless, they suggest that during the early twentieth century, when Ireland's population was just over three million, the circulation of Irish story papers such as the *Irish Packet, Ireland's Own*, the *Irish Emerald*, and the *Shamrock* "varied between 30,000 and 80,000 copies per week."[5] The *Irish Packet* was first published in 1903, and its last issue appeared in December 1909. As such, it was part of a new wave of publications of Irish literary magazines between 1892 and 1922, peaking in 1904, during which such magazines appeared in a quantity not seen since before the Famine. Although a lifespan of little over six years might not sound impressive, it was a relatively extensive run for a literary magazine at the time, as "the average lifespan" during the period rose "from ten to thirty months" (a maximum of two and a half years). Nevertheless, the *Irish Packet* has received little scholarly attention.[6] The magazine appeared weekly, comprised twenty-four pages, and, typical for a story magazine, was priced at a penny per regular issue. Although primarily an outlet for prose fiction and poetry, the *Irish Packet* contained nonfiction as well, including historical essays on influential Irish politicians and important events, a weekly "Chat with the Editor" column, and women's pieces. "The Ancient Tongue" was a weekly feature, with bilingual pieces written by Douglas Hyde and J. J. O'Kelly. Contributions concerning the fields of journalism and law, both fictional and nonfictional, also frequently appeared; examples include anecdotal pieces such as the recurring "A Session in Parliament" or the long series "Famous Irish Trials." The editor of the magazine, Matthias McDonnell Bodkin (1849–1933), a barrister, journalist, author, and later judge, was responsible for this specific angle, and many of the pieces on the practice of law were penned by him. This was also the case for numerous "Famous Irish Trials" pieces, which were collected into one volume of the same title in 1918. Bodkin was leader writer for the *Freeman's Journal* as well.[7]

From 1880, it became possible for writers to earn a living through writing short fiction, and the writing and publication of short stories became more frequent in Ireland and Britain. By the 1890s, there was a new generation of illustrated monthly miscellanies, which tended to avoid the serialization of long novels. This development was due to several factors: technological innovations and changes in periodical publishing, the increase in size of the reading public because of educational reforms, and the declining popularity of the Victorian three-decker.[8] In the *Irish Packet*, the shift in balance between long and short fiction was visible; although longer narratives did feature in the magazine, much of its fictional content consisted of short stories. The *Irish Packet* featured pieces by unknown or anonymous writers and by well-known authors, sometimes posthumously: writings by Jane Barlow, Justin McCarthy, Katherine Tynan, Thomas Moore, Sheridan Le Fanu, and Charles Kickham graced its pages. From across the Atlantic, the *Irish Packet* reprinted stories by Mark Twain and the already deceased Edgar Allan Poe. It regularly included Finley Peter Dunne's then-popular Irish American sociopolitical satire, the "Mr. Dooley" columns.

Many stories in the *Irish Packet* focused on Irish rural life of the past, including the Famine; the latter also appeared in other materials included in the magazine. In 1903, the magazine contained William Smith O'Brien's "Never Despair" (1848), a poem written on the day the author was sentenced to death. That same year, "A Song for the Irish Militia" (1845), a poem by Thomas Davis (1814–45) that glorifies sacrifice for Ireland, was reprinted. Young Ireland was praised by Alice Harriman in her poem "Thomas Francis Meagher 1823–1867" (1905). Such content can be seen as part of the attempt made by Irish story papers including the *Irish Packet* to compete with imported British story papers by "emphasizing their Irishness."[9]

Narrative Frameworks, Witnessing, and Lasting Impact

The prose stories in the magazine set in the rural Ireland of the past are stylistically similar. They use a framework narrative typically placed in an unspecified present with a firsthand witness who offers memories of famine. The framework adds an oral quality to the narrative, further underscored by use of colloquial speech—or "brogue"—and a register of everyday language. Examples of narratives with these characteristics besides Allen's "The Frenzy of Famine" include "Home to Her Mother" (1903) by Miriam

Williams and Michael MacNamara's "Irish Paddy" (1904). MacNamara's story is presented as a traditional *seanchas* oral narrative relating the adventures of a kindhearted rogue driven into the fairy world by famine and consequent hardships; Williams's story is discussed in more detail below.[10]

Similar framework structures are found beyond the pages of the *Irish Packet* and in earlier publications as well, demonstrating that by the turn of the century, this narrative structure had become an established feature of writings including the Famine. In Edward N. Hoare's *Mike: A Tale of the Great Irish Famine* (1880), the framework narrative is set during Christmas probably in the late 1870s, and Mike's story of famine suffering is told by the family that adopted him as a beloved servant. In Justin H. McCarthy's *Lily Lass* (1889), the narrator is an American reporter who encounters personal recollections of the Young Ireland rebellion decades after the event and feels such an ardent connection to Lilias Geraldine (the titular Lily Lass), the rebels, and their nationalist ideology that he decides to piece together the narrative. This plot device highlights the transatlantic dimension of Irish nationalism, suggests the plot's historicity, and provides metafictional reflections on the tension between verisimilitude and the imaginative power of the author. Margaret Brew's *The Chronicles of Castle Cloyne; or, Pictures of the Munster People* (1885) and F. H. Clayton's *Scenes and Incidents in Irish Life* (1884) also contain framework narratives in which narrators stress the long-lasting (emotional) effects of the Famine and/or the veracity of the account; in the latter case, this framework is presented as autobiographical.[11]

In Allen's "The Frenzy of Famine" (1904), the reader encounters the story's two narrators in a "comfortable parlour." The first remains unnamed and asks his friend James Daly for his recollections of the Great Famine. Daly describes how in his youth, neighbor John Davis once came to the Daly family's cabin. The Dalys are doing relatively well; throughout the story, they do not seem to face the threat of starvation or disease. Seeing that Davis is starving, the father of the house offers his neighbor stirabout, which the visitor consumes "with the ferocity of a wild animal." When the charitable host refuses to give his neighbor more food, fearing that Davis's emaciated body will succumb to sudden abundance, the hunger-maddened Davis almost kills Daly's father and storms out. Concerned for Davis's and his family's well-being, Daly's father sends his son to the Davis cabin with food. James comes in time to help Davis's wife and daughter, and both survive the Famine. In the end, Davis's daughter makes an appearance in the framework narrative as well, now James Daly's wife.[12]

Bearing witness verbatim to famine is a key element of the narrative, as the first narrator retells Daly's story "word for word." Moreover, throughout the narrative, the focus is on Daly as focalizer: the verb "to see" is used repeatedly in connection to James Daly, making us aware that we are seeing events through his eyes and placing him as direct witness. Although young Daly is our eyes and ears in the story, his function as witness is limited: at a crucial moment, he indicates that he cannot do exactly that—cannot bear (to) witness. En route to the Davis's house, young Daly finds his neighbor on the side of the road in his final and agonizing moments of famine suffering:

> "I procured some bread and hurried across to Davis's house. As I ran along by a ditch that was covered with briars I beheld a slight commotion in the briars a little ahead of me. I stopped, rooted to the spot, for there, lying in the briars, lay John Davis in the agony of death, and even as I looked his eyes rolled in his head, his arms fell to his sides and he—
>
> "Oh!" exclaimed James Daly, and he put his hands to his eyes as if to shut out that awful scene, and when he withdrew them there were tears in his eyes. He continued in a shaken voice:—
>
> "I could look no longer. I turned aside and ran as fast as my trembling limbs would take me till I reached Davis's house."[13]

Here, the witness has a paradoxical function. He is employed to witness historical trauma but can only deliver a fragmented image, an absence. This absence is reflected in the manner through which the text is interrupted, indicated by omission ("he—"). The adult Daly attempts to describe Davis's death throes but is physically incapable of finishing the description of the scene he sees in his mind's eye.

Roy Brand defines witnessing trauma as "stand[ing] in proximity to an event that escapes representation but calls for communication nevertheless." John Durham Peters calls a witness "a paradigm medium—the means by which experience is supplied to others who lack the original."[14] These statements have two implications: through the firsthand witness, the experience of the original is passed down to others, while the use of the firsthand witness also points out that the listener in the story—and by extension, the reader—lacks access to the original. Such is the achievement of Allen's story. It communicates the horrors experienced by Daly but points to the impossibilities of representing the period and really knowing what it was like for those receiving Daly's account at a mediated distance and temporal remove.

Furthermore, the passage above demonstrates the great potential affect of the scenes Daly experienced in his youth. Too overcome to tell his story uninterruptedly, Daly "puts his hands to his eyes as if to shut out that awful scene" and cries in the narrative's present. Thus, although the framework securely places the events that occurred during the Famine in the past, their affect does not remain rooted in history and is central to the reader's narrative experience. The acknowledgment of prolonged affect features more broadly in fiction of the period. For example, in "The Little Boy of the Powers (The Returned American's Story)," included in the *Irish Packet* in 1903, the protagonist, a return migrant in his fifties, feels a "stab of pain to the heart" when, decades after the Famine, he remembers how his mother suffered. And in "Jimmy Hackett's Temptation: A St. Patrick's Day Story of Uskamore," published in the *Irish Emerald* in 1896, an elderly mother is still overpowered by memories of the death of her baby during the Famine: after waking up from her nightmares, "she shed tears ere she slept again."[15]

Affect and witnessing are crucial to "The Holy Well," written by Bodkin himself and included in the *Irish Packet* on December 3, 1904. The narrative opens in the "great drawingroom of Knockmaroon House, the stately seat of the MacDermotts of Mayo," where the lady of the house, Mabel MacDermott, recounts her memories of a famine period some ten years earlier. The date of the scene is not specified. The reader learns that MacDermott used to be an absentee, living in London with her son instead of on their estate in Mayo. She is not represented as the stereotypical rack-renting absentee often found in Irish rural fiction, rather as a kind but misinformed landlady who has learned the error of her ways, having been too trusting of her agent, who secretly "ground the faces off the poor in [her] name."[16] MacDermott describes what her tenantry went through during that famine.

> "Well, this year that I tell you of was the worst of all. The potato crop and the oats crop, on which they mainly depended for food, wholly failed, and something like famine came upon the people. But our agent . . . did not spare them the least on that account. If they failed to pay their rent for their poor patches of bog and mountain on the poorest parts of the estate, they were evicted without mercy, summer or winter, sunshine or rain, or snow or frost, it did not matter in the least to him. They were driven out of their humble homes as trespassing cattle are driven out of a field; driven out to shiver and starve by the roadside, or take a refuge in the poorhouse or the grave. Can you fancy how I felt when I heard of those things, for which before God I was responsible, for I let them be done."[17]

Having discovered the true situation on the estate, Mabel MacDermott and her son return to Ireland to take care of their tenantry. In the narrative's present, the reader finds them "living happily amongst [their] own people."[18] This narrative of restoration, as chapter 2 has shown, had already become unfashionable before the story was published.

In the internal narrative, Mabel MacDermott focuses on one tenant family's distress; in so doing, famine suffering becomes individuated. Paradoxically, the character-narrator implies the sheer magnitude of the distress experienced by the tenantry by focusing on the story of a single family, or else the "story will never end." The internal narrative concerns widow Bridget O'Connor and her daughter, Eileen. Having already "suffered the worst pangs of poverty and cold and hunger," they now find their hunger coupled with "fear of threatening famine, and fear of [the] agent."[19] Catholicism is combined with mythical elements: hoping to save her family, Eileen goes to the holy well to pray. After accidentally dropping her rosary in the well, she finds at its bottom a golden bracelet that once belonged to a mythical princess. With the help of the local priest, the girl sells the bracelet and thus saves herself and her mother from starvation. "The Holy Well" also implies the transformative power of the press, as Mabel Mac-Dermott and her son learn of the distress on their family estate because the story of the holy well is covered in the London papers; the story brings them back to Mayo.

While the inclusion of the fantastical at first glance comes across as an ill-fitting intermezzo in an otherwise realistic (as in probable) tale and, in that sense, seems to weaken the power of the plot, its veracity is underscored by its supposed reproduction in the papers. Moreover, McDermott claims the story to be real: "I know it is true, every word, as I have told it to you."[20] The story shows concordances with what we now know as the genre of magic realism, in which real and fantastic are combined and the fantastic is narrated in realist tones, fully plausible within the confines of the story world.

Besides the story's similarity with images popular during the Gaelic Revival, its use of the mythical as a deus ex machina device is influenced by oral and folk memory: as Cathal Póirtéir demonstrates, "legend and lore" played an important part in how survivors and their descendants gave shape to famine recollections. Moreover, the inclusion of the mythic is shaped by local-color writing. Josephine Donovan argues that local-color fiction often resists the normalizing and standardizing tendencies of dominant cultural capitals, advocates of modernity and rationality dating back to the Enlightenment. Sanitizing nature, these dominant narratives made it a measurable object fit for scientific study, classification, and, most importantly, domination rather than an animate force in its own right. Hence, little room was left for the folkloric and mythic, known for relying on the supernatural and irrational. As Donovan writes, "much of the animus in local-colour literature is directed against the imposition of these standards, affirming instead regional deviancy as valuable and sometimes superior to the ways of modernity."[21] We can read the infusion of the mythic in "The Holy Well" (and other works of Irish regional or local-color fiction) as a way of reaching back to older understandings of the world and nature and a means of resisting the homogenizing tendencies of dominant cultural modes and temporalities. In that sense, the inclusion of the mythic underscores the narrative's specific Irish dimension and strengthens rather than weakens it on the basis of questioning the superiority of an Enlightenment-inspired (British) ontological paradigm.

Mabel McDermott's absence from Ireland during the worst famine years makes her a more problematic witness than James Daly in "A Frenzy of Famine." Her emotional response to tenant suffering occurs when she learns of events through the media—through the eyes of direct witnesses, not her own. Thus, in her double role as absentee/witness, she embodies the difficulties of representing the unrepresentable. In Brand's terms, her testimony fills the "gap between event and representation."[22] Yet as with James Daly, MacDermott's response to the ordeal that her tenants experienced ten years earlier remains one of agitation: "It makes me heart sick, even now to remember it."[23] This sentiment is fueled by MacDermott's realization of her own moral failure and the immoral transgressions committed in her name.

Although both fictions consist of multiple narrative frames securely placing events in the past, their affect does not remain rooted in history. Susannah Ketchum-Glass speaks of memory as a "palimpsest." Although this term has become a commonplace in memory studies, her definition offers an additional semantic layer: "palimpsestuousness" both "examin[es] the past" and means "to scrape again." In that double capacity, memory impacts present identities.[24] James Daly's firsthand and Mabel McDermott's indirect memories function as palimpsests: they not only reveal the layering inherent to the character's identity but also demonstrate that disruptive memories continue to penetrate, remaining as abrasions to the character's present identity. For McDermott, they are transformative, having changed her relationship to her tenantry and altered her role as landowner. For Daly, famine recollections are an integral part of his memory and, by extension, his present identity. The narratives show a dual temporal orientation, simultaneously directing readers toward the past and present. The framework places events in the past, while the narrative contents locate affect in the present.

As shown in these readings, first-person narration and focalization have the potential to stimulate identification, facilitating readerly engagement with a narrator or protagonist (if these entities are not morally or emotionally objectionable). By contrast, an increase of narrative embeddedness—the incorporation of additional narrative layers between the reader and the narrativized figure of the famine sufferer—can impede identification.[25] In "The Frenzy of Famine" and "The Holy Well," the authors opt for first-person narrators who are not the famine sufferers at the core of the narratives. They also include several narrative layers between the famine victim and the reader. Together, these structural interventions serve to impede vicarious identification between audience and famine victim.

The framework format and witness figure work together to establish a truth effect. Of course, fiction's truth claims on reality are inherently problematic; that, however, does not mean that fiction does not contain a truth or that readers read fiction as only being fictional. Indeed, fiction writing and history writing are equally indebted to the real, and both can impact the real. While a work of fiction is fiction, it still makes claims to truth in the form of verisimilitude, and the witness frameworks of these narratives enhance that claim.[26] When discussing the narrativization of the past, Jeffrey C. Alexander explains that "we like to believe in the verisimilitude of our accounts, but it is the moral frameworks themselves that are real and constant, not the factual material that we employ to describe them."[27] In the stories discussed above, what remain real and constant are indeed those moral frameworks, which expose the inequalities between tenants and landlords, the effects of repeated famines on the Irish poor, and the lasting emotional affect of the Famine. For the *Irish Packet* and other literary magazines that contained moral fiction, claims to connections to the real and verisimilitude were central. Through techniques from the mode of fiction writing, a sense of historicity was achieved.

The connection to reality is established on another level in these stories: the future time to which the stories allude temporally aligned with the actual present of the reader. Large-scale crop failures and famine conditions continued to plague parts of Ireland. From the first reading of the Land Purchase Bill onward, commentators found consolation in the bill's "partial recognition" of Ireland's rights but nevertheless strongly criticized the shortcomings of the bill and later Land Purchase (Ireland) Act.[28] The New York *Irish World* denounced the Wyndham Act, opining that it would not suffice to solve Ireland's land issues and that famines, poverty, and emigration would remain staples of Irish life until substantial amendments were made. Critics felt that the land purchasing price should be lowered, that the act served the interests of landlords rather than tenants, and that Irish taxpayers, through yearly increases of taxes to England, undeservedly would be made to foot the bill.[29] The *Irish-American* criticized the Land Act in 1903, also on the basis of Ireland paying for it dearly while England profited: "But the effect is, as was said of the terms of the Act of Union, to make Ireland pay for the knife that cuts her own throat. At the same time, the English government poses before the world as the generous benefactor of the Irish people." Furthermore, concluded the newspaper, since the union, "Ireland has been paying into the English Treasury, at the rate of from ninety to a hundred millions [*sic*] of dollars a year, in over-taxation, in excess of what should have been demanded of her. . . . Irish tenants should never be asked to pay a single penny for land that they have purchased a hundred times over, by their sweat and toil."[30] Perhaps most importantly, the measure did not provide the panacea, "the only possible remedy" to Ireland's miseries: Home Rule.[31] If around the time of its passing the Land Act was seen favorably, this often was more for its function as a stepping stone to Ireland's legislative independence than for what it could achieve in the short term.[32]

In January 1904, the Dublin *Freeman's Journal* showed serious concern about whether the Land Act would solve rural Ireland's chronic distress; in the recurring article "Land Purchase Finance," it stated that the new act allowed landlords to "extract exorbitant prices" from tenants to whom they planned to sell their land.[33] At the close of that year, the *Freeman's Journal* again wrote that "during the past sixty years," the Irish had experienced "recurring famines."[34] Extending the *Freeman's Journal*'s political rhetoric to the *Irish Packet*, its sister paper, suggests that the moral lessons offered by works of fiction in the latter were of contemporary relevance. The historical distress described in these narratives underscored the continued impact and presence of such hardships. While the futures suggested by the stories—caring landlordism in Bodkin's, for example—did not necessarily align with real-world possibilities, the moral frameworks they offered advocated for a humane treatment of the rural Irish tenantry. In so doing, they premediated meaning-making processes in relation to readers' contemporary sociopolitical issues.

The familiar cultural storehouse of famine imagery includes a frequent focus on parts of the human frame rather than the victim in full form—what Christopher Morash has called the "fragmented body" in famine writing.[35] Other oft-employed images of victimhood connected to famine writing include the anthropomorphosis of famine as a monstrous figure stalking the land, madness, dehumanization of victims, and, as discussed in chapter 3, a focus on female victims. The *Packet* stories combine localized, individuated narratives with such images and mythical elements, familiar from larger national and possibly even global contexts. In so doing, the stories operate on what Niall Ó Ciosáin calls the popular level of representation. Through the use of known imagery, the *Irish Packet* stories not only collaboratively generate representations of famine suffering but also become part of the larger repertoire of famine writing. In this repertoire, the repeated use of imagery across texts—which Jerome Bruner refers to as "narrative accrual"—enhances their truth effect, a process aligned with the cotextual effect but taking place at a larger scale.[36] So while the use of familiar imagery shows the constructed, artificial nature of a narrative, it also provides plausibility to the imagery presented. In this manner, existing imagery becomes associated with new connotations.

The passage of time necessitates renegotiation in how to represent highly disruptive events or periods. Here, Holocaust studies offers valuable insight—though, as mentioned in the previous chapter, borrowing from that field should not suggest a comparison between the Holocaust and the Irish Famine on my part. About Holocaust literature from the late twentieth century, Froma L. Zeitlin writes that "now invention has become an increasing necessity in order to compensate for the ever-receding horizons of the event in time, and the absence of a firsthand memory now dictates a reliance on myth and icon as well as on fact." Likewise, Marianne Hirsch speaks of the "need to rely on canonization and repetition in our postmemorial discourse."[37] Authors like Bodkin (born in 1850) and Jane Barlow (discussed below) did not have a personal register with direct recollections of the Famine but could rely on the communal repertoire of famine imagery to enhance verisimilitude in their fiction.[38]

A potential hazard to the use of a collective mnemonic frame of established imagery is the deindividuation of suffering and victimhood: the use of common and generic images can depersonalize the specific scene of suffering. This section demonstrates how the *Packet* stories combine different scales of cultural production and successfully deal with this tension between individuation and deindividuation.

Several stories by Jane Barlow were reprinted in the *Irish Packet*, including "Herself" and "Con the Quare One." These works exemplify the popular level of representation, positioned between the local and the global. Moreover, as Elke D'hoker explains, through their narrator, Barlow's stories mediate "not only between traditional, rural, and modern, urban life, but also between Irish protagonists and the English or American readers."[39] Barlow (Dublin, 1857–Bray, 1917) was a poet and writer who frequently contributed to journals such as the *Dublin University Review*, the *Nation*, and the American *Literary Digest* and *Eclectic Magazine*. She lived a quiet life, leading Douglas Hyde to describe her as "the great 'incognita.'" Much of Barlow's fiction was likely inspired by Irish rural scenes she witnessed during her extensive travels through Ireland and walking holidays along the west coast.[40]

Barlow was an acclaimed writer during her time and, in 1904, was the first woman to receive an honorary doctorate from Trinity College Dublin. Her *Irish Idylls* (1892) was an instant success; Stephen Gwynn stated that because of the book, "the public took her gently to its bosom."[41] *Irish Idylls* went through at least eight editions in Barlow's lifetime, "had a larger sale than any other Irish story collection in the period," and was also read in Germany, France, Britain, and the US.[42] As Heidi Hansson points out, appreciation for Barlow's work unfortunately declined: while at first she was seen as a sympathetic outsider writing about rural Ireland, later in life, her work was perceived as politically ambiguous, its representation of language considered incorrect and its tone registered as aloof by influential figures within the Revival movement. Nevertheless, *Irish Idylls* and *Strangers at Lisconnel* (1895) continued to be reprinted as late as 1984.[43] Their continued popularity, evidenced through this long reproduction history, suggests that these stories not only tapped into the larger existing transatlantic storehouse of famine memory but also, in their turn, maintained and shaped this fund of memory, functioning as new media through which familiar tropes were disseminated.

"Herself" and "Con the Quare One" were not written for the *Irish Packet*—both had been published previously. "Herself" first appeared in *Irish Idylls* and "Con the Quare One" in *Strangers at Lisconnel*; both collections function as connected short story cycles and deal with the lives of characters in the fictional Connemara hamlet of Lisconnel. Barlow's novels are "usually critical of the Irish landowning class"; by contrast, in the Lisconnel stories, this critical dimension is largely absent, and the stories contain an "idealization of village life" in which characters are attached "to life in Lisconnel, despite the hardships it presents."[44] "Herself" and "Con the Quare One," however, offer a more critical dimension, focusing especially on the continued hardships endured by the Irish rural poor. The reprinting of these specific stories of famine suffering in the *Irish Packet* attests to the popularity of rural fiction in the magazine and the stories' continued popularity for the periodical-reading public of Ireland. Additionally, it suggests that their republication was done on the basis of perceived sociopolitical relevance. The latter becomes clear from consideration of the *Freeman's Journal*'s content of 1905, the same year the *Irish Packet* included Barlow's two stories. In that year, the newspaper continued to be critical about the effects of the Wyndham Act: "While the Act was calculated to bring increased comfort and prosperity to those already secure in their happy homesteads, it had brought no relief to the victims who had sacrificed their all in the land war of the last five and twenty years."[45]

Barlow's collections typically "dramatize and question community life," and the use of the brogue for direct speech provides the narratives with local color.[46] The position and style of the narrator emphasize the narratives' indebtedness to oral storytelling. The narrator takes the stance of a sympathetic onlooker to the Lisconnel community and addresses the reader in a colloquial manner. She might be a frequent visitor but does not seem to be part of the narrative action or the community. As Hansson explains, although Barlow at times uses a brogue-tinged English for the descriptions and contemplations provided by the narrator, the narrator at other times displays a far more sophisticated linguistic register that paradoxically distances her from the Lisconnel villagers.[47]

In her narrative representation of the effects of famine, Barlow uses the trope of madness, also a key plot element in Allen's "The Frenzy of Famine." Another well-known example of famine fiction that deals with madness is Kickham's *Sally Cavanagh* (1869). The scene in which the male protagonist finds his maddened wife roaming a famine graveyard was reprinted in the *Irish Packet* in 1904. The story "Sown in Tears; or, The Secret Chamber in the Devil's-Hoof: A Tale of Ireland in the Days of the Famine" (1896), by Ethel Greene, references a maddened mother eating her child during the Famine, a combination of the tropes of famine-induced madness and cannibalism found in John Mitchel's writings on the Famine as well.[48]

In Barlow's "Con the Quare One," the titular character experiences mental unsettlement. When Con is a young boy, he is sent to live with his grandmother. Feeling homesick, Con returns home and finds his family members dead or dying from famine and famine-related disease:

> Con rushed at her head foremost, crying "Och mammy darlint, I've come home this long way . . . And where's daddy if he isn't working? And musha what for is Nannie and Johnny in bed?"
>
> He pulled at her shawl because she did not look round at him, and immediately she dropped down prone on the floor as heavily and helplessly as he had seen the white shawl fall. She had in truth been dead for hours but Con ran out screaming that he was after killing his mammy, and nothing would persuade him otherwise. Vainly the neighbour averred that "the crathur was starvin' herself this great while to keep a bit for the childer, let alone her heart bein' broke from frettin' after her poor husband and little Pat, who were took from her wid the fever, both of them in one day."[49]

After this startling scene, the young boy's "mind was shut fast into [that] dreadful moment," and he contracts brain fever. He recovers and finds that all his relatives, except his sister Katty (who later emigrates to the US), have died. The narrator states that "from this time dated the springing up among his neighbours of a suspicion that he was not all there—a suspicion which developed into an accepted article of belief." Consequently, the Lisconnel people refer to Con as "cracked," a "crathur," and "the quare one." As the narrator remarks, Con grows up into a "strange, small figure" the neighbors liken to a "leprechaun."[50] This classification of Con as not fully human, as a sort of fairy changeling, distances him from the community by both isolating and dehumanizing him. After the death of his mother, Con becomes a wandering figure seemingly incapable of anything but incoherent conversation who comes into town only occasionally before he disappears, never to reappear again, further underscoring his liminal position.

Con's supposed madness stays ambiguous, for community opinion about his mental state differs. He remains emotionally tied to another famine survivor, the widow O'Driscoll, the protagonist of Barlow's "Herself." After Con saves her young son from a supposed drowning, Mrs. O'Driscoll's devotion to him is ensured. Unable to connect with other community members, these two outsiders turn to each other. The villagers imply that the widow too has become mad, yet this implication remains ambiguous. She has gone through so much hardship—two famines, great poverty, the loss of family members to death or departures, and eviction—that her mental distress appears inevitable. Indeed, the neighbors report that after experiencing such ordeals, "she was never the same woman again, . . . never herself again."[51] Previously a beacon of health and industry at the center of

Barlow's fictitious community, the widow's experiences have transformed her into an isolated and frail old woman. In long conversations with a local crazy figure, the widow O'Driscoll speaks of her loved ones as gone only temporarily, while the story reveals that after a while, they stop contacting her and never return to Ireland. These conversations lead some to conclude that her mind must be slipping. However, as with Con, the widow's neighbors qualify her seeming deterioration: "All the while you could perceive she knew right well she was just persuadin' herself agin' her reason."[52]

Barlow's stories suggest that the experience of famine is so disruptive to the sense of self that victims no longer hold coherent identities and are relegated to the fringes of their communities, ill-fitting outcasts in a post-famine world. In that sense, the trope of madness serves as a metaphor for famine suffering and perhaps even a form of death (on the level of identity and growth) rather than as only a literal aftereffect. While Barlow does not use the term herself, her emphasis on liminality and the prolonged disruption of identity caused by a devastating event can be read as early literary engagement with what we classify today as Freudian-inspired trauma discourse. Notably, Barlow limits her descriptions of emotional affect to the level of individual characters and does not mark the whole community as traumatized; the same can be said for the *Packet* narratives discussed earlier in this chapter.

Relatedly, D'hoker explains that this focus on individual rather than community impact characterizes both of Barlow's story cycles from which these narratives are taken. In her view, it "add[s] a tinge of unreality," as real-world "past upheavals and political turmoil" do not "impinge on life in Lisconnel."[53] "Con the Quare One" and "Herself" give room for a modification of this argument. Granted, contemporary upheavals such as famine and emigration largely take place outside the confines of the narratives themselves; for example, the two famines are only briefly described as "series of bad seasons."[54] Nevertheless, Barlow does suggest that they seriously impact individual members of the Lisconnel community: Con and his family and the O'Driscolls. Through this partial and individualized acknowledgment of famine's impact, Barlow's narratives—and, by extension, those by Bodkin and Allen—can be read as early engagements with the notion of individual rather than cultural trauma.

The *Packet* stories use the trope of the suffering mother. Barlow's widow O'Driscoll works exceptionally hard to care for her stepchildren, while Con's mother stints her own food intake to give her family a better chance at survival. The selfless maternal image furthermore features in the story "The Little Boy of the Powers" (1904), in which a "withered and witch-like little mother had often gone hungry that her child might eat."[55] And as in Bodkin's "The Holy Well," in Miriam Williams's story "Home to Her Mother," the mother and child figure are at the center of the narrative. Like MacNamara's "Irish Paddy" and Bodkin's "The Holy Well," "Home to Her Mother" was included in a Christmas issue, indicating that this time of year was considered especially apt for the inclusion of such moralizing tales.

The *Irish Packet* frequently included opportunities for readers to enter contests, be that by solving puzzles and riddles or submitting stories. Such competitions were very popular in the late nineteenth and early twentieth centuries and could boost circulation. Rains explains that the *Irish Packet* ran them from the beginning, which suggests that the inclusion of amateur fiction was part of its business plan. As figure 4.1 shows, "Home to Her Mother" was a prize-winning story.[56]

In Williams's story, adult narrator Sally recollects her youth and the deaths of her father, stepmother, and younger sister. The loving parents try to provide for their family by working a "straggling, stony piece of ground, where, within the memory of man, nothing ever grew but nettles [sic] docks, and thistles." The family is doing relatively well until "the month of October 1845 . . . when . . . the food of the earth was turned to poison." With "nothing but starvation before" them, the father and brother go to work on the public roads scheme. Sally's mother saves all food for her family, frequently skipping her own meals. After the father dies, the already enfeebled mother works even harder by doing backbreaking work "for the sake of earning enough to keep [the family] alive." She eventually contracts fever and dies, after which her four-year-old daughter refuses to eat and succumbs to starvation. The deaths of both mother and daughter are presented as acts of divine benevolence; thus, Sally's stepmother is rewarded for her selfless acts in the afterlife.[57]

In death, Sally's stepmother seemingly meets a worse end than Barlow's widow O'Driscoll and Mrs. Powers in "The Little Boy of the Powers," but on reconsideration, it must be noted that the latter two face a harder fate. While not succumbing to starvation or disease, they are not offered divine benevolence and survive to toil and suffer until their last day. The effects of famine on these female figures remain limited to "local and domestic terms"; their suffering is not presented as part of a larger pattern of economic or political causation.[58] As such, and contrary to Maud Gonne's use of the female figure in her nationalist and anti-imperialist discourse

That was a pleasant place where I was born, though 'twas only a thatched cabin by the side of a mountain stream, where the country was so lonely in summer the wild ducks used to bring their young ones to feed on the bog, within a hundred yards of our door; and you could not stoop over the bank to raise a pitcher full of water, without frightening a shoal of beautiful speckled trout.

Well, 'tis long ago since my brother Richard, that's now grown up a fine, clever man, God bless him!—with grown-up sons to look up to him and honour him—and myself used to set off together up the mountain to pick bunches of the cotton plant and the bog myrtle, and to look for birds' and wild bees' nests.

'Tis long ago, and though for many a long year afterwards I was happy and well off, living in the big house as own maid to the young ladies, who, on account of my being foster-sister to poor, darling Miss Ellen, that died of decline, treated me more like their equal than their servant, and gave me the means to improve myself, still, in bygone times, especially when James Sweeney, a dacent boy of the neighbourhood, and myself took walks together through the fields in the cool and quiet of a summer's evening, I could not help thinking of the times that were passed, and talking about them to James with a sort of peaceful sadness, more happy, maybe, than if we had been laughing aloud.

For many years, every evening before I said the Rosary, I used to read in the New Testament that Father Ryan gave me the words—"And God shall wipe away all tears from their eyes; and death shall be no more mourning, nor crying, nor sorrow shall be any more; for the former things are passed away." The words made me think of them that were gone—of my father, and his wife, that was a true, fond mother to me, and, above all, of my little sister, poor Mary, the colleen bawn that nestled to her bosom.

I was a wild slip of a girl, ten years of age, and my brother Richard about two years older, when my father brought home his second wife. She was the daughter of a farmer up at Locke-, and was reared with care and dacency. My father held his ground at a rackrent, and the difference that was between him and the head landlord did not pay his own rent, so that the place was ejected, and the farmer collected every penny he had, and set off with his family to America.

My father had a liking for the youngest daughter, and well become him to have it, for a sweeter creature never drew the breath of life. But while her father passed for a strong farmer, my father was timorous-like about asking her to share his little cabin. However, when he found how matters really stood with her father, he didn't lose much time in finding out that she was willing to be his wife, and a mother to his boy and girl.

That she was—a patient, loving one. Oh! old as I am now, it often sticks me like a knife when I think how many times I fretted her with my foolishness and my idle ways, and how 'twas a long time before I'd call her "mother." Often when my father would be going to chastise Richard and myself for our provoking doings, especially the day that we took half-a-dozen eggs from under the hatching hen to play "Blind Tom" with them, she'd interfere and say—

"Tim, aisagh, don't touch them this time; sure 'tis only arch they are; they'll get more sense in time."

And then after he was gone out, she'd advise us for our good so pleasantly, that a thundercloud itself couldn't look black at her.

She did wonders, too, about the house and garden. They were both dirty and neglected enough when she first came over them, for I was too young and foolish, and my father too busy with his outdoor work, and the old woman that lived with us in service too feeble and too blind to keep the place either clean or dacent. But my mother got the floor raised, and the green pool in front drained, and a parcel of roses and honeysuckles planted there instead.

West of us there was a straggling, stony piece of ground, where, within the memory of man, nothing ever grew but nettles, docks, and thistles. One Monday, when Richard and myself came in from school, my mother told us to set about weeding it, and to bring in some baskets full of good clay from the banks of the river. She said if we worked well at it until Saturday she'd bring me a new frock and Dick a jacket from the next market-town; and, encouraged by this, we set to work with right good will, and didn't leave off till supper-time. The next day we did the same, and by degrees when we saw the heap of weeds and stones that we got out growing big, and the ground looking nice and smooth and and red and rich, we got quite anxious about it ourselves, and we built a nice little fence round it to keep out the pigs. When it was manured, my mother planted cabbages, parsnips, and onions in it, and, to be sure, she got a fine crop out of it, enough to make as many a nice supper of vegetables stewed with pepper, and a small taste of bacon or a red herring. Besides, she sold in the market as much as bought a Sunday coat for my father, a gown for herself, a fine pair of shoes for Dick, and as pretty a shawl for myself as e'er a colleen in the country could show at Mass.

Through means of my father's industry and my mother's good management, we were, with the blessing of God, as snug and comfortable a poor family as any in Munster. We paid but a small rent, and we had plenty of potatoes to eat, good clothes to wear, and cleanliness and decency in and about our little cabin.

Five years passed on in this way, and at last little Mary was born. She was a delicate, fairy thing, with that look, even from the first, in her blue eyes, which is seldom seen, except where the shadow of the grave darkens the cradle. She was fond of her father, and of Richard, and of myself, but the love in the core of her heart was for her mother. No matter how tired, or sleepy, or cross the baby might be, one word from her would set the bright eyes dancing, and the little rosy mouth smiling, and the tiny limbs quivering, as if walking or running couldn't content her, but she must fly to her mother's arms. And how that mother doted on the very ground she trod! I often thought that the Queen in her state carriage, with one of her children alongside of her, could not be one bit happier than my mother, when she sat under the shade of the mountain ash near the door, in the hush of the summer's evening, singing and cronauning her only one to sleep in her arms.

In the month of October, 1845, Baby Mary was four years old. That was the bitter time, when first the food of the earth was turned to poison; when the gardens that used to be so bright and sweet, covered with the purple and white potato blossoms, became in one night black and offensive, as if fire had come down from heaven to burn them up. 'Twas a heartbreaking thing to see the labouring men, the crathurs! that had only the one half-acre to feed their little families, going out, after work, in the evenings to dig their suppers from under the black stalks. Spadeful after spadeful would be turned up, and a long piece of a ridge dug through, before they'd get a small kish full of such withered crohauneens as other years would be hardly counted fit for the pigs.

It was some time before the distress reached us, for there was a trifle of money in the savings' bank that held us in meal, while the neighbours were next door to starvation. As long as my father and mother had it they shared it freely with them that were worse off than themselves. But at last the little penny of money was all spent, the price of flour was raised, and, to make matters worse, the farmer that my father worked for, at a poor eight pence a day, was forced to send him and three more of his labourers away, as he couldn't afford to pay them even that any longer.

Oh! 'twas a sorrowful night when my father brought home the news. I am a feeble, bowed-down old woman now, but I remember, as well as if I saw it yesterday, the desolate look in his face when he sat down by the ashes of the turf fire that had just baked a yellow meal cake for his supper. My mother was at the opposite side, giving Baby Mary a drink of new milk out of her little wooden piggin, and the child didn't like it, being delicate and always used to sweet milk, so she said:

"Mammy, won't you give me some of the nice milk instead of that?"

"I haven't it, asthore, nor can't get it," said her mother; "so don't ye fret."

Not a word more out of the little one's mouth, only she turned her little cheek in towards her mother, and stayed quite quiet, as if she was hearkening to what was going on.

"Judy," said my father, "God is good, and sure 'tis only in Him we must put our trust; for in the whole wide world I can see nothing but starvation before us."

"God is good, Tim," replied my mother; "He won't forsake us, and His holy Mother will pray for us."

Just then Richard came in with a more joyful face than I had seen on him for many a day.

"Good news!" says he, "good news, father! There's work for us both on the Drouncarra road. The Government works are to begin there to-morrow; you'll get eight-pence a day, and I'll get six-pence."

If you saw our delight when we heard this you'd think 'twas the free present of a thousand pounds that came to us, falling through the roof, instead of an offer of small wages for hard work.

To be sure the potatoes were gone, and the yellow meal was dear and dry and chippy—

Figure 4.1. Williams, "Home to Her Mother," *Irish Packet*, December 12, 1903, 269. Image courtesy of the National Library of Ireland.

(see chap. 6), these stories locate the representation of the suffering Irish mother in a moral register and consequently depoliticize this gendered form of famine-related suffering.

Memory, Morality, and Meaning Making

The use of common imagery, or "collective mnemonic frames," from both nonfiction and creative writing in literary stories demonstrates the productive interplay between collective memory and the imagination, a process in which memories become incorporated in and adjusted to new contexts.[59] The stories in the *Irish Packet* guard against the depersonalization of victimhood by combining different scales of memory and employing techniques and devices from fiction writing. While they frequently employ known imagery to represent famine suffering, they also individuate suffering by giving victims identities and substantial presence in the narrative: John Davis, Bridget and Eileen O'Connor, the widow O'Driscoll, the Powers, and Con are all distinct characters with backstories and families. Thus, in these stories, we are dealing not with nameless walking skeletons or fragmented faceless bodies but rather with individual subjects.

The contemporary sociopolitical relevance of the *Irish Packet* stories is not formulated explicitly within the confines of the narratives; it becomes clear when viewed in light of the pieces detailing the renewed threat of famine and the effects of the Wyndham Act disseminated through the *Freeman's Journal* and other critical periodicals at the turn of the twentieth century. Moreover, the relative absence of an explicit sociopolitical message in the *Irish Packet* offers the audience the possibility of engaging in a posteriori meaning-making processes surrounding these stories and the famine memories they contain.[60]

The *Packet* did direct its audience in these processes in another way, suggesting how to relate to the past. Processes of meaning making were aided by genre characteristics and the format of the *Irish Packet* as a story paper. Indeed, as the current chapter has shown, many of the stories follow similar patterns and show comparable characteristics. While some stories—like Barlow's—were written for earlier publications, they fit these characteristics. Moreover, the similar narrative format and content of new creative texts on famine and Irish rural life written specifically for the *Irish Packet* imply that creative works included in the magazine earlier prescribed or premediated the format and content of newer inclusions. This, by extension, shows the temporality of the medium to be backward looking: new narratives become embedded in known structures, making the new a "variation within a known system."[61] The fact that one of the stories was included as the result of winning a competition further supports the value awarded in the *Irish Packet* to the Famine as subject matter and to stories containing well-known imagery and narrative frameworks.

By representing both narrators and characters as heavily impacted by famine experiences, the narratives in the *Irish Packet* acknowledge the overpowering effect famine memory still had over half a century later. Marianne Hirsch and Dominick LaCapra warn against the danger of vicarious appropriation; they underscore the morally suspect nature of such appropriation and stress the importance of retaining the "otherness of the other" in cross-generational acts of recollection. The stories in the *Irish Packet* provide guidance in how to maintain this boundary. The framework nature of these narratives extends the boundary between own and others' memories to the reader's experience, as narrative embeddedness impedes easy identification. Through embedding and an emphasis on lasting affect, the narratives suggest that the moral responsibility of the generation(s) after is to affectively engage with historical hardships and consider them part of their cultural memory without falling into the trap of overidentification through "vicarious victimhood." Later generations are positioned as "recipients of someone else's trauma" rather than implicated in that trauma directly; in that manner, a distance is maintained.[62]

Notes

This chapter is an adapted and extended version of the article "From Silence to Plenty" published in *Éire-Ireland*.

1. Cole, "One Hundred Years," April 13, 236. Armstrong, "Friend in Need," April 16, 1, 4. "Piper's Gift," March 17, 262–63. I briefly discuss this story in chapter 5.

2. Nothing is known about author Harry Allen. Analyzing works of famine fiction between 1892 and 1921, Christopher Cusack explains that many authors who had not experienced the Famine emphasized the factuality of their narratives by stating that their work was based on eyewitness accounts ("Memory, History, and Identity," 41).

3. Ricoeur, *Time and Narrative*, vol. 3, 187–88, 186.

4. Hirsch, "Surviving Images," 11; Dominic LaCapra uses the term "vicarious victimhood" (*Writing History, Writing Trauma*, 47).

5. Rains, "Going in for Competitions," 139.

6. Clyde, *Irish Literary Magazines*, 33. In his comprehensive *Irish Literary Magazines*, Clyde does not discuss the *Irish Packet*. Rains discusses the paper in her blog *Irish Media History* ("*Irish Packet*, 1903–1910") and "Going in for Competitions."

7. Larkin, "Matthias McDonell Bodkin," n.p.

8. D'hoker and Mourant, "Introduction," 9; Law, *Serializing Fiction in the Victorian Press*, 32; Law and Patten, "Serial Revolution," 167. Malcolm and Malcolm, "British and Irish Short Story," 9.

9. O'Brien, "Never Despair," December 5, 220. Davis, "Song for the Irish Militia," December 5, 233. Harriman, "Thomas Francis Meagher," October 14, 68. Harriman wrote from

Helena, Montana, so apparently the *Packet* was read across the Atlantic. On Irish story papers more broadly, see Rains, "Do You Ring?," 18.

10. Williams, "Home to Her Mother," December 12, 269–70. MacNamara, "Irish Paddy," December 3, 238–40.

11. *Mike* was published posthumously; Hoare died in 1877. *Scenes and Incidents* was published under the pseudonym An Irishman. Little is known about the author behind that pseudonym, F. H. Clayton, so it is unclear whether the autobiographical form of the framework narrative is based on the author's life or whether Clayton used the device to simulate the veracity of an otherwise fictional account.

12. Allen, "Frenzy of Famine," 567.

13. Ibid.

14. Brand, "Trauma Witnessing in Film," 198; Peters quoted in ibid., 208.

15. "Little Boy of the Powers," March 19, 589; K. O'L. G., "Jimmy Hackett," March 21, 178.

16. Bodkin, "Holy Well," 224.

17. Ibid.

18. Ibid.

19. Ibid., 224, 225.

20. Ibid., 226.

21. Especially see chapter 17, "Of Curses, Kindness and Miraculous Food," in Póirtéir's *Famine Echoes*; Donovan, "Local-Colour Literature," 43. Additionally, Corporaal mentions "narrative 'templates' of conflict" at the heart of regional fiction ("Relocating Regionalism," 158), and Cusack discusses the antimodern "non-normative relation to the temporality of modernity" of regional fiction, specifically in Seumas MacManus's work ("Seanachie to the New World," 10).

22. Brand, "Trauma Witnessing in Film," 199.

23. Bodkin, "Holy Well," 224.

24. Ketchum-Glass, "Witnessing the Witness," 21–22.

25. For narrative embedding or textual hierarchy and focalization, see Mieke Bal, "Laughing Mice," 204. Martha Nussbaum notes that "compassion can be blocked by a sense of distance and unlikeness" (*Upheavals of Thought*, 447).

26. Ricoeur, *Time and Narrative*, vol. 3, 191, 192. Levine, *Forms*, 14.

27. Alexander, "On the Social Construction," 262.

28. On "partial recognition," see, for example, the comments by Davitt and the *Providence Telegram* quoted in "Irish Land Bill," *Irish World*, April 4, 1903 1, 2.

29. "Davitt on the Land Bill," April 25, 1903, 6. W. M. C., "Compromise with the Landlords," May 2, 1903, 6. "Audacious English Lying," April 18, 1903, 1.

30. "New Land Policy," February 21, 1903, 4.

31. "Only Possible Remedy," February 20, 1904, 1, 2; See also "Irish Nation Speaks Out," *Irish World and American Industrial Liberator*, April 25, 1903, 1, 2.

32. On December 24, 1904, secretary of the American United Irish League John O'Callaghan explained the act to readers of the *Irish World*: "Nevertheless, with all its shortcomings, it is putting a new and more contended and prosperous appearance on the condition of the Irish land problem, and in the opinion of the best judges of social and political affairs in Ireland, whether native of the soil or belonging to the ascendancy party formerly, is destined within a few years to make the winning of Irish legislative independence a matter of absolute certainty" ("Land Purchase Act," 2).

33. See, for example, "Land Purchase Finance," January 12, 1904, 5.

34. "One of the Resolutions . . . ," December 16, 7. The newspaper was likely referring to Maud Gonne's comments on Queen Victoria's reign displayed in "Famine Queen" a few years earlier. See chapters 1 and 6 on Gonne's article.

35. Morash, "Famine/Holocaust."

36. Bruner, "Narrative Construction of Reality," 228–29.

37. Zeitlin, "Vicarious Witness," 8; Hirsch, "Surviving Images," 30.

38. In Bodkin's *Recollections of an Irish Judge* (1915), scenes of famine suffering do not feature. The aforementioned authors Margaret Brew (born in 1850; author of *Castle Cloyne*) and Justin H. McCarthy (born in 1860; author of *Lily Lass*) also did not experience or witness the Famine.

39. D'hoker, *Irish Women Writers*, 125. In his PhD dissertation, Cusack discusses two other texts by Barlow in light of how the author incorporated famine memory into her fiction ("Memory, History, and Identity").

40. Luddy, "Jane Barlow," n.p.; Clarke, "Barlow, Jane," n.p.; Hyde quoted in Luddy, "Jane Barlow," n.p.

41. Clarke, "Barlow, Jane," n.p.; Gwynn, "Looking at Ireland," *Irish Times*, September 14, 1946.

42. D'hoker, *Irish Women Writers*, 120. Frances Clarke states that *Irish Idylls* ran "into nine editions" ("Barlow, Jane"). Hansson, "Our Village," 60.

43. Hansson, "Our Village," 66–67, 60.

44. Luddy, "Jane Barlow," n.p.; D'hoker, *Irish Women Writers*, 124. D'hoker discusses the format of the short story cycle in detail in chapter 5 of *Irish Women Writers*; she also discusses Barlow's story cycles.

45. "Working of the Land Act," May 1, 11.

46. D'hoker, *Irish Women Writers*, 112.

47. Hansson provides a detailed analysis of the different linguistic registers and their political dimension in the Lisconnel stories, demonstrating how they create distance between narrator and characters and ambiguity regarding Barlow's position as author. See Hansson, "Our Village."

48. Kickham, "Scenes and Characters," October 22, 83. Greene, "Sown in Tears," *Irish Emerald*, January 4, 2.

49. Barlow, "Con the Quare One," 298. Nannie and Johnny are Con's siblings.

50. Ibid., 298, 299, 300.

51. Barlow, "Herself," April 8, 1905, 27.

52. Ibid., April 15, 1905, 50.

53. D'hoker, *Irish Women Writers*, 124.

54. Barlow, "Herself," April 8, 1905, 26; April 15, 1905, 50.

55. "Little Boy of the Powers," 589.

56. Rains, "Going in for Competitions," 138–41.

57. Williams, "Home to Her Mother," 269, 270.

58. Kelleher discusses the potential depoliticization of representations of female suffering; she explains that in several famine novels, female victims remain detached from larger sociopolitical contexts. Focus on their suffering effectively depoliticizes the respective novel's representations of famine. See Kelleher's discussion of Carleton's *Black Prophet* in *Feminization of Famine*, 35–39.

59. Pickering and Keightley, "Communities of Memory," 122. Cultural memory scholars have reflected in detail on the use of narrative templates in the construction of cultural memory. See, for example, Wertsch, "Narrative Organization of Collective Memory" and *Voices of Collective Remembering*.

60. Speaking specifically about cultural trauma, Alexander explains how the audience is implicated in bridging the gap between event and representation ("Toward a Theory of Cultural Trauma," 11–12).

61. Mussell, "Cohering Knowledge," 97, 101.

62. LaCapra, *Writing History, Writing Trauma*, 47. I borrow the phrase in the final sentence from Paul Frosh and Amit Pinchevski, who discuss media witnessing in our own time ("Introduction," 13).

Section II
Diasporic and Transnational Connections

5

"FAMINE, OR FARMS"

McGee's Illustrated Weekly and the Betterment
of the Poor Laborer's Lot, 1876–82

IN EARLY 1878, *McGEE'S ILLUSTRATED Weekly: Devoted to Catholic Art, Literature and Education* looked back on the previous year, reflecting that it had been "one of depressed trade and continuous commercial anxiety both at home and abroad."[1] This situation had been building for several years. Since the onset of industrialization, Britain had been world leader in industrial output; however, by the end of the nineteenth century, the position had shifted to the US. America's road to dominance was not without hurdles. During the 1860s and early 1870s, Irish American newspapers showed concern over labor issues, and concerns over the rights and condition of poor laborers intensified as the 1870s progressed. After the Panic of 1873, a depression ensued in Europe and North America. During the late 1870s, laborers in the US grew increasingly dissatisfied, which resulted in the establishment of labor parties and trade unions advocating the rights of both rural and urban laborers. These developments led to the great rise in popularity of the Knights of Labor, a movement that advocated for the rights of US laborers across ethnic and cultural lines and in which many Irish Americans were involved.[2]

At this time, engagement with the Irish Land Question increased in both Ireland and Irish America, a development for which John Devoy's "New Departure" of 1878 was a major turning point. As chapters 2 and 3 have shown, in addition to worsened economic conditions, Ireland experienced several crop failures between 1877 and 1879, famine

137

in 1879, and the Land War of 1879–82. The popular American political economist Henry George (1839–97) drew parallels between Ireland and the US in his 1881 pamphlet *The Irish Land Question*: noticing that inequality in the US had only increased during the country's unprecedented industrial expansion, George warned that the conditions that had caused the Irish land problem were emerging in the US.[3] George, a member of the American Land League, reasoned that "the Irish land question is not a mere local matter between Irish landlords and Irish tenants . . . but the great social problem of modern civilisation" and furthermore argued that poverty in the US and Ireland was caused by "centralized ownership of land in the hands of the few instead of the many."[4] This view was widely shared, as Margaret Dixon McDougall's criticism on land monopoly demonstrates, for example. George gained much support, especially from the Irish American and Irish communities. However, it should be noted that while George propagated an end to private property, most Irish radicals in the Land League did not opt for this relatively extreme socialist ideal but rather for the "more equitable distribution of land."[5]

Periodicals in North America provided frequent coverage of developments in Ireland, including rural unrest, evictions, and Land League rallies, as well as speaking tours of Irish orators in the US. A visual example of such coverage can be found in figure 5.1, taken from *McGee's Illustrated*. This two-page image shows one of the beautiful large illustrations often included in the magazine; in depicting contemporary famine in Mayo, it is indicative of *McGee's* concern with the Irish poor.

Recollections of suffering in Ireland were incorporated into sociopolitical discourses on the plight of the Irish American urban poor. This chapter investigates the diasporic use of recollections of Irish hunger in service of US rhetoric on labor and land conditions in the late 1870s and early 1880s. On the pages of *McGee's Illustrated*, famine memories were used to argue for changes in US labor conditions and to provide better prospects for not only poor Irish immigrants in the US but also those in Ireland contemplating emigration.

While in Ireland the Land League strove to improve the rights of the rural population, in the US an initiative to improve the lot of poor Irish American laborers—and of their peers in Ireland—gained popularity: Catholic colonization, or the attempt to establish (Irish) Catholic communities in America's interior. The Land League and Catholic Colonization Association were considered rival initiatives by some, as both sought

Figure 5.1. R. C. Woodville, "The Famine in Ireland—Distributing Relief Tickets in the Turf Market, Westport, County Mayo," *McGee's Illustrated*, April 10, 1880, 328–9. Reproduced from the original held by the Department of Special Collections of the Hesburgh Libraries of the University of Notre Dame.

support in the US and Ireland and operated with similar goals. Both struggled to secure land and ownership rights and better living and working conditions for the rural-minded Irish; however, they envisioned radically different locations and ways for achieving these goals.[6]

During the period, the "continual interplay of events, ideas, and people in Ireland and the United States . . . profoundly impacted both Irish and American society"; Ely M. Janis demonstrates that such exchanges formed a transatlantic "Greater Ireland."[7] Besides analyzing the comparative diasporic utilization of recollections of Irish hunger, this chapter explores tensions in the debate on the Catholic Colonization Association and Land League in the pages of various Irish and Irish American periodicals. It takes as its central publication *McGee's Illustrated*, an avid proponent of the colonization movement. By focusing on a literary magazine, the chapter demonstrates the need to cotextually analyze nonfiction, prose fiction, and poetry and argues for the consideration of literary magazines when exploring sociopolitical debates.

McGee's Illustrated Weekly and the Plight of the Poor American Laborer

McGee's Illustrated Weekly was founded in 1876 by proprietor James A. McGee, who had left his native Ottawa some years earlier and, by the time publication of his magazine began, had become a notable printer, seller, and publisher of Catholic books.[8] The devoutly Catholic weekly magazine counted sixteen pages and had a cover price of six cents. The magazine tried to be accessible to a wide readership; in its ads, *McGee's* boasted that it was not just the "only illustrated Catholic paper in America" but also the "cheapest" one.[9] The advertisements on the final pages of each issue demonstrate an orientation to the area of New York, where most of the companies and institutions buying ad space in the magazine were located. However, parties from other regions also featured. The lists of traveling agents included in the magazine reveal that *McGee's* was sold in many US states as well as in Canada; in his memoires, the editor of *McGee's* verified this Canadian audience. The magazine's subscription and postage rates furthermore show that it was possible to have *McGee's* mailed across the globe.[10]

While focusing on prose fiction and poetry, the magazine also contained illustrations, opinion pieces (editorials and letters sent in by readers), articles on current events, and items of general interest; the latter were often of a religious nature. For the majority of its run (1876–82), *McGee's* was edited by Maurice Francis Egan (1852–1924). Egan was a second-generation Irish American whose father—a County Tipperary native turned successful businessman in the US—had come from Ireland during the 1820s or 1830s. Like his parents, Egan was a devout Catholic. He regularly contributed to magazines, and in addition to editing *McGee's*, he edited the *Illustrated Catholic American*, the *Catholic Review*, and the American *Freeman's Journal*; for the latter, he was an associate editor. Egan authored several works of genteel fiction meant to show readers how to live a virtuous, Catholic middle-class life in America. He taught literature as a professor at the Catholic University of Washington, DC, and the University of Notre Dame. An international career followed these academic positions, as Egan was appointed American ambassador in Copenhagen. As such, he was an important Roman Catholic author, editor, intellectual, and diplomat.[11]

It seems that editor Egan and proprietor McGee were not always on the same page. Egan's *Recollections of a Happy Life* (1924) shows that he considered McGee's taste "not impeccable." This memoire reveals that the proprietor of *McGee's* regularly copied illustrations from other periodicals such as "the London *Illustrated News*, the *Graphic*, *L'Illustration*, and *Le Monde Illustre*." Egan felt that McGee did not always include these images in *McGee's Illustrated* in a sensible or appropriate manner.[12]

The "Letter of Introduction" included in the first issue of *McGee's* explained the establishment of the magazine from the conviction that Catholics (Irish specifically) in the US were still dealing with religious opposition on a regular basis and that within the existing fund of Catholic magazines in the US, "something [was] wanting to complete the line of defenses which Catholics were endeavouring to throw up for themselves and their children against the combined assaults of the advocates of heresy, infidelity and atheism." The magazine was to function as a moral guide to Irish Catholics in America, illustrated by its intent to supply proper reading material for its flock—a service denominational magazines typically provided: "We intend . . . to make the principal feature of our paper the publication of tales, stories and poetry, which, selected primarily for their healthful moral tone, will be also sufficiently artistic and meritorious in construction to attract and amuse the young while edifying the more fastidious and experienced."[13] The magazine's didactic streak was further evidenced by the regular inclusion of strongly moralizing editorials in which readers were instructed on how to act virtuously and be good Irish Americans.

Some of the materials included in *McGee's* suggest that it stressed the latter element; its readership should be Americans first, Irish second.

Because of this, Egan and *McGee's* can be seen as part and product of the "lace-curtain Irish" community.[14] The piece "With Whom Shall We Sympathize?"—which *McGee's* took from the Waterford *Celt* and which sparked a series of follow-up pieces and reader responses—made it clear that siding with the Russians against the Turks in the Russo-Turkish War (1877–78) was not only the Irish and anti-British course but also the American way to go: "One thing is certain, the side against which England will be arrayed will have the active sympathy and moral support of the greater part of the civilized world. With Americans particularly the recollection of the perfidious conduct of England, before and during our late civil war, will not easily be effaced."[15]

In an editorial response copied from the *San Francisco Monitor* to which *McGee's* added the telling title "Sound Sense on Irish Politics," this identificatory stance again featured. Putting in his place a reader who had declared himself ready to die for Ireland, the editorial instructed said reader to leave Irish politics to Irish politicians, for "the men at home know most about the national cause and are quite competent to conduct its fortunes." The author quipped that the periodical had "no strong objection that our correspondent should commence the dying," for it would mean that he would cease to write questionable letters to newspapers. Most importantly, the reader was told to do his "duty . . . as an American citizen, and to engage in no enterprise illegal or against the peace and dignity of this nation."[16] In other words, being an Irish firebrand was not only illegal but also undignified behavior for an American subject.

Rather than singling out the Irish specifically, *McGee's* regularly showed concern for all European immigrants in the US. James E. McGee's poem "The Immigrants," included in the first issue of *McGee's*, underscored the common plight of the newly arrived: all "gathered nations / shall, united, learn to pray," protected by the "gracious mother" and "Queen of Nations" "Columbia."[17] On October 18, 1879, the magazine spoke of a "new tide of emigration" that was to hit the US. Rather than sounding the alarm, *McGee's* showed that its version of America was an inclusive one, home for all newcomers—as long as they integrated and adhered to American values.[18] With such pieces, the magazine provided inroads for multidirectional considerations of these peoples, their interactions, and the overlaps in their past experiences.

When *McGee's* spoke on behalf of laboring communities, its focus was often on poor urban laborers in eastern US cities or their rural peers in Ireland. Public opinion on Irish laborers in the US was not always supportive.

In nativist rhetoric and discourses oppositional to immigration and organized labor, Irish American labor activism became easily conflated with nationalist resistance, and the representation of Irish violence was coded in racialized terms of inherent irrationality and aggression. Such representations became more prominent during the 1860s and 1870s, as the Molly Maguires, a secret society involved in labor activism, committed various violent acts. Many Catholics disapproved of these acts.[19] As such, *McGee's* defense was situated in ongoing, complex societal negotiations of the figure of the laborer—and of the Irish American laborer specifically.

In its support for the worker, the magazine drew links beyond the Irish-diasporic connection. In the 1877 Christmas issue, "An English Christmas Story" was published. In the story, poor English town laborers go through an episode of famine during the late 1840s. The protagonist family is saved by an investment in the father's business—he is a gifted but unemployed cobbler—by a wealthy fellow Catholic. The family survives the ordeal. The story then fast-forwards three decades: the cobbler's son has become the prosperous mayor of the adjoining town and is a highly respected—Catholic—member of his community. The story shows that in the 1840s, other regions were hit by famine as well, drawing a transnational link between the suffering of the Irish and English poor (Catholics). Moreover, by focusing on town life and town laborers, it draws analogies between rural and urban poverty. Crucially, by seeing investment by rich employers in poor laborers as the solution, the narrative provides an implicit indictment of (US) capitalist individualism.[20]

McGee's expressed disappointment at the lack of concern for the poor displayed by many better-off Irish Catholics in US cities. Borrowing the words of the St. Paul (Minnesota) *Northwestern Chronicle*, the magazine condemned this perceived apathy: "Are your Catholic hearts so calloused with life's many concerns that you cannot feel for these [poor laborers]? are your ears so deadened with the whir of industry's wheels and the clink of the money tables, that ye will not heed the cry of your brethren for help?"[21] Even if Catholic philanthropists showed concern for the Irish poor in cities, *McGee's* had opined a year earlier, this concern often fell short: rarely did privileged members of society "give a thought to the practical amelioration of the condition of their co-religionists" beyond city limits.[22] McGee's call for understanding asked members of its readership to make an effort by imagining themselves in the position of those in need of help and highlighting their moral obligation to their fellow men on the basis of religious ties.

One of the ways in which *McGee's* sought to help the laboring poor was through Catholic colonization. Assisted emigration schemes and specifically Catholic colonization efforts were not new phenomena in the 1870s. Such ideas were voiced by Daniel O'Connell and the North American Colonial Association of Ireland in the 1830s and 1840s, and in the mid-1850s, the Irish Emigrant Aid Society attempted to settle Irish emigrants in New York state and Pennsylvania. These schemes were unsuccessful and met with opposition, most notably from Archbishop John Hughes of New York. Consequently, they were not developed further. However, in the mid-1870s, the situation looked different, as Hughes had died in 1864 and the global economic crisis had worsened laborers' circumstances. In Ireland, assisted emigration initiatives were devised once more, now by the Tuke Committee and John Sweetnam, a rich Irish philanthropist. Such schemes were opposed by the Catholic clergy and the Irish and American Land Leagues. The league reasoned that assisted emigration was akin to the involuntary renunciation of one's holding followed by forced emigration, a line of reasoning that failed to acknowledge that many struggling Irish tenants would welcome an escape from their difficult living conditions.[23]

Reflecting on internal migration in the US, Bishop Coadjutor John Ireland of St. Paul (Minnesota) wrote in the late 1870s that "the surplus populations in our cities, the depression of business, the scarcity of employment, the poverty, suffering and discontent attending thereon, the magnitude of labor strikes, and the dread of their repetition, have made the question of immigration to the land from our over-crowded cities of pressing, national interest."[24] In 1875, he established the Catholic Colonization Association. Its aim was to provide the Irish poor in the cities of the eastern US with assistance and means to buy their own farms. Until the mid-1880s, the association established various Catholic "colonies," especially in Minnesota. Catholic colonization was at its peak during the period from 1876 to 1881. The facts that John Ireland was directly involved, that several Irish American bishops supported the undertaking, and that the association established Catholic priests in each of the colonies gave weight to the endeavor for Irish Catholics who feared that moving westward would mean a disconnect from their religious communities.[25]

The term "colonization" aligns with the larger phenomenon of the spiritual empire, in which a special role was assigned to Ireland. Prominent figures including the itinerant orator Father Burke envisioned a Catholic empire in North America specifically. In this narrative of religious empire building, mass emigration from Ireland provided the island with the status of "martyr nation" and the Irish with a divine destiny. The Irish would form new congregations of the Catholic Church and establish Catholic institutions wherever they settled, helping to build a global Catholic empire.[26] As Sarah Roddy explains, those who spread the faith across the globe not only sent remittances back home; they also were a source of pride to the church at home and "reinforc[ed] the popular self-conception of the Irish as 'the most intensely religious and practical Catholics in the world,'" an identity fortified by the devotional revolution of the third quarter of the nineteenth century.[27]

Irish American author Dillon O'Brien (1817–82) functioned as the executive secretary of the Colonization Bureau. He wrote pamphlets and articles in support of Catholic colonization, was responsible for the daily administration of the association, guided newly arrived Irish settlers to their destinations, and, like John Ireland, lectured on the scheme on many occasions. Because of his great involvement, James P. Shannon calls O'Brien the "true director" of the Colonization Bureau. O'Brien was not a blindly optimistic advocate and realized that the climate of Minnesota—characterized by harsh winters and hot, humid summers—could be taxing, especially on those unaccustomed to it. Moreover, social isolation was a serious issue on the prairies. In his pamphlets and articles, O'Brien warned those considering the move westward to truly think about their intentions. John Ireland was also optimistic yet realistic, as he made clear to those intending to come to the colonies that it would be hard, even impossible, to come without funds.[28]

Catholic colonization received much attention in the Irish and Irish American press through advertisements, articles, sent-in letters, and fiction, demonstrating how the press version and religious version of "Greater Ireland" overlapped and impacted one another. At first, John Boyle O'Reilly of the Boston *Pilot* disapproved of Catholic colonization, and disapproval by an outlet as influential as the *Pilot* weighed heavily on the movement. O'Reilly later became supportive and acted as a member of the board of directors of the Irish Catholic Colonization movement. He did continue to denounce assisted emigration from Ireland, seeing it as forced banishment.[29] In O'Reilly's rhetoric, a difference was made between internal migration in the US and Irish emigration across the Atlantic. Several Irish American periodicals presented the scheme in a positive light. Patrick Ford of the *Irish World and American Industrial Liberator* believed Irishmen in

America "had neglected the soil—their natural heritage" and supported the movement.[30] The New York *Celtic Monthly* lauded the scheme. *McGee's Illustrated* included ads and editorials about it on a weekly basis and considered it a potentially beneficial influence on the societal standing of the Irish in the US.[31]

Cotextual Connections in Creative Writings and Nonfiction: US Labor Issues, Catholic Colonization, and Famine Memory

McGee's frequently expressed concern with regard to the health and moral development of Irish immigrants in cities. Arguing that the East was overcrowded, that the "labor market . . . of New York and other large cities, is and is likely to be for a long time, overstocked," and that "the triple temptation of poverty, evil associates and the vices of large communities" loomed in urban areas, the magazine asked support to take the poor laborer and his family out of the "degradation and sorrow" of tenement living and move them to "where his labor is in demand, and where he can rear up his family in sobriety and comfort." As the magazine stated, "the true field for honest industry and assured personal independence is to be found, not in the workshops of New York, the mines of Pennsylvania nor the factories of New England, but in such states as Texas, Missouri, Kansas, Iowa and Minnesota, and further westward."[32] Effectively, *McGee's* proposed an old cure: trading the toxic influence of the city for the wholesome effect of the country.

In 1878, Dillon O'Brien wrote a letter to the editors of the Irish American press, which was included in *McGee's*. In the letter, O'Brien explained that the colonization effort was going well but asked for additional support to help the "large surplus population" of "every Eastern city" he visited on his tour, for the remedy to their ills was "the immigration to the land, of those of our people adapted for agricultural life."[33] In his 1879 pamphlet, Bishop Ireland wrote that "there is about the same difference between the moral atmosphere of the rural Catholic colonies to which we invite our people, and the back streets and alleys of the over-crowded city, as there is between the pure air of the prairie and the foul air of the city lane." Moreover, an added benefit would come to those who stayed behind. In rhetoric familiar from the argument that emigration from Ireland could provide those who stayed behind with a better quality of life, Bishop Ireland argued that "the immigration of those of our people adapted to agricultural life from the city to the land will be a benefit, not alone to themselves, but to those they leave behind. By this healthful drain the latter will be left more room, and have more opportunities to better their condition."[34] The benefits of exchanging urban squalor for rural life had been voiced earlier: in 1861, the New York *Tablet* had included a letter by Rev. Dr. Sweeny, bishop of St. John (New Brunswick). Bishop Sweeny, then president of the Emigrant Aid Association, advocated assistance for newly arrived immigrants to relocate to New Brunswick to "ameliorate both their moral and temporal condition" and keep them safe from the "evil influences of our large cities and towns."[35]

In 1879, *McGee's* included the cover image "On a Farm / Along the Docks" (fig. 5.2), which equally idealized the country and condemned the city. The full-page illustration was accompanied by a lengthy explanation that clarified that "On a Farm" was "no Arcadian idyll (fig. 5.3). The counterpart of it can be seen a thousand times over in any of the Irish settlements in Kansas, Iowa or Minnesota." "On the Docks," unfortunately, was also drawn from life: "It is no caricature, but a stern reality. . . . Some friendly and charitable hand must be extended to aid him [the Irish American urban laborer], otherwise he perishes. And his little ones, what of them? If not kidnapped and proselytized by the Aid Societies, their future destiny points to the workhouse or the penitentiary. Who can look on this sketch from real life and say that it is overdrawn?" Likely, the idea of proselytization did not sit well with Irish readers who had experienced or heard of conversion attempts in exchange for sustenance during the Great Irish Famine. Unfortunately, the illustration had a side effect *McGee's* tried to circumvent. "On the Docks" shows an Irishman with simianized features; *McGee's* sought to dispel the existing connotations of this stereotype on the basis of social determinism, arguing that these features were not innate qualities but the product of a detrimental environment. Nevertheless, the stereotype could not be rewritten that easily, and some readers considered it offensive.[36]

Explicitly drawing the link to Catholic colonization, below "On a Farm / Along the Docks" was printed a reference to an article on Catholic colonization included later in that same issue. As figure 5.3 shows, that article was printed next to the explanation of the illustration. Thus, through proximity, this choice in layout cotextually fortified the nexus between the problem and its solution, as propagated by *McGee's*.

Two years earlier, the article "Famine, or Farms" had been included in *McGee's*; it reflected on the Great Uprising, the nationwide railroad and labor strikes that took place in the US in July 1877.[37] These strikes were suppressed by federal troops and state militia, and, as John Rogers Commons points out, "brought labour face to face with an openly hostile government." The strikes led to the establishment of many working men's parties.[38] *McGee's* argued

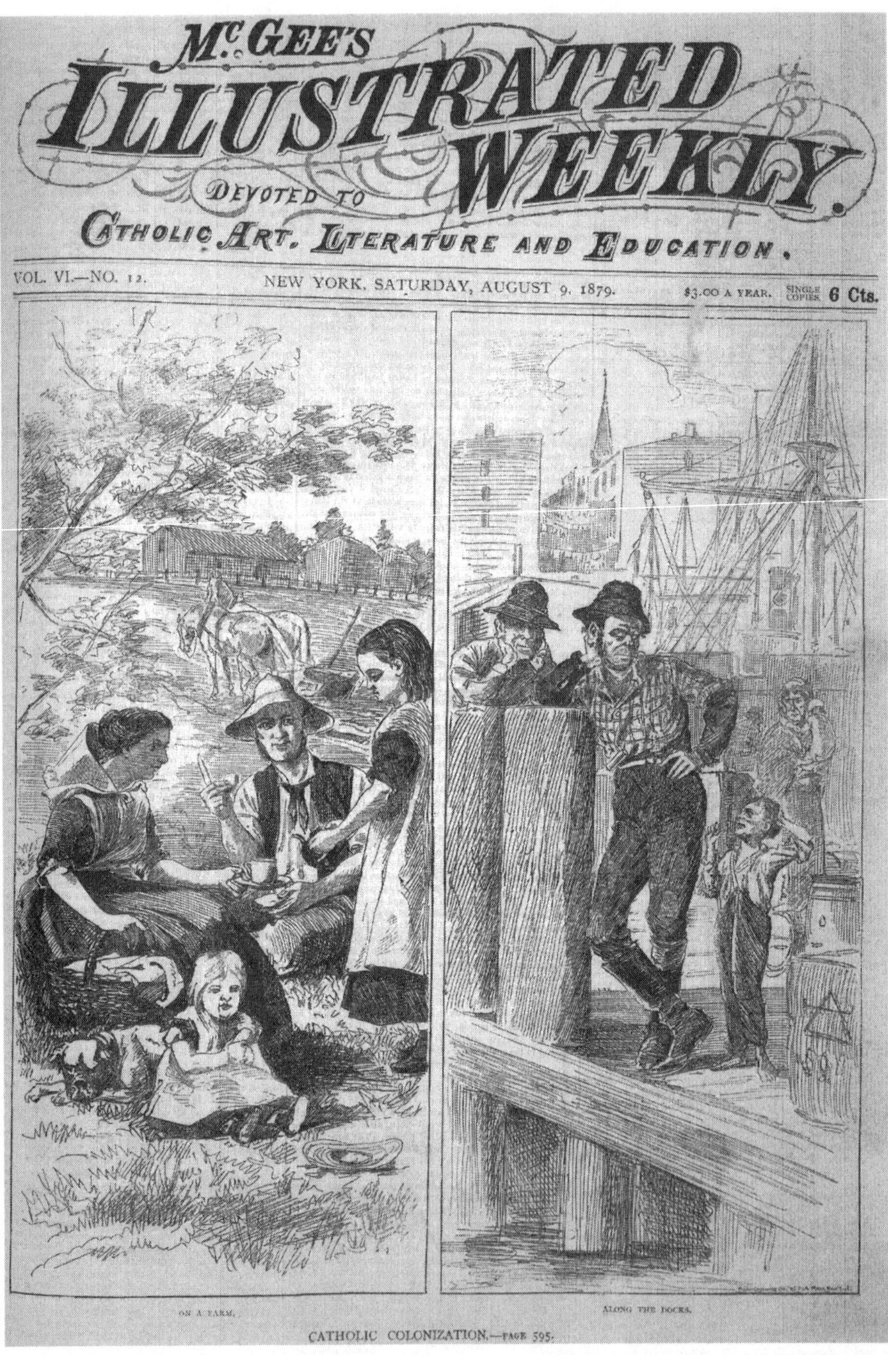

Figure 5.2. "On a Farm / Along the Docks," *McGee's Illustrated*, August 9, 1879, 593. Below the image, a reference to Catholic colonization is included. Reproduced from the original held by the Department of Special Collections of the Hesburgh Libraries of the University of Notre Dame.

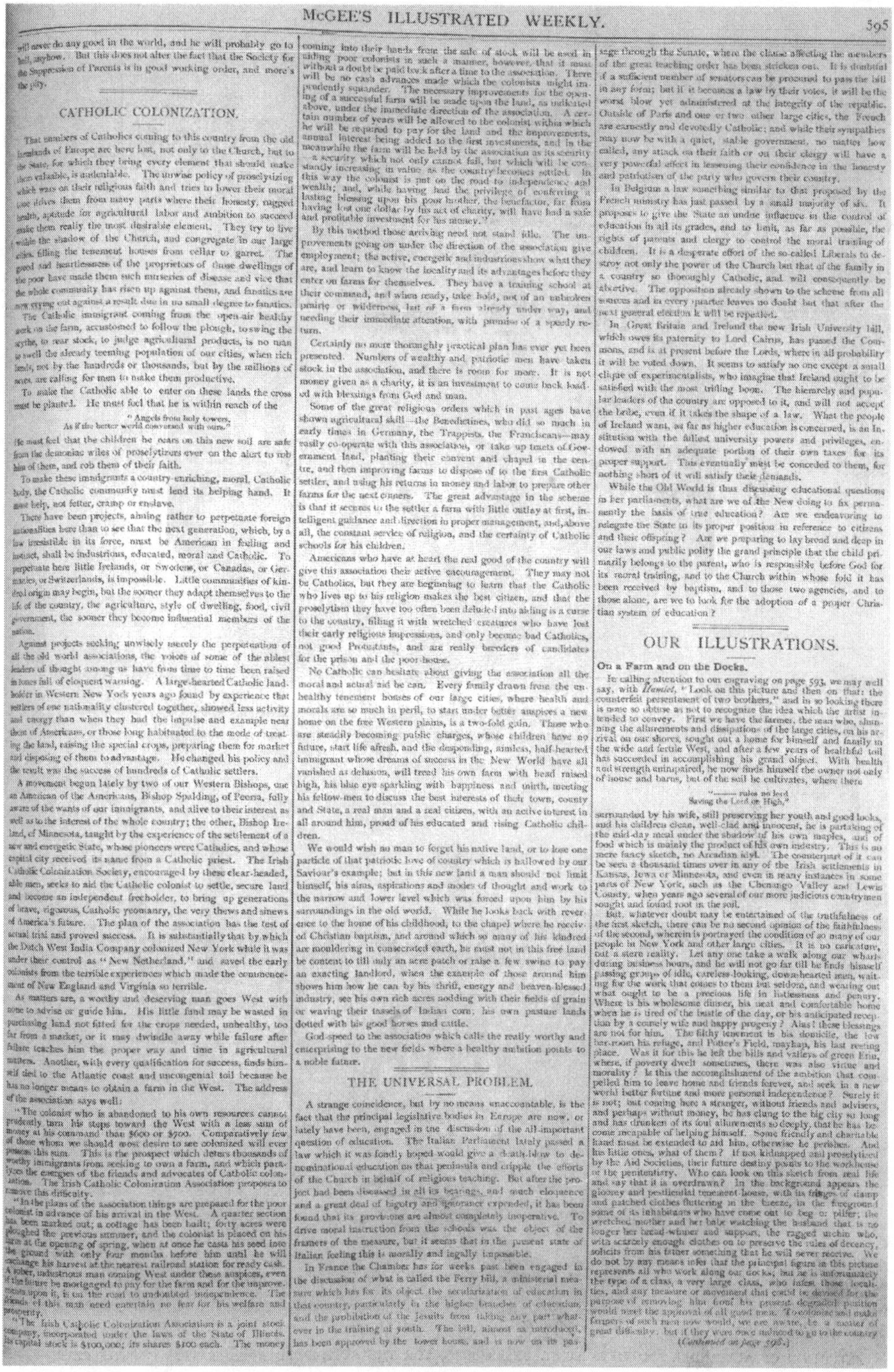

McGEE'S ILLUSTRATED WEEKLY. 595

will never do any good in the world, and he will probably go to hell, anyhow. But this does not alter the fact that the Society for the Suppression of Parents is in good working order, and more's the pity.

CATHOLIC COLONIZATION.

That numbers of Catholics coming to this country from the old lands of Europe are here lost, not only to the Church, but to the State, for which they bring every element that should make them valuable, is undeniable. The unwise policy of proselytizing which wars on their religious faith and tries to lower their moral tone drives them from many parts where their honesty, rugged health, aptitude for agricultural labor and ambition to succeed make them really the most desirable element. They try to live within the shadow of the Church, and congregate in our large cities, filling the tenement houses from cellar to garret. The greed and heartlessness of the proprietors of those dwellings of the poor have made them such nurseries of disease and vice that the whole community has risen up against them, and fanatics are now crying out against a result due in no small degree to fanatics.

The Catholic immigrant coming from the open-air healthy work on the farm, accustomed to follow the plough, to swing the scythe, to rear stock, to judge agricultural products, is no man to swell the already teeming population of our cities, when rich lands, not by the hundreds or thousands, but by the millions of acres, are calling for men to make them productive.

To make the Catholic able to enter on these lands the cross must be planted. He must feel that he is within reach of the

"Angels from holy towers,
As if the better world conversed with ours."

He must feel that the children he rears on this new soil are safe from the demoniac wiles of proselytizers ever on the alert to rob him of them, and rob them of their faith.

To make these immigrants a country-enriching, moral, Catholic body, the Catholic community must lend its helping hand. It must help, not fetter, cramp or enslave.

There have been projects, aiming rather to perpetuate foreign nationalities here than to see that the next generation, which, by a law irresistible in its force, must be American in feeling and instinct, shall be industrious, educated, moral and Catholic. To perpetuate here little Irelands, or Swedens, or Canadas, or Germanies, or Switzerlands, is impossible. Little communities of kindred origin may begin, but the sooner they adapt themselves to the life of the country, the agriculture, style of dwelling, food, civil government, the sooner they become influential members of the nation.

Against projects seeking unwisely merely the perpetuation of all the old world associations, the voices of some of the ablest leaders of thought among us have from time to time been raised in tones full of eloquent warning. A large-hearted Catholic landholder in Western New York years ago found by experience that settlers of one nationality clustered together, showed less activity and energy than when they had the impulse and example near them of Americans, or those long habituated to the mode of treating the land, raising the special crops, preparing them for market and disposing of them to advantage. He changed his policy and the result was the success of hundreds of Catholic settlers.

A movement begun lately by two of our Western Bishops, one an American of the Americans, Bishop Spalding, of Peoria, fully aware of the wants of our immigrants, and alive to their interest as well as to the interest of the whole country; the other, Bishop Ireland, of Minnesota, taught by the experience of the settlement of a new and energetic State, whose pioneers were Catholics, and whose capital city received its name from a Catholic priest. The Irish Catholic Colonization Society, encouraged by these clear-headed, able men, seeks to aid the Catholic colonist to settle, secure land and become an independent freeholder, to bring up generations of brave, vigorous, Catholic yeomanry, the very thews and sinews of America's future. The plan of the association has the test of actual trial and proved success. It is substantially that by which the Dutch West India Company colonized New York while it was under their control as "New Netherland," and saved the early colonists from the terrible experiences which made the commencement of New England and Virginia so terrible.

As matters are, a worthy and deserving man goes West with none to advise or guide him. His little fund may be wasted in purchasing land not fitted for the crops needed, unhealthy, too far from a market, or it may dwindle away while failure after failure teaches him the proper way and time in agricultural matters. Another, with every qualification for success, finds himself tied to the Atlantic coast and uncongenial toil because he has no longer means to obtain a farm in the West. The address of the association says well:

"The colonist who is abandoned to his own resources cannot prudently turn his steps toward the West with a less sum of money at his command than $600 or $700. Comparatively few of those whom we should most desire to see colonized will ever possess this sum. This is the prospect which deters thousands of worthy immigrants from seeking to own a farm, and which paralyzes the energies of the friends and advocates of Catholic colonization. The Irish Catholic Colonization Association proposes to remove this difficulty.

"In the plans of the association things are prepared for the poor colonist in advance of his arrival in the West. A quarter section has been marked out; a cottage has been built; forty acres were ploughed the previous summer, and the colonist is placed on his farm at the opening of spring, when at once he casts his seed into the ground with only four months before him until he will exchange his harvest at the nearest railroad station for ready cash. A sober, industrious man coming West under these auspices, even if the future be mortgaged to pay for the farm and for the improvements upon it, is on the road to undoubted independence. The friends of this man need entertain no fear for his welfare and prosperity.

"The Irish Catholic Colonization Association is a joint stock company, incorporated under the laws of the State of Illinois. Its capital stock is $100,000; its shares $100 each. The money coming into their hands from the sale of stock will be used in aiding poor colonists in such a manner, however, that it must without a doubt be paid back after a time to the association. There will be no cash advances made which the colonists might imprudently squander. The necessary improvements for the opening of a successful farm will be made upon the land, as indicated above, under the immediate direction of the association. A certain number of years will be allowed to the colonist within which he will be required to pay for the land and the improvements, annual interest being added to the first investments, and in the meanwhile the farm will be held by the association as its security—a security which not only cannot fail, but which will be constantly increasing in value as the country becomes settled. In this way the colonist is put on the road to independence and wealth; and, while having had the privilege of conferring a lasting blessing upon his poor brother, the benefactor, far from having lost one dollar by his act of charity, will have had a safe and profitable investment for his money."

By this method those arriving need not stand idle. The improvements going on under the direction of the association give employment; the active, energetic and industrious show what they are, and learn to know the locality and its advantages before they enter on farms for themselves. They have a training school at their command, and when ready, take hold, not of an unbroken prairie or wilderness, but of a farm already under way, and needing their immediate attention, with promise of a speedy return.

Certainly no more thoroughly practical plan has ever yet been presented. Numbers of wealthy and patriotic men have taken stock in the association, and there is room for more. It is not money given as a charity, it is an investment to come back loaded with blessings from God and man.

Some of the great religious orders which in past ages have shown agricultural skill—the Benedictines, who did so much in early times in Germany, the Trappists, the Franciscans—may easily co-operate with this association, or take up tracts of Government land, planting their convent and chapel in the centre, and then improving farms to dispose of to the first Catholic settler, and using his returns in money and labor to prepare other farms for the next comers. The great advantage in the scheme is that it secures to the settler a farm with little outlay at first, intelligent guidance and direction in proper management, and, above all, the constant service of religion, and the certainty of Catholic schools for his children.

Americans who have at heart the real good of the country will give this association their active encouragement. They may not be Catholics, but they are beginning to learn that the Catholic who lives up to his religion makes the best citizen, and that the proselytism they have too often been deluded into aiding is a curse to the country, filling it with wretched creatures who have lost their early religious impressions, and only become bad Catholics, not good Protestants, and are really breeders of candidates for the prison and the poor-house.

No Catholic can hesitate about giving the association all the moral and actual aid he can. Every family drawn from the unhealthy tenement houses of our large cities, where health and morals are so much in peril, to start under better auspices a new home on the free Western plains, is a two-fold gain. Those who are steadily becoming public charges, whose children have no future, start life afresh, and the desponding, aimless, half-hearted immigrant whose dreams of success in the New World have all vanished as delusion, will tread his own farm with head raised high, his blue eye sparkling with happiness and mirth, meeting his fellow-men to discuss the best interests of their town, county and State, a real man and a real citizen, with an active interest in all around him, proud of his educated and rising Catholic children.

We would wish no man to forget his native land, or to lose one particle of that patriotic love of country which is hallowed by our Saviour's example; but in this new land a man should not limit himself, his aims, aspirations and modes of thought and work to the narrow and lower level which was forced upon him by his surroundings in the old world. While he looks back with reverence to the home of his childhood, to the chapel where he received Christian baptism, and around which so many of his kindred are mouldering in consecrated earth, he must not in this free land be content to till only an acre patch or raise a few swine to pay an exacting landlord, when the example of those around him shows him how he can by his thrift, energy and heaven-blessed industry, see his own rich acres nodding with their fields of grain or waving their tassels of Indian corn, his own pasture lands dotted with his good horses and cattle.

God-speed to the association which calls the really worthy and enterprising to the new fields where a healthy ambition points to a noble future.

THE UNIVERSAL PROBLEM.

A strange coincidence, but by no means unaccountable, is the fact that the principal legislative bodies in Europe are now, or lately have been, engaged in the discussion of the all-important question of education. The Italian Parliament lately passed a law which it was fondly hoped would give a death-blow to denominational education on that peninsula and cripple the efforts of the Church in behalf of religious teaching. But after the project had been discussed in all its bearings, and much eloquence and a great deal of bigotry and ignorance expended, it has been found that its provisions are almost completely inoperative. To drive moral instruction from the schools was the object of the framers of the measure, but it seems that in the present state of Italian feeling this is morally and legally impossible.

In France the Chamber has for weeks past been engaged in the discussion of what is called the Ferry bill, a ministerial measure which has for its object the secularization of education in that country, particularly in the higher branches of education, and the prohibition of the Jesuits from taking any part whatever in the training of youth. The bill, almost as introduced, has been approved by the lower house, and is now on its passage through the Senate, where the clause affecting the members of the great teaching order has been stricken out. It is doubtful if a sufficient number of senators can be procured to pass the bill in any form; but if it becomes a law by their votes, it will be the worst blow yet administered at the integrity of the republic. Outside of Paris and one or two other large cities, the French are earnestly and devotedly Catholic; and while their sympathies may now be with a quiet, stable government, no matter how called, any attack on their faith or on their clergy will have a very powerful effect in lessening their confidence in the honesty and patriotism of the party who govern their country.

In Belgium a law something similar to that proposed by the French ministry has just passed by a small majority of six. It proposes to give the State an undue influence in the control of education in all its grades, and to limit, as far as possible, the rights of parents and clergy to control the moral training of children. It is a desperate effort of the so-called Liberals to destroy not only the power of the Church but that of the family in a country so thoroughly Catholic, and will consequently be abortive. The opposition already shown to the scheme from all sources and in every quarter leaves no doubt but that after the next general election it will be repealed.

In Great Britain and Ireland the new Irish University bill, which owes its paternity to Lord Cairns, has passed the Commons, and is at present before the Lords, where in all probability it will be voted down. It seems to satisfy no one except a small clique of experimentalists, who imagine that Ireland ought to be satisfied with the most trifling boon. The hierarchy and popular leaders of the country are opposed to it, and will not accept the bribe, even if it takes the shape of a law. What the people of Ireland want, as far as higher education is concerned, is an Institution with the fullest university powers and privileges, endowed with an adequate portion of their own taxes for its proper support. This eventually must be conceded to them, for nothing short of it will satisfy their demands.

While the Old World is thus discussing educational questions in her parliaments, what are we of the New doing to fix permanently the basis of true education? Are we endeavoring to relegate the State to its proper position in reference to citizens and their offspring? Are we preparing to lay broad and deep in our laws and public polity the grand principle that the child primarily belongs to the parent, who is responsible before God for its moral training, and to the Church within whose fold it has been received by baptism, and to those two agencies, and to those alone, are we to look for the adoption of a proper Christian system of education?

OUR ILLUSTRATIONS.

On a Farm and on the Docks.

In calling attention to our engraving on page 593, we may well say, with *Hamlet*, "Look on this picture and then on that: the counterfeit presentment of two brothers," and in so looking there is none so obtuse as not to recognize the idea which the artist intended to convey. First we have the farmer, the man who, shunning the allurements and dissipations of the large cities, on his arrival on our shores, sought out a home for himself and family in the wide and fertile West, and after a few years of healthful toil has succeeded in accomplishing his grand object. With health and strength unimpaired, he now finds himself the owner not only of house and barns, but of the soil he cultivates, where there

"—— rules no lord
Saving the Lord on High,"

surrounded by his wife, still preserving her youth and good looks, and his children clean, well-clad and innocent, he is partaking of the mid-day meal under the shadow of his own maples, and of food which is mainly the product of his own industry. This is no mere fancy sketch, no Arcadian idyl. The counterpart of it can be seen a thousand times over in any of the Irish settlements in Kansas, Iowa or Minnesota, and even in many instances in some parts of New York, such as the Chenango Valley and Lewis County, when years ago several of our more judicious countrymen sought and found root in the soil.

But, whatever doubt may be entertained of the truthfulness of the first sketch, there can be no second opinion of the faithfulness of the second, wherein is portrayed the condition of so many of our people in New York and other large cities. It is no caricature, but a stern reality. Let any one take a walk along our wharfs during business hours, and he will not go far till he finds himself passing groups of idle, careless-looking, down-hearted men, waiting for the work that comes to them but seldom, and wearing out what ought to be a precious life in listlessness and penury. Where is his wholesome dinner, his neat and comfortable home when he is tired of the bustle of the day, or his anticipated reception by a comely wife and happy progeny? Alas! these blessings are not for him. The filthy tenement is his domicile, the low bar-room his refuge, and Potter's Field, mayhap, his last resting place. Was it for this he left the hills and valleys of green Erin, where, if poverty dwelt sometimes, there was also virtue and morality? Is this the accomplishment of the ambition that compelled him to leave home and friends forever, and seek in a new world better fortune and more personal independence? Surely it is not; but coming here a stranger, without friends and advisers, and perhaps without money, he has clung to the big city so long and has drunken of its foul allurements so deeply, that he has become incapable of helping himself. Some friendly and charitable hand must be extended to aid him, otherwise he perishes. And his little ones, what of them? If not kidnapped and proselytized by the Aid Societies, their future destiny points to the workhouse or the penitentiary. Who can look on this sketch from real life and say that it is overdrawn? In the background appears the gloomy and pestilential tenement-house, with its fringes of damp and patched clothes fluttering in the breeze, in the foreground some of its inhabitants who have come out to beg or pilfer; the wretched mother and her babe watching the husband that is no longer her bread-winner and support, the ragged urchin who, with scarcely enough clothes on to preserve the rules of decency, solicits from his father something that he will never receive. We do not by any means infer that the principal figure in this picture represents all who work along our docks, but he is unfortunately the type of a class, a very large class, who infest those localities, and any measure or movement that could be devised for the purpose of removing him from his present degraded position would meet the approval of all good men. To colonize and make farmers of such men now would, we are aware, be a matter of great difficulty, but if they were once induced to go to the country

(Continued on page 598.)

Figure 5.3. Page with "Catholic Colonization" (top left) and the explanation of "Our Illustrations," including "On a Farm / Along the Docks" (bottom right), *McGee's Illustrated*, August 9, 1879, 595. Reproduced from the original held by the Department of Special Collections of the Hesburgh Libraries of the University of Notre Dame.

that since the strikes, the situation had only deteriorated, and US capitalists had simply found new ways of "subduing and impoverishing labor," showing little care for the poor as long as their own property was not affected. The article then transformed into a plea for making available more tracts of arable land in America's interior. Stressing once more that laborers' funds were limited, *McGee's* asked employers, businesses, and the government to financially support their relocation. Earlier, the magazine had recognized that calls for governmental intervention were un-American: "Under ordinary circumstances, and in our country particularly, the relation between employer and employed is wisely considered a matter of private regulation, of supply and demand, but the present instance is an exceptional one, and we hold that the governments, both Federal and State, constituted by and for the people, are in duty bound to take such steps as will prevent the appalling scenes of suffering and death which periodically afflict so many of the misgoverned people of the old world. Prompt action in this direction will save much affliction and remorse hereafter."[39] The magazine posited Catholic colonization as a solution to contemporary labor issues. As figure 5.4 shows, this link was further strengthened by the inclusion of an article on the colonization scheme on the same page as "Famine, or Farms."

In "Famine, or Farms," the following reference is made to hunger: "We hate mobs and abhor those who would counsel the laborer to resort to violence; but we have some knowledge of human nature and of the state of society in our large cities, and we are satisfied that famishing men will not, cannot, long remain hungry, when bread is to be obtained by force and even criminal violence. . . . Aid them [the people] to leave the cities and to go upon the land."[40] The article's references to hunger and famishing are of a general nature, suggesting that they can be read as diffuse famine references and extending the scope of divergent temporality to a diasporic dimension. Additionally, the juxtapositional combination of the terms "famine" and "farms" in the title ties the hardships experienced by the Irish American urban poor to their peers fighting for peasant proprietorship and the revision of land legislation in Ireland at the time of publication. It is also likely that these references to famine and hunger would have had specific effects on *McGee's* diasporic readership. As Joep Leerssen explains in the context of national character formation, old memories, when not explicitly recalled, "remain subliminally present in the social discourse and can always be reactivated should the occasion arise."[41] Recollections of a recent and highly disruptive event such as the Famine would have been triggered in many Irish American immigrants.

McGee's Illustrated Weekly.

A Paper of sixteen pages, devoted exclusively to the publication of Original and Selected Tales, Stories, and Poetry; Biography and History; with notices of the progress of the Arts, Science and General Literature.

BEAUTIFULLY ILLUSTRATED.

PRICE, PER COPY,	SIX CENTS
MAIL SUBSCRIBERS, for One Year,	$3.00.
MAIL SUBSCRIBERS, for Six Months,	1.50.

☞ In all cases Mail Subscribers will receive their paper *free of postage.* ☜

ADVERTISING RATES.

Transient Advertisements per line for each insertion, 15 cents; if on the sixteenth (last) page, 25 cents per line. Special Notices, 40 cents; and Editorial Notices, 50 cents per line for each insertion. Cards of twelve lines, one year, inside page, $50; of six lines, one year, $40. Cards of twelve lines, one year, sixteenth (last) page, $45; of six lines, one year, $35; payable semi-annually in advance.

☞ Special arrangements made with Colleges, Academies, Schools and Charitable Institutions.   Address,

JAMES A. McGEE, Proprietor.
P. O. Box, 2120.   **7 BARCLAY STREET, N. Y.**

SATURDAY, SEPTEMBER 8, 1877.

TRAVELLING AGENTS.

We have appointed the following gentlemen as resident and travelling agents, to solicit subscriptions and procure subscribers for the States and districts set opposite their names. They will also supply our publications, and take orders for books, pictures, statues, etc., sold by us.

C. E. PARISEAU—Chicago, and places west of that city.

MICHAEL O'SHEA—Territory of Dakota.

A. H. TENCE—St. Louis, Mo., Southern Indiana and Southern Illinois.

W. H. BARRY—States of Kentucky and Tennessee.

JOHN J. GILLIGAN—Western Virginia.

JOHN K. BURKE—Massachusetts.

J. D. HARTNEY (Springfield)—State of Ohio.

C. S. MAGUIRE—Rhode Island.

PATRICK McDONNELL—152 York St., Jersey City.

ANSWERS TO CORRESPONDENTS.

"J. H. C. and D. C.," Albany, N. Y.—We have not mentioned the matter to which you allude, because, while having no faith whatever in identity of the person claiming illegitimacy, we prefer to treat with silence a scandal evidently concocted to injure the Church and its ministers. As a falsehood travels so fast that truth seldom can overtake it, we do not propose to join in a useless chase, but choose rather to await the normal course of events.

An editorial friend writing from the West, amongst other things, says of our journal: "It is really too handsome to put my editorial scissors in; therefore please advise me upon what terms you will send me an extra copy for preservation." We shall be happy to send our polite correspondent an extra copy occasionally, and also one to any editorial brother who desires to preserve it for his own use and for similar aesthetic reasons.

BACK NUMBERS.—Back numbers containing the early chapters of Sister Mary Francis Clare's story can be procured from the AMERICAN NEWS COMPANY, Chambers Street, New York, or on application to this office.

ARCHBISHOP BAYLEY.—The steamship "Russia," which arrived at this port August 21st, had among her passengers the Most Rev. J. R. Bayley, Archbishop of Baltimore, Rt. Rev. Francis McNeirny, of Albany, N. Y., Rev. Messrs. B. J. McManus, McMurray, A. J. McConomy, Conroy and Maguire. The party embarked from Queenstown on the 12th, and though the voyage was unusually propitious, we regret to learn that the venerable Archbishop suffered from ill-health during the entire passage. On his arrival, Dr. Bayley proceeded to Seton Hall College, Orange, N. J., where he intends to remain some weeks before reassuming charge of his diocese, now in care of his coadjutor, Bishop Gibbons.

THE ORDINATION OF REV. JOSEPH HENDRICK took place in Rochester, N. Y., August 6th, in the presence of a large number of clergymen and an immense congregation, among which were many non-Catholics. All the members of the reverend gentleman's family were present, with the exception of two, who were unavoidably hindered from attending: Sister Aloysia, a member of the Community of the Sisters of St. Joseph of the diocese of Buffalo, and Miss Therese C. Hendrick, of New York city.

"PROGRESS OF THE WAR."—We omit this week our usual column of news under this head, for the very satisfactory reason that there has been little or no progress in the war-like movements of the Turks and Russians for the past week. Each combatant seems to be strengthening his positions, bringing up his reserves, and preparing for a grand, and mayhap decisive battle in Bulgaria. Nicsics has not been taken by the Montenegrins, the Russians still hold the Schipka Pass and Hobart Pasha, ex-blockade runner, is cooling his heels in the antechambers of the Sultan. The neutral powers have made no demonstrations of their intentions to interfere, but, like ourselves, are waiting for the latest news. Everything is significant of the lull that precedes the storm.

FAMINE, OR FARMS.

In every respect but one the late strikes were failures. They succeeded in destroying the lives of numerous innocent persons and large amounts of property, but have left the condition of the average workingman worse than it was before. Wages have neither been increased nor guaranteed; great corporations have been only scared into new devices of oppression, not frightened into measures of justice; and the feeling of bitterness and hostility which previously prevailed between employer and employed has been intensified and largely developed.

The worst feature, however, which has become painfully perceptible in our present social and industrial condition, is that while capitalists are inventing new methods of subduing and impoverishing labor, and thus, as they vainly suppose, rendering it helpless, men of good social standing, wealth and influence seem utterly indifferent to the destitution and misery which prevails around them in their myriad forms. They think that as long as their property has not suffered, nor their comforts been interfered with, they ought to have no concern for the thousands of their fellow-creatures around them who are suffering for the common necessaries of life. Let those selfish men not deceive themselves. Let them not lay the flattering unction to their souls, that the present state of things can exist long without some radical change. What that change is to be will depend mainly on the choice of the "upper" or "better classes," as they are called, for in their hands alone rests the power to do good or permit evil to be done. Should they continue to remain callous and blind to the signs of the times, devoting their efforts to hoarding money and their leisure to squandering it on useless pleasures, then, as sure as the sun shines at noon, they will wake up some morning to find themselves in the midst of a proletarian insurrection to which the rising of the Communists of Paris was but the play of children. We are not an alarmist, nor do we write for sensational purposes; we hate mobs and abhor those who would counsel the laborer to resort to violence; but we have some knowledge of human nature and of the state of society in our large cities, and we are satisfied that famishing men will not, cannot long remain hungry, when bread is to be obtained by force and even criminal violence.

In common with many of our cotemporaries, we have endeavored to point out one of the measures which might be adopted to remove honest unemployed men from temptation, and the snares of the demagogue and the disorganizer. Aid them to leave the cities and to go upon the land. There is yet enough soil left unoccupied to enable tens of thousands to obtain from it food, homes and a reasonable return for their labor. Plenty of stalwart, energetic men are willing to turn their hands to the fertile West, but they have not money to pay their way to their destination. Give it them, and it will be money well spent; give them also information where and how to go, and you will have removed one of the worst cankers that is now gnawing at the vitals of society—the vices of idleness and dissipation. But let them remain as they are, without hope, ambition or employment—a seething mass of human discontent—and depend upon it the time is rapidly approaching when they will care little for the barriers of law and religion, and less for the property of those who now revel in ease and luxury.

Nor is it a moment too soon to apply the remedy. The public land of the United States is fast passing into the hands of railroad corporations or monopolists, and comparatively very little is even now left for actual settlement. Major Powell, in charge of the geological survey of the Territories, recently made a statement that there is but comparatively a small area of arable land owned by the United States. This statement has been frequently controverted. Major Powell is preparing for Congress, at the direction of the Committee on Public Lands, an accurate statement of this question, in which he will maintain his assertion. He divides the United States into three regions, with respect to agriculture: The humid, or arable, the sub-arid and the arid. In the arable portion, which includes the country east of a line from the eastern point of Lake Superior to the Gulf, the United States owns no lands not taken up. The belt of country, 350 miles in width, from Canada to the Gulf, adjoining that belt on the west, is the sub-arid division. In this the United States owns a considerable quantity of land, which may be cultivated by irrigation. West of that, in the immense arid belt extending from the Rocky Mountains into Eastern California, only two per cent. of the land can be cultivated, and of this per cent., one per cent. has already been taken up!

Shall we have action now, or shall we wait till all merely human efforts will be of no avail?

THE I. C. B. U.

The annual Convention of the Irish Catholic Benevolent Union will meet in Richmond, Va., on the 19th of September, and already extensive preparations have been made in that city to receive the various delegations, and to make their visit not only useful, but agreeable. That the aims and purposes of this organization may be clearly understood, we quote the words of one of its most intelligent and influential members, who, in reply to a question, writes: "We are laboring to bind all Catholic benevolent associations in our land into one body, in which, while the individual objects of each, whether of piety, charity or temperance, may be pursued untrammelled, the whole shall be bound to render aid and counsel, each to all and all to each, as necessity may require. We antagonize none, accept all, and ask no questions but these: 1. Are you exclusively Catholic? 2. Do you give benefits to your disabled, sick and unfortunate? If so, you are welcome, and for a pittance of less than ten cents a head per annum, your members may join a society in which 40,000 Catholics are enrolled, all pledged to give you substantial aid whenever and wherever you need it—within the limits of their organization."

It is unnecessary for us to attempt to add to the simplicity and force of this statement. The benefits arising from a union of Catholic societies are obvious; for union not only gives strength, but directness of purpose, mutual and judicious support, and that harmony of feeling which should ever exist among people of the same faith. We hope, therefore, that the delegates who have been already appointed will be promptly at their posts, and that those societies which have not yet selected representatives will lose no time in doing so. From the character of the gentlemen in Richmond who have charge of the arrangements, and the former hospitable renown of that beautiful city, a trip to it at this season of the year will undoubtedly prove very pleasant to all parties concerned.

CATHOLIC COLONIZATION.

A fact of importance in connection with the colonization idea, which is just now attracting considerable attention throughout the country, is that a Catholic Colonization Society has been formed in St. Louis to help such worthy Catholic poor of that city as desire to become colonists. The society expects to conclude, soon, the purchase of a hundred thousand acres in Texas, at an average price of a dollar and twelve cents an acre.—*Boston Pilot.*

We are happy to receive this interesting piece of news, and congratulate the people of St. Louis on their common sense and public spirit. Let us have a similar society started in every large city on the eastern seaboard, particularly in New York. We have promised to give *five hundred dollars* as a commencement to such an organization, and we are sure there are many of our fellow-citizens who would give more. Who will begin the good work?

THE IRISH "OBSTRUCTIVES."

The English House of Commons, during its centuries of existence, has been the theatre of many exciting and uproarious scenes; but there are none on record so utterly without precedent, and yet so entirely within parliamentary rules, as that which lately took place during the discussion of the South African Bill. The object of that measure was to give legal sanction to the incorporation into the overgrown British Empire of the Transvaal or Dutch Colonial Republic of Africa, without the consent or even knowledge of the greater portion of its citizens, and thus so closely resembled the destruction of the legislative independence of Ireland at the opening of this century, that a few of the more advanced Irish Nationalists resolved to oppose its passage by every means in their power.

This little body of Parliamentarians, albeit one of their number had taken his seat but a few days previously, never numbering at any time more than eight, and sometimes as few as three, kept the Commons in continuous session for twenty-six hours, caused any number of divisions, and after exhibiting wonderful knowledge of the rules of the house, adroitness in silencing their crowd of opponents, and great physical endurance, finally retired, when, to use the words of Mr. Parnell, "the bill had been forced through almost at the point of the bayonet." The names of this hardy little band, who defied all the sneers, jeers, rhetoric, logic and brow-beating which so eminently distinguish the House of Commons when an Irish question comes up or an Irish member rises to address it, are Messrs. Gray, O'Donnell, Biggar, O'Gorman, Nolan, O'Connor Power, Parnell and Sullivan.

Though prominent Irishmen like Mr. Butt have expressed their dissent from the system of obstructive tactics thus so successfully inaugurated, there is little doubt that the sympathy and suffrage of the great majority of the people are with its projectors. If this be so, and if the Home Rulers continue to put into execution the plan they propose at the next sitting of Parliament, they will do more to bring the British Ministry to terms, and to increase the chances of ultimate success, than could be accomplished by protests and petitions in a whole century. As soon as the Irish people understand that the policy of obstruction is the only one to be pursued within the law, they will be eager to give a cordial support to its originators; and when the obtuse mind of the average Anglo-Saxon becomes at length convinced that there is in Parliament a resolute, unflinching minority, who will have the interests of their country considered with proper care and at opportune hours, "or know the reason why," it will begin to consider whether, after all, it would not be better to let that Spartan band meet in their own capital and legislate for their own people.

The Paris *Univers*, the leading Catholic paper of Europe, very justly says: "It is well known how Ireland has been treated by England since, as well as before, the days of O'Connell. Whenever a Whig or a Tory Ministry is in danger, it remembers that there is such a thing as an Irish minority. A few flattering words from the Government, a few gracious promises to local deputations, a few attractive smiles from the interested Minister, accentuate the position of the Irish members who may happen to have an important notice on the order of the day book. But, the storm past, the redoubtable cape of an adverse vote doubled—Tory or Whig, the Government saved—what becomes of the promises? All wrongs which Ireland suffers are put off till a more opportune time. Is it astonishing that, fatigued and embittered by the tyranny of English majorities, some Irish members have determined to take a sort of revenge in crowding up the order of the day with amendments, questions and speeches and to reply to the brutality of numbers by the persecution of indefinitely speaking? The English Parliament thrown out the bills of interest to Ireland. Well, the Irish put off the solution of English questions with the assistance of never-ending debates. It is not our business to pronounce to-day on the worth of such tactics from an Irish point of view. That is exclusively for the men whom the Irish people have chosen to represent them, and who can afford to despise the sympathy of M. Louvaine. [A Franco-English writer in the *Journal des Débats.*] What right

---

Figure 5.4. Page with "Famine, or Farms" (top middle) and "Catholic Colonization" (top right), *McGee's Illustrated*, September 8, 1877, 242. Reproduced from the original held by the Department of Special Collections of the Hesburgh Libraries of the University of Notre Dame.

The likeliness of these references evoking specific recollections of the Great Irish Famine is not just supported by the continued presence of famine memory in Irish and Irish American creative writing (as evidenced in chap. 1) and the fact that the Great Famine had only happened a few decades earlier and was therefore very much alive—as lived memories or recollections passed down to the second generation—in the magazine's readership. *McGee's* perceived a preoccupation with the Irish past in its readers, evidenced by a strong allegiance to the old land. The magazine showed concern that this allegiance might hamper Irish Americans' success as farmers in the US interior; for this reason, it emphasized that Catholic colonization should not lead to the creation of "little Irelands" (or little Swedens or little Germanies, etc.) but should entail adaptation to the new home country.[42]

For both Dillon O'Brien and John Ireland, the transatlantic and transhistorical links forged in the pages of *McGee's* reflected their own lives. Both were born in Ireland: O'Brien in Kilmore (County Roscommon) in 1817 and Ireland in Burnchurch (County Kilkenny) in 1838. Ireland likely saw disturbing instances of famine suffering in his youth—in Kilkenny, "such scenes by 1848 had become a grisly commonplace," as Marvin R. O'Connell writes in his biographical work.[43] Ireland came to Canada with his family in 1849 and later moved to the US. O'Brien's life was seriously impacted by the Famine. As the son of a prosperous Catholic landowner, he had lived as a country squire on one of the family holdings. The Famine ruined the O'Briens, and because of their efforts to support their Catholic tenants—and probably also because of the Poor Law Extension Acts during the Famine—the family was landless by 1850. Shortly after, O'Brien and his wife and children emigrated to the US. In 1863, the family settled in St. Paul, where O'Brien edited the *Northwestern Chronicle* and later became active for the Catholic Colonization Bureau. In 1866, O'Brien published the novel *The Dalys of Dalystown*, in which he had his upper-class protagonist condemn the role of the British government during the Famine.[44]

The link to recollections of the Great Famine was further strengthened by the fiction included in *McGee's* that year. On March 17, 1877, the magazine included M. M. Armstrong's "The Piper's Gift: A Tale of the Irish Famine." The use of the definite article and lack of modifier in the story's title highlights the Great Famine's central position in Irish American cultural memory at the time. In Armstrong's story, a poor piper receives money from relatives already in the US and uses it to pay for his transatlantic passage and to save a poor widow and her child from starvation.[45]

Between August and October 1877, *McGee's* serialized Margaret Anna Cusack's romantic-didactic novel *From Killarney to New York; or, How Thade Became a Banker.* Cusack (1829–99) was born in Coolock, County Dublin, in 1830 and wrote under several pen names, including "the Nun of Kenmare" and "Sister Mary Francis Clare." Cusack was quite famous in her time. She was a devoted social worker, early feminist, writer, poet, publisher, and, for some time, a Catholic nun. During the smaller famine of 1879–80, she raised funds and developed a network of relief committees, contributing significantly to assisting the starving Irish. She was an extremely effective individual campaigner for aid, apparently driven by altruism and narcissism. James A. McGee published her *Advice to Irish Girls in America* in 1872, and *McGee's* commissioned Cusack to write *From Killarney.* The story proved very popular, as it was republished multiple times.[46] It traces the life of Thade O'Halloran, a young boy who survives the Famine but loses his family and eventually emigrates to America with the help of a wealthy American banker. In the US, he becomes a successful banker and marries the American banker's Catholic daughter. The narrative does not advocate for a continued rural life for the Irish emigrant, but it does support privately assisted emigration. Moreover, the narrative's working subtitle was "How Thade Became a Yankee," showcasing an initial focus on national identity rather than profession in line with the American orientation advocated through *McGee's* at large.[47]

The first part of *From Killarney to New York* is set during the Famine, and it describes the Famine as "the slayer of thousands." The local priest's experiences with famine are described with stock imagery:

> Heartrending scenes had come before him. He had found a poor mother on the roadside, almost unconscious, with a dead babe in her arms and a dead child clinging to her skirts. She was just so far on her road to the poor-house when she fell insensible, and but for the timely arrival of the priest she had died as she lay.
>
> He had been in a house where comfort and plenty once reigned, and there he had found the living and the dead lying together on the same bed of straw and covered with a piece of old baize that had once been a table-cover.[48]

When the Famine hits, Thade's mother dies. Tim, Thade's father, refuses to let himself or his son be converted to Protestantism in exchange for sustenance, catches famine fever, and dies. Soon after, Thade's elderly grandmother dies of heartache. The orphaned Thade is exposed to repeated conversion attempts by Protestant proselytizers but cannot be made to betray his religion.

In the September 8 issue, a poetic epigraph prefaces chapter 8 of Cusack's narrative; this epigraph displays the typical image of female and child victims, including the lines

> Famine slaughtered were plenty reigned,
> Starved mothers died ere their babes were born.[49]

The chapter ends by detailing the emigration to the US of trusted Irish servant Mick O'Grady, who earlier had saved Thade from proselytizers.[50] In Cusack's narrative, the Famine is cast as an era from which to learn and functions as a test of faith that spans generations: because Tim died of starvation rather than letting himself and his family be converted, in America his son Thade finds the land of promise. By the late 1870s, tropes such as female and child victims, Souperism, selfless clergymen, and the anthropomorphosis of famine had become part of a representative repertoire connected to the Great Famine, further solidifying the link between Cusack's narrative, *McGee's* as its outlet, and famine memory.

Chapter 8 of Cusack's novel featured in the same issue as "Famine, or Farms." In the pages of *McGee's*, *From Killarney* provides two lessons. It shows that emigration, Catholic virtue, and an American mentality of self-sufficiency can provide a joint solution to rural hardships in Ireland. Additionally, as a cotext to "Famine, or Farms," it explicates the link between current labor issues, the hardships of the urban poor in America, and the famine suffering of the Irish in Ireland.

In 1879, *McGee's* drew an additional parallel between the current famine, the Great Famine, and future prospects in the US, writing that "the great flood of emigration to the United States which began in 1847 is, to all appearances, to be renewed." This renewal was to come "with a difference": "Great things have been done by the emigrants of 1847–'48. . . . Greater yet may be done by the emigrants of 1879–'80."[51] Like Cusack, *McGee's* incorporated famine memory in an upward diasporic trajectory, the idealized success story of the Irish American diaspora. As the terrible hardships of the Famine had caused the felicitous entrance and integration of many hardworking Catholic Irish laborers in the US, current hardships in Ireland were bound to do the same.

As such, in *McGee's*, prose fiction, poetry, nonfiction, and illustrations together created a cotextual effect. Crucial to this combination was the inclusion of famine memory, which established a truly diasporic support for the betterment of the condition of the Irish American laboring poor and for the Catholic colonization effort specifically.

THE TRANSATLANTIC DEBATE: CATHOLIC COLONIZATION ASSOCIATION VERSUS LAND LEAGUE

In 1880, the *Irish-American* included a work of fiction portraying American country life as a solution to Irish starvation. In the anonymously written "Thade M'Sweeney; or, A Tenant Farmer's Trials: A Story of the Great Famine," the titular character loses all he has during the Famine, including his wife, who is "stricken down with malignant fever." After these hardships, Thade M'Sweeney sails for the US, where he does not settle in one of the cities but starts over on a small farm and soon is "well and hearty." Writing home, Thade displays modest pride in his new life as a farmer and landowner in America, a position unobtainable for him in Ireland: "I own a farm—it isn't big, but it's mine."[52]

In the current section, the discussion of Catholic colonization moves from a cotextual contextualization to a diasporic and even transnational one. In Ireland, some outlets equally considered emigration a potential solution to Irish issues. The *Irish Times* did not support the emigration of the young by themselves but did see reason in the emigration of full families.[53] In his letter to the editor of the Dublin *Freeman's Journal*, F. R. Cruise, MD of Trinity College, underscored the message of "Famine, or Farms." Doing his "duty in these disastrous times," Cruise wrote: "Deeply as we grieve to see the country drained of the wealth of its bone and sinew, we cannot help recognising the sad fact that 'Necessity has no law,' and the sadder reality that multitudes of our people must emigrate or starve. . . . When the future prospect includes an occasional run of bad harvests and their results, with famine and pestilence to follow, accompanied by a cool recommendation to the world's charity as a remedy, it ceases to be a marvel that man become desperate and emigration popular, for 'Hope deferred sickens the heart.'" Besides reiterating the choice between starving and leaving Ireland, Cruise noted a parallel between famine and emigration in 1880 and the 1840s. He by no means intended to endorse wholesale emigration, for that would lead to a "storm [bursting] over his head." Pragmatically, he argued "that if the people must emigrate, at least let them do so wisely. Let them so lay their plans as not to become waifs on the face of the country to which they are driven, but with such wisdom and method that humanity may be reverenced, and their dearest feelings—natural, national, and above all religious—shall be well cared for." The latter, he felt, could best be done in the Catholic colonies of the West, not "the great cities of the Eastern coast." For those intent on the eastern cities, it was "far better for them to die of starvation in the old country than to stay in New York or other large cities."[54]

As Cruise argued, Catholic colonization should be considered a diasporic movement, as Catholic settlements provided a future prospect for the Irish not only in America but also in Ireland. In Cruise's rhetoric, the threat of starvation became the push factor for those Irish emigrating to the US and settling in the colonies of the West. As such, Cruise considered the recurring threat of Irish hunger key to the establishment of rural communities in the US.

The diasporic potential of Catholic colonization was acknowledged by the Colonization Bureau as well, and to better guide the Irish not yet in the US, the bureau disseminated advertisements through Irish newspapers and set up a branch in Liverpool led by Father James Nugent, editor of the *Catholic Times*. Nugent printed the Minnesota pamphlet many times and distributed it in England, Galway, and Belgium, extending the initiative's reach even beyond the diasporic and into the transnational dimension. Like Cruise, Nugent, O'Brien, and John Ireland emphatically stated that they did not mean to encourage emigration, but rather that they intended to find suitable homes for those who had already left Ireland or had made up their minds to leave. These explicit statements regarding intent were necessary, as Catholic colonization, and support for emigration more broadly, received substantial backlash. Land League leaders and sympathizers often opposed the scheme, which to them it constituted "a form of treason against the homeland" and "only alleviated surface symptoms. By depleting Ireland's manpower, they argued, Catholic colonization rendered the country less capable of solving her economic problems."[55]

Clearly, opinions on emigration varied greatly; author Charlotte Grace O'Brien's views illustrate this divide well. Involved in migrant aid on both sides of the Atlantic, she wrote in 1883 that she was "utterly opposed to the English policy of state-aided emigration. I believe it to be fatal and misleading, useless in itself, and only to turn the attention from the more potent remedies of Land reform, industrial revival, and before and above all, self-government. But I cannot close my eyes to the fact that a large part of Ireland is in deep distress; that starvation is, in parts, imminent; that the steamship companies have lowered their fares, and that in America there is fair prosperity."[56]

In its prose fiction and poetry, *Young Ireland* magazine rejected emigration and the Minnesota scheme specifically while simultaneously supporting the Land League. In the aforementioned "His Honour's Word; or, A Victim of 'Painful Duty': A Tale of the Times" (1881), author M. Mackey used famine memory to draw a parallel between tenant suffering during the late 1840s and early 1880s. The story suggests that, unless tenants join the Land League, a similar lot will continue to befall them. All characters in the narrative join the league save James Burke, who mistakenly trusts his landlord's promise not to evict him and his family. As the Burkes' hardships increase, they can count on their community and on the Land League, for the league, although Burke refuses to join, "procure[s] seed for him to sow his farm."[57] Thus, the league represents community spirit and unconditional support.

Although the protagonist likens hardships and initiatives to support the Irish poor during the early 1880s to their Great Famine counterparts, the narrative suggests that this time, it is not simple repetition that will lead to naught. Matters do not end well for the Burkes. The landlord—with the ridiculous telltale name Lord "Fitzturfclamp"—evicts the family and offers them assisted emigration to Minnesota. Two of Burke's children die en route. In Minnesota, focalization shifts to Burke's remaining son, innocent victim of landlord malpractice and his father's outdated notions. We read of his inner turmoil: "The boy has experienced, in his short life, cold, sorrow, hunger: but never did he feel so cold, so sorrowful, so desolate as now that he stands looking at the miles and miles of snow-encumbered plain, the monotony of which is unbroken by aught living. . . . 'I'll earn money— I'll go home—I can't stand it,' he moaned." The narrative ends with Burke on his deathbed elated at the successes of the Land League. Contrary to Fitzturfclamp's intention to evict all tenants and ship them off to Minnesota, the league has made sure that all "tenantry evicted last May . . . have been readmitted to their holdings on the most favourable conditions. Arrears have been forgiven, law costs blotted out—the existing rents reduced by one-third."[58]

Thus, in Mackey's story, the Minnesota scheme is considered an option for landlords in Ireland to rid themselves of poor tenants. In similar vein, in 1882, the *Wexford People* vehemently rejected Catholic colonization, stating that "this rate of banishment is cheaper to the English Government than exciting a rebellion and slaughtering the people, or arranging for a famine and starving them." It considered Catholic colonization "the most dangerous and most destructive of all the English methods of ruining Ireland." What was needed to truly better the situation in rural Ireland, argued the newspaper, was a system of small proprietary farms and the diversification of industries.[59] Catholic colonization was considered another English tool to ruin Ireland; in the rhetoric of the *Wexford People*, it was a method on a par with, or indeed perhaps even superseding, famine as a weapon. As such, the opinion represented by the *Wexford People* can be read as the extreme end of a broader hardening of Irish public opinion on emigration. Due to the Famine and frustration with the government's failure to fully grant land reforms during the 1870s and early 1880s, emigration was considered part of a supposedly willful British policy to depopulate Ireland.[60]

Texts such as "Famine, or Farms" and *From Killarney to New York* also explored the link between starvation and emigration but aimed to subvert the discourse by presenting emigration not as forced or part of intentional English policy but as a safety valve and positive contribution to Ireland's spiritual empire, more in line with prefamine considerations of emigration.[61] These examples show that within a short span of time, the use of famine memory to give shape and meaning to a phenomenon—in this case, migration—could vary significantly.

Because of the development of the railroad system, colonies in the US interior would have been established even without the Catholic colonization scheme; nevertheless, interventions in the settlement of the US interior by men such as Ireland and O'Brien did impact the (religious) character of settlement. Although it is hard to give exact numbers, Shannon estimates that between 1875 and 1885, some four thousand Catholic families settled in the newly established Minnesota colonies. The colonies proved not to be the intended havens for poor laborers, as many people lacked the required funds to make the move and establish themselves on colony lands. Also, the goals of those organizing the scheme and of the settlers varied; the latter were more inclined to work as day laborers than farm their own lands. In the end, many gave up their farms to work for the railroads. Additionally, more affluent Irish Americans were never sufficiently convinced of the colonization scheme to back it financially, and their peers of lesser means were never persuaded into believing that "it was a more deserving charity than the resettlement of cottiers in Ireland."[62]

For *McGee's*, the decision between supporting Catholic colonization or the Land League stood in line with its juxtaposed rhetoric concerning national allegiance, in which Irish Americans should prioritize American issues but were failing to do so. In this argument, lack of financial backing for Catholic colonization from fellow "countrymen and co-religionists" was caused by an archaic allegiance to the old land. The magazine observed caustically that "we have, of course, . . . patriots at every turn," but they "are so engaged with Irish affairs three thousand miles away, that they have no time to waste on such trifles."[63] Lack of financial support from the Irish American community was one of the main reasons Catholic colonization never became the success Ireland and O'Brien had originally envisioned. After O'Brien's death in 1882, and due to Bishop Ireland's increasingly pressing clerical obligations, the association lost steam and ceased to exist in 1886.[64]

In the pages of *McGee's*, famine memory was used to advance prospects and living conditions for the Irish urban poor in America. The use of famine memory for specifically American political ends would be repeated later; Christopher Cusack and I have shown that famine recollections were used to voice pro-US democratic rhetoric in Irish American fiction of the 1890s.[65] *McGee's* use of famine recollections displays what Emilie Pine calls "anti-nostalgia." Typically, nostalgia provides escapism, a "welcome break from the demands of the present." Conversely, in antinostalgic use of the past, the future "becomes the idealised space."[66] While Pine focuses on Irish culture of the twenty-first century, her concept can be applied to the use of famine memory in the Catholic colonization debate in the pages of periodicals during the late nineteenth century as well. In *McGee's*, famine memory inspires antinostalgia. The magazine's treatment of the US labor question and its concomitant vision for the Irish in America direct its readers toward the possibilities of the (near) Irish American future rather than having them reluctantly gaze back at their lives in Ireland, even showing that such an orientation would be un-American. The future-oriented use of famine memory in the magazine thus combines the national and diasporic scales of memory formation, emphasizing the latter, as famine memory is used to incite societal change across the Atlantic. In the process, it becomes part of a reorientation: from what famine memory means for the American Irish to how that fund of memory can inform the (future) lives of the Irish *as Americans*.

This chapter's exploration of the debate on Catholic colonization as played out in periodicals is illustrative of two types of involvement. It shows how closely intertwined US and Irish labor and land initiatives were beyond the well-documented transatlantic involvement with the Land League and the Knights of Labor. Moreover, on the level of the periodical medium, the analysis carried out in this chapter makes clear that when exploring the diasporic sociopolitical debate on Irish and Irish American access to land, it is crucial to equally consider nonfiction and creative works and to include literary magazines as potentially influential outlets in such debates.

1. "Ireland in 1877," January 26, 146.

2. Parfitt, *Knights across the Atlantic*, 1, 27, 28. Examples of engagement with labor issues in newspapers can be found in the Boston *Pilot*, which published the articles "Miners of Pennsylvania" (March 21, 1863, 4), "Profit and Loss of Strikes" (December 26, 1863, 4), "Strikes—Difficulty among the Coal Miners" (September 23, 1865, 4), "Ten Hour Movement" (November 17, 1866, 1), and "Labor Movement" (November 17, 1867, 1). The *American Celt* published "Labour Question" (October 22, 1870, 145). Demands for improvement included an eight-hour workday, more stringent factory inspection, regulation of prison labor, prohibition of child labor under fourteen years of age, creation of a labor bureau, and payment of wages in cash. See Commons, *History of Labour*, 249–51. As Parfitt shows, the Knights evolved into a global movement with branches in Britain and Ireland (Parfitt, *Knights across the Atlantic*, 16).

3. O'Donnell, "Though Not an Irishman," 416–17. Janis, *Greater Ireland*, 60.

4. Janis, *Greater Ireland*, 130, 131; the quote by George can be found on 130.

5. O'Donnell, "Though Not an Irishman;" the quote is taken from Janis, *Greater Ireland*, 115.

6. As this chapter shows, the Catholic Colonization Association advocated its cause in Ireland and Europe as well. As previous chapters have shown, the Land League also canvassed for support in the US, and several leagues were established across the Atlantic. Support was sought not only through initiatives such as Parnell's fundraising tours but also through the actions of his sister, Fanny Parnell, and the American Ladies' Land League (McCarthy, *Respectability & Reform*, 3).

7. Janis, *Greater Ireland*, 3.

8. "What One Man Has Done for Catholic Literature" (reprinted from *Irish Canadian*), *McGee's Illustrated*, December 2, 1876, 27.

9. "Subscribe for McGee's," February 15, 1879, 208. Readers could subscribe by mail for $1.50 per six months or $3 per year. See, for example, "McGee's Illustrated Weekly," January 13, 1877, 114. By contrast, the highly popular illustrated magazine *Harper's Weekly* had a cover price of ten cents per issue in 1876 (see, for example, the cover of November 26, 1876).

10. Egan, *Recollections of a Happy Life*, 110. For example, a smoking tobacco company from Durham (NC), the University of Notre Dame (South Bend, IN), and Seton Hall College (South Orange, NJ) purchased ad space in the magazine; see "Subscribe for McGee's," February 15, 1879, 207, 208. Roman Catholic colleges did so repeatedly. The reach of *McGee's* in North America is demonstrated in the editorial of October 12, 1878: "Our subscribers in Toronto, Brantford, Stratford, Guelph, Oshawa, Paris, Dundas, Coburg, Brocton, in the Province of Ontario, will please pay no more money to Thos. J. Keaveny, as he is no longer our Agent. They will please remit the amount of their subscriptions direct to this office" (322).

11. Fanning, *Irish Voice*, 198–99. Loeber and Loeber, with Mullin Burnham, *Guide to Irish Fiction*, 432.

12. Egan, *Recollections of a Happy Life*, 109–10.

13. "Letter of Introduction," November 11, 1876, 2.

14. Peter D. O'Neill explains that this group of white-collar bourgeois Irish Americans "preferred to leave Ireland behind and much of their Irish heritage" in favor of an orientation toward the US. He mentions Egan as a fiction writer who captured the "lace-curtain rebuff of the old country" like no other (O'Neill, *Famine Irish*, 134–35).

15. "With Whom Shall We Sympathize?," July 28, 1877, 146.

16. "Sound Sense on Irish Politics," August 4, 1877, 166.

17. Not to be confused with the publisher of the magazine, James A. McGee. McGee, "Immigrants," November 25, 1876, 10.

18. "Tide of Emigration," 754.

19. Kenny, *Making Sense of the Molly Maguires*, 6, 12. By the Civil War, the term "Molly Maguires" had "become ubiquitous for labor activism, violence, and social disorder" (ibid., 102).

20. "An English Christmas Story," December 29, 90–91.

21. "Agitate! Agitate!," December 22, 1877, 67. See also "Who Will Help the Poor?," December 23, 1876, 66, and "Remember the Poor," December 30, 1876, 82. All articles were included around Christmas time.

22. These words were written in response to a sent-in letter titled "Candid Answer" (December 22, 1877, 67).

23. Roddy, *Population, Providence and Empire*, 38–39, 47. Moran, "In Search of the Promised Land," 137. Shannon, *Catholic Colonization*, 256. Janis, *Greater Ireland*, 85–86, 88.

24. Ireland, *Catholic Colonization*, 4. The pamphlet originally appeared in 1877.

25. Moran, "In Search of the Promised Land," 138. Shannon, *Catholic Colonization*, 264. John Ireland became bishop in 1884 and archbishop of St. Paul in 1888.

26. Colin Barr uses the term "Greater Ireland" for this international spiritual Irish Empire ("Devotional Revolution in Greater Ireland" and *Ireland's Empire*); see also Cusack, "Memory, History, and Identity," 228. Barr, "Devotional Revolution," 96.

27. Roddy, *Population, Providence and Empire*, 213, 183, 187; Roddy quotes Catherine Aherne, 205.

28. Shannon, *Catholic Colonization*, 185, 274. Ireland's pamphlet included detailed calculations of the funds needed to establish oneself on a Minnesota farm: it stipulated a little over $400 as starting capital (Shannon, *Catholic Colonization*, 35). John Sweetnam likewise calculated that between $400 and $500 was needed (ibid., 106). In various articles, the Catholic Colonization Bureau stressed this point as well, using it as a reason to solicit funding from readers.

29. Shannon, *Catholic Colonization*, 285; Janis, *Greater Ireland*, 88. Several Irish American leaders rejected assisted emigration, seeing the potential influx of the poor as having a detrimental effect on their community's respectability. They also feared immigrants would take scarce jobs and cause a lowering of wages (Janis, *Greater Ireland*, 88).

30. Rodechko, *Patrick Ford*, 70. Chapter 7 of *Periodical Famines* includes more information on Ford and his newspaper.

31. See, for example, "Following Brief Item . . . ," in which the *Celtic Monthly* congratulates Bishop Ireland and his associates for "doing work that will live in America and Irish history long after them. God speed their work!" (July 1879, 90). On page 91, Thomas O'Neil Russell's letter of support was included ("Mr. T. O'Neill Russell . . ."). In October 1880, the magazine praised both Catholic colonization and O'Brien ("Editorial Department," 378) and endorsed the establishment of facilities in Ireland to inform the Irish back home about the colonies (McClure, "Irish of Ulster," 439–40). "Rays of Hope," *McGee's Illustrated*, September 22, 1877, 274. As Rodechko explains, this positive sentiment was shared by several Irish leaders in the US (*Patrick Ford*, 69); see also Shannon, *Catholic Colonization*, 108–109.

32. "Emigration and Colonization," May 19, 1877, 403.

33. O'Brien, "To the Editors of the Irish-American Press," March 23, 295.

34. Ireland, *Catholic Colonization*, 12, 13.

35. Sweeny, "Letter of Rt. Rev. Dr. Sweeny," February 9, 10. The idea that American cities were hotbeds of sin and temptation was widespread in postfamine Irish American discourse. In literature, an example can be found in influential author Mary Ann Sadlier's *Bessy Conway*, which describes these places as "these great Babylons of the West" (iii).

36. "Our Illustrations," August 9, 595, 598.

37. "Famine, or Farms," September 8, 242. Parfitt, *Knights across the Atlantic*, 1.

38. Commons, *History of Labour*, 240.

39. "Who Will Help the Poor?," December 23, 1876, 66.

40. "Famine, or Farms," 242.

41. Leerssen, "Rhetoric of National Character," 278.

42. "Catholic Colonization," August 9, 1879, 595.

43. O'Connell, *John Ireland*, 12.

44. The Poor Law Extension Acts meant that the cost of the poor law system fell on landowners. Loeber and Loeber, with Mullin Burnham, *Guide to Irish Fiction*, 990. For the protagonist's condemnation of British governmental action, see O'Brien, *Dalys of Dalystown*, 499. Marguérite Corporaal discusses the novel's criticism in more detail in "Political Economy?" (83).

45. Armstrong, "Piper's Gift," 262–63. This story was reprinted in the *Irish-American* on April 19, 1902, under the title "A Friend in Need; or, The Piper's Gift: A Tale of the Irish Famine."

46. Geary, *Land War*, 68, 97, 130–31; Maume, "Cusack, Margaret Anna"; "Sister Mary Francis Clare," *McGee's Illustrated*, August 11, 1877, 180. Loeber and Loeber, with Mullin Burnham, *Guide to Irish Fiction*, 342. The preface to the 1878 novel edition indicates the commission by *McGee's Illustrated*. *Guide to Irish Fiction* lists the following publishers for the narrative, also published as *Tim O'Halloran's Choice; or, From Killarney to New York*: Burns, London; M. H. Gill, Dublin; D. O'Loughlin, New York and Boston; G. Robertson, Melbourne: Fotheringham, Paris (ibid., 343). As stated in chapter 1, the novel was also reprinted in the London *Universe* in 1877.

47. "Our New Story," July 7, 1877, 98. For a detailed analysis of Cusack's novel and how it questions the concept of the Famine as the Irish American origin myth, see my article "Diasporic Identifications."

48. Cusack, *From Killarney*, August 11, 1877, 182.

49. P. O'C. Mac. L. quoted in ibid., September 8, 1877, 246.

50. The chapter ends in the next installment (September 15, 1877, 262).

51. "Tide of Emigration," October 18, 754.

52. "Thade M'Sweeney," April 10, 3.

53. Moran, "In Search of the Promised Land," 140–41.

54. Cruise, "Emigrant Question," July 3, 1880, 3.

55. Shannon, *Catholic Colonization*, 64. The Catholic colonies were also inhabited by Catholics from other European countries. Cruise refers to hostile reactions to Nugent ("Emigrant Question," 3). The quotes are taken from Shannon, *Catholic Colonization*, 71.

56. Letter dated January 9, 1883; included in Gwynn, "Introductory Memoir," 79.

57. Mackey, "His Honour's Word," September 17, 593.

58. Ibid., 595, 596.

59. "Banished for £5 a Head," November 29, 3.

60. Roddy, *Population, Providence and Empire*, 43, 50.

61. Roddy explores the shift from prefamine support for emigration to postfamine rejection by Irishmen religious in the first chapter of *Population, Providence and Empire*.

62. Shannon, *Catholic Colonization*, 262, 261, and 252–54. The numbers indicated by Shannon constitute not just Irish Catholics but also members from other (immigrant) communities; the quote is taken from 254. Janis explains that the funds raised for Catholic colonization "paled in comparison with" the money collected on behalf of the Land League (*Greater Ireland*, 89).

63. "Case in Point," October 6, 1877, 306.

64. On pages 252–54 of *Catholic Colonization*, Shannon gives a clear summary of the reasons for the end of the Catholic Colonization Association.

65. Cusack and Janssen, "Famine, Home, and Transatlantic Politics."

66. Pine, *Politics of Irish Memory*, 8.

6

HUMILIATING THE NATION

Imperial Oppression, Gender, and Hunger in Maud Gonne's
Periodical Writings on Ireland and South Africa, 1898–1904

IN 1898, NATIONALIST AND ACTIVIST Maud Gonne (1866, Tongham, Surrey–1953, Clonskeagh, Dublin) visited districts affected by agrarian distress in the West of Ireland to report on famine conditions and help the suffering. To her surprise, she found that some locals were afraid of her. A local curate told her the reason: supposedly, a "woman dressed in green" would come during a time of famine to "preach the revolt." After this, "men would rise and there would be fighting and many killed but . . . the English would in the end be driven out." Gonne, indeed dressed in green, thus became identified as the woman of the prophecy. This was not the first time she had been given such a label; when traveling around Donegal to help evicted tenants in 1888, Gonne had been called "the woman of the Sidhe." The combination of gender and myth would continue to feature in Gonne's nationalist and anti-imperialist politics.[1]

In speeches and writings for various Irish newspapers in Ireland, the US, and France, Gonne frequently stood up for the Irish poor. She also wrote and spoke about other regions and peoples impacted by British imperialism and, in doing so, made repeated references to famines in India and the Second Boer War in South Africa (1899–1902). As a staunch opponent of Britain's declaration of war on the Transvaal and its treatment of the Boers during the war, Gonne, together with independent nationalist Arthur Griffith (1871–1922), founded the Transvaal Committee in 1899. This committee consisted of nationalists and was established to promote

163

the military exploits of the Irish Transvaal Brigade against the British and to provide and stimulate support for the Boers.[2]

When awoken in the middle of the night by a Dublin police inspector to be told that a Transvaal Committee pro-Boer meeting planned for the next day had been banned, Gonne was characteristically unfazed, asking, "And you really think it is worth while to disturb me at this hour for that?" In the morning, Gonne and fellow committee members James Connolly and John O'Leary went to the location of the meeting, Beresford Place. Carrying a Transvaal flag, they drove right through the police cordon, quickly pledged their full assistance to the Boers, and became central figures in the public protest against the presentation of an honorary degree to Joseph Chamberlain, the British colonial secretary.[3]

As a tireless nationalist force, Gonne was an active participant in European and transatlantic press networks. She started her own paper—*L'Irlande Libre*—in Paris, wrote for the Dublin *Freeman's Journal*, and was closely involved with the Dublin *United Irishman: A National Weekly Review* as a journalist and financial contributor; she also held an important role in overseeing the latter paper's content. Patrick Ford and his sister Ellen regularly collaborated with Gonne, and as this chapter shows, contributions by Gonne repeatedly ended up in the pages of Ford's New York–based *Irish World and American Industrial Liberator*.[4]

While also including several newspapers from Ireland and the US, this chapter focuses on Gonne's outlet the *United Irishman*, the paper cofounded by Griffith in 1899. Griffith saw himself as carrying on the legacy of the Young Ireland movement of the 1840s and established the *United Irishman* as a successor to John Mitchel's militant 1848 publication of the same title. The paper soon grew from a half-penny weekly to an eight-page penny weekly with international distribution in Belfast, London, Paris, New York, Brooklyn, and Philadelphia. This rapid expansion, as Trish Ferguson explains, can be attributed to Gonne's networking skills.[5] The *United Irishman* was of great value for Gonne; during the first ten months of the paper's existence, her pieces were included almost every other week. It also republished many of her articles from *L'Irlande Libre* and provided coverage of the activities of the Inghinidhe na hÉireann (Daughters of Ireland), the nationalist women's movement founded by Gonne in 1900.[6]

In exposing injustices caused by imperial aggressor Britain, Gonne argued that Irish famines were examples of England's willful destructive policies. This chapter explores the connections she drew between colonial oppression in South Africa, Ireland, and elsewhere around the Second Boer

War. When one compares the discursive use of Irish famines to the representation of hardships experienced by the Boers in Gonne's writings for the *United Irishman*, the *Irish-American*, and other periodicals, a gendered dimension arises. In nationalist discourse, the nation is often depicted as a muse to fight for or a mother to cherish and protect; both figures can be found in different interpretations of Ireland's Cathleen Ni Houlihan figure. Hence, the subjugation of the nation can be rendered symbolically as subjugation of the native female by the male colonizing power. After being cast as a woman of prophecy in Donegal and Mayo, Gonne played the leading role of Cathleen Ni Houlihan in W. B. Yeats's and Lady Gregory's eponymous one-act play of 1902. She also harnessed the symbolic potency of the female embodiment of the nation in her writings.[7] Equally, pieces in the *United Irishman* dealing with the humiliation of women through hunger and poverty in both Ireland and South Africa received a dimension of national allegory.

Typical British imperial discourse on the family sphere and gender roles emphasized ideals of femininity, motherhood, and domesticity for women, which, it was argued, were not sufficiently met by (to be) colonized peoples.[8] Around the turn of the twentieth century, women's—and not least Irishwomen's—societal and political positions were very much limited but hotly contested and undergoing significant change. During this transformative period, Gonne's rhetoric on the effects of imperialism on gender patterns subverted British imperial and Irish traditionalist discourses on male and female roles, but in discrepant ways. British imperialist intervention, argued Gonne in the *United Irishman*, did not correct atavistic imbalances between men and women; rather, it disturbed otherwise adequately functioning gender patterns. Her argument rested on an appreciation for traditional gender roles in Boer and Irish society, which resulted in a problematic tension between her progressive ideas on female participation in politics, society, and war on the one hand and her retention of a traditionalist, domestic position for women on the other.

Gonne, her nationalism, and her anti-imperialism have been the subject of much scholarship. This chapter seeks to innovatively showcase Gonne's transnational and transhistorical combination of gender and recollections of hunger in anti-imperialist and nationalist periodical writings. In so doing, it explores unresolved gendered tensions in Gonne's rhetoric by considering how she represented the effects of imposed hunger on the Irish and Boer peoples—and especially on their women. First, Gonne's reports on distress in the West of Ireland in 1898 are discussed. Then, by way of a cotextual analysis of the famous aforementioned article "The Famine Queen" (1900), the chapter investigates how Gonne and the *United Irishman* combined representations of Irish and Boer hunger and deprivation during 1899–1902. Finally, it demonstrates how Gonne's argument on the subjugation of colonized women through starvation found its way into her literary writing as well.

In 1898, Gonne visited districts affected by agrarian distress in the West of Ireland. She wrote about her experiences in Mayo in 1898 for various newspapers and took it on herself to request aid from the Irish in America, thereby functioning as "the voice of these helpless victims of England's policy, [speaking] for them before the world."[9] Much of her journalism can be associated with the "new journalism" of the time, "concerned with exposing social ills and injustices." Gonne's reports tap into a familiar popular register of famine imagery to underscore the disquieting condition of the people. Using this register, coupled with some of her rhetorical effects, earned her a comparison with Lady Wilde's writings for the *Nation* during the Great Famine, as W. B. Yeats called her "the New Speranza."[10] In Gonne's journalism, sufferers are described as "living skeleton[s]" and "crowds of famishing creatures, whose ragged garments fluttering in the wild Atlantic wind scarcely hid their gaunt limbs, and whose blue lips implored help, [who] seem already . . . like some terrible nightmare vision." Reiterating an argument made repeatedly since the Famine, her letters regularly mention how cattle and pastures had replaced people and their plots of land; Gonne argued that the Irish must starve because the English market had a greater need for cattle than for them.[11]

The task of writing about famine conditions in 1898 "seemed too big for me," Gonne stated in her 1938 autobiography, *A Servant of the Queen.*[12] She utilized a narrative device commonly associated with representations of the Great Famine: the unrepresentability of the event. "Words fail to describe this struggle for a foothold of life on the brink of death of almost the whole population of the western seaboard," wrote Gonne; the "suffering of the people is simply beyond description."[13] Gonne transhistorically extended discourse highlighting the gravity of the Great Famine on the basis of its unrepresentability to this later period of local distress. She combined the national scale (the Great Famine) with the regional scale (the 1898 distress in the West of Ireland), demonstrating that although the scope and impact of both events differed significantly, connotations of the former could premediate descriptions of the impact on the human consciousness of the latter, as the distress of 1898 still exceeded her representational capabilities.[14] As such, we can read Gonne's descriptions of famine in 1898 as indicative of a temporality of repetition. Moreover, Gonne's writing crucially demonstrates that around the turn of the twentieth century, unrepresentability had become a discursive device for Irish famines more generally, a temporally diffuse shorthand for indicating the severity of a period of agrarian distress and hunger.

Female, child, and elderly victims receive much attention in Gonne's reports.[15] When visiting Erris (County Mayo), she was struck by the impact of the government relief works on Irish families. In the Dublin *Freeman's Journal* of March 9, 1898, she wrote:

> What shocked me most on the relief works was that women should be engaged on them. There they were; old, bent women of sixty, young, slight girls of sixteen working away with pickaxes and spades under the pouring rain, or worse, carrying great stones or sods of turf on their backs. I questioned several of them. One said her father was too old and feeble, and she had come in his place; another that her husband was dead and that the children must be fed; a third, a woman of over sixty, Mary Conway, said she was the youngest of three sisters—they would starve but for her work. One delicate-looking girl of about sixteen, who was carrying sods, told me her home was six miles away, which meant she had to walk 12 miles a day—72 miles a week—and do work which would be hard for a man during eight hours, to help her mother and younger sisters, and all she gets to eat is a piece of Indian corn bread twice a day.[16]

Only the head of the household could work on the relief works, which, as the letter shows, often meant backbreaking labor and long journeys on foot. If the male head of the household could not fulfill his duty, a female would work instead.[17] Gonne felt this order of things, "this shameful cruelty," went against women's natural purpose and intended place in the family. Stressing feminine fragility, she argued that "women are physically unfitted for such work; nature intended them to be mothers, and exertion of this kind is calculated to do them serious and permanent injury." The article was partially republished in the New York *Irish World and American Industrial Liberator* (see fig. 6.1) as an appeal to Irish American women to help their sisters back home; to the republished article, Gonne added "a sadder sight I never witnessed."[18]

In the final years of the nineteenth century, Gonne resolutely repudiated Irishmen who fought in the British army. In her view, Irishmen in the British army were maintaining existing imperial hierarchies, oppressive

Figure 6.1. Page 1 of *Irish World*, April 2, 1898, which includes Gonne's letter. The accompanying illustration was taken and adapted from the Dublin *Freeman's Journal*. This reproduction was derived from the collections of the Boston Public Library.

systems their peers were suffering under back home. In a speech held in Parnell Square and reported in the *United Irishman*, Gonne opined that those who fought in the British army "brought disgrace on their country by winning England's battles for her against Ireland's friends."[19]

Gonne argued that their reason for joining the army was hunger, thereby rhetorically turning Irish hunger into a deliberate element of Britain's conscription policy[20]:

> One of the reasons why England organises the famines and destroys the means of existence of our people is to force them into the army. This year [1898], when the famine was at its height in the West of Ireland, when the people were dying of starvation, . . . I found the recruiting agents in each of the miserable villages I visited, trying to get the starving people to join the army or navy.
>
> When one is starving the temptation must be terrible, and I wondered at and admired the courage and endurance of those poor peasants who, though face to face with death, and seeing people dying of hunger around them, shut the door of their desolate cabins against the British agent, preferring hunger and perhaps death to the shame of wearing the English livery.[21]

On April 7, 1900, the *United Irishman* repeated the causal connection between Irish famine and joining the British army: in "Recruiting," a poem reprinted from the *Celt*, "Ether" wrote of "fierce pangs by hunger bred," "living ghosts / That prowled along the plain," and grain hoarded by the English while Irishmen were lured "to fight in England's cause."[22]

The "Famine Queen" Issue of the *United Irishman* as a Cotextual Manifesto

"Recruiting" appeared in the same issue as Gonne's article "The Famine Queen" (see fig. 6.2). While Ireland was readying itself for Queen Victoria's visit in April 1900, Gonne published a *numéro exceptionel* of her monthly Parisian paper *L'Irlande Libre* in which she fiercely criticized the Queen's upcoming trip across the Irish Sea.[23] The *United Irishman* commended the special issue of Gonne's Parisian publication for its critical frontispiece illustration of the Queen and accompanying caption, which included numbers for famine deaths, emigration, and evictions during her reign.[24] Before being translated for and reprinted in the *United Irishman*, "The Famine Queen" appeared in this special issue. As chapter 1 has shown, in that article, Gonne placed blame for a long history of famine and evictions on Queen Victoria. The English-born Irish nationalist described the Queen as a decrepit old woman with a "vile and selfish and pitiless soul."[25] Gonne argued that hunger was not only a tool for conscription but also a weapon in service of British imperial oppression.

Gonne ended her inflammatory article by taking up the voice of the Irish people, promising vengeance toward Britain and rejecting those Irish who sided with the British. She wrote:

> Queen, return to your own land; you will find no more Irishman ready to wear the red shame of your livery. In the past they have done so from ignorance, and because it is hard to die of hunger when one is young and strong and the sun shines, but they shall do so no longer; see! Your recruiting agents return unsuccessful and alone from my green hills and plains, because once more hope has revived, and it will be in the ranks of your enemies that my children will find employment and honour! As to those who to-day enter your service to help in your criminal wars, I deny them! If they die, if they live, it matters not to me, they are no longer Irishmen.[26]

Gonne considered Irishmen who joined the British army perpetrators of an "awful crime" against Ireland. Nevertheless, her articles show that, with hunger as a driving factor, judgment about these men could not unproblematically be placed in a straightforward victim versus perpetrator paradigm in which an Irishman would cross from the former to the latter category after joining the British army. Rather, when choosing between joining the British army or the threat of starvation in Ireland, these men did not have a free choice to do the former; Gonne's rhetoric, although firm in its denunciation, makes it more apt to see these Irishmen as victims of British imperialism at best and "implicated subjects" at worst.[27]

The issue of the *United Irishman* that contained "The Famine Queen" included several more examples of hunger, misrule, and oppression in British imperial territories, stretching from the 1840s until the present. Indeed, as a whole, the April 7 issue can be read as an anti-imperialist, Irish nationalist manifesto in which the majority of articles cotextually support that message in transhistorical and/or transnational ways. These connections can be drawn across articles but also feature within single pieces. The article "An American Letter" transitions from a description of famine conditions in India, where one sees "skeletons traversing the plain in search of corn husks," to the argument that India provided "many men and much money to Her Gracious Majesty's Government to help defeat the Boers." Later in that same article, Father Ryan's rousing nationalist poem "Erin's Flag" is included, extending the connection to Ireland, where "thousands . . . famished, unfed / Died down in the ditches while howling for bread."[28]

THE FAMINE QUEEN.

"The Queen's visit to Ireland is in no way political," proclaims the Lord Lieutenant, and the English ministers. "The Queen's visit has no political significance, and the Irish nation must receive her Majesty with the generous hospitality for which it is celebrated," hastens to repeat Mr. John Redmond, and our servile Irish members whose nationality has been corrupted by a too lengthy sojourn in the enemy's country.

"The Queen's visit to Ireland has nothing at all to do with politics," cries the fishmonger, Pile, whose ambitious soul is not satisfied by the position of Lord Mayor and who hankers after an English title. "Let us to our knees, and present the keys of the city to her Most Gracious Majesty, and compose an address in her honour."

"Nothing political! nothing political! let us present an address to this virtuous lady" echo 30 town councillors, who when they sought the votes of the Dublin people called themselves Irishmen and Nationalists, but who are overcome by royal glamour. Poor citizens of Dublin! your thoughtlessness in giving your votes to these miserable creatures will cost you dear. It has already cost the arrests of sixteen good and true men, and many broken heads and bruised limbs from police batons, for you have realised—if somewhat late—the responsibility of Ireland's capital, and, aghast at the sight of the men elected by you betraying and dishonouring Ireland, you have, with a courage which makes us all proud of you, raised a protest, and cried aloud, "The visit of the Queen of England is a political action, and if we accord her a welcome we shall stand shamed before the nations. The world will no longer believe in the sincerity of our demand for national Freedom!"

And in truth, for Victoria, in the decrepitude of her eighty-one years, to have decided after an absence of half-a-century to revisit the country which her hatred and whose inhabitants are the victims of the criminal policy of her reign, the survivors of sixty years of organised famine, the political necessity must have been terribly strong; for after all she is a woman, and however vile and selfish and pitiless her soul may be, she must sometimes tremble as death approaches when she thinks of the countless Irish mothers who, shelterless under the cloudy Irish sky, watching their starving little ones, have cursed her before they died.

Every eviction during sixty-three years has been carried out in Victoria's name, and if there is a Justice in Heaven the shame of those poor Irish emigrant girls whose very innocence renders them an easy prey and who have been overcome in the terrible struggle for existence on a foreign shore, will fall on this woman, whose bourgeois virtue is so boasted and in whose name their homes were destroyed. If she comes to Ireland again before her death to contemplate the ruin she has made it is surely because her ministers and advisers think that England's situation is dangerous and that her journey will have a deep political importance. England has lived for years on a prestige which has had no solid foundation. She has hypnotised the world with the falsehood of her greatness; she has made great nations and small nations alike, believe in her power. It required the dauntless courage and energy of the Boers to destroy for ever this illusion and rescue Europe from the fatal enchantment. To-day no one fears the British Empire, her prestige has gone down before the rifles of a few thousand heroic peasants.

If the British Empire means to exist she will have to rely on real strength, and real strength she has not got. England is in decadence. She has sacrificed all to getting money, and money cannot create men, nor give courage to her weakly soldiers. The men who formerly made her greatness, the men from the country districts have disappeared; they have been swallowed up by the great black manufacturing cities; they have been flung into the crucible where gold is made. To-day the giants of England are the giants of finance and of the Stock Exchange, who have risen to power on the backs of a struggling mass of pale, exhausted slaves.

The storm approaches; the gold which the English have made out of the blood and tears of millions of human beings attracts the covetousness of the world. Who will aid the pirates to keep their spoils? In their terror they turn to Victoria, their Queen.

She has succeeded in amassing more gold than any of her subjects; she has always been ready to cover with her royal mantle the crimes and turpitude of her Empire, and now, trembling on the brink of the grave, she rises once more at the call. Soldiers are needed to protect the vampires. The Queen issues an appeal to England, the struggling mass of slaves cry "Hurrah;" but there is no blood in their veins, no strength in their arms. Soldiers must be found, so Victoria will go herself to fetch them; she will go over to Ireland—to this people who have despised gold, and who, in spite of persecutions and threats, have persisted in their dream of Freedom and idealism, and who, though reduced in numbers, have maintained all the beauty and strength and vitality of their race.

Taking the Shamrock in her withered hand, she dares to ask Ireland for soldiers—for soldiers to protect the exterminators of their race!

And the reply of Ireland comes sadly but proudly, not through the lips of the miserable little politicians who are touched by the English canker, but through the lips of the Irish people:

"Queen, return to your own land; you will find no more Irishmen ready to wear the red shame of your livery. In the past they have done so from ignorance, and because it is hard to die of hunger when one is young and strong and the sun shines, but they shall do so no longer; see! your recruiting agents return unsuccessful and alone from my green hills and plains, because once more hope has revived, and it will be in the ranks of your enemies that my children will find employment and honour! As to those who to-day enter your service to help in your criminal wars, I deny them! If they die, if they live, it matters not to me: they are no longer Irishmen."

MAUD GONNE.

"UNDER THE UNION JACK."

For several days previous to the arrival of the Queen of England, placards and hand-bills had been distributed through Dublin, signed on behalf of the Nationalist societies, calling on the people to refrain from any act of hostility on Wednesday, but to assemble at Lower Abbey-street and march thence in procession through the city in the evening to protest against the attempt to misrepresent Ireland as being "loyal to the Empire." Though the police had been busily engaged in tearing down the placards and endeavouring to intimidate those who were engaged in the distribution of the handbills, no proclamation had been issued by the Castle against the gathering, nor had any notification of any kind been given to the organisers that the police would interfere with the procession. At 7.30 on Wednesday evening a crowded meeting was held at the Transvaal Committee Rooms. Mr. O'Leary Curtis took the chair on the motion of Mr. Arthur Griffith.

The Chairman said it was their duty to show that the display of loyalty which was made in the streets that day did not represent, and to show that it did not reflect, the sentiment of the National citizens of Dublin (hear, hear).

Mr. M. J. Quinn proposed the following resolution:—"That this meeting of citizens of Dublin declares that the Loyalist pageant of to-day in no wise reflects the sentiments of the people of Dublin, and, unawed by the display of force and uncorrupted by the treacherous suggestions of reform, we once more affirm our resolve to continue the struggle for our full national independence." He said they were determined to maintain now, and in the future as hitherto, hostility to the Government that had over-ridden this country for the last seven hundred years (hear, hear). That day reminded him of '98, when martial law was proclaimed in the streets of Dublin.

Mr. James Connolly seconded, and Mr. Francis Dorr supported the resolution, which was passed.

The street outside was held by a force of 200 policemen. A cordon was drawn across either end to prevent the people gaining access to Lower Abbey-street. On the conclusion of the indoor meeting the doors were thrown open and about fifty men bearing lighted torches walked out into the street. Immediately, without warning, the police charged upon them. An exciting scene ensued. The torchbearers were knocked down, kicked, and in two instances batoned on the ground. Messrs. Connolly and Dorr were felled by the police, and Messrs. Curtis and Griffith struck. Mr. M'Namara, a resident in the street who was proceeding home from work, was attacked, knocked down, and kicked. The policemen then rushed into the hall and up stairs, striking and kicking all whom they met. At the same time a body of young men who attempted to make their way to the assembly-place were batoned by the police in O'Connell-street.

The procession, however, succeeded in starting. While the police were engaged in their baton work in Abbey-street a body of Nationalists, headed by torch bearers, appeared in Capel-street, and, followed by an immense crowd, marched through Little Britain-street, Halston-street, and King-street, as far as Church-street, where the police, who had hastily gathered, charged the people with batons. Some heavy fighting occurred; a number of the oil torches were smashed on the ground and the street seemed for a few moments as if on fire. Women and children were struck down by the police; but a great portion of the people forced their way through to Bridge-street. Here the police were massed in overwhelming force. Portion of the people succeeded in reaching Lord Edward-street, and thence Dame-street and College-green, where bodies of Nationalists marched to and fro, singing National songs and cheering enthusiastically for the Boers. A body of Loyalists, escorted by the police, marched past at one time, cheering for Queen Victoria.

Many exciting scenes occurred in the streets during the evening. In Grafton-street a number of the garrison were badly beaten by the people, and trophies and flags were torn down. In O'Connell-street a body of loyalists carrying Union Jacks were smashed up and their flags torn. The decorations on one side of O'Connell-bridge were torn down. Those at the City Hall and Nassau-street corner were destroyed. In Abbey-street a number of soldiers and Cockneys who were cursing the Boers were stripped of their hats and sticks and soundly punished. The hats, with some scores of loyal flags were flung into the Liffey. In Phibsboro' the decoration displayed by the toadies were pulled down. In Brunswick-street a number of howling Loyalists, after being chastised by the people, were with grim humour deposited under the tombstones in a monumental sculptor's yard, and advised to sing "God Save the Queen" there. Black and Boer flags were displayed from houses in King-street, Thomas-street, Wentworth-place, The Coombe, Jervis-street, and other places. A tramcar in Grafton-street was seized by the people, who hoisted a Boer flag from the top. Up to an early hour in the morning crowds paraded the streets singing "God Save Ireland" and cheering for the Boers. All the bridges were held by bodies of policemen, and all "strategic points" occupied by special constables. The military were held in readiness to turn out. In Upper Abbey-street the police batoned the Socialist Republicans. Such was the "enthusiastic reception" of the virtuous Queen.

SLIM PIET.

I was standing one January day outside the Grand National Hotel, Pretoria, watching the passing of the funeral of Commandant Pretorius, the hero of Elandsfontein. A crowd of chattering, laughing, jibing well-dressed Englishmen and Englishwomen were around me. As I raised my hat when the gallant soldier's coffin, draped with the flag of his country, passed, they stared at me insolently, and made jeering references to the dead officer,—for such is the nature of the British uitlander.

I followed the funeral procession across the Kerk-square, down Kerk-street West, past the Presidency to the cemetery. The crowd was enormous, and I could not approach the grave. I heard a voice suddenly up-raised and then a hush fell upon all.

I have heard many great singers, many great actors, and many great orators, but never had I heard a voice like the one which reached my ears that evening in the cemetery of Pretoria. Its sweetness, its richness, its tenderness, its pathos, its nobleness—it was music—music of the gods.

Not one word did I understand—for it was the voice of a Dutchman speaking in the taal, and I was a newcomer to the Republic. But though it did not speak to my understanding, it spoke to my soul. It spoke of patriotism, heroism, gentleness, and devotion. When it ceased, the voices of the people swelled in a hymn, and as the twilight fell a rifle-volley rang out above the soldier's grave, and they turned away.

I pressed in to look upon the owner of that glorious voice. I found him gazing sadly on the grave of his comrade. An old, white-bearded man, seeming small and slight, beside the herculean frame of President Kruger, who stood next him. He turned his head as he heard my step behind him, and his eyes seemed to pierce me through. Once only had I met so piercing a glance, and that was from Charles Stuart Parnell.

That evening as I wandered past the Presidency with a friend I saw my angel voiced sitting on the stoep with the President and some ladies. "That is—?" I asked. "Slim Piet—General Joubert," returned my friend.

"Shrewd Peter," as the burghers called him, was a familiar figure in the streets of Pretoria. Commandant-General; he never, save on extra-official occasions wore anything like uniform. In a little pony carriage he drove about the town dressed in sober black and wearing a white helmet. He was fond—very fond—of Irishmen, and liked to have them about him. His secretary, Hogan, was one—the editor of his paper, Land en Volk, —O'Brien—was another.

Joubert represented for a long time what was called the "Progressive Party" amongst the Boers. In 1893 he contested the Presidentship with Kruger, and was beaten only by a few votes. It was considered certain that he would become President at the next election—and he might have, but for the Jameson raid and the rise of Schalk Burger.

The Jameson Raid damned Joubert's chances of being elected head of the State. Even "Slim Piet" had been deceived by the English, whom he had been urging on his countrymen were honourable men, with whom it should be their ambition to live and work in harmony. Practically what Joubert had been preaching for years was "Let us guard our independence—and live in trust with the English"—what Kruger had been saying was, "Guard your country from England. Distrust the English. They are enemies always." The Raid proved Oom Paul's wisdom, and the General, though he never lost his place in the affections of his countrymen, lost caste as a politician.

Schalk Burger took his place with a section—young, clever, thoughtful, travelled, and deeply read Burger dreamed of making the Transvaal the peer of European nations. He regarded, not too wisely, the old time beliefs and conservatism of the Boers as an obstacle to the progress of the country, and appealed to the younger section, who largely rallied round him. At the election of '98 he stood for the Presidency against Kruger. So did Joubert. But the old man was returned over both his opponents by a majority of four to one.

One of the most beautiful incidents of that election was the fact that while they were fighting hard against each other for the headship of the State, the three patriots lived on close terms of friendship. During the thick of the contest I have seen them time after time in the evenings drinking their coffee, smoking their pipes, and chatting and laughing together on the President's stoep, with their friends and supporters gathered round them. Not one single word of disrespect was uttered by any one of them during the campaign of either of his opponents. On the contrary, each paid in his speeches generous tribute to the patriotism of the others. Would we were half as civilised here!

One little incident, I recollect well, may illustrate the difference in attitude of Oom Paul and Slim Piet towards the English. The capitalist gang at one time thought they would nobble the Boers. They gave a banquet, to which they invited the President and the General. Speeches were delivered by the Englishmen, full of fulsome and insincere praise of their guests, and urging them to rely on the generosity, magnanimity, and inherent nobility of the great English people for the independence of the Republic. Joubert, in reply, spoke highly of the English nation. Then the old man rose and thanked his hosts. He had listened, he said, with interest to what they had said about the magnanimous desire of the English people to safeguard his little country. He was thankful to the great English people. "But, gentlemen," he added grimly, "we are a nation, and we rely for the safe-guarding of our independence not upon the generosity of the English, but upon the *man with the gun!*"

May the turf of Rustenburg lie light on Slim Piet! His lion-heart has ceased to beat—his patriot soul has fled—his angel-voice is hushed; but his name will go thundering down the ages.

ISR.

Figure 6.2. Page containing Gonne's "The Famine Queen," *United Irishman*, April 7, 1900, 5. Image courtesy of the National Library of Ireland.

A substantial part of the April 7 issue was taken up by the plight of the Boers and recent developments in the Boer War. More specifically, the page that contained Gonne's article (see fig. 6.2) was fully taken up by three articles that functioned as a transition from the Irish Famine to the South African Boer War, thus serving as an effective cotextual integration of these issues. After "The Famine Queen," the article "Under the Union Jack" detailed recent protests in Dublin during which protesters not only rallied against Queen Victoria's visit but also showed their support for the Boers by parading in the streets while "singing 'God Save Ireland' and cheering for the Boers" as Boer flags were displayed from several houses. In the third article, regular contributor to the newspaper "Ier," an Irishman who had lived in South Africa for a long time, criticized the recently deceased commandant general and vice president of the Transvaal Petrus Jacobus Joubert for too easily trusting the English and praised "Slim Piet" ("Shrewd Pete," a nickname for Joubert) for his efforts in service of the Transvaal.[29]

"The Ireland of Africa": The Boer War as Hope for Ireland

After the discovery of gold and diamonds in South Africa in the late 1860s, British need for labor in the mines increased, as did desire for centralized state control and control of land. These needs eventually led to the Second Boer War, considered a "war over land and labor."[30] The Boer War was the first major British war to take place after the advent of mass literacy, and the (newly) literate masses were eager to learn about the war from the rapidly expanding new media. The popular press frequently covered and extensively scrutinized the war and thus contributed greatly to its impact. Although public opinion in England and Scotland was strongly prowar until the middle of 1901, public opinion shifted in the later stages of the war; media coverage of wartime hardships, transgressions, and embarrassments significantly stimulated antiwar sentiment. In Ireland, many nationalist, intellectual, and cultural leaders expressed antiwar criticism and pro-Boer sentiments. Nevertheless, Irishmen also joined the British war effort; some Irish considered the empire "an arena in which the Irish could prosper."[31] The Second Boer War turned out to be a much more substantial and protracted affair than originally envisioned and negatively impacted public opinion on British imperialism, causing the latter to lose "the moral high ground."[32]

The Boer War was also a conflict between two modes of life: the traditional, secluded, rural lifestyle of the Boer community and the life and labor required by the British Empire. In British critical writings from before and during the war, the Boers and their lifestyle are represented as backward and uncivilized, justifying British imperial domination in the region on the basis of social Darwinist reasoning.[33] These representations show parallels to the Irish situation—not just in the contest over land but also in the public image building of the Boers and Irish as inferior Other. It shows concordances in the clash of temporalities as well, as traditional Boer and rural Irish life did not align with the pace and changes of British modernization and industrialization.

In 1899, French politician and journalist Hector Depasse stated that the takeover of the Transvaal by Britain would create "another Ireland" in the heart of South Africa. In 1900, politician, journalist, and Gonne's former lover Lucien Millevoye called colonial secretary Chamberlain a "bandit, inspired by greed instead of patriotism" and an "audacious charlatan." He wrote that South Africa had become "the Ireland of Africa."[34] Depasse's article had appeared earlier in *L'Echo de Paris* and Millevoye's piece in his Paris newspaper, *La Patrie*, before being translated for the *United Irishman*. The latter regularly included articles and bits of information taken from French sources. This close connection between the *United Irishman* and the Parisian press was largely the product of Gonne's life and ties in the French capital and her link to Millevoye and *La Patrie* on the basis of shared advanced nationalism.

Several commentators in Irish newspapers on both sides of the Atlantic drew comparisons between Ireland and South Africa based on their respective positions vis-à-vis the British Empire. Senia Pašeta writes that the "effect of the Boer war on Irish nationalism was vital." While Irish conservatives continued to employ a conciliatory approach to the Irish Question, the Second Boer War and the resistance of the Boers fueled more extremist Irish nationalism. The *United Irishman* served as a "medium through which [these] advanced nationalists railed against British Imperialism and lauded the bravery of the Boers."[35]

In the *United Irishman*'s anti-imperialist critique, all victims of British imperial dominance together form a "race of the oppressed."[36] In the article "Toleration," Gonne implored the world to no longer tolerate the evil caused by imperial practices in Ireland, India, South Africa, and elsewhere around the world and explained that "to those living under the British flag, the sight of murder is so habitual that it no longer appalls—it is part of the system."[37] Highly critical anti-imperialist remarks had already been made in earlier issues of the *United Irishman*. For example, the aforementioned Ier subverted imperialist discourse by calling the English "white barbarians" for how they treated the Irish and the Matabele, a people in South Africa who had recently experienced two bouts of war with the English.[38]

According to Gonne, there was an important difference between the Transvaal on the one hand and Ireland and India on the other. In 1900, she wrote that Ireland and India had been worn to the last degree by starvation and were therefore easily subdued. She stated that starvation in these countries was the result of England's "famine policy" and spoke of "manufactured" famines in India.[39] By contrast, the Transvaal had not yet arrived at that level of suffering and therefore was still capable of resisting British rule. Had the Boers not resisted, Gonne was convinced, "the world would soon become as familiar with accounts of South African famines as it is with accounts of Irish and Indian famines."[40] Moreover, the Irish and Indian peoples had been fooled by the "falsehood of England's [imperial] greatness" and, through continual oppression, no longer believed that "freedom is worth fighting for." The courageous Boers, who had not been fooled, still grasped the value of freedom and were fighting for it.[41]

This multidirectional comparison of imperial suffering turned Irish and Indian hunger into a rhetorical device to mobilize resistance by and in service of the Boers. As a next step, it was meant to boomerang Boer opposition into a battle cry for Ireland. In what Gonne considered a demonstration of "dauntless courage and energy," the Boers had been able to "destroy for ever this illusion [of imperial grandeur] and rescue Europe from the fatal enchantment. To-day no one fears the British Empire; her prestige has gone down before the rifles of a few thousand heroic peasants."[42] In "Signs of Hope," Gonne wrote that Ireland had been the "Mother of Exiles" and the "Mother of Sorrows" long enough; following the Boer example would allow a different connotation to the female symbol of the Irish nation.[43]

For Gonne, as for many other Irish nationalists, the Boers became a glorious example, and the Boer War—especially when the outcome of the war had not yet been decided—signified hope, the promise of independence through armed struggle. In America, imperialist expansion was hotly debated at that time, and Gonne and Irish Transvaal Brigade commander John MacBride (1868–1916) traveled across the Atlantic in 1901 for a lecture tour during which they repeatedly spoke about Boer and Irish freedom.[44] During the first lecture of the tour, held at the Academy of Music in New York, the "Irish Joan of Arc" asserted that Ireland was "a dying nation now. Her population is decreasing. After thirty years of parliamentary agitation she is suffocating from it." Transforming her lament into a call to action, Gonne continued: "On the verge of the grave the Irish people have awakened. They realize now that there is no freedom to be obtained without fighting for it. Revolution means action, not words. The Dutch are leading the way. Let not the Irish stand back."[45] Gonne tied together the destinies of Ireland and the republics of the Transvaal and the Orange Free State, commenting that MacBride had "done more for Ireland by organizing the Irish brigade in the Transvaal than any living man."[46] The tour helped mobilize support for the Boers and raised money for the *United Irishman*. Nevertheless, Gonne did not feel satisfied afterward, for she had found that "the men in high places" were more inclined to support constitutional politicians, and while "they were full of sympathy with the Boer Republic," this support was "not to the extent that MacBride and I had hoped for."[47]

Before successful resistance could take place, Gonne had written earlier in the *United Irishman*, the Irish had "work to do at home": "we must prepare men's minds for war." Then Ireland would, "through the smoke, and the fire, and the darkness," find her way toward "life, light, and regeneration." Later in 1901, the *Irish-American* again argued that the Boer War would be advantageous to the Irish struggle for independence. The newspaper quoted Michael Davitt, who had spent eight months among the Boers and through that experience had become more ardent in his quest for self-government: "'I am satisfied,' [Davitt] said, 'that the evolution of events now in progress will result in giving Home Rule to Ireland. When the Boer War is over, the English people will see that it will be to their advantage to give Ireland such a government as Canada has. . . . For myself, I have enlarged my claim. I was satisfied to have Home Rule: but, when I saw what a fight the Boers could make against England, I declared that I wanted independence for Ireland.'"[48]

Even after the defeat of the Boers, hope continued: the *Irish-American* wrote that if Chamberlain would not grant the Boer generals what they wanted—"to pledge British credit for the purpose of re-establishing the Boers in their country on such a scale of liberality as they think necessary"—the Boer generals would not only contact the US to increase pressure on the British but also join Irish nationalists to form an "Irish Boer alliance" meant to topple the empire. The newspaper concluded that Ireland's time to rise was nigh: "The Irish question is now advancing into the front rank on the political stage."[49] As the frequent references in various newspapers and the threat of exercising political pressure in the influential *Irish-American* cited in this section show, newspapers played a vital part in representing and fueling Irish and Irish-diasporic antiwar and anti-imperial sentiments and fostering renewed engagement with Irish independence. In so doing, they considerably aided in placing these matters center stage.

STARVE THE WOMEN, HUMILIATE THE NATION

Imperialism is undeniably a gendered phenomenon, as acts of colonization have been predominantly carried out by men, and imperialist discourse is often gendered. Colonial oppression does not equally affect men and women; colonized women have often experienced more simultaneous forms of oppression and had fewer rights than their male counterparts, underscoring the importance of considering histories of colonial subjugation from an intersectional perspective. Anne McClintock writes in her feminist study *Imperial Leather: Race, Gender and Sexuality in the Colonial Contest* (1995) that one of the governing themes of Western imperialism was "the transmission of white, male power through control of colonized women."[50]

The discourses and practices of nationalism are also gendered. As McClintock writes: "no nationalism in the world has granted women and men the same privileged access to the resources of the nation-state. So far, all nationalisms are dependent on powerful constructions of gender difference."[51] Nationalism was no different in Ireland during the period this chapter covers. Since the decline of the Ladies' Land League, Irishwomen had been largely excluded from nationalist organizations, leading them to establish their own nationalist periodical, the *Shan van Vocht* (1896–99), and their own organization, Inghinidhe na hÉireann, in 1900. The latter campaigned against recruitment of Irishmen in the British army; it also sought to merge the nation's and women's rights, but a tension remained between the two in which nationalist concerns were generally more prominent. Irish nationalism of the time not only excluded women from participation but also limited how women could apply themselves in the nationalist struggle: before the establishment of Inghinidhe na hÉireann, women were confined to a passive patriotism. Gonne and other progressive female nationalists had to navigate this traditional situation, and it was not until the start of the Boer War that Gonne was able to establish herself as "a figure of primary importance at nationalist meetings."[52]

Such progressive efforts with regard to gender divisions did not mesh with the appreciation of traditional gender relations in Boer society expressed by Gonne and the *United Irishman*. However, this appreciation might have been meant not to emancipate Boer women but rather to counter British claims of ill treatment of women by Boer men. As Philippa Levine argues, "one of the characteristics seen to define colonial peoples and to relegate them to a lesser status was their apparent lack of respect for women. . . . The mistreatment of women came to be seen as definitive of primitive societies, and one of the many reasons justifying the need for colonial authority."[53] Ier wrote that the British press told "blackguardly lies" about the Boers ill treatment of Englishwomen. Sarcastically, he stated that these views came from "the Englishman, whose respect for women is so well understood in the Rand."[54] In *The Brunt of the War*, British feminist, pacifist, activist, and relief provider Emily Hobhouse (1860–1926) included many letters and petitions by Boer women, and one of these underscores Ier's criticism. It describes "the cruel and barbarous manner in which the British officers and soldiers behave towards defenceless women and children," removing them from their homes, forcing them to undertake long marches with little to no clothing on, and separating the women from their children.[55]

While in several Irish creative and journalistic writings, focus on tropes of powerless female and child victims could lead to a depoliticization of famine, in her pleas for the Irish and Boer peoples, Gonne fully utilized the "rhetorical power" of the "feminization of famine," to again use Margaret Kelleher's key phrase.[56] Gonne's anti-imperialist critique combines a focus on female and child victims familiar from a broad register of depictions of hunger with a gendered dimension of imperialism and nationalism. In Gonne's rhetoric concerning imperial oppression in Ireland and beyond, periods of hunger are part of England's "old policy of extermination."[57] As such, underlying imperial policy is presented as static and hunger consequently as repetitive across many decades; together, they disturb established gender norms.

This disturbance negatively impacted both colonized and colonizing females, a point further emphasized through cotextual reference in the *United Irishman*. In the "Famine Queen" issue, a comment on recent famine in India was included. It showed how famine could radically subvert the maternal role, turning infanticide into an act of maternal mercy: "Harrowing, indeed, were the scenes depicted of mothers murdering their offspring to bring merciful oblivion to their horrifying aid."[58] The impact of famine on women in power is pithily explained in "The Famine Queen." Gonne held Queen Victoria responsible for decades of evictions and organized famine; in this argument, the Queen's policy defied traditional gender patterns. Gonne included that she could not help but wonder if the Queen was ever sensible to feminine sentiments: "For after all she is a woman, and however vile and selfish and pitiless her soul may be, she must sometimes tremble as death approaches and she thinks of the countless Irish mothers who, shelterless under the cloudy Irish sky, watching their starving little ones, have cursed her before they died."[59] Thus, Gonne implied that the Queen was failing to live up to her role as mother to all her people.

The use of the mother figure is crucial, as a rhetoric of familial ties shaped imperialist as well as national discourse and the family was often seen as the cornerstone of the nation. As McClintock explains, "nations are frequently figured through the iconography of familial and domestic space," and by extension, "nations are symbolically figured as domestic genealogies." The cult of domesticity and patriarchal model were transplanted from the imperial center to the colonies, where the English considered "the family as the model of social order."[60] In this ideology, children function as the promise of the nation. Hunger, explained Gonne, disturbed established gendered patterns and killed all promise for the emerging nation. Reflecting on hunger in South Africa, India, and Ireland, she wrote that the death of children through starvation meant the destruction of "the flower-crown of hope."[61] Gonne's argument that the British Queen could not fulfill her role as a mother to all her people, then, is meant to show that the imperial power itself was incapable of maintaining the familial ideology it propagated.

The Second Boer War "was in many respects waged as a war on Boer women," and the "massive cruelty inflicted on Boer mothers was a key episode in the politics of gender in Britain."[62] This view was put forward in the first years of the twentieth century by Hobhouse, who stated that the experience of the Boer women "is unique. Never before has the entire womanhood of a white nation been uprooted and placed in circumstances of such difficulty"; "never before have women and children been so warred against."[63]

In "The Boer Women," included in the *United Irishman* on March 17, 1900, Gonne explored the involvement of Boer women in the war and attempted to paint them as valiant figures rather than victims. She used General Joubert's wife as a case in point, "a picture of the true Boer woman—the faithful wife, the devoted mother, the fearless companion—who braves the awful carnage of war and amid whistling bullets and bursting shells provides, like the careful housewife that she is, for her husband's table. For the Boer women go to battle with their husbands and fathers." Linking caretaking and ideal womanhood to the provision of food, Gonne commended Mrs. Joubert as she "forgot danger and fear and remembered only that the men who were fighting for freedom were starving."[64] Shortly after, through a reprinted excerpt from the Johannesburg *Standard and Diggers News*, the *United Irishman* included that Boer women not only cared for their own sons but also extended this maternal trait beyond their own people, giving provisions to the Irish fighting on their behalf.[65]

Gonne's discussion of women's roles in the war in "The Boer Women" was deeply ambivalent: Gonne wrote that the Boer women adopted a purely supportive role and were "not essaying the role of Amazons. They are only trying to soften some of the horrors of battle, to ease the pangs of suffering and cheer and comfort the well. So it happens that many of them, like the wife of their General, are engaged in home-making even amid the din of war."[66] Conversely, Gonne called the Boer woman equal to the "Spartan woman." In a paragraph that should be quoted in full to appreciate the complexity of Gonne's depiction of female roles, the Boer women are described as follows:

> But the difference between her and her sister [the Boer woman and her urban counterpart] is merely a thin veneer of civilisation. At heart they are the same. And each is religious, each loves her country better than her life. For that reason both of them are now on the battlefield. Each of them has been taught two things—to use her Bible and her pistol. In her hour of need she trusts in both of these. Days spent in the excitement of the chase have taught her endurance. She has wonderful physical courage. Disdaining a saddle she rides all day by the side of her brother, and uses rifle or pistol with the skill of a sharpshooter. Tall, strong, with muscles like iron, she does not know the meaning of fatigue. With all this she is strictly a domestic woman. She is satisfied by her own fireside. Her whole heart is centred in the little world that she calls by the sacred name of home. It is big enough to hold all her ambitions, all her hopes, all her dreams. It is now an important factor in the Transvaal War. She has the same old spirit, modified and beautified by Christianity, that animated the Spartan woman. They are pure in heart, simple in life, strong in faith.[67]

Gonne's reference to the Spartan woman implies an aggressive and masculine dimension, oppositional to the role of the supportive caretaker and transgressing the traditional division between men and women. When describing the capabilities of the Boer women in an earlier battle against the Matabele, Gonne praised these women's tactical abilities, as they could be seen "riding round and inspecting the plans of defense." These "women, and delicate young girls and feeble mothers and grandmothers," loaded weapons "with lightning-like precision" and "were as cool as soldiers."[68]

Nevertheless, the Boer woman was "strictly domestic," wrote Gonne; it seems the paragraph quoted above makes a distinction between the

Boer woman's identity and gender role in peacetime (supportive angel of the house) and wartime (Christian Spartan woman). This distinction, however, does not align with the supposedly innate powerful and assertive qualities typically associated with masculinity Gonne also assigned to these women. Moreover, from the perspective of Gonne's lobbying for women's rights and participation in the sociopolitical sphere, this divided womanhood remains problematic. With acknowledging these women's masculine qualities—they could ride, shoot, and do battle alongside their brothers—Gonne allocated them a prominent position in nationalist and anti-imperialist struggles, a place she herself also aimed to occupy. However, by stating that, under normal conditions, these women would choose a secluded domestic life, Gonne immediately rejected any sustained change in women's social positioning. As such, her attempt to not portray the Boer women as victims is at once very progressive and deeply conservative. This failure to consolidate a progressive repositioning for women can be considered a result of the transitional and unstable nature of the period regarding women's roles in society and politics.

Turning the Boer women into symbols, Gonne wrote that "women of this kind . . . have been the mothers of the great nations of the earth." By extension, her vision of the Boer woman can be linked to the icon of the *volksmoeder* (mother of the people), a paradoxical figure that simultaneously suggests a mother's power and the female's position within the domestic sphere.[69] In any case, if the Boer women were cast as volksmoeders, that image did not meet the ideal of passive femininity and domesticity put forward in British gender discourse. In the popular British press, gendered ideology concerning the nation frequently featured, perhaps best exemplified by the icons Hibernia and Britannia. Amy Martin demonstrates that during and after the Fenian Rising, the British press coded revolutionary Irish violence as masculine and aggressive, while counterinsurgent violence by the state was represented as feminine and legitimized on the basis of being reactionary (female) rather than aggressive (male).[70] Gonne's rhetoric in "The Boer Women" can be understood as an attempt to revise these gendered connotations to rebellion, thereby posing insurgent Boer violence as feminine and reactionary (legitimized) and British counterinsurgent state violence as masculine, aggressive, and transgressive (unjustified).

The unclear positioning of Boer women also influenced their reception by the British. While Gonne lauded female heroics, British critics of Boer resistance argued that through such acts, Boer women "forfeited the right to be considered non-beligerents" and were considered potential military participants. This attitude in British rhetoric could consequently imply that these women had given up the right to "considerate treatment."[71] Their treatment at the hands of the British was thus influenced by their inability to meet feminine ideals disseminated through British imperialism.

British troops burned Boer farms; in an initial attempt to provide relief, over forty concentration camps were established toward the end of 1900. Due to inhumane living conditions, these camps soon became a controversial element of the war. Some four thousand Boer women and twenty-two thousand Boer children died in these camps, mostly due to disease epidemics. These numbers constituted about one-quarter of the total population of women and children of the two Boer republics.[72] Elizabeth van Heyningen explains that "a common feature of the camps was the 'faded flowers,'" children who slowly perished. Some parents believed that their children's deaths were deliberate, and such beliefs became part of camp mythology. Hobhouse visited several concentration camps in South Africa to provide aid and report her experiences; her graphic descriptions of the mass deaths in the camps were reported in full in the *Manchester Guardian*, the *Speaker*, and other liberal journals and had a strong impact on public opinion.[73]

Soon after arriving, Hobhouse realized that the English at home misunderstood conditions in South Africa and sought to show them the reality of the situation. She wrote that the English public were led to believe that people in South Africa had "a sufficient allowance, and were all comfortable and happy," while she "knew that they were miserable and under-fed, sick and dying." Moreover, as far as deaths of Boer women and children were acknowledged in the British press, they were considered as stemming from Boer mothers' insufficient knowledge of hygiene and nutrition.[74] In her influential reports, meant to provide "an outline of the recent war, from the standpoint of the women and children" on whom "fell the brunt of the war," Hobhouse at length described the overcrowded and deplorable conditions in the camp at Bloemfontein, concluding that "soon . . . the facts loomed large. I realised that the barest necessities of life were lacking or inadequately supplied." Hobhouse made similar observations about other camps. She also noted that the numbers of women and children entering the camps were rising so quickly that relief could not be organized satisfactorily and that sanitary conditions were insufficient. A few weeks later, she revisited Bloemfontein and found the women and children in much deteriorated conditions, with "disease and death stamped on their faces." Hobhouse urged the British government to provide more financial support, pointing out that it was the government's duty to provide for the people whose means it had destroyed.[75]

A year after writing about the valiant mien of the Boer women and reading Emily Hobhouse's reports, Gonne again likened South Africa to Ireland: "In those refuge camps in South Africa the English are trying, by overcrowding and squalor and filth, and by the presence of their soldiers, to humiliate those noble Boer women, and rob death of its dignity and calm. Ireland is weak, sick unto death from British rule; the presence of the English King would be a last humiliation. The Boer women are wailing among their dying children, Ireland is wailing amid her ruined homes. The anger of the people is rising. When will the toleration of evil cease?"[76] A sense of intentionality and the words "humiliation" and "toleration" are key to Gonne's argument. By using the latter—also the title of the piece—Gonne implied the complicity of those who might not be perpetrators of imperialism but who nevertheless carried some of the blame: their inability or unwillingness to act against imperialism, their passive toleration of misdeeds justified through the imperial endeavor, aided in the continuation of British imperialist expansion.

Zoë Denness writes that critical British discourse focused on the internment of only Afrikaner women and children during the Boer War and excluded nonwhite victims. As a result, "black victims of the concentration camp system were forgotten." Gonne's sympathy had similar limits—despite her keen awareness of the oppression of the Boers, she "showed little awareness" of the effect of white, both Dutch and British, colonialism on the native population. Humiliation of Britain seems to be what mattered to Gonne, as Steele explains.[77]

Like Gonne, the "feminist-leaning" *United Irishman* was of the opinion that the British had an intentional practice of humiliating opponents through their women.[78] In "England Starving the Boer Women and Children," the newspaper reflected on the reported seizing of sacks of American flour meant to aid the Boers. It wrote that the English reasoned as follows: "The Boers have wives and tender children, and if these can be starved of every comfort and every delicacy, if these can be deprived of white bread and thrown back on the Yellow Meal, so dear to English Policy from the Shannon to the Tugela, if hard fare and coarse food can pinch the Boer's children and undermine the health of the nursing mother, oh then, there will be a triumph of English Valour and English Statecraft."[79]

The mention of yellow meal undoubtedly provided a poignant reminder of its distribution by the British government during the Great Famine.

According to the *United Irishman*, the English intended to "kill the nits less they become lice," an approach familiar to the Irish. Moreover, the newspaper opined that English policy to seize food supplies rested on the following logic: "to starve the Boer's household is to embarrass the Boer's army in the field."[80] In the construction of *Afrikanerdom* (Afrikaner cultural identity), the family household was the sacred, final bastion against British control.[81] In imperial discourse, the hunger experienced by women and children was coded as an inability of Boer men and women to support their families. Thus, the disruption of traditional family structure and the inability of oppressed women to feed their families were extended into emblems of national humiliation.

Hunger and Humiliation in Gonne's Later Creative Writing

In 1904, the discourse of hunger and humiliation returned in Gonne's revisiting of her 1898 visit to Mayo. Gonne's famine play *Dawn* was intended for the Inghinidhe na hÉireann but would never be performed; it did appear in the *United Irishman* on October 29, 1904.[82] A combination of creative writing and recollection, the piece constitutes another fascinating example of the diffuse boundary between journalism and fiction and the possibility of achieving a standing-for an absent history through the combination of these modes of writing. Moreover, "*Dawn* performs a direct appropriation of famine to the story of nationalism."[83]

Dawn includes expressions of the shame and inhumanity of forcing females to work on the relief works reminiscent of Gonne's article "Relief Work in Erris." One of the men employed on the relief works remarks: "It's a shame seein' the women at such work as carrying the stones and some of them with big sons standing around looking for hire, but it's what the Stranger says, only the heads of families are to be employed, and he says he likes to see the women work. He had Brideen turned off the relief works last week because she is with Bride, and it's Bride herself he says should come; he wants to humble her."[84]

Underscoring Gonne's conviction that famines were a recurrent feature in Ireland, the play remains temporally undefined, and its representation of starvation can be considered a manifestation of a diffuse temporality. In three tableaux—"Sunset," "Night," and "Dawn"—the prophetic play follows a group of Irish poor under the power of their evicting landlord and England, both indicated with the moniker "the Stranger." These Irish poor tell of their work on "famine roads that lead to nowhere," emigration, and the demise of loved ones. Central to the play is Bride, an evicted mother who functions as a symbol for Ireland and who will never emigrate because "it's not money she cares for, it's her land she wants. It is vengeance for the dead she wants." Emphasizing that the people should follow their mother, her adult daughter, Brideen, although starving, refuses to leave. Soon, Bride comes to function as mother to her community, the male members of which have not left the country and thus "have been faithful to [her]." During the deathbed scene of her daughter, Bride prophesizes: "See, Brideen, see, the dawn is coming, the red dawn. The river of blood must flow, but there is freedom on the other side of it, and the Strangers are driven away like clouds before the sun. Brideen, it is you and the mighty dead who are driving back the clouds." Shortly after, neighbors promise to avenge Brideen and their other dead and to fight for the Irish nation, to make "Bride of the Sorrows Bride of the Victories."[85]

Thus, in its hunger, Gonne's microcosmic Irish society finds the resolve to resist, and the play harnesses the activating potential of the Cathleen Ni Houlihan figure in the guise of the ever-suffering but battle-ready mother. The excerpt indicates that "the Stranger" wishes to "humble" Bride by evicting her, forcing her family to become dependent on English relief works and suffer from hunger. The analogy again points out that England employs a willful "policy of extermination" to demean Ireland.

In Gonne's writings included in Irish and Irish-diasporic periodicals, transnational affiliations are forged on the basis of shared suffering. While Gonne did not suggest a hierarchy of suffering, it should be noted that the connections established through her anti-imperialist rhetoric are formulated to first and foremost support the call to end British rule in Ireland: therefore, Gonne's rhetoric does showcase at least an emphasis on the personal and national rather than the global context. Nevertheless, in her journalistic writings, the Irish and Boers are considered equal in their humiliation by the English. Whether it is the oppression of the Boer volksmoeder or Christian Spartan woman or the Irish Bride as Mother of Sorrows or Mother of Exiles, for Gonne the humiliation of the oppressed female through hunger symbolized a spiritual starvation and signified the ultimate form of national humiliation.

NOTES

1. The quotes are taken from Gonne, *Servant of the Queen*, 240–41; Father Munelly is quoted on 240. Ferguson points out that during Gonne's early lectures in France, she had already started to connect her own martyrdom to that of the nation (*Maud Gonne*, 17, 26–27).

2. Steele, *Maud Gonne's Irish Nationalist Writings*, xxiii; O'Callaghan and Nic Dháibhéid, "MacBride, (Edith) Maud Gonne," n.p.

3. Ferguson, *Maud Gonne*, xii–xiv; Gonne, *Servant of the Queen*, 297–302; the quote is taken from 297.

4. Ferguson, *Maud Gonne*, 6. Gonne was able to personally finance the *United Irishman* (ibid., 3, 41). In her autobiography, Gonne mentions writing to Ellen Ford to appeal for financial aid for the famine-stricken areas (*Servant of the Queen*, 233). Ford's paper is discussed in the following chapter.

5. Quinn, *Young Ireland*, 132. Ferguson, *Maud Gonne*, 40–41.

6. Ward, *Maud Gonne*, 58. Ward, *Unmanageable Revolutionaries*, 47. O'Callaghan and Nic Dháibhéid, "MacBride, (Edith) Maud Gonne," n.p.

7. Ferguson describes Gonne as "acutely aware of the power of mythology and its role in political activism" (*Maud Gonne*, 52).

8. Denness, "Women and Warfare," 257–58.

9. Gonne, "Appeal to the Women of America!," *Irish World and American Industrial Liberator*, April 2, 1.

10. Ferguson, *Maud Gonne*, 27–28.

11. Gonne, "Appeal to the Women of America!," 1; "Letter from Maud Gonne," *Irish World*, April 9, 1898, 5.

12. Gonne, *Servant of the Queen*, 233.

13. Gonne, "Appeal to the Women of America!," 1; "Situation Is Horrible!," *Irish World*, April 9, 1898, 1. The problematics of representation are widely acknowledged in famine writings of the nineteenth and early twentieth centuries and in recent scholarship. For example, during the Famine, American philanthropist Asenath Nicholson remarked that the imagination falls short to describe the sufferers she witnessed on her travels through Ireland (*Annals of the Famine*, 37). In the preface to *The Chronicles of Castle Cloyne; or, Pictures of the Munster People*, novelist Margaret Brew reflected on the complexities of representing the Famine:

> It may be said that I have painted the great Irish Famine in colours that are too gloomy, and in language that it too strong. But to this I answer that the story of the Irish Famine could not be told with a pen dipped in rose-water, even in a work of fiction. But there are many still living who remember that calamitous epoch in Irish history, who will bear testimony that I have in no way exaggerated its horrors, or made its details more painful than was warranted by strict truth. They will say that on the contrary, I have passed over them as lightly as it was possible to do, consistently with the proper working out of the story (vol. 1, vii).

With regard to scholarship on the problematics of representing the Famine, see for example Lloyd, "Indigent Sublime," and Morash, "Afterword on Silence."

14. In this case, Gonne did not make explicit references to the Great Famine; she did make a link to the Land War era, saying that because of government negligence, "on the Western seaboard of Ireland we are face to face with the most serious famine we have had since 1879" ("Letter from Maud Gonne," 5).

15. For a specific focus on the child victim, see the article "Letter from Maud Gonne: We Live under a Hard Government," *Irish World*, July 16, 1898, 5. In this letter, Gonne wrote about her visit to schools in the West of Ireland, remembering "the poor little skeleton forms and hollow famine brightened eyes" she had seen two months earlier.

16. Gonne, "Relief Work in Erris," reprinted in Steele, *Maud Gonne's Irish Nationalist Writings*, 124.

17. Kelleher, *Feminization of Famine*, 121.

18. Gonne, "Relief Work in Erris," 124; Gonne, "Appeal to the Women of America!," 1.

19. Quote from Gonne, "Irishmen and the English Army," October 20, 1900, 5. See also Gonne, "Famine Queen," 5.

20. Gonne, "Reward of Serving England," *United Irishman*, October 21, 1899, 5.

21. Gonne, "Irishman and the British Army," *Worker's Republic*, September 24, 1898, reprinted in Steele, *Maud Gonne's Irish Nationalist Writings*, 48–49.

22. Ether, "Recruiting," 6.

23. This was the March–April issue of *L'Irlande Libre*. Gould, "Playing at Treason," 47.

24. "*L'Irlande Libre*," April 7, 1900, 4.

25. Gonne, "Famine Queen," 5.

26. Ibid.

27. Gonne, "Ireland and Her Foreign Relations," December 22, 1900, reprinted in Steele, *Maud Gonne's Irish Nationalist Writings*, 179; Rothberg, *Implicated Subject*.

28. De. Grey, "An American Letter," 3.

29. "Under the Union Jack," 5; Ier, "Slim Piet," 5. "Ier" is Dutch or Afrikaans for "Irishman."

30. McClintock, "No Longer a Future," 106, 109.

31. Morgan, "Boer War," 2, 1, 10–11, 13–14. Judd and Surridge, *Boer War*, "Introduction: An Irrepressible Conflict?," n.p. The quote is from Crosbie, "Networks of Empire," 997.

32. Morgan, "Boer War," 11.

33. Denness, "Women and Warfare," 256. Morgan, "Boer War," 5. Morgan explains that in the British popular press, this image became more balanced as the war went on, and there was a "growing admiration for social and moral qualities of the Boer peoples." Some British officers shared this admiration (ibid.).

34. Depasse, "Europe, England and the Transvaal," *United Irishman*, September 9, 1899, 4; Millevoye, "From Pretoria to Pekin," *United Irishman*, October 13, 1900, 4.

35. Pašeta, "Nationalist Responses," 489.

36. Gonne, "World's Justice," August 25, 1900, reprinted in Steele, *Maud Gonne's Irish Nationalist Writings*, 176.

37. Gonne, "Toleration," July 9, 1901, 6.

38. Ier, "Civilising the Kafir," December 9, 1899, 3.

39. Gonne, "India," *United Irishman*, May 12, 5; "Her Subjects" (part 2), *United Irishman*, April 28, 5.

40. Gonne, "Her Subjects" (part 2), 5.

41. Quotes from Gonne, "Signs of Hope," *United Irishman*, January 13, 1900, reprinted in Steele, *Maud Gonne's Irish Nationalist Writings*, 162. Gonne, "Ireland To-Day," *United Irishman*, September 28, 1901, 2.

42. Gonne, "Famine Queen," 5.

43. Gonne, "Signs of Hope," 163.

44. Ward, *Maud Gonne*, 60.

45. "For a Free Ireland," *Irish-American*, February 23, 1901, 4. The image of Gonne as the Irish Joan of Arc had arisen during her first American tour in 1897 (Ferguson, *Maud Gonne*, 37).

46. Gonne, "Ireland and Her Foreign Relations," *United Irishman*, December 22, 1900, reprinted in Steele, *Maud Gonne's Irish Nationalist Writings*, 179.

47. Ward, *Maud Gonne*, 61; Gonne, *Servant of the Queen*, 322–24.

48. Gonne, "In the Event of War," *United Irishman*, December 22, 1900, 4. "Home Rule for Ireland," *Irish-American*, September 7, 1901, 4. Canada held dominion status and was an autonomous community within the British Empire.

49. "Irish Boer Alliance," September 30, 1902, 4.

50. McClintock, *Imperial Leather*, 1, 3.

51. McClintock, "No Longer a Future," 105.

52. McCarthy, *Respectability & Reform*, 111, 112. Ward, *Unmanageable Revolutionaries*, 69–70, 86, 87, 249; quote taken from 47.

53. Levine, *British Empire*, 158. While not denying the wrongs they had committed in the past, Hobhouse spoke favorably of the virtues of Boer men in her time (*Brunt of the War*, 313).

54. Ier, "Blackguarding the Boer," *United Irishman*, October 14, 1899, 5. Journalist W. T. Stead published (controversial) accusations that British troops had raped Boer women (Judd and Surridge, *Boer War*, "Introduction," n.p.).

55. Hobhouse, *Brunt of the War*, 220.

56. Kelleher, *Feminization of Famine*, 35–39, 121.

57. Gonne, "Relief Work in Erris," 124.

58. De. Grey, "An American Letter," 3. A reference to "Madame Curzoni" suggests that the article refers to recent famine conditions, as Lord Curzon was viceroy of India between 1898 and 1905.

59. Gonne, "Famine Queen," 5.

60. McClintock, *Imperial Leather*, 357, 17, 239.

61. Gonne, "Ireland and the Children," *United Irishman*, June 7, 1902, reprinted in Steele, *Maud Gonne's Irish Nationalist Writings*, 135.

62. McClintock, *Imperial Leather*, 378; Morgan, "Boer War," 11.

63. Hobhouse, *Brunt of the War*, 316, 317. Hobhouse's letters were based on her observations while visiting South Africa to provide relief and were read by subscribers to the Distress Fund for South African Women and Children she had set up (*Brunt of the War*, 123–24).

64. Gonne, "Boer Women," reprinted in Steele, *Maud Gonne's Irish Nationalist Writings*, 164.

65. "The Transvaal Irish Brigade," April 7, 1900, 2.

66. Gonne, "Boer Women," 164.

67. Ibid., 166.

68. Ibid., 165.

69. Ibid., 166; McClintock, *Imperial Leather*, 378. McClintock, "No Longer a Future," 109.

70. Martin, *Alter-Nations*, 134–39.

71. *Times* quoted in Denness, "Women and Warfare," 264.

72. Heyningen, "Tool for Modernisation?," 1; Denness, "Women and Warfare," 262; Morgan, "Boer War," 12. Morgan adds that these lives were lost in the span of about fifteen months.

73. Quote from Heyningen, "Tool for Modernisation?," 1. Morgan, "Boer War," 11.

74. Hobhouse, *Brunt of the War*, 124. Morgan writes that the *Times* often misrepresented the Boer War ("Boer War," 3, 11).

75. Hobhouse, *Brunt of the War*, xv, 116, 122, 118.

76. Gonne, "Toleration," *United Irishman*, July 6, 1901, 6. This excerpt refers to speculations about an upcoming visit of Edward VII; the visit took place in 1903.

77. Denness, "Women and Warfare," 275; Steele, *Maud Gonne's Irish Nationalist Writings*, 161.

78. Ferguson, *Maud Gonne*, 41.

79. The article appeared in the section "Foreign Notes" (January 13, 1900, 1).

80. Ibid.

81. Isabel Hofmeyr's work referred to in McClintock, "No Longer a Future," 110.

82. Ferguson, *Maud Gonne*, 58.

83. Kelleher, *Feminization of Famine*, 125.

84. Gonne, *Dawn*, 205.

85. Ibid., 204, 206, 207, 210, 212.

7

IMPERIALISM VERSUS ECONOMIC PROGRESS

The *Irish World and American Industrial Liberator* and

Robert Ellis Thompson on Famines in Ireland and

India at the Turn of the Twentieth Century

IN 1904, MICHAEL DAVITT PRAISED the New York *Irish World and American Industrial Liberator* and especially its editor Patrick Ford (1837–1913) for their efforts regarding the Irish Land Question. Davitt wrote, "*The Irish World* has been a tower of strength in every conflict of the past quarter of a century in which the great principle of 'the land for the people' was fought for and upheld, and its name and giant efforts in a historic social and national revolution will always be linked with the name and achievements of the Irish Land League."[1] Ford's *Irish World* was the most popular Irish American newspaper of its time. Scholars including James Paul Rodechko and Ely M. Janis have demonstrated the great importance of this newspaper and its editor and proprietor for the Irish American and Irish communities. In such studies, the 1870s and 1880s have received the most attention because of Ford's substantial influence in the Irish Land and National Leagues during those decades. The current chapter picks up in the mid-1890s, further exploring how Ford did not limit the *Irish World*'s orientation to the Irish and Irish-diasporic communities and their issues but was also concerned with the oppressed worldwide.[2] In so doing, the *Irish World* made transnational connections between the plights of the Irish and various other colonized groups across the globe, including the Boer, Indian, Cuban, and Filipino peoples.

In the decade surrounding the turn of the twentieth century, the *Irish World* used memories of Irish famines to illustrate concordances between

188

the detrimental effects of imperialist endeavors on native populations across the globe; as in Gonne's journalism discussed in the previous chapter, Irish famine memories were put in service of a larger anti-imperialist critique. Representations of famine and imperial suffering in the *Irish World* belong to different scales of cultural construction: individual, regional, national, and international. Therefore, this chapter also explores the "multi-scalarity" at the heart of the *Irish World* during the period.[3]

The second part of the chapter focuses specifically on links drawn in periodicals between famines in Ireland and India. In the late nineteenth century, an "elaborate web of contact, dialogue and exchange was fashioned between nationalist spokesmen in Ireland and India," and their growing awareness of shared economic and political goals drew public attention to the failures of the British Empire.[4] Additionally, contemporary commentators frequently juxtaposed famines in Ireland and India, which, as Peter Gray argues, "suggests a significant phenomenon worthy of further investigation."[5] The chapter focuses on the terms of the transnational connections forged through such comparisons. Irish American early sociologist and contributor to the *Irish World* Robert Ellis Thompson (1844, Lurgan, County Down–1924, Philadelphia, PA) witnessed famine suffering during his childhood and used his personal recollections to critique the global effects of imperialism, landownership, and free trade policies; for this reason, his contributions to the *Irish World* receive special attention.

The *Irish World*: Ford's Vehicle to Combat Oppression and Inequality

Patrick Ford was born in 1837 in Galway, came to the US with his parents in 1845, and never returned to Ireland. The Ford family settled in Boston. Ford served as a printer's devil to William Lloyd Garrison's abolitionist newspaper the *Liberator,* where he "found his vocation as a publisher and editor who would use his paper to promote social justice." He then became editor and publisher of the *Boston Tribune* and served in the Union army during the Civil War. Subsequently, Ford edited the *South Carolina Leader,* a paper geared to the welfare of newly freed slaves, and the Irish American *Charleston Gazette.* Ford moved back north, settled with his family in New York, and founded the *Irish World* in 1870.[6]

The *Irish World* counted twelve pages and cost $0.05 per issue or $2.50 per year, making purchase within reach for the working classes. Many items included in its pages were clipped from other newspapers and magazines, including news from several Indian, British, and US newspapers as well as textual and visual material from New York's *Harper's Weekly* and London's *Pall Mall Gazette*. The *Irish World* also frequently reused copy from Irish newspapers, especially the *Freeman's Journal*. In the paper's early days, items were reused because Ford did not have much funding. However, such scissors-and-paste journalism was still frequently practiced on the pages of the *Irish World* in the 1890s and early twentieth century, illustrative of this then-widespread process in periodical composition. Conquering initial financial issues, the *Irish World* eventually became the biggest Irish American newspaper; its competitors had, at most, a quarter of the *Irish World*'s readership. In 1876, the paper reportedly had a circulation number of 35,000. In 1878, this number grew to 50,000, in 1882 to 60,000. In the 1890s and early 1900s, this figure more than doubled and regularly ran up to 125,000—some issues could boast circulation numbers of over one million copies. Additionally, at this time, the paper had a circulation of about 20,000 in Ireland. Around the turn of the twentieth century, the *Irish World* was at its peak in terms of the size of its readership.[7]

Ford's intention with the newspaper was to spread information among and educate workers regarding their plight. In his opinion, all people were entitled to equality of opportunity; he therefore advocated several causes in his newspaper, including "women's rights, African-American rights, and temperance," and showed himself a strong proponent of labor and industrial movements.[8] Ford's concerns were of both a diasporic and a transnational nature, and he showed deep engagement with his own community's and other communities' well-being in Ireland, the US, and elsewhere. As a diasporic publication, the newspaper was a "formidable political force for Ireland in the US."[9] The Irishman's inferior status in the US was a prime concern for Ford, and he saw his newspaper as a means to improve his fellow countrymen's standing. This status was closely tied to the position of the Irish in Ireland: according to Ford, the relatively low position of the Irish in America was caused by the continued subservience of the Irish to the English across the Atlantic. The "destruction of British domination" in Ireland therefore was not only essential to Ireland but also "conducive to the honor of the Irish race in all lands."[10]

In Ford's view, the land belonged to the people, and as a result, he was a great supporter of the Land League in the 1880s, the No Rent Manifesto of 1881, and the Plan of Campaign of 1886. He "continuously pushed Irish leaders to expand the goals of the movement beyond its calls for rent reductions and peasant proprietorship and into a drastic reconfiguration of the existing land system that linked radical agrarian reform in Ireland inextricably to the urgent need for land reform in the United States." He established many branches of the Irish Land League and later United Irish League in the US, including his own, meant to rival less radical branches. Ford set up various fundraising campaigns throughout his editorship of the paper, and in 1898, he established a Famine Fund to which many readers of the *Irish World* contributed. While such funding initiatives were first and foremost set up for altruistic purposes, they also conveniently functioned to amp up Ford's public persona.[11]

As an editor, Ford continually reformulated his ideology and adjusted the newspaper to his changing views. During the 1880s, the editor moved from radicalism to reform, and by 1890, he had lost much of his radical streak, rejecting violence in favor of a more peaceful constitutional and parliamentary approach to achieve change, and strove toward middle-class respectability for the Irish in America. Despite Ford's changing ideology, the *Irish World* never diminished its attention to the Irish Land Question, nor did its anti-imperialist colors dull. Janis has demonstrated in detail how Ford and likeminded reformers in the US during the 1870s and 1880s drew connections between the Irish Land Question and the plight of the Irish poor on the one hand and labor issues and growing discrepancies in the distribution of wealth and land in the US on the other; chapter 5 of *Periodical Famines* has demonstrated *McGee's Illustrated Weekly*'s involvement in this matter.[12] The current chapter furthers scholarly understanding of the *Irish World*'s transnational dimension by focusing on multidirectional global connections made in the paper in the 1890s and early 1900s.

In his realization of the importance of the Land Question for not just peasants and laborers of Ireland but also workers of other nations, Ford was influenced by Henry George. Both men saw parallels between Ireland and the US: Ireland was dealing with the issues of "monopolized land, social unrest, hollow democratic institutions, and degraded farmers and laborers," a situation also emerging in the US. For this reason, Ford argued that "the struggle in Ireland . . . is radically and essentially the same as the struggle in America—a contest against legalized forms of oppression."[13] In the 1880s, Ford argued that Ireland's Land Question could be solved by land nationalization rather than peasant proprietorship. In so doing, an attempt was made to shift the Irish American conception of British oppression from a "cultural-religious one (Anglo-Protestants in Ireland and America), to a socioeconomic one (any illegitimate monopolizer of resources that belong to all of society)." During this period, Ford came to support trade tariffs as a means to protect domestic industries and the people's well-being.[14]

In 1898, the *Irish World* formulated an understanding of famine (in Ireland) as the man-made product of imposed economic policy; in an article titled "The Distress in Ireland," it stated that "in a strict sense, Ireland is not and never has been a land of famine. A national famine means a general scarcity of food in a country. There was a famine in the land of Canaan, when Jacob sent his sons with money to buy food in Egypt. It is the other way in Ireland. In Ireland, taken as a whole, there is always food enough for the whole population; and when people in Ireland die of hunger, it is because the food produced in Ireland is shipped to England." The *Irish World* upheld a rhetoric of cumulation meant to explicate that under the British, bent on "destroy[ing] or displac[ing] the Irish people," Ireland had become a "land of famines," and the recurrence of famine could only be solved by allowing Ireland to govern herself.[15]

In "The Distress in Ireland," the Great Famine was mentioned: "In the Black '47, when more than a million of the Irish people died of hunger, Ireland exported to England her annual tribute of twenty million (20,000,000) bushels of wheat—all to pay the accursed blackmail to absentee Anglo-Irish landlords. Even to-day England draws from Ireland more food, in the shape of beef, pork, mutton and poultry, than comes to her from all other countries put together." Little under a year later, the newspaper again adopted such cumulative rhetoric, this time quoting Irish Home Rule politician John Dillon's phrase "periodical famines" (see "Introduction").[16]

Five years later, the paper reused copy from the *Philadelphia Ledger* in which a history of oppression, starting with Cromwell's invasion, was offered to explain "the extreme of human misery as it is shown in Ireland to-day." Seeing the Great Famine as the most excessive example of "merciless exploitation," it again drew a link between that period and current distress: "Between 1845 and 1848 a million of them died. After the famine years, matters were even worse. Landlords, despairing of the regular rents from the starving people, drove them out of large tracts, which they now gave over to pasturage. Today, out of 15,000,000 acres of arable land in Ireland, less than 2,500,000 acres is under the plow. The best land is given to cattle. The people are in many regions huddled together in bogs, trying to eke out a living out of mudholes such as an American farmer would turn over to his pigs for a wallow."[17] These examples demonstrate that through historical accumulation, the *Irish World* adopted a well-known Mitchelite rhetoric regarding the dangers of free trade policies and food exports from Ireland during the Great Famine and extended this argument to the turn of the century.[18]

The idea of excessive food exports during the Famine has been revised by more recent scholarship. Of course, shipping food from a famine-stricken country is in itself morally questionable in that it implies precedence of economic policy over humanitarian aid. Nevertheless, the amount of grain exported from Ireland during 1846 and 1847 would not have counterbalanced the number of potatoes lost to the blight. Cormac Ó Gráda offsets grain exports against the regular yield of potatoes and calculates that "the exported grain would still have filled only about one-seventh of the gap left by the potatoes during these two crucial years."[19] It should be considered that grain exports from Ireland during the Famine were significantly reduced compared to previous years and that grain imports greatly exceeded exports after 1846. In an insightful biopolitical reading of government policy and famine relief, David Nally argues that colonial famines can be considered "regulated" events with "functions as well as causes" but crucially adds that this does not "condone the radical nationalist view of calculated genocide"; rather, the concept of regulation emphasizes that strategies for relief and improvement could be used as colonial biopolitical tools for societal regeneration. Despite these vital modifications, the Mitchelite argument of mass food exports remains widespread, feeding into the genocide thesis.[20]

Even in light of its scholarly corrective, the discourse on excessive food exports highlights the validity of Amartya Sen's argument. Hunger and famine are not just reliant on the amount of food per capita: "hunger is best seen in terms of failure of 'entitlements' of people, that is, the failure to establish command over an adequate amount of food and other necessities."[21]

THOMPSON'S ANTI-IMPERIALIST DISCOURSE

Robert Ellis Thompson was born in Lurgan, County Down, in 1844 and came to Philadelphia with his parents when he was thirteen. He worked at Penn University as professor of mathematics, history, and English literature. He married Mary Neely in 1874; when, in that same year, a professorship of social science—what we today call sociology—was created at the university, Thompson was elected for that position as well, becoming a pioneer in an emerging field. He lectured at Harvard and Yale between 1884 and 1887 and the Princeton Theological Seminary in 1891. Thompson worked at Penn until resigning in 1892. He took up the post of president of Central High School in Philadelphia and retained that position until he was forced by state law to retire in 1920. After this, he received an emeritus appointment as a lecturer on ethics and political science. This appointment extended students "the privilege of attending lectures by the great master" until his death in 1924.[22] Thompson is described as an outstanding teacher with great influence over his students, apparently stimulating more of them to choose a career in scholarship "than any other teacher at Pennsylvania in a generation."[23] Indeed, the addresses made at his memorial meeting by his former students, pupils, and friends are full of praise, including that "Dr. Thompson devoted his entire life to the supreme calling of education. He spent his whole time and effort in teaching and preaching. All that he did was for the uplift of mankind, constantly inspiring the rising generation to the highest ideals. He always used his great talents for the good of others."[24]

The quote shows that Thompson was also an esteemed preacher. The deeply spiritual Presbyterian clergyman was an outspoken defender of labor unions and was in favor of female suffrage. His interests were broad, and he taught and published on a range of topics including "social science, political economy, protection and the tariff, ethics, church history, and literature." Although Thompson had an impressive intellectual command, it does not seem he boasted about his abilities or knowledge: he is described as a man of courage and principle in his convictions, always displaying modesty, humility, and simplicity.[25]

Thompson contributed regularly to newspapers and magazines and edited the *Penn Monthly Magazine* from 1870 to 1880 and the *American* from 1881 to 1882. His periodical contributions included publications in the *Penn Monthly*, the *North American Review*, and the *Irish World*; he was on staff for the latter.[26] Thompson explained his views on society and economics in works such as *Social Science and National Economy* (1875) and *Elements of Political Economy* (1881). The former, a comparative discussion of economic circumstances in various regions at various times, Thompson argued that since the Middle Ages, famines "owe much of their desolating force to the bad economic management that has kept the whole people to a single occupation, or made them dependent upon a single crop, for a failure or a series of failures of that crop must produce dreadful misery." He summarized "the specifics of famine" as the absence of "enlightened government and modern civilization": "Where they exist, scarcity will never result in depopulation. Where they do not, the utmost endeavors of government may mitigate but they cannot avert."[27] Imperial government, in Thompson's view, was not enlightened, nor did it bring modern civilization. He demonstrated that while populations had grown, famines had actually lessened or even disappeared; as a result, the issue was "the disproportion of the opportunities of employment to population," not "the disproportion of natural resources and land to the population."[28]

After the turn of the twentieth century, Thompson still opined that Ireland was and would continue to be plagued by "recurrent famines" and "perennial poverty" unless English misgovernment ended. The 1903 Wyndham Land Act had made "some provisions for relief of the West Coast" but was not as "peremptory as it should be" and, in the short term, was insufficient to check emigration from Ireland, according to Thompson.[29] A "firm advocate for home-rule for Ireland," he felt that an end to imperial rule was key.[30] However, it would not suffice to solve Ireland's long-standing distress; Ireland's home industries needed to be protected, and Ireland needed to diversify its industries. For several decades, Thompson had been a firm proponent of the diversification of industry. Reflecting on the Irish Land War and smaller famine in 1880, he equally argued that the Land League should focus not only on agrarian reform but also on the development of Irish industry and manufactures.[31] Ireland served as an example of Thompson's broader theories on economic reform. Diversification would give the Irish, and any population in a similar economic bind, recourse to more options to overcome starvation and stave off enduring poverty, giving subjects better entitlement to the sustenance needed to survive by having either more foodstuffs at their disposal or more commodities available to exchange for food.[32] Other commentators picked up on the need to stimulate home industries as well; in 1901, Maud Gonne wrote that the opening up of the Irish market for English trade while "our own people are starving for want of work" was a type of "extermination policy" geared to the "systematic destruction of Irish industries."[33]

Thompson belonged to the school of American Political or National Economy, which he considered a subdivision of sociology. The British and American schools of Political Economy were distinct, in his opinion, and this distinction was based on a key methodological difference. Feeling that British Political Economy, premised on a deductive methodology, did not stand in connection to real-world developments, Thompson relied on American and German Political Economy. According to him, these followed an inductive approach to studying the workings of a national economy and proposed a broad study of real-world events and developments, which lent themselves to the formulation of general economic laws or principles.[34]

Defenders of British Political Economy explained the deductive approach as following the doctrine's purportedly nonsectarian and nonpolitical approach. For these supporters, in Political Economy, the interests of the individual, that individual's class, and the nation coincided through the "automatic and dispassionate operation of the market mechanism, through *laissez-faire*, rather than through regulative agency." As such, the pursuit of self-interest also served the interests of the larger collective.[35] This form of Political Economy had a strong moral dimension with a perverse edge: it aligned wealth with "personal rectitude" and poverty with "atonement for sin."[36] Its laws were considered "natural laws and hence universal"; however, as Thomas A. Boylan and Timothy P. Foley have written, Political Economy was in fact "partisan, prescriptive, tendentious." Moreover, many nineteenth-century critics argued that while Political Economy might be suitable for industrially advanced societies, it was unfit for supposedly economically backward agricultural societies such as Ireland—demonstrating that "Political Economy had a nationality."[37] The disconnect between the natural laws or universal principles of British Political Economy and real conditions perceived by Thompson demonstrates that in his view, British Political Economy was a static and inflexible system that reasoned from the atemporal heights of theory and was therefore unable to accommodate real circumstances. In other words, for Thompson, a mismatch existed between the temporalities of British Political Economy and of the actual Irish economy. As a result, the application of British Political Economy would lead to repetition, to "perennial famines" in the real world.

Both Thompson and the *Irish World* provided a steady flow of strong anti-imperialist critique toward the US and Britain; imperialism was a form of "modern cannibalism" Thompson ironically considered to be "the loftiest enjoyment open to a civilized nation."[38] Examples of anti-imperialist comparisons printed in the paper include Davitt's piece of November 12, 1898, in which he pointed out that both Cuba and Ireland had suffered much and were equally deserving of freedom.[39] On June 6, 1903, the *Irish World* condemned British presence in South Africa and called that country "another Ireland"—a comparison made by Lucien Millevoye and Hector Depasse and included in the Dublin *United Irishman* a few years earlier, as the previous chapter has shown.[40]

The typical layout of the *Irish World* very aptly demonstrates cotextuality; the layout frequently served to underscore the shared plight of the colonized. Often, various articles on imperialist oppression and abuses in different regions would be included on the same page. For example, the first page of the issue of February 4, 1899, featured an article that criticized

Figure 7.1. Illustration included on the first page of the *Irish World*, October 31, 1903. The image was taken from *Il Fischietto* (The Whistle), an illustrated magazine from Turin, Italy. This reproduction was derived from the collections of the Boston Public Library.

the US "administration's intention of acquiring the Philippines against the wishes of the inhabitants." In its rejection of US imperial policy in the East, the article emphasized how the US had let itself be persuaded by Britain to take up action in the Philippines and "now depends upon England to keep other powers off its back."[41] This article was paired with two articles on the success of the United Irish League and continued abuses such as evictions and land grabbing in Ireland.[42] These pieces used a similar rhetoric, questioning who held the right to own the land in Ireland and the Philippines. Harsh in its critique of US expansionism, the *Irish World* was often even more acerbic in its pieces on British imperialism, calling England a world-wide "land grabber" more than once (see fig. 7.1).[43]

As noted earlier, at the heart of Thompson's convictions was an ardent belief in protectionism and the importance of protective tariffs to guard and stimulate domestic markets—a view he shared with Ford. For the former, "all history illustrates that the chief growth of the state is from within. Nations have often imparted to each other wholesome and stimulating impulses, but beyond a certain limit foreign influence has always been a hindrance." Rather, all nations should focus on the well-being of their own economies; this conviction informed Thompson's overall anti-imperialist stance.[44]

Thompson had argued in *Social Science and National Economy* in 1875 that famines were a necessary corollary of unenlightened (imperial) government. His comparisons between conditions in Ireland and India can be placed in this larger transnational and transhistorical rhetoric; additionally, they are part of a longer history of comparative periodical writings on the detrimental effects of British imperial policy. During the Irish Famine, the Boston *Pilot* opened an issue with the cartoon in figure 7.2. The *Pilot* wrote that England was focused on its "pet" and "victim" "young Africa" but continued to oppress Ireland and India. The paper condemned the "carnage, the robberies, and spoliations of India" and the "sturdy foot upon Ireland, [which] tells the tale of seven hundred years of oppression."[45] Equal in their treatment by England, in the cartoon in figure 7.2, India and Ireland figure as footstools for John Bull. Tellingly, the foot oppressing famine-stricken Ireland is clad in a robust cavalry boot, while the foot on India is in a cast, suggesting damage and danger to the colonizing power itself through imperial oppression. The image shows Young Africa being fed with John Bull's "abolition pap." The paper's proprietor and editor, Patrick Donahoe (1811–1901), was a Democrat and advocate of the gradual emancipation of slaves; therefore, the cartoon does not seem to advocate an anti-abolitionist stance but rather suggests that England was using the abolition of slavery to pacify Africa.[46]

In 1866, a large part of India was hit by what became known as the Orissa famine. Estimates indicate that about 8 percent of the affected region's population of almost twelve million died within the year.[47] The Dublin *Nation* compared famines and saw both the Great Irish Famine and the Orissa famine as "periodical" events and as evidence of British political

Figure 7.2. "Brother Bull, with One Foot on Old Ireland, Another on India, and Young Africa in His Arms," Boston *Pilot*, July 29, 1848, 1. The newspaper reused the image; it appeared again on the cover of the issue of June 29, 1861. Image derived from the collections of the Boston College Libraries (a digital version can be found at https://newspapers.bc.edu/).

malpractice and use of famine as "an agent of civilized progress." The article transposes several stock images of Irish famine discourse to India. In describing the sufferers there, focus is placed on bodily fragmentation: sufferers "raise their fleshless hands and gaunt, hunger-pinched faces in suppliance before the Eternal Throne." Equally, the "dead . . . lying by the road-side and in the streets of the towns unburied," the eating of "herbage by the roadside," and suggestions of cannibalism and the destruction of the mother-child bond ("mothers had eaten their dead children, and children gnawed at the mother's breasts from which they had been wont to draw life's nutriment") show parallels to representational tropes of Irish famine. The *Nation* argued that, like Ireland, the stricken district in India was in fact fertile and that, on top of that, there was enough food in neighboring districts, but nothing was being done to alleviate suffering. This complaint is explicitly linked to the Mitchelite interpretation of food exports during the Great Irish Famine: it is "a well-known fact that in the famine years, Ireland, the 'sterile,' produced double the food sufficient for the maintenance of her people and that England was daily importing her produce, while her own children were sinking on the earth with starvation, like the poor Hindoo of today."[48]

A decade later, the Madras famine of 1876–78 affected more than fifty million people, and between 6.1 and 10.3 million perished.[49] On February 23, 1877, the Montreal *True Witness and Catholic Chronicle* wrote that the famine "is assuming alarming proportions in India. British rule in that country has been as disastrous as it has been in our own. All authorities agree in saying that before India came under the British crown, famine was unknown."[50] On October 3 of that year, Irish Cardinal Cullen asked *True Witness* readers hailing from Ireland, "so often famine stricken herself" and having received "a munificent contribution" from the people of Madras during the Great Famine, to contribute to a famine relief fund for India.[51] In that same issue, special correspondence was included stating that "a more fearful calamity has never descended on any people, probably, for the last century."[52]

Twenty years later, India experienced a period of five years of successive droughts that hit 65 percent of the country and led to major famines in 1896–97 and 1899–1900.[53] At the start of 1900, the Dublin *United Irishman* shared the conviction that famine relief in India could be compared to the failed relief system in Ireland during "the Black 'Forty-Seven.'" As had been the case in Ireland, relief works in India typically consisted of the construction of roads that, stated the paper, "as a rule" were of a "useless character." The paper included that Ireland and India held sufficient natural wealth, but their potential was not developed by the imperial powers. In this context of the waste of natural resources, an exaggerated estimate of grain exports during the Great Famine was included: "Corn, to feed twice over the victims of the potato blight, was carried out of Ireland for the British rents and the British taxes." It summarized: "So there it is in a nutshell. The Indians perish, as the Irish perished, *because English Government stands between the nations and the rational utilisation of the natural resources of their own land.*"[54]

The analysis provided by the *United Irishman* again suggests the use of existing and well-known representations from the Irish context to give meaning to ongoing famine elsewhere: as had been the case for the *Nation* in 1867, in 1900, the *United Irishman* transposed the Mitchelite rhetoric regarding imperial economic policies in a transhistorical and transnational manner from Ireland to India. Moreover, the examples included in this section demonstrate the application of images from the national sphere to the global scale of cultural construction. Arguments resting on deliberate British imperial policy continued to feature: in 1905, for example, the New York *Gaelic American: A Journal Devoted to the Cause of Irish Independence, Irish Literature, and the Interests of the Irish Race* drew further comparisons between Ireland and India in articles such as "Murderous British Rule in India."[55] In her writings, Gonne also argued that since "the accession of Victoria to the throne," "famines have gone on recurring with ever increasing rapidity" in Ireland and India.[56]

"FREE TRADE SLAYS MILLIONS"

In the article "Free Trade Slays Millions," included on page 5 of the *Irish World* on February 20, 1897 (and reproduced as an appendix to this book), Thompson provided his reflections on India's 1896–97 famine through the combined lens of Ireland's history and his own childhood memories of the Great Famine. The piece blends the modes of fiction, history, and journalistic writing with economic theorization, combining various scales of representation. The mixing of writing styles and discursive registers is typical for Thompson's essays for the *Irish World*, but "Free Trade Slays Millions" is exceptional in the inclusion of a personal dimension. The transcultural comparison between Ireland and India that runs throughout the essay is further solidified in its narrative structure. Through these characteristics, the piece develops into a rich, multilayered, and dynamic feat of writing. In "Free Trade Slays Millions," a combinatory effect is established on the level of the singular essay through the combination of different textual types and discursive registers to support one argumentative point. Periodicals of the time were not clearly distinguished based on which textual types and modes of writing were acceptable for either a newspaper or a magazine. In this context, Thompson's essay can be considered a small-scale version of many of the cotextual processes of recollection and writing found in Irish, Irish American, and Irish Canadian periodicals between the mid-nineteenth and early twentieth centuries, which are at the heart of *Periodical Famines*.

The Indian famine of 1896–97 was caused by drought and, while not as devastating as the Madras famine of 1876–78, was severe. A relief fund set up by the government of India raised £1.7 million; in comparison to the

£10 million spent on the celebration of Queen Victoria's Diamond Jubilee in 1897, this government-provided relief sum was seen in an unfavorable light.[57]

"Free Trade Slays Millions" starts with transnational comparisons, pointing out that India's current famine could only be equaled by the contemporary famine in China and that the death toll was sure to surpass the number of deaths caused by the Armenian (or Hamidian) massacres of 1894–97. Seeing in the Indian famine another example of "English greed," Thompson argued that the situation was caused by the detrimental effects of imperial oppression, free trade, and laissez-faire. This relationship between imperialism and economic policy was the inverse of professor of Political Economy and archbishop of Dublin Richard Whately's vision, expressed some seventy years earlier. Advocating the beneficial effects of colonization on the economic prosperity and societal advancement of the "savage," Whately had argued that "on looking around us and examining all history, ancient and modern, we find . . . that no savage tribe appears to have risen into civilization, except through the aid of others who were civilized."[58] By contrast, according to Thompson, India had possessed "plenty of manufacturing industry" and a thriving cotton industry before the British had arrived, and it was British intervention—especially ending the India tariff—that had put an end to this industry. Favoring its own manufacturers and traders, England had "destroyed the resources of the Indian people" and left them "without a single resource if the yearly rains of the wet season do not fall," effectively turning India into a "famine country," a phrase Thompson had used earlier to describe Ireland's problems caused by British imperial rule.[59]

For Thompson, in both Ireland and India, "human misrule" and "English greed" were the causes of famine. With regard to the assigning of blame and meaning by British politicians and members of the press, Thompson made another link: in both cases, "the *Times* and other representatives of officialdom" blamed "providence" for the occurrence of famine.[60] The *Times*' providentialist rhetoric would have been very familiar to Irish audiences, as well-known commentators had resorted to the divine argument in the late 1840s. Perhaps the most (in)famous example can be found in assistant secretary to the treasury Charles Trevelyan's beliefs. On October 9, 1846, Trevelyan, inspired by providentialist and Malthusian rhetoric and driven by the laissez-faire economic principles of his time, wrote that "a remedy has already been applied to that portion of maladies of Ireland which was traceable to political causes" by "the direct stroke of an all-wise

Providence."[61] Later, John Mitchel pithily retorted that "the Almighty, indeed, sent the potato blight, but the English created the famine," a remark that would become a shibboleth of Irish anti-British sentiment.[62] Giving some credit to how the English were dealing with contemporary famine in India, Thompson acknowledged that in contrast to Ireland fifty years ago, while the *Times* continued to see providence rather than British imperial misgovernment as the cause, the British government did now propose "to correct its blunders" in India.[63] Political Economy and laissez-faire policies increasingly received criticism in the latter half of the nineteenth century, which likely led to the change in approach between Ireland in the 1840s and India in the final decade of the nineteenth century.

"Perennial hunger and recurrent famine" "never fall upon countries whose manufactures give them the means to draw upon the resources of other land in the hour of need," only plaguing parts of the world characterized by a lack of diversified industries and sole reliance on agriculture.[64] Thompson believed that it was not enough to provide aid for famine relief, as "one-fifth" of the Indian population was hungry "the round year [*sic*]." What was needed, then, was to end the "uniformity of occupation" and stimulate domestic manufactures. Industries needed to be diversified and the domestic market stimulated and protected, the latter through (the reinstatement of) protective tariffs. If these steps were realized, a country would be governed on the principles of enlightened government and "for the good of its own people"; it "would have no such insoluble problem for its rulers to solve."[65] This conclusion echoes advice Thompson repeatedly gave with regard to Ireland's distress during the 1880s; in 1897, he again expressed that tariffs would be good for both countries.[66] The acknowledgment that a substantial part of the Indian population was undernourished throughout the year implies a static condition; in the context of Thompson's broader argument on what causes countries to become famine countries, his comments additionally suggest that where there is (imperial) misgovernment and too great a trust in free trade and laissez-faire, a deviant temporality sets in, which in the case of India manifested itself as static. As such, Thompson's argument proposes that this kind of divergent temporality could be used not only to describe Ireland's problematic positioning in relation to British imperial temporality but also more broadly as a temporality of the colonized.[67]

Thompson wrote "Free Trade Slays Millions" in February 1897, when India was still in the midst of famine.[68] As a result, his descriptions of that famine and his estimations of its death toll have a prefigured quality. The first parts of the essay use imagery from the European literary canon and recollections of the midcentury Irish Famine and display a more florid, literary style of writing. Thompson at length described the effects of starvation on a community, using metaphorical language such as "at last the home is a charnel house" and speculative generalizations about how extreme hunger haunts sufferers in their sleep.

At the same time, use of the phrase "It Would Take a Dante to Picture its Horrors"—also used as a section header—hints at the problematics of representation when it comes to "death by starvation": famine suffering cannot be adequately described through conventional modes of nonfictional representation, so a literary register is needed to approximate its horrors, to be able to achieve an adequate standing-for.[69] As the previous chapter has shown, Maud Gonne applied the concept of unrepresentability to the distress in the West of Ireland in 1898 as well. In 1900, she used similar language to describe famine in India. After reiterating comments made in the House of Commons on the unrepresentability of famine conditions in India, Gonne wrote: "I have never been to India, and imagination, however strong, fails before the awful realities of British Imperial Famine."[70]

Gonne's and Thompson's writings demonstrate that by the turn of the twentieth century, Irish commentators on both sides of the Atlantic were employing the concept of unrepresentability as a discursive device not only in representations of Irish famines but also in the context of a broader, transnational representational framework concerning famines. Unrepresentability had, in fact, become a generalized representational trope in its own right, which is further supported by the fact that after acknowledging unrepresentability, both Gonne and Thompson nevertheless went on to describe in some detail starvation and death in Ireland and India. This discursive contradiction existed more broadly: while unrepresentability is "perhaps the most frequent observation on the Famine, . . . there is, nonetheless, an abundance, a surplus of representations of it."[71] Moreover, as Christopher Morash writes, even if each individual text's representational paradigm "can be said to have failed, the plurality of views" in texts that claim unrepresentability together constitute a multifaceted representational storehouse "with more extensive claims to adequacy than any one of its constituent parts."[72] Finally, Thompson's use of recollections of the Great Irish Famine to represent famine in India suggests that the former gives shape and meaning to the latter event and thus holds not only representational but also premediational power.

Including a reference to the "Tower of Hunger" connects "Free Trade Slays Millions" to what Niall Ó Ciosáin calls the popular level of representation, providing an intertextual connection to Canto 33 of Dante's *Inferno*. In Canto 33, the author provides a fictional rendering of the fate of Count Ugolino, locked in a tower with his sons and grandsons and left to starve. Dante's work was enthusiastically taken up by several British Romantic authors and artists such as Byron, Shelley, and Blake, reinvigorating appreciation of Dante's writings and helping this imagery of hunger to become part of the British literary and artistic canon. In 1875, Annie Keary had also referred to "Ugolino's Famine Tower" in *Castle Daly*.[73] "Misgovernment," wrote Thompson, "sowed these towers of hunger broadcast over Ireland then, as it is sowing them broadcast over India now. Hundreds have perished already, and yet the terrible harvest is but beginning."[74] In this instance, the figurative language adopted inverts common associations, with harvests now yielding not nourishment but rather the deaths of many. Thompson's brief reference to the *Inferno* would trigger a more substantial literary frame of reference based on readers' familiarity with Dante's work. Thus, it could aid readers' processes of meaning making by providing another avenue for premediation, understanding the contemporary famine in India through the mold of a literary tale of imposed familial tragedy and starvation rendered in Gothic tones.

No temporal or geographical demarcations are provided for Thompson's descriptions of starvation and suffering in the first section of the essay, leading the reader to assume that he is describing the current situation in India. Only when the reader moves into the consecutive section, "That Was the Tragedy Enacted Fifty Years Ago in Myriads of Irish Cabins," do they understand that Thompson has in fact transitioned into a description of the Great Irish Famine. Starting from a generalized discourse on famine suffering, the essay transitions into a literary mode of writing and uses literary intertext, after which it shifts to argumentative journalism, then into personal childhood recollections. It closes with economic theorization. In so doing, Thompson not only crosses the reality boundary—a technique known from literary journalism—but also cleverly utilizes the structure of his essay to link the midcentury Great Irish Famine and the contemporary famine in India. Thompson's temporal conflation simultaneously strengthens his anti-imperial economic argument and becomes extended in a transnational manner.

Thompson witnessed scenes of starvation and suffering in his early years and used his memories to represent the consequences of British policy and famine in India: "It is that England may prosper that India is thus exposed to the perils of famine and the plague which follows in the wake of famine, as dysentery and typhus following in Ireland in those black and terrible winters of my boyhood. Almost the earliest of my childish recollections is the pleading of poor mothers for a mouthful of wholesome food for their sick children, and I am proud to be the son of one who so spent his substance to save his poor neighbors from their fate, that, financially, he never could get on his feet again." This reference makes use of Thompson's status of direct witness. Use of personal memory points to the proximity between the personal and the global and gives an added sense of veracity to his more general descriptions of famine conditions. Additionally, he employed and contributed to existing cultural storehouses of memory and literature to represent, predict, and warn against the effects of the current famine in India on its population.

His piece again demonstrates affiliations between the modes of history and fiction writing explored by Ricoeur and discussed in more detail in chapter 4. Moreover, Thompson's essay showcases the multiscalarity of communal processes of cultural production. On the personal/local level, it uses Thompson's own boyhood memories set in Lurgan. It is here that the piece also briefly switches to first-person narration from an overall more detached third-person perspective, a narratological choice that may stimulate readerly engagement. On the cultural level, it uses generalized descriptions of suffering during the Great Irish Famine. On the international level, it draws on the European literary canon as well as references to other regions. Consequently, the personal/local, cultural, and international/canonical premediate the representation of India's 1896–97 famine as it was going on. Irish and literary scenes are woven into Thompson's warnings for what might happen in India—and not only in India. In the context of his body of socioeconomic thought, this transnational act of signification becomes part of a global anti-imperialist critique.

Famine as Memory Imperative

Comparisons with other collective groups and their suffering can be accompanied by a hierarchical approach: nationalist and antiabolitionist Mitchel's remark that the Irish slave (poor laborer) had it worse than the "fat and happy lot" of Black slaves in Brazil serves as a famous example.[75] On the pages of the *Irish World*, hierarchical interpretations of Ireland's suffering were also found. In his letter of April 16, 1898, titled "The Murder Famine of '48: But This Sort of Thing Is Sure to Last While English Rule in

Ireland Lasts," Denis L. Mayer, a reader of the newspaper and Great Famine survivor, praised the *Irish World* for "standing guard" against English abuse of Ireland. Now long settled in the US, Mayer stated that he had "left that persecuted land in 1848. In that year, also, there was a famine, and now, after fifty years, we have the same sad story." Elaborating on what he perceived to be a transhistorical injustice done to Ireland, Mayer wrote: "A good deal is now said about Spanish cruelty in Cuba; but if all that is charged were true, the *Irish World* knows that England has been ten times more savage in her dealings with Ireland, and is so to this very day."[76] Indignity at the eagerness of the US to interfere with Spanish rule at the behest of Cuba during the Spanish-American War of 1898 was not an idiosyncrasy of Mayer. As Matthew Frye Jacobson demonstrates, several Irish American commentators wondered why Cuba received much attention and why the US readily took up arms against the Spanish imperial aggressor and not against "perfidious Albion" in Ireland.[77] For these commentators, in international comparison, Ireland was at the top of a hierarchy of suffering caused by imperialist practices.

The transnational nature of these processes of cultural production says little about the sentiment behind them. While Mitchel's and Mayer's examples show a limiting and skewed approach, Thompson's "Free Trade Slays Millions," as well as the earlier articles on famine in India included in this chapter and Gonne's journalism discussed in the previous chapter, are equally transnational but not competitive. In fact, "Famine in India and Ireland" (included in the Dublin *Nation* in 1867 and discussed above) considers India's Orissa famine more severe than the Irish Famine, for it happened during a shorter period and in a smaller region but still cost the lives of an estimated 1.5 million people. Additionally, in "India's Awful Visitation," an article included in the *Irish World* on the same page as "Free Trade Slays Millions," famine in India is described in graphic detail, and it is included that "no famine within a century has proved half so terrible."[78]

Michael Rothberg laments that "transcultural memory often seems primarily to be a place of bitter contestation, competitive claims, and righteous victims."[79] He advocates instead for a multidirectional approach that acknowledges that memories are not owned by groups and that different funds of collective memory inflect each other. Both the earlier articles included in this chapter and Thompson's rhetoric achieve just that: in their arguments, Irish famine memory functions as a premediating mold for the representation of the Indian famine of 1896–97, allowing the connotations of injustice, colonial oppression, and erroneous economical approaches

(British Political Economy's laissez-faire principles in their most extreme manifestation) of the former to provide form and signification for the latter.

Through the use of the Great Irish Famine as a transnational mold for premediation, the memory of that period is taken out of its original socio-historical context. Rothberg explains that as "acts of remembrance are pre-mediated by prior image repertoires," they are consequently "remediated in ways that both confirm their place in the canons of cultural memory and reroute them on new and unexpected itineraries."[80] While at the time of writing, Thompson's connection between Ireland and India was in no way unexpected, his multiscalar use of Irish famine memory does follow Roth-berg's double trajectory: it both solidifies the existing storehouse of famine memory and demonstrates its egalitarian multidirectional potential. By consequence, it establishes unrepresentability as a transnational representational device for famine.

Daniel Levy and Nathan Sznaider argue that there exists a "global memory imperative," a "universal code" that gives shape to "a global concern for human rights."[81] I do not intend to draw easy connections between more recent and historical understandings of human rights, nor between Levy and Sznaider's discussion of memories of the Holocaust and my discussion of memories of the Irish Famine. Keeping important distinctions regarding victims, perpetrators, and motives in mind, I do believe that in Thompson's argument, the memory of the Irish Famine functions in similar ethical fashion as Levy and Sznaider's global memory imperative. In Thompson's rhetoric, the Great Famine has the connotation of failure to prevent human rights abuses caused by imposition of ill-suited imperial economic principles on the subjected country. By extension, through what Avishai Margalit calls "thin relations," transcultural comparisons to the mid-nineteenth century Irish Famine at the end of the nineteenth century underscore a shared humanity and identify the injustices done under the cover of imperialism and free market economics in other times and places.[82]

N O T E S

1. Davitt, *Fall of Feudalism*, 716.
2. Ford was the strongest anti-imperialist voice among Irish American nationalists of his time (Silvestri, *Ireland and India*, 19).
3. De Cesari and Rigney, "Introduction," 5.
4. Crosbie, "Networks of Empire," 1002.
5. Gray, "Famine and Land in Ireland and India," 194.
6. Murphy, "Ford, Patrick"; Legg, "Ford, Patrick"; Rodechko, *Patrick Ford*, 34. The quote is taken from Murphy.

7. Rodechko, *Patrick Ford*, 38, 39; Janis, *Greater Ireland*, 116; Murphy, "Ford, Patrick," n.p. The circulation numbers are taken from Jacobson, *Special Sorrows* (57), Rodechko, *Patrick Ford* (48–49), and Murphy, "Ford, Patrick," n.p. See also Ní Bhroiméil, "Presidents, Protection, and Politics," 154–55.

8. Janis, *Greater Ireland*, 122. Rodechko, *Patrick Ford*, 86. The quote is taken from Janis, *Greater Ireland*, 116.

9. Murphy, "Ford, Patrick," n.p.

10. Rodechko, *Patrick Ford*, iv; Ford is quoted on 56.

11. Ibid., 197; Janis, *Greater Ireland*, 135–36 (includes quote), 121–22. For the Land League, Ford set up some twenty-five hundred branches in the US and by 1882 had raised about $343,000 for the league. The *Irish World* did not miss any opportunity to boast about Ford's accomplishments as a fundraiser, for example by frequently including letters of thanks in which the editor was lauded as Ireland's protector. Rodechko points out that in the 1880s already, the *Irish World* was very active in claiming and stimulating respect for Ford and his paper in relation to the success of the Irish Land League (*Patrick Ford*, 186, 44). For examples of the many pieces in the *Irish World* appreciative of Ford's actions, see Michael Davitt's letters "Distressed Districts of Ireland," June 18, 1898, 5, and "Davitt's Answer on Coercion," November 12, 1898. In the latter, Davitt calls Ford "my good friend" (1, 9).

12. Rodechko, *Patrick Ford*, 26, 91, 199, vi, 215. See chapter 5 in Janis, *Greater Ireland*, 112–36.

13. Rodechko, *Patrick Ford*, 187; O'Donnell, "Though Not an Irishman," 415, 416; Ford is quoted on 416.

14. Murphy, "Ford, Patrick"; Janis, *Greater Ireland*, 118. Quote from O'Donnell, "Though Not an Irishman," 416. Rodechko, *Patrick Ford*, 89–90, 142.

15. "Distress in Ireland," April 2, 4.

16. Ibid.; "People of Ireland Demand Unity," January 14, 1899, 1.

17. *Philadelphia Ledger* quoted in "Irish Land Bill," April 4, 1903, 2.

18. Mitchel, *Ireland since '98*, 124.

19. Ó Gráda, *Black '47 and Beyond*, 124.

20. Quotes from Nally, "That Coming Storm," 714, 733. Kelleher, "Irish Famine," 89. On pages 89–90 of her essay, Kelleher provides a useful summary of revisionist scholarship on food exports and government relief. For biopolitics, also see O'Neill, *Famine Irish*, 21.

21. Sen, "Political Economy of Hunger," 351. See also Sen's *Poverty and Famines*.

22. "Robert Ellis Thompson, 1844–1924," n.p.; Bossard, "Robert Ellis Thompson"; quote from Hepburn, "Robert Ellis Thompson," 22.

23. Bossard, "Robert Ellis Thompson," 239.

24. Austin, "Address," 4.

25. "Robert Ellis Thompson, 1844–1924," n.p. Bossard, "Robert Ellis Thompson," 240–42; the quote is taken from Bossard, 241–42. Thompson held the first professorship in social science created in the US. During his memorial meeting, Thompson was described as having a "deep spirituality" (Montgomery, "Address," 8). McDevitt, "Address," 11–12.

26. Bossard, "Robert Ellis Thompson," 241; "Robert Ellis Thompson, 1844–1924"; Hepburn, "Robert Ellis Thompson," 22.

27. Thompson, *Social Science and National Economy*, 59, 60.

28. Lord Dufferin quoted in ibid., 59–60, 315.

29. Thompson, "Most Distressful Country," *Irish World*, December 24, 1904, 5; "Irish Dispersion," *Irish World*, October 3, 1903, 5.

30. Hepburn, "Robert Ellis Thompson," 23.

31. Thompson, "Most Distressful Country," 5; Janis, *Greater Ireland*, 55.

32. Sen explains the entitlement approach to famine in *Poverty and Famines*; see especially chapter 5.

33. Gonne, "Ireland To-Day," *United Irishman*, September 28, reprinted in Steele, *Maud Gonne's Irish Nationalist Writings*, 81.

34. Bossard, "Robert Ellis Thompson," 244; Thompson, *Social Science and National Economy*, 31.

35. Boylan and Foley, *Political Economy*, 130, 114.

36. Bigelow, *Fiction, Famine, and the Rise of Economics*, 4.

37. Boylan and Foley, *Political Economy*, 2–3, 2, 8.

38. Thompson, "Modern Cannibalism," August 13, 1898, 4.

39. Davitt, "Objections and Principles Good," 4. In *Special Sorrows*, Matthew Frye Jacobson explores reactions in the Irish American press to America's foreign policy around the turn of the twentieth century. See especially chapters 4 and 5.

40. "South Africa Another Ireland," 6.

41. "Republican Revolt," 1, 6. Ní Bhroiméil argues that the *Irish World* still saw "the primacy of Britain in the evil canon of imperialism as unsurpassed" and felt that newer colonizing powers were learning from Britain ("Presidents, Protection, and Politics," 175).

42. "West's Awake!," 1; "On the Rock of Cashel," 1, 6.

43. See, for example, "England Wants the Earth," January 4, 1896, 5.

44. Thompson is described as an "ardent protectionist" by Hepburn ("Robert Ellis Thompson," 23); Thompson quoted in Bossard, "Robert Ellis Thompson," 248. Ní Bhroiméil writes that during the period 1890–1913, according to the *Irish World*, isolationism and economic nationalism were two core US principles ("Presidents, Protection, and Politics," 179).

45. "England and Young Africa," July 29, 1848, 6.

46. Rouse, "Donahoe, Patrick," n.p.

47. Mohanty, "Orissa Famine of 1866," 55.

48. All newspaper article quotes in this paragraph are from "Famine in India and Ireland," February 23, 1867, 12. Morash discusses representational fragmentation of the body in "Famine/Holocaust." The eating of grass and nettles is repeatedly referred to in representations of the Irish Famine; for a literary rendering, see William Carleton's story "Fair Gurtha; or, The Hungry Grass," which appeared in the *Dublin University Magazine: A Literary and Political Journal* in 1856 and was reprinted in the *Irish-American* in 1876. See also Ó Gráda, *Eating People Is Wrong*, 36. On the (assumed) practice of cannibalism and its use in a metaphorical sense with regard to the Irish Famine and periods of famine elsewhere, see Ó Gráda, *Eating People Is Wrong* (especially chap. 1).

49. Mishra et al., "Drought and Famine in India," 2079.

50. "Famine in India," 1.

51. "Ireland and the Indian Famine," 1.

52. "Indian Famine," 1.

53. Mishra et al., "Drought and Famine in India," 2077–78.

54. All quotes are taken from "The Foreign Secretary," "Foreign Notes: Piracy in Africa and Famine in India," January 6, 1 (emphasis in original).

55. "Murderous British Rule in India," 4.

56. Gonne, "Her Subjects," *United Irishman*, April 21, 1900, 5. Gonne drew links between Ireland and India on the basis of a shared struggle for independence (Steele, *Maud Gonne's Irish Nationalist Writings*, 161). The analogy had an even longer life, as Kelleher has demonstrated that links between the Bengal famine of 1943–44 and the Great Irish Famine were drawn as well. See Kelleher, *Feminization of Famine*, chapter 4 especially.

57. Burge McAlpin, *Subject to Famine*, 208. Mishra et al. write that the 1896–97 famine affected 69.5 million people and caused the deaths of 5 million ("Drought and Famine in India," 2079). See Brewis on the relief fund ("Fill Full," 899).

58. Whately, *Introductory Lectures on Political Economy*, 124.

59. Thompson, "Free Trade," 5.

60. Ibid.

61. Trevelyan, "Letter of Charles Edward Trevelyan."

62. Mitchel, *Ireland since '98*, 152.

63. Thompson, "Free Trade," 5.

64. Thompson, "Most Distressful Country," 5. Thompson in Devoy et al., "Irish Comments on an English Text," 298. In 1884, Thompson wrote: "That a diversified industry is necessary to the national well-being, has been conceded by free-trade authorities from Adam Smith's time till our own" (Thompson in Roach, Thompson, and Dingley Jr., "Benefits of the Tariff System," 391). Thompson used the phrase "perennial hunger and recurrent famine" often. See, for example, his contribution to Devoy et al., "Irish Comments on an English Text," 297, and "Most Distressful Country," where he described Ireland's condition using the phrase.

65. Thompson, "Free Trade," 5.

66. "England and India," *Irish World*, September 4, 5. To criticize sole reliance on farming in Ireland, Thompson wrote: "The root of Irish misery—as all impartial observers, free traders not excepted, are now coming to agree—is to be found not in over-population, not in a bad land system, not in faults of creed or character of the Irish people, but in the absence of anything but farming to employ the people. . . . If the land were divided among its people it would give them only $14.00 worth a head, and its ownership would not suffice to put a stop to perennial hunger and recurrent famine" (Thompson in Devoy et al., "Irish Comments on an English Text," 297). And when arguing for the benefits of protectionism for Ireland, Thompson stated that "the Free Traders simply despair of the future of the island; Protectionists have a well-founded confidence that the method of protection to home industry, which lifted America from sinking into a similar slough in 1783–89, would be the economic salvation of Ireland" (ibid.).

67. On May 12, 1900, Gonne also spoke of "a chronic state of famine in India" ("India," reprinted in Steele, *Maud Gonne's Irish Nationalist Writings*, 169).

68. Mishra et al., "Drought and Famine in India," 2079.

69. Ricoeur, *Time and Narrative*, vol. 3, 186.

70. Gonne, "India," reprinted in Steele, *Maud Gonne's Irish Nationalist Writings*, 171.

71. Lloyd, "Indigent Sublime," 161. Additionally, Cusack demonstrates that the concept of silence has a similar function to unrepresentability in Irish famine discourse and paradoxically became an oft-used trope ("Memory, History, and Identity," 50).

72. Morash, *Hungry Voice*, 37.

73. In "popular representation," "informants draw on a repertoire of images, motifs, and short narrative, many of which . . . are part of a wider international narrative repertoire" (Ó Ciosáin, "Famine Memory," 102). I discuss Ó Ciosáin's distinctions between the local, popular, and global in more detail in the introduction. The reference to Count Ugolino again ties in with cannibalism, as in the *Inferno*, Dante consigns him to hell for having eaten his own children, among other crimes. Ó Gráda points out that forensic DNA analysis of the real thirteenth-century count has since absolved him of cannibalism (*Eating People Is Wrong*, 18). Saglia, "From Gothic Italy," 76. Keary, *Castle Daly*, vol. 3, 1–2.

74. Thompson, "Free Trade," 5.

75. Mitchel felt that Black slaves in Brazil were "merchantable slave[s]" who had a much better life than the slaves he saw back home, for at least the former had "real money value" (*Jail Journal*, 170).

76. Mayer, "Murder Famine of '48," n.p.

77. Humphrey Desmond of the *Catholic Citizen* quoted in Jacobson, *Special Sorrows*, 149. Jacobson explains this "Ireland first" rhetoric in chapter 4 of his book (see especially 148–50). He also includes Ford in this discussion, as Ford acknowledged that there were enough horrors happening in wartime Cuba but argued that in Ireland, "men women and children at this moment are enduring sufferings as great and as horrible as any recorded in our consular

reports from Cuba" while the country was officially at peace (Jacobson, *Special Sorrows*, 149–50).

78. "Famine in India and Ireland," 12. Quote from "India's Awful Visitation," February 20, 1897, 5.

79. Rothberg in Moses and Rothberg, "Dialogue on the Ethics," 32.

80. Rothberg, *Implicated Subject*, 175.

81. Levy and Sznaider, *Human Rights and Memory*, 4.

82. Margalit recognizes that morality, which establishes "human respect," can be afforded to those connected to us through what he calls "thin" relations. "Thick" relations are predicated on close relationships, such as kinship, friendship, and national ties; "thin" relations are based on the concept of a shared humanity (*Ethics of Memory*, 7).

CONCLUSION

Traveling Irish Famine Memories in
Transatlantic Periodical Culture

Temporalities: Medium, Memory, Aggregate

Through an exploration of periodical materials covering about seven decades and spanning the Atlantic, *Periodical Famines* demonstrates the extent to which famine memory from early on penetrated different strata of
Irish and Irish North American writings. This spread of famine memory is
illustrated from a quantitative perspective in chapter 1, which makes evident the period's presence in Irish and Irish North American periodical
and book publications for the full period this book covers. Additionally,
that chapter's tracing of the publication journeys of Annie Keary's, John
Mitchel's, and William Carleton's works shows that famine memory traveled in popular creative works and nonfiction between both sides of the
Atlantic and beyond, as evidenced by the European editions of Keary's and
Carleton's novels.

From the Famine onward, periodicals were an avenue of publication
that featured a diverse range of texts and visuals reaching vast and varied
audiences. Engagement with famine memory was not limited to specific
genres or modes of writing but happened in many different textual forms
and in both creative works and nonfiction, ranging from historical essays,
opinion pieces, and journalism to poetry and short and long prose fiction.
As chapter 1 on famine memory's global periodical infrastructure and the
case studies in chapters 2–7 reveal, periodicals were an especially popular outlet to engage with famine memory during later times of hardship

and struggle. Chapter 1 demonstrates the need to also consider the book publication market in this regard. It provides a combined view, which in this case focuses mostly on prose fiction and poetry but could be extended to nonfiction, further demonstrating the continuous presence of famine memory in the Irish transatlantic book and periodical markets.

In their representations of the Great Irish Famine, many of the periodical sources consulted for this book saw Irish life as marked by stasis or repetition. As I have argued, divergent temporalities were caused by the incompatibility of an Irish temporality—or even a temporality of the colonized more broadly, as chapters 6 and 7 suggest—and British imperial temporality. These temporalities often existed at the same time; their simultaneity has roots in real-world discrepancies and can be traced back to long-term issues within economic and political governance by the British Empire in Ireland and its colonies. More specifically, this coexistence of temporalities translated into the overlap of various organizing principles. British laissez-faire economics were at odds with the continuation of a precapitalist collective feudalism, leading to clashes between their respective temporalities. Moreover, such ordering structures affected the generic forms fiction took and the possibilities and future outlooks that came with these forms. For example, chapter 2 shows that during the 1880s, clashing temporalities were accompanied by tensions between the traditionalist parameters of the Big House narrative and national marriage plot and real-world future outlooks in which the establishment of a Catholic upper class in rural Ireland was fast becoming outdated.[1]

Imperial time can be seen as a form of institutional time, which is future-oriented and progressive. Nevertheless, as many of the Irish and Irish North American periodical writings discussed in *Periodical Famines* show, its application in Ireland can often be interpreted as paving the way for stasis or repetition. The temporal structure in which the Famine becomes embedded is informative regarding its status within Irish and Irish North American constructions of cultural memory. The different temporal constellations around famine memory found in Irish and Irish North American periodicals between the Famine and the early twentieth century demonstrate that within the transatlantic Irish community, discourse surrounding the Irish Famine and its impact had not yet solidified. The era *Periodical Famines* covers witnessed engagement with famine memory by second and third generations, which further contributed to the composite nature of this fund of memory and its perceived impact on Irish life at home and in diaspora. Different interpretations came with their own visions for the future and specific connections. Sometimes, transhistorical links were made; at other times, the diasporic or transnational potential of famine memory was utilized. Several sources combined temporal and geographic comparative dimensions: examples can be found in periodical contributions by Maud Gonne and Robert Ellis Thompson.[2]

What the Famine meant varied per outlook; to be sure, its gravity and human cost were acknowledged across different periodical outlets, but ideas of what the Famine could mean for present and future Irish lives at home and in diaspora were not uniform. Within the bounds of transatlantic Irish periodical culture, the coexistence of differing interpretations becomes especially visible, as well as when adopting a cotextual analytic lens and combining focus on creative works and nonfiction. Studying periodical contributions in isolation, or with a narrow focus on a specific author, genre, or another delineating concept, would result in a less varied understanding of the functions and presences of famine memory in transatlantic periodical culture. As a necessarily composite medium, the periodical does not facilitate a singular narrative. In the inclusion of different textual genres by a variety of contributors ranging from professionals such as editors, literary authors, and journalists to story prize competitors and letter writers, the periodical allows for the coexistence of a great many voices and discourses from different locations and periods. Reading "sideways" different periodical texts that engage with Irish famine memory shows that, although these texts taken together often work toward a specific set of ideological convictions that underscore the political coloring of a periodical, these voices and discourses do not necessarily cohere on the level of detail.[3]

The inherent plurality of the medium supports different functions and interpretations of famine memory and its historical contextualizations. Regarding recent commemorative culture and monuments to the Famine in a global context, Emily Mark-FitzGerald writes that "the legacy of the Famine in Ireland will never be resolved and neatly compartmentalized; nor should it."[4] As *Periodical Cultures* demonstrates, the simultaneously concluding and prescriptive sentence offered by Mark-FitzGerald holds true for transatlantic Irish periodical culture between the Famine and the early twentieth century as well. As both carriers and shapers of memories and identities, the magazines and newspapers investigated in this study suggest that between the mid-nineteenth and early twentieth centuries, cultural memories of the Famine should be considered an "aggregate" rather than a "shared" notion. Shared memory is an integrated form of memory in which different individual memories are recalibrated; aggregated memory consists of a collection of memories of people who have experienced or recollect a communal event or episode individually.[5]

From Temporalities to Cultural Trauma Discourse?

The consulted periodical materials show the existence of various interpretations of the starting point of temporal discord in Ireland, which do not lend themselves to a one-dimensional view. More specifically, Ireland's hunger-related hardships are seen either as a characteristic of Irish life before the Famine reaching a high point during the late 1840s or as heralded by the Famine. This discrepancy underscores that historical embedding of the Famine is not a given or an inherent characteristic of famine memory; rather, such decisions are an act of narration.[6] Between the mid-nineteenth and early twentieth centuries, we cannot speak of a consensus view on the Famine's historical placement or on Irish people's capabilities to grapple with the event. Some considered it so severe in its immediate and long-term impact that the period receives a disconnected, exceptional quality and exceeds conventional forms of representation. Many emphasized that the Famine was part of a longer line of colonial hardships, predating and succeeding the period and sometimes extending beyond Ireland's boundaries, which suggests continuity and historical embeddedness.

If the periodical materials had clearly indicated the Famine as the beginning of a divergent Irish temporality, this concordance would validate seeing the period as so disruptive as to constitute a cultural trauma in the Freudian sense, perhaps even a charter myth with regard to the Irish American community.[7] In problematizing the Famine as cultural trauma, Oona Frawley provocatively asks us to "consider *when* it is that the Famine became traumatic." My analyses support the argument that not only is the term "cultural trauma" a twentieth-century construct but also that applying the term and its connotations to the Irish Famine is an equally a posteriori phenomenon.[8]

On the basis of the periodical corpus, a stronger and more convincing argument can be made for considering foreign rule as the main disruptor to Irish temporality, society, demography, and progress. In that sense, the Famine is seen as an example of what results when British and Irish temporalities clash under the strain of imperial dominance. Seeing imperial policy as the root cause for the existence of discordant temporalities and the Famine as a manifestation—granted, an extreme manifestation—of the effects such clashes can have in the aftermath of a natural disaster more firmly roots the Famine in history, in a sequence of events. This historical embedding, in turn, complicates considering the Famine as atemporal and so exceptional that it comes to serve as cultural trauma. Indeed, although the newspapers and magazines analyzed in this book acknowledge that the Famine could be a traumatic event for the individual and that experiencing the Famine could impact communal responses to later events, grander claims of communal silence, repression, and amnesia that typically form the basis of the common cultural trauma paradigm are harder to find.

As a collective corpus, these transatlantic periodicals resist essentializing impulses connected to cultural trauma. Wulf Kansteiner finds fault with the term because it "conflates the experiences of victims, perpetrators and spectators of traumatic events." If we consider the proprietors, editors, authors, and contributors involved in transatlantic Irish periodical culture as part of the "carrier group" responsible for denoting the Famine's status and impact in the context of Irish identity formation, seeing Irish trauma as collective does not do justice to the plurality of interpretations expressed by this in-group.[9]

In the context of the historical periodical materials and authors discussed in this book, what seems necessary is a way to classify the Famine and its causes, impacting factors, and aftermath as more than just a demographically and socially disruptive event without tapping into the inherent psychoanalytic connotations of the label "cultural trauma." In this regard, David Lloyd's term "colonial catastrophe" seems appropriate. Lloyd writes that "the Famine was clearly not simply a natural disaster but the effect of intersecting vectors of social change that precede and succeed the years of starvation, but in radically different forms. . . . The horrific death-toll, the inevitable destruction and scattering of a people and of cultural formations incommensurable with modernity, becomes less a question of intentions than of the structural effects of colonialism itself. The Famine, whatever else we wish to say about its contours and meaning, must be seen as a colonial catastrophe."[10]

As I have written elsewhere, "colonial catastrophe" as a term acknowledges the root causes and great cost of the Famine while avoiding the undesired blanketing effect the term "cultural trauma" has in both theoretical and common parlance.[11] The concept of intersecting vectors moreover provides a parallel to the notion of coexisting, overlapping, and clashing temporal trajectories. While Lloyd's 2009 article reflects on the then-recent years of famine commemoration, *Periodical Famines* shows the validity of his term for the ways in which the Famine was remembered and famine memories were already (re)used in the postfamine nineteenth and early twentieth centuries. Suggestions of reparations—in financial or political form—for famine suffering certainly feature in Irish and Irish North American periodical writings, suggesting a wish for recovery, in more recent times typically seen as characteristic for how we deal with trauma. Nevertheless, the frequent use in periodicals of famine memory to foster transnational sympathy or empathy and to stimulate acts of philanthropy, and the antinostalgic use of that memory to envision and realize future change for the Irish at home and in the US, seems to suggest a wish for a "non-therapeutic relation to the past, focused on the notion of survival or living on, rather than recovery."[12]

Diasporic and Transnational Connections: Memories of the Irish Famine as Tools for Change

In exploring transnational connections forged through memories of the Irish Famine, *Periodical Famines* demonstrates the global dimensions of famine memory, thereby strengthening and extending the claims of scholars such as Cian T. McMahon and Pauline Collombier-Lakeman in novel ways. The examples in the previous chapters show that famine memory was not only crucial for the formation of Irish cultural identities and the defense of Irish rights at home and in diaspora; famine memories also functioned as significant discursive tools to provide meaning for hardships elsewhere, strengthening concomitant calls for labor rights in a US diasporic context and anticolonial criticism in a global sphere. By extension, transnational comparison demonstrates that Irish famine memory functioned as a means to establish affiliative connections premised on "social and political conviction, economic and historical circumstances, voluntary effort and willed deliberation," connections that traversed cultural groups and national boundaries.[13]

This study has shown that famine memory travels transnationally through its function as a premediational format. A representational storehouse of images related to the Irish Famine—including a focus on the fragmented body, mother and child victims, consumption of grass and herbs as famine foods, and Mitchelite interpretations of food provision and imperial economic relief policies—become transposed on situations elsewhere. Through this process of narrativization, the gravity of the Irish situation migrates and inflects how new events are understood. As such, the representational storehouse can be considered a transnational manifestation of a repertoire of temporally undefined famine imagery.

Rothberg provides an important point for critical attention in relation to acts of memory comparison. While multidirectional approaches are preferable to competitive discourses, such approaches run the risk of "downplaying historical heterogeneity." Moreover, in considering present events through the lens of a past event that took place elsewhere, "the present loses its potential as a locus of novelty." So, while cumulative transnational political rhetoric helps strengthen individual claims for the rectification of injustice, its combinatory nature can also serve to reduce difference to sameness for both the newer event or period and the older mnemonic referent.[14] The frequent use of an established repertoire of imagery for representations of the Great Irish Famine between the time of the event itself and the early twentieth century, as well as the threat of sameness inherent to the periodical format, arguably showcases that on the pages of Irish and Irish North American periodicals, famine memory indeed becomes universalized.[15] Famine memory loses its specificity through acts of cultural memory formation from an emic perspective, undermining a sense of uniqueness in suffering.

However, and more importantly, famine memory also gains a broader discursive and critical potential. While it is important to be aware of reductive pitfalls to acts of transnational comparison in recollection, this awareness should not refute the crucial positive potential of comparative uses of recollections of the Famine—or other historical catastrophes, for that matter. Writing his study "under the sign of optimism," Rothberg argues that acts of multidirectional memory can further the expression in the public sphere of memories previously relegated to marginal positions. He adds that a multidirectional approach harnesses "the legacies of violence in the interest of a more egalitarian future" and is "often the very grounds on which people construct and act upon visions of justice."[16]

In a similar vein, this book shows how Irish famine memory was used to bring examples of colonial suffering elsewhere to the attention of Irish and Irish-diasporic audiences. Such acts of comparison are inherently ethical as they are premised on instigating awareness and improvement of labor and human rights. Chapter 5 argues that the use of famine recollections in service of a diasporic argument to advance the prospects and living conditions of the Irish American urban poor displays a form of what Emilie Pine calls "anti-nostalgia." In its critical and productive character, comparative use of Irish famine memory in global anti-imperial contexts also displays an antinostalgic approach. Engagement with the Irish past maintains the inherent instability of the past and the catastrophic dimensions of the Famine because it maintains "the pedigree and authenticity of the Irish nation, forged in pain." At the same time, antinostalgia provides a potentially positive approach to what is yet to come, "a future-centric cultural outlook."[17] *Periodical Famines* shows how historical Irish hardships were enlisted in the service of positive change in the present and near future. Taking the future-centric antinostalgic perspective from Irish studies scholarship and combining it with the concept of multidirectionality from memory studies, *Periodical Famines* innovatively demonstrates that Irish famine memory had radical, transformative potential not only for the Irish themselves but also beyond Irish and Irish-diasporic communities and their futures. The book shows that this potential was acknowledged in periodicals from shortly after the occurrence of the Great Famine. The antinostalgic use of the Great Irish Famine in diasporic and transnational contexts opened new pathways, as the hardships of the past became the impetus of a potentially new anti-imperial temporality capable of breaking through stasis/repetition, of breaking temporal trajectories in which countries would stay famine countries.[18] This insight supports the connection between the transhistorical and transnational dimensions of the current study.

Through comparison, the devastation and magnitude of the Famine are acknowledged in a global context. The multiperspectivity offered by the political discourses in which the Irish Famine is integrated often goes beyond the boundaries of the singular text and does not confine itself to a narrow set of textual genres. Through fully recognizing cotextuality as a key characteristic of the periodical medium and adopting it as an analytic lens, *Periodical Famines* has shown that the historical periodical is the quintessential medium to show the multidirectional workings of Irish famine memory and chart how famine memory travels. Without an eye to cotextuality specifically, *Periodical Famines* would not only have failed to do justice to the nature of the periodical medium; essentially, it also would not have been able to fully explore the breadth and depth of combinatory rhetoric as provided conjunctly by news articles, poetry, opinion pieces, images, journalistic essays, sent-in letters, special correspondence, and prose fiction.

NOTES

1. On the overlap of ordering principles and their possibilities or "affordances" in the real world and in fiction, see Levine's *Forms*.
2. Mullen, *Novel Institutions*.
3. Hughes, "SIDEWAYS!"

4. Mark-FitzGerald, *Commemorating the Irish Famine*, 281.

5. Margalit, *Ethics of Memory*, 50–51.

6. Following Frederic Jameson, Rothberg points out that historical periodization "turns on the deployment of narratives" (*Multidirectional Memory*, 10).

7. Kelleher, "Hunger and History," 268; Janssen, "Diasporic Identifications."

8. Frawley, "Introduction," 10.

9. Kansteiner, "Genealogy of a Category Mistake," 193. The term "carrier group" as used here aligns with Alexander's terminology (*Trauma: A Social Theory*, 4).

10. Lloyd, "Colonial Trauma/Postcolonial Recovery?," 220, 221.

11. Janssen, "From Silence to Plenty."

12. Lloyd, "Colonial Trauma/Postcolonial Recovery?," 219–20.

13. Said, *The World, the Text, and the Critic*, 24–25.

14. Rothberg, "From Gaza to Warsaw," 538–39.

15. Mussell, "Repetition," 351.

16. Rothberg, *Multidirectional Memory*, 21, 19.

17. Pine, *Politics of Irish Memory*, 8.

18. Thompson, "Free Trade," *Irish World*, February 20, 1897, 5.

APPENDIX I:

Margaret Dixon McDougall, "A Tour through Ireland," *Daily Witness*, April 16, 1881

A Tour through Ireland.

Along a Mountain Road—Why the Rent Was Raised—
Turning Farms into Pastures—St. Colomb Kill—Taking
the Census—Aching for a Joke—Irish Hospitality
(From Our Own Correspondent.)[1]

Tarmon, March 28th.

The 26th rose sunny and cold, and I decided to hire a horse and guide to go to Derryveigh, made memorable by Mr. John George Adair.[2] The road lay through wild mountain scenery. Patches of cultivated fields lay on the slopes, hungry whin-covered hills rose all round them, steep mountains rank upon rank behind, deep bog lands full of treacherous holes lay along at the foot of the mountains here and there. The country is wild beyond description. Not a tree for miles in all the landscape. On some of the lower hills men were ploughing with wretched looking horses. Men were delving with spades where horses could not keep their footing. The houses were wretched, some only partly roofed, some with the roof altogether gone and a shed erected inside, but for the most wretched of all the hovels rent is exacted. Every bit of clearing was well and carefully labored. The high, broad stone fences round hillside fields were all gathered from the soil. At

223

one place, I was told that the brother of the occupant had sent him, from America, money to make the house a little more comfortable. He roofed it with slate. The rent was raised from £2 9s 4d to £13 10. I may remark here that the tenants complain that

THE PRESENT EARL,

through his agent Captain Dobbin, is even more oppressive in a steady, cruel manner than the late Earl. The late hard years, the cruel famine has led to the sacrifice of all stock, so that some of these people have not a four-footed beast on their holding. Another thing that is against Lord Leitrim's tenants just now, as the guide informed me on the road to Derryveigh, was this. When Lord Leitrim was murdered there was a disputed succession; there were three who claimed heirships. The people were afraid to pay their rent for fear of being required to pay it over again. Then the hard years and the famine came and they sacrificed everything to live. Now the arrears are against them, the cost of eviction processes, they are sued for the seed given to them a year ago, and there is so little with which to [illegible] all this that they are dreadfully worried.

As we wound along among the hills my guide spoke of getting another man to accompany us, who was well acquainted with the way to Derryveigh, and we stopped at his place accordingly. He came to the car to explain that he was busy [illegible] up corn or he would be only too glad to come. In a subdued whisper he told my guide of Captain Dobbin having been at his house, with his bailiffs and body-guard of police, threatening the wife, he said. He then told of the sacrifices he had made of one thing and another to gather up one year's rent. He had to pay five shillings for cutting turf on his own land, and one shilling for a notice served on him. Poor little man, he had a face that was cut out for mirthfulness, and his wofulness [sic] was both touching and amusing. So we left him and went our way.

Along the road winding up and down among the hills, by sudden bogs and rock crags still more desolate and lonely looking. We came upon a cultured spot, now and then, where a solitary man would be digging around the edges of the rocks. Again we were among wild mountains heaving up their round heads to the sky and looking down at us over one another's shoulders. It brought to my mind the Atlantic billows during the last stormy February. It is as if the awful rolling billows mounting to the sky were turned into stone and fixed there, and the white foam changed into dark heather. After driving some time the landscape softened down into rolling hills beautifully cultivated, and sprinkled here and there with grazing cattle. We are coming to Gartan lake, and where there is a belt of trees by the lake shore stands the residence of Mr. Stewart,

ANOTHER LANDLORD,

He, when cattle became high-priced, thought that cattle were much preferable to human beings, so he evicted gradually the dwellers who had broken in the hills, and entered into possession, without compensation, of the fields, the produce of others' toil and sweat. His dwelling is in a lonely, lovely spot, and it stands alone, for no cottage home is at all near. He has wiped out from the hill sides every trace of the homes of those who labored on these pleasant fields and brought them under cultivation. Since the Land League agitation began he has given a reduction of rents, and the whole country side feels grateful and thankful. There is no solitude so great that we do not meet bailiffs at their duty, or policemen on the prowl. Stopping to enquire the way from a solitary traveller, my guide began in Irish to sympathize with him of some great sorrow, when the man burst into tears and walked on without a word. He had just lost his wife, who left him with a large small family and new-born twins. He is one of Mr. Adair's shepherds. We are now nearing Derryveigh. There are two lakes lying along the valley connected with a small stream. My guide informed me that both lakes once abounded with salmon. The celebrated St. Colomb Kill was born on the shores of the

GARTAN LAKE.

Being along the lake one day he asked some fishermen on the lower lake to share with him of the salmon they had caught. They churlishly refused, and the saint laid a spell on the waters, and no salmon comes there from that day to this. They are plentiful in Upper Gartan Lake, and come along the stream to the dividing line, where the stream is spanned by a little rustic bridge; here they meet an invisible barrier, which they cannot pass. I told my guide in return the story of the Well of St. Keyne, but he thought it unlikely, so there is a limit to belief.

Since Mr. Adair depopulated Derryveigh, and gave it over to silence, the roads have been neglected, and have become rather difficult for a car. The relief works in famine time have been mainly road-making, and there are smooth hard roads through the hills in all directions, so the people complain of roads that would not be counted so very bad in the Canadian backwoods. However, the difficulty being of a rocky nature, we left our car at the house of a dumb man, the only one of the inhabitants spared by Adair. He and his sister, also dumb, lived together on the mountain solitudes. She is dead, and a relative, the daughter of one of the evicted people, has come to keep house for him. He made us very welcome, seeing to it that the horse was put up and fed with sheaf oats. I and my guides, for we were now joined by the man who had had the oats to fan; he had got his brother to take his place and came a short cut across the hills to meet us, so we all three set out to walk over Derryveigh.

It was a trying walk, a walk to be measured by ups and downs, for the Derryveigh hamlets were widely scattered. There they were, roofless homes, levelled walls, desolation and silence. My guides told me story after story of

THE WOES THAT FOLLOWED THE EVICTION.

How one man, Doherty, died behind a ditch, for no neighbor dare harbor him a night, or admit any of them under a roof for fear of eviction themselves. And this has been done; human beings have died under the protection of English law. Many of these people lost their reason and are in the asylum at Letterkenny. Some are still *coshering* here and there among their charitable neighbors yet, while many are bitter-hearted exiles across the sea. After walking up and down amid this pitiful desolation, and hearing many a heart-rending incident connected with the eviction, a sudden squall or hail came on, and we were obliged to take shelter on the lee side of a ruined wall till it blew over. To wile away the time one of the guides told me of a local song made on the eviction, the last line of each verse being "Five hundred thousand curses on cruel John Adair." I must get a copy of it. Here was I, an utter stranger, away in the wilds of Derryveigh with two strange guides. Well, they were both courteous and kind as gentlemen of the hills could be.

Across the Gartan Lake we could see from our partial shelter the point to which Mr. Steward wasted the people off his estate. Mr. Stewart's is a handsome lonely place, but when one hears all these tales of spoliation it prevents one from admiring a fine prospect. "He is dealing kindly with the people now," said my guides, "whatever changed his heart God knows." The shower being over we returned to the house of the dummy, who met me with warning gestures, for the ubiquitous policeman was following us from the hills. He turned out to be taking the census and followed us into the dummy's for that purpose. He was a nice-looking lad with the dandy air common to the force, and a mark near his eye as if he had been in a scrimmage. He did his duty and then lingered a little as if he were curious about us, and not sure what was his duty concerning us. It is very cold among the hills, and my hostess had filled a jar with hot water for my feet. The guides were half inclined to pretend to hide the jar to make the policeman suspect poteen. I wonder what misery could prevent Irishmen from joking. I rather suspect that there is illicit drinking going on among the mountains, though I saw no sign of it. In our absence,

DINNER

was prepared for us at the dummy's. She had not plates, but the table on which she laid out oat cakes was as white as snow. She gave us a little butter which, by the signs and tokens, I know to be all she had, boiled eggs, made tea of fearful strength, and told us to eat. My guides enjoyed the mountain fare with mountain appetites. I tried to eat, but somehow my throat was full of feelings. I had great difficulty to make this mountain maid accept of a two shilling piece for her trouble.

It was stated through the press that Mr. Adair traced the murderers of his employee, Mr. Murray, from where he was killed to the village of Derryveigh. This is altogether impossible. The way is long, across mountains and hill sides, and stony hollows covered with heather where a track either booted or barefooted could not be traced by any white man. We returned by the way we came to a point where we had a view of a rectory which was pointed out to me as the abode of another good rector. These people do seem to feel kindness very much. Here we took another road to visit Glenveigh and see Adair's castle.[3] On the way we were informed by a woman, speaking in Irish, that a process-server near Creeslach was fired at through the window of his house.[4] He had been out serving processes, and was at home sitting with his head resting on his hand. Three shots were fired, two going over his head and one going through the hand on which his head was resting. Two men are taken up to-day.

NOTES

In the title, McDougall refers to Saint Columbkille.

1. From the Montreal *Daily Witness*, April 16, 1881, 2. This reproduction has been derived from the digital version of the *Witness* newspaper, digitized by the Bibliothèque et Archives nationales du Québec, and can be freely accessed through the BAnQ website: https://numerique.banq.qc.ca/patrimoine/details/52327/3625856.

2. Derryveagh.

3. Glenveagh.

4. Creeslough.

APPENDIX 2:

Margaret Dixon McDougall, "A Tour through Ireland," *Daily Witness*, July 27, 1881

A Tour through Ireland.

Remembering the Great Famine—The "Planted"

Scotch Farmers—A Beautiful Edifice

(From Our Special Correspondent)[1]

Deciding that I would not take another post car to drive to Ballycroy, I returned to Mulraney again along the same road in the shadow of the mountains, leaving the prospective Land League meeting and Ballycroy behind me. On to Newport we drove, back over the road winding along the side of Clow Bay, and across the head of the bay through the lonely country back to Westport. The driver, a weather beaten man in a weather-worn drab coat, entertained me with tales of the clearances made in the famine time that left the country-side so empty. It is hard to believe that ever human beings were so cruel to other human beings in this Christian land, and that it passed unknown, or comparatively unknown, to the rest of the world. This man told, with a certain grim satisfaction, of what he called God's judgments which had fallen on

"EXTERMINATORS."

The common people of the West have a firm belief that God is on their side, no matter what trouble he allows to come over them. "Sure, I do feel my heart afire when gintlemen sit on my car driving through this loneliness an' talk of over-population." "Over-population! And the country empty!" I wish I could remember all this old man said, but I can only recall snatches here and there. It is most amazing to think that, when the world at large was sending help to save the Irish alive in the awful visitation, so many were throwing their tenants out on the road to die. And these people had by hard toil won a living here and paid rent. Every rood of this land, every cabin had helped to swell princely revenues, until the finger of God came down in famine and, then, when the revenue stopped, there was no pity, and it seemed to these poor people that there was no one that regarded. I do not wish to ever come to that time of life when I can hear of the scenes that wasted this country without feeling a passion of sorrow and regret. I spoke of these things to a worthy gentleman resident in another part of the country and he brushed it aside as if it were a fly, saying, "Oh, that is long past, thirty years and more." Memory is very strong among people who seem to have little to look forward to—the past seems the principal out-look. Every incident of the French landing here so far back as '98 is told to me in the west here with a freshness of detail as if it happened a few years ago; one can imagine, therefore, how the cruel evictions of the famine time fit themselves into the memory of the people, especially as the rush of fresh evictions are awaking all the horrors of the past. It seemed a gloomy satis-faction to this man to tell over what he considered

GOD'S JUDGMENTS

which had fallen on exterminators. He pointed out to me many who seemed doomed to be the last of their race. At last we passed the long dead wall which encloses the magnificent demesne of the Marquis of Sligo and drew up at Westport once more. The local papers which await me are full of Miss Gard-ner [Gardiner] and her war with her tenants—more evictions, emergency men from Dublin to hold possession—and all the rest. If ever the land Bill become law, if there is any relief contained in it which the educated cannot evade when contending with the ignorant, there will be few left comparatively speaking to receive the benefits of it. I wonder much at what a stronghold this lady Miss Gardner has, as yet, in the hearts of the people. Unmeasured is the abuse poured upon the head of Miss Pringle, who gets the weight of all the blame. If words of many syllables and of the strongest meaning which can be found in any dictionary had power to injure that same lady, she would be a sufferer. I was introduced by a Protestant clergyman to a gentleman con-nected with the executive of the law for a quarter of a century. He knows the heart-rending inner history of legal eviction. This gentleman has a wonderful tenderness in his heart for Miss Gardner. "Sure she grew up among us. The other one (Miss Pringle) found her as kindly a woman as was on God's earth and has made an ogre of her." I will give an extract or two out of the softest part of the statement he has drawn up for me. He tells of a landlord who evicted whole townlands in 1847. He hated the people because the famine swept over them. He became possessed with the same ideas as other landlords of this period, whose income had diminished through the visitation of God, that if the present possessors were rooted out and the depopulated

LAND PLANTED WITH SCOTCHMEN

their skill and capital would prevent a recurrence of famine. Now it is a fact freely attested to me by clergymen of different denominations that the planted people of Mayo required help, and help to a very large amount, to keep them from starvation during the last scarcity. On many estates in Mayo and the adjoining parts of Sligo the Protestant population would have died of hunger but for the large help given both denominationally and otherwise. They could not have seeded their grounds but for seed freely given them. Fields in Mayo this season are lying bare because the wretched people are not able to get seed to put in the ground. Some of the planted people complained to me that though when they settled on their present lands they got them cheap, two shillings and sixpence an acre for wild land, yet as they improved their land the rent was raised to five, to seven and six, to fourteen, and now to over a pound an acre. These men also complained that they could not possibly exist at all during these last seasons and pay the rent which was laid on them in consequence of the improvements done by their own labor. I find by the most conclusive proof that a difference of religious belief did not enable the settlers any more than the natives to pay a rent that could not be produced from the soil. The desire to change the nationality and religion of his tenants was so strong in one landlord that, in the words of my informant, "A scene of ruthless havoc began among his tenantry. To stimulate the slowness of the crowbar brigade, he was known to tear down human habitations with his own hands. I remember these poor people standing in the market in

THOSE DARK DAYS OF FAMINE,

Having their bits of furniture for sale on the streets and there were none to buy. I have heard the wailing of men, women and children on the coach-top day after day, when these fortunate unfortunates were escaping from their native land forever, I saw those who could not go in the agonies of death in the fever sheds. These scenes happened over thirty years ago, but they will never be forgotten. Four large townlands, on which eighty homes had been, became a wilderness of grass and rank weeds. No Scotch were forthcoming for the wrecked farms. There was a Nemesis in store for him. His day of eviction came about, and in his troubles his tenants saw retribution. As charity kept some of his tenants alive, so he also was indebted to the charity of friends, and passed away to meet his tenants at a bar where high blood or aristocratic connections does not sway the Judge who sits on the throne of justice, nor does party prejudice blind his eyes. When Miss Gardner came of age it took all the property of her father to pay the money secured to her by her mother's settlement, and she entered into possession in his stead. Like Queen Elizabeth, whom Miss Gardner greatly resembles, she had in her youth known troubles; sympathy for these trials, so well known to the peasantry, made them receive her with open arms and open hearts. In the interval between

MISS GARDNER ENTERING INTO POSSESSION

and her coming under the influence of Miss Pringle she set herself to repair the havoc made by her predecessor, and was the idol of her tenantry. She was near neighbor to the model farm and orphanage presided over by the Scotch ladies. Philanthropy collected the vast sums which bought and stocked the model farm at Ballinglen. When their mode of managing matters there could be no longer hidden from the Presbyterian Church which they misrepresented, the mission came out largely indebted to these ladies. It took all the stock to pay off its indebtedness to one lady, and the farm itself to pay the other. It is the lady who got the farm as her share, that lives with Miss Gardner, and gets the credit of her every unpopular act. She has divided between her and her only friend in the dark days. This Scotch hag found her a kind-hearted woman, and has made her into an ogre." Some of this communication, the hardest of it, I shall reserve. Also several confirmatory anecdotes given me at Westport.

In mercy to the readers, I will only say that Miss Gardner has intense courage and an intellect of masculine strength, and resembles Queen Elizabeth in more ways than one. It is a great pity that she has not Queen Bess's popularity or care for her people.

WESTPORT

when I have time to look at it, is a very pretty town. Its buildings, its hotels and the warehouses on the quay look as if it once had an extensive and flourishing trade, or was prepared for and expecting it. There was, I am told, once a flourishing linen trade here, but it has gone to decay. The town is a little hollow, with pleasant and tree-crowned green hills rising all round it: at one side is the demesne of the Marquis of Sligo, which is open to the public. These grounds extend for miles, and are as beautiful as gorgeous trees, green grass, dark woods, waters that leap and flash, spanned by rustic bridges, can make them. There are winding walks leading through the green fields, under trees, into woods, up hill and down, into shady glens, where you might wander for miles and lose yourself in green-wood solitudes. Crowds of Westport folk, in the calm evening, saunter through the grounds and enjoy their beauty. I noticed a statue erected on one of the streets by the grateful Westporters to the memory of one of its departed inhabitants. None of the present inhabitants remember the good deeds for which he is so honoured as far as I could discover. The little town has a subdued expression of prosperity. You feel conscious that some business is going on that enables the inhabitants of the town to live comfortably and to dress respectably. You hear of the mills of the Messrs. Livingstone, of their business in trading and land-owning, until you are convinced that they are the centre round which this little world revolves. I had a lady pointed out to me here as being in such embarrassed circumstances, owing to the non-payment of rent, that her son was obliged to join the police force to earn a living. I heard also great sympathy expressed for another gentleman in Dublin who has many sons, whom he has brought up to do nothing, and who has been reduced by the strike against rent to absolute poverty. I am told that banks in Dublin are glutted with family silver left as security for loans. These people are to be pitied, for poverty is poverty in purple or in rags: but when poverty comes to actual want, it is still more pitiful. The Westporters' sympathies, as far as I had an opportunity of hearing, are more exercised on

THE EMBARRASSMENTS OF THE UPPER CLASS

than the wants of the lower. Mr. Smith, who shot his father's would-be assassins, is quite a hero in their eyes, and Mr. Smithwick, who shot a poacher, is also very popular because of it. He is said to allow the widow something a year. A lady remarked to me that the widow of the man who was shot was very fortunate to get such an allowance. "Do you think," I asked, "that she was glad to receive money to pay her for her husband's death?" "Of course," said the lady, "she would naturally feel sorry for losing her partner, but he never when alive brought her £20 a year." It is quite a treat to walk or drive through the Marquis of Sligo's demesne. There are some beautiful monuments of fine marble in a small burying ground close to a dilapidated church in the demesne. One in particular, a reproduction in modern sculpture of an ancient recumbent cross, is beautifully wrought in reddish marble. There is a fair white cross erected to a deceased Marchioness of Sligo, who seems to have been much beloved. Near to the demesne, indeed in a corner of the demesne, is a new church finished in a more costly manner and with greater elaboration of ornament than any church edifice which I have yet seen. The carvings round the different entrances are very fine, almost as fine and elaborate as lace work. The end of the church behind the platform is almost semicircular, and is panelled with arches of polished marble of a pale chocolate color, divided from each other by pillars of darker marble exquisitely carved. Above these panels are slabs of snow white marble,

EACH SLAB A PICTURE

of evangelist, or apostle, outlined after the manner of ancient pictures, in black and gold. Over these the ribbed roof with all its gilded arches comes to a point in a golden rose. Along the side walls are great slabs of the same white marble, row above row, each with its picture illustrating a parable of our Lord. Here the sower scatters the good seed, there the good Samaritan has the hereditary enemy of his people on his ass taking him to the inn to take care of him. Again there is a picture representing Lazarus rising from "the charnel grave" at the voice of the All Powerful. The worshippers here sit among pictured remembrances of the records of the mercies of our Lord. The embrasures of the doors are lined with tiles of the same beautifully polished white marble with arabesque patterns traced on them in black. The whole church is marvelously perfect and beautiful. A magnificent organ in remembrance of the Marchioness of Sligo, as recorded by a gilt inscription on it, adds harmony to all this beauty. Both the grand organ and the magnificently beautiful marbles were a gift of the Marquis of Sligo. I enquired where the marble used in these decorations came from. "From Italy," I was told. There is exquisite pink marble in Donegal, and green marble of every possible shade in Connemara. I wished that some of Erin's beautiful marbles had found a place in this gem of a church.

THE BEAUTY OF THIS LITTLE CHURCH,

the perfection of its finish from roof to floor, the rich windows, the doorways, triumphs of the sculptor's art, made me think of the descriptions I had read of the costly perfection of foreign churches. And it was foreign in a sense, for the workmanship and material which made it so exquisite were foreign. I think the Irish marble very beautiful. The panels of the railing before the great altar in Sligo Cathedral were of green Connemara marble, and very beautiful it looked, its pale green shadings contrasting with the white dividing pillars. I had an intense longing to go back and get a second glimpse at the workmanship of this church. I felt like saying also to the Master, "Lord, behold what manner of stones and what buildings are here." I did not manage to spare time to go back for another look, but I heard a sermon there on the Sabbath Day. I heard the grand tone of the organ that blends with its notes a plea for remembrance of the dead and gone great lady. I heard also some good singing. The congregation were dressed, to match the church, faultlessly. There were some very handsome ladies handsomely attired. The people looked wealthy, authoritative, official. I composed myself and listened with keen enjoyment, feasting both eyes and ears. A colony of young jackdaws in the steeple, or the surrounding trees, began to make fun of us, and were hushed by discordant scoldings from the wiser and more respectful elders. The loveliest building which I have seen yet in my four months' sojourn here is undoubtedly the little church in Westport, Mayo, enriched by the costly gifts of the Marquis of Sligo.

Note

1. From the Montreal *Daily Witness*, July 27, 1881, 2. This reproduction has been derived from the digital version of the *Witness* newspaper, digitized by the Bibliothèque et Archives nationales du Québec, and can be freely accessed through the BAnQ website: https://numerique .banq.qc.ca/patrimoine/details/52327/3625941.

APPENDIX 3:

Robert Ellis Thompson, "Free Trade Slays Millions," *Irish World and American Industrial Liberator*, February 20, 1897

FREE TRADE SLAYS MILLIONS

—

It Would Require the Extirpation of the Whole Armenian Race to Equal the Mortality of the Anglo-Indian Famine of 1876–78

—

AND THAT OF THIS YEAR WILL BE EVER MORE DESTRUCTIVE!

—

This Was the Tragedy Enacted Fifty Years Ago in Myriads of Cabins in Ireland.

—

THE LONDON "TIMES" BLAMES PROVIDENCE.

—

English Greed, Which Destroyed the Resources of the People of India, the Root of It All.

—

UNIFORMITY OF OCCUPATION THE FINAL CAUSE.

—

One-Fifth of the People of India Go Hungry All the Year Round.

—

MANUFACTURES THE FIRST SAFEGUARDS AGAINST FAMINE

—

(IRISH WORLD STAFF CORRESPONDENT.)[1]

—

The awful realities of an Indian famine are once more tugging at the heart strings of the human race. There is but one calamity in the world fit to be named beside it, and that one is a famine in China. The disasters which attend great floods, vast earthquakes, volcanic eruptions, and the rest destroy but a few lives, as compared with a great famine, and that with relatively little pain. The Christian world, outside the diplomatic circles of a few European governments, was horrified by the wholesale slaughter of innocent and unarmed Armenians which the Turks have perpetrated during the last few years. But it would require the extirpation of the whole Armenian race to equal the mortality of the Indian famine of 1876–78, and that of the present year is certain to prove more destructive than even that was.

It Would Take a Dante to Picture Its Horrors

It would take a Dante to depict the horrors of death by starvation, when the parents see their children pine away in suffering and sit powerless to help or deliver those for whose lives they gladly would give their own. Day after day passes and the terrible blending of pain with weakness grows more poignant. Broken and unrefreshing sleep brings dreams of food, which make the needs of waking hours only the more bitter. First, the feeblest, sickliest, and therefore most loved, of the poor children succumb; then the others follow one by one, the living having no strength to bury out of their sight their dead, whom they are soon to follow in death. At last the home is a charnel house and the pitying, but enfeebled, neighbors put down its poor ruins over the occupants as the only means they have of burying them.

That Was the Tragedy Enacted Fifty Years Ago in Myriads of Irish Cabins.

That was the tragedy which was enacted fifty years ago in myriads of Irish cabins in that terrible Winter. Dante has portrayed the tragedy which gave one building in Pisa—the Tower of Hunger—its terrible associations. One wicked noble there shut up another there with his grandsons and left them to perish of hunger; and the old man's heart broke as his loved ones cried to him for bread. Misgovernment sowed these towers of hunger broadcast over Ireland then, as it is sowing them broadcast over India now. Hundreds of thousands have perished already, and yet the terrible harvest is but beginning.

The Times Says Providence, Not England, Is to Blame.

Sir William Wederburn, in the English House of Commons, has moved an inquiry into the causes of such famines, to the great indignation of the

Times and other representatives of officialdom. To the Times the cause is as clear as can be. Under the beneficent rule of England population in India has grown so fast that it has outrun the means of subsistence, and when providence chooses to send a drought the surplus must die, unless the generous aid of Government and of individuals interferes. It is a sign of moral growth that the Times allows of the interposition of Government to check the ravages of famine. Fifty years ago those who started from such premises were logical. They declared against any Government interference with the laws of this "Providence" of theirs, and censured individuals for the weakness of aiding those whom natural law had sentenced to extinction. Now the Times only blames Providence for the evil and proposes to correct its blunders—to use no stronger word—out of the generosity of the English rulers of India and the rest of mankind.

English Greed the Cause of It All.

It is not Providence which has sentenced millions of the Hindoos to die of a lingering and painful death this Winter. It is human misrule. It is the English greed, which destroyed the resources of the Indian people, for the sake of a profit to their own manufacturers and traders, and which has left the country without a single resource if the yearly rains of the wet season do not fall. It is that England may prosper that India is thus exposed to the perils of famine and the plague which follows in the wake of famine, as dysentery and typhus following in Ireland in those black and terrible winters of my boyhood. Almost the earliest of my childish recollections is the pleading of poor mothers for a mouthful of wholesome food for their sick children, and I am proud to be the son of one who so spent his substance to save his poor neighbors from their fate, that, financially, he never could get on his feet again.

Uniformity of Occupation Is the Ultimate Cause.

It showed the right spirit in Sir William Wederburn to raise the question: "Why should such calamities mark our humane and beneficent rule in India?" But he need not have called for a fresh investigation: the matter has been probed to the bottom before this. More than ten years ago a Famine Commission reported in India. It was made up chiefly of English servants of the Crown. It made a report which was signed by every Commissioner. It stated the plain truth that the final cause of Indian famines is the uniformity of occupation among its people, and that their recurrence must be expected until the means were found to divert a fair share of the people from agriculture to manufacture. But it went on to say that, of course, the commission did not advocate a protective tariff for India. It only wanted the end, but not the means to that end!

So far as I could learn at the time, the report was received with entire indifference. The poor space of seven years which had elapsed since the Hindoos were dying by millions was enough to destroy all interest in the subject. It was only in America that the report got even a fair notice and was treated as an important document. And now it is so far forgotten that Sir William Wederburn, although kindly disposed toward the Hindoos, appears never to have heard of it, and knows nothing of its sane suggestions. His own plan is to induce or compel the village communities to insure themselves against famine by storing away food or money in good years. He is not aware that they are all underfed now, and that one-fifth of them, the report says, are hungry the round year. [*sic*]

Manufactures Are the First Safeguards against Famines.

Manufactures are the first safeguards against famine—the indispensable safeguard in a country as densely populated as India now is, or even as it was in the days of the English invasion. At that date the country had plenty of manufacturing industry. Nearly the whole population in many districts took part in the manufacture of cotton fabrics which India was supplying to the world. But England crushed out these manufactures by breaking down the India tariff in 1804, and thus driving the millions of its people to agriculture as the only staff of life. That made India under English rule a famine country, although it never had been such under any of its previous rulers. That made the question of annual rainfall a question of life or death for millions of the people.

It is true that the authorities in both India and England are now awake to the awful peril of their Hindoo subjects. But the evil has gone too far to be met and remedied without frightful loss of life. The country is but poorly supplied with railroads. The natives are so closely attached to their own hearthstones that they cannot be got to travel any considerable distance, even by the peril of death from starvation. Food cannot be got to them by any human agency in time to save the lives of hosts of sufferers. But neither should it have been necessary to effect this. India, if wisely governed, and for the good of its own people, would have no such insoluble problem for its rulers to solve.

ROBERT ELLIS THOMPSON.

NOTE

1. From *Irish World and American Industrial Liberator*, February 20, 1897, 5. This reproduction was derived from the collections of the Boston Public Library.

APPENDIX 4:

Chronological List of Creative Works That Contain Famine

This list contains titles that refer to the Great Irish Famine and/or other episodes of famine in Ireland, including more general mentions of famine. That being said, the titles predominantly refer to the 1840s Famine.[1]

The list is a compilation of works of poetry and prose fiction found during online and on-site archival research for *Periodical Famines* and from the following sources (in alphabetical order):

- Marguérite Corporaal, *Relocated Memories of the Great Famine in Irish and Diaspora Fiction, 1847–70*
- Christopher Cusack, PhD diss., "Memory, History, and Identity in Irish and Irish-Diasporic Famine Fiction, 1892–1921"
- Charles Fanning, *The Exiles of Erin: Nineteenth-Century Irish-American Fiction*
- Charles Fanning, *The Irish Voice in America: 250 Years of Irish-American Fiction*
- Melissa Fegan, *Literature and the Irish Famine 1845–1919*
- Lindsay Janssen, PhD diss., "Famine Traces: Memory, Landscape, History and Identity in Irish and Irish-Diasporic Famine Fiction, 1871–91"
- Margaret Kelleher, *The Feminization of Famine: Expressions of the Inexpressible?*
- Rolf and Magda Loeber, with Ann Mullin Burnham, *A Guide to Irish Fiction 1650–1900*

- Christopher Morash, *The Hungry Voice: The Poetry of the Irish Famine*
- Christopher Morash, *Writing the Irish Famine*

For full bibliographic details, please consult the bibliography.

When a title was published by multiple publishers in the same year and has no known earlier publications, I indicate "first publication" for all publications of that title in that year (see, for example, Charles Lever's *The Martins of Cro' Martin* in 1856). When a periodical serialization of a title spans multiple years, each year is counted as one publication. When a title is published in multiple locations in the same year, each place is counted as one publication. If not all publication details can be provided, I indicate where I encountered the work in the comments column. Poetry is indicated with regular text; prose is indicated in **bold.**

Note

1. For a digital version of this list, please consult my website: https://lindsaybjanssen.wordpress.com/.

Chronological List of Creative Works That Contain Famine

Year of publica-tion	Author	Title	Publ. details	Publ. location	First publ. or republ.	Publ. in periodical or book	Comments
1845	Ellen Mary Patrick Downing	The Sleeping Warriors	*Nation* 4, no. 162 (Dublin, Nov. 15)	Ireland		Periodical	
1845	William Pembroke Mulchinock	The Famine, the Fever, and the Priest	*Nation* 4, no. 162 (Dublin, Nov. 15)	Ireland		Periodical	
1846	Anon.	The Potato Crop, 1846	*Illustrated London News* 9, no. 244 (Aug. 29)	England		Periodical	
1846	William Carleton	***The Black Prophet: A Tale of Irish Famine***	*Dublin University Magazine*	Ireland	First publ.	Periodical	
1846	Ireland	**Narrative of Malcolm McGregor**	*Northern Star* (Oct. 17–Dec. 16)	Ireland		Periodical	
1846	James Clarence Mangan	The Warning Voice	*Nation* 4, no. 176 (Dublin, Feb. 21)	Ireland	First publ.	Periodical	
1846	James Clarence Mangan	Siberia	*Nation* 4, no. 184 (Dublin, Apr. 18)	Ireland	First publ.	Periodical	
1846	James Clarence Mangan	The Peal of Another Trumpet	*Nation* 4, no. 186 (Dublin, May 2)	Ireland	First publ.	Periodical	
1846	James Clarence Mangan	The Peal of Another Trumpet	*Pilot* 9, no. 23 (Boston, Jun. 6)	United States	Republ.	Periodical	
1846	William Pembroke Mulchinock	The Famine	*Nation* 4, no. 178 (Dublin, Mar. 7)	Ireland		Periodical	
1847	Anon.	The Song of the Famine	*Dublin University Magazine* 30, no. 175 (Jul.). London: Hurst and Blackett.	England, Ireland	First publ.	Periodical	
1847	Anon.	**The Widow O'Leary: A Story of the Present Famine**	Cork: G. Nash	Ireland		Book	
1847	William Carleton	***The Black Prophet: A Tale of Irish Famine***	*Dublin University Magazine*	Ireland	First publ.	Periodical	

(continued)

Chronological List of Creative Works That Contain Famine (*continued*)

Year of publication	Author	Title	Publ. details	Publ. location	First publ. or republ.	Publ. in periodical or book	Comments
1847	William Carleton	***The Black Prophet: A Tale of Irish Famine***	London and Belfast: Simms and M'Intyre	England, Ireland	Republ.	Book	
1847	William Carleton	***The Black Prophet: A Tale of Irish Famine***	New York: Burgess, Stringer	United States	Republ.	Book	
1847	William Carleton	***De zwarte profeet: Een verhaal uit den tijd van den Ierschen Hongersnood***	Niewe Diep: C. Bakker	Netherlands	Republ.	Book	Dutch translation of *The Black Prophet*.
1847	William Carleton	**A Middleman Magistrate of the Old School and His Clerk (from *The Black Prophet*)**	*Telegraph and Connaught Ranger*	Ireland	Republ.	Periodical	Excerpt.
1847	Chloe	Enigmatica: A Riddle	In *Enigmatica; or, Original Rhymes and Riddles*. Bideford: W. Cole	England		Book	
1847	C. C. T.	Untitled [Sketches in the West of Ireland]	*Illustrated London News* 10, no. 250 (Feb. 13)	England		Periodical	Part of famous article with illustrations by James Mahony.
1847	C. S.	The Famished Land	*Nation* 5, no. 224 (Dublin, Jan. 23)	Ireland		Periodical	
1847	Jane Elgee (Lady Jane Francesca Agnes Wilde, "Speranza")	The Stricken Land	*Nation* 5, no. 224 (Dublin, Jan. 23)	Ireland	First publ.	Periodical	Republished as "The Famine Year."

1847	Jane Elgee (Lady Jane Francesca Agnes Wilde, "Speranza")	France in '93: A Lesson from Foreign History	*Nation* 5, no. 233 (Dublin, Mar. 27)	Ireland	First publ.	Periodical
1847	Jane Elgee (Lady Jane Francesca Agnes Wilde, "Speranza")	A Supplication	*Nation* 5, no. 272 (Dublin, Dec. 18)	Ireland	First publ.	Periodical
1847	John De Jean Frazer	The Spring Flowers	*Nation* 5, no. 234 (Dublin, Apr. 3)	Ireland	First publ.	Periodical
1847	Mrs. Hoare	**A Sketch of Famine**	*Howitt's Journal* (London, Apr. 24)	England	First publ.	Periodical
1847	Ireland	***A Tale of Irish Famine in 1846 and 1847: Founded on Fact***	Reigate: William Allingham	England		Book
1847	Denis Florence MacCarthy	A Mystery	*Nation* 5, no. 245 (Dublin, Jun. 19)	Ireland	First publ.	Periodical
1847	Martin MacDermott	A Very Old, Old Man	*Nation* 5, no. 272 (Dublin, Dec. 18)	Ireland		Periodical
1847	James Clarence Mangan	Lamentation of Jeremias over Jerusalem	*Duffy's Irish Catholic Magazine* 1, no. 3 (Apr.)	Ireland		Periodical
1847	James Clarence Mangan	Pompeii	*Duffy's Irish Catholic Magazine* (Apr.)	Ireland		Periodical
1847	James Clarence Mangan	A Vision of Connaught in the Nineteenth Century	*Nation* 5, no. 250 (Dublin, Jul. 17)	Ireland		Periodical
1847	James Clarence Mangan	The Song of the Albanian: 1826	*Nation* 5, no. 254 (Dublin, Aug. 14)	Ireland		Periodical
1847	T. D. McGee	The Living and the Dead	*Nation* 5, no. 244 (Dublin, Jun. 5)	Ireland		Periodical

(continued)

Chronological List of Creative Works That Contain Famine (*continued*)

Year of publication	Author	Title	Publ. details	Publ. location	First publ. or republ.	Publ. in periodical or book	Comments
1847	Thomas D'Arcy McGee	Life and Land [The Famine in the Land]	*Nation* 5, no. 236 (Dublin, Apr. 17)	Ireland	First publ.	Periodical	
1847	Miro	Patrick's Day, 1847	*Nation* 5, no. 234 (Dublin, Apr. 3)	Ireland		Periodical	
1847	Richard D'Alton Williams	Kyrie Eleison, Christe Eleison!	*Duffy's Irish Catholic Magazine* 1, no. 2 (Mar.)	Ireland		Periodical	
1847	Richard D'Alton Williams	Dominica and Vesparas	*Duffy's Irish Catholic Magazine* 1, no. 5 (Jun.)	Ireland		Periodical	
1847	Richard D'Alton Williams	Vesper Hymn	*Duffy's Irish Catholic Magazine* 1, no. 7 (Aug.)	Ireland		Periodical	
1848	Anon.	How Shall We Hail the Spring?	*United Irishman* 1, no. 7 (Dublin, Mar. 25)	Ireland		Periodical	
1848	Anon.	The Plucking of the Shamrock	*Nation* 6, no. 286 (Dublin, Mar. 25)	Ireland		Periodical	
1848	Britannicus	Erin Go Bragh!	*Nation* 6, no. 297 (Dublin, Jun. 10)	Ireland		Periodical	
1848	William Carleton	***Der schwarze Prophet: Aus den Zeiten irisher Hungersnoth***	Dresden: Arnoldische Buchhandlung	Germany	Republ.	Book	German translation of *The Black Prophet* by Friedrich Gerstäcker.
1848	William Carleton	***The Emigrants of Ahadarra: A Tale of Irish Life***	London and Belfast: Simms and M'Intyre (Parlour Library, no. 11)	England, Ireland	First publ.	Book	

1848	Jane Elgee (Lady Jane Francesca Agnes Wilde, "Speranza")	The Enigma		*Nation* 6, no. 293 (Dublin, May 6)	Ireland	First publ.	Periodical
1848	Jane Elgee (Lady Jane Francesca Agnes Wilde, "Speranza")	The Voice of the Poor		*Nation* 7, no. 294 (Dublin, May 13)	Ireland	First publ.	Periodical
1848	Jane Elgee (Lady Jane Francesca Agnes Wilde, "Speranza")	Attendite Populæ		*Nation* 6, no. 295 (Dublin, May 27)	Ireland	First publ.	Periodical
1848	John De Jean Frazer	The Harvest Pledge		*Nation* 6, no. 301 (Dublin, Jul. 8)	Ireland		Periodical
1848	John Frazer	The Three Angels		*Cork Magazine* 1, no. 10 (Aug.)	Ireland		Periodical
1848	John Keegan	To the Cholera		*Cork Magazine* 2, no. 13 (Nov.)	Ireland		Periodical
1848	L.	Untitled [Mortality in Skibbereen]		*Illustrated London News* 10, no. 5 (Jan. 30)	England		Periodical
1848	James Clarence Mangan	A Voice of Encouragement: A New Year's Lay		*Nation* 6, no. 274 (Dublin, Jan. 1)	Ireland		Periodical
1848	James Clarence Mangan	A Vision: A. D. 1848		*United Irishman* 1, no. 3 (Dublin, Feb. 26)	Ireland		Periodical
1848	James Martin	A Dialogue between an Irish Agent and a Tenant		Dublin: privately printed	Ireland		Book
1848	Thomas D'Arcy McGee	A Harvest Hymn		*Nation* 6, no. 298 (Dublin, Jun. 17)	Ireland		Periodical
1848	William Pembroke Mulchinock	A Lament		*Cork Magazine* 2, no. 13 (Nov.)	Ireland		Periodical

(continued)

Chronological List of Creative Works That Contain Famine (*continued*)

Year of publication	Author	Title	Publ. details	Publ. location	First publ. or republ.	Publ. in periodical or book	Comments
1848	William Pembroke Mulchinock	The Old Story	*Cork Magazine* 2, no. 14 (Dec.)	Ireland		Periodical	
1848	Paul Peppergrass (John Boyce)	***Shandy M'Guire; or, Tricks upon Travelers, Being a Story of the North of Ireland***	New York: Edward Dunigan and Brother	United States	First publ.	Book	
1848	A. Southern	On the Death of the Rev. Robert Traill, D. D.	In *Lays for Patriots*. Dublin: Samuel B. Oldham	Ireland		Book	
1848	A. Southern	The Irish Emigrant's Farewell in the Famine Year	In *Lays for Patriots*. Dublin: Samuel B. Oldham	Ireland		Book	
1848	A. Southern	The Summer of 1847 in Ireland: The Second Famine Year	In *Lays for Patriots*. Dublin: Samuel B. Oldham	Ireland		Book	
1848	Richard D'Alton Williams	Lord of Hosts	*United Irishman* 1, no. 15 (Dublin, May 20)	Ireland		Periodical	
1849	Anon.	Thanatos, 1849	*Irishman* (May 5)	Ireland		Periodical	
1849	Anon.	Be Free	*Irishman* 1, no. 31 (Aug. 4)	Ireland		Periodical	
1849	Anon.	Lines Written the Day before the Queen's Arrival in Dublin	*Dublin University Magazine* 34, no. 201 (Sep.)	Ireland		Periodical	
1849	Anon.	***Paddy's Leisure Hour in the Poor House; or, Priests, Parsons, Potatoes and Poor Rates***	Dublin: Hodges and Smith	Ireland		Book	
1849	J. W. Bourke	Present and Future	In *Echoes from Parnassus: Selected from the Original Poetry of the Cork Southern Reporter*. Cork: Southern Reporter	Ireland	Republ.	Book	

1849	Jane Elgee (Lady Jane Francesca Agnes Wilde, "Speranza")	Foreshadowings	*Nation* 7, no. 2 (Dublin, Sep. 8)	Ireland	First publ.	Periodical
1849	Jane Elgee (Lady Jane Francesca Agnes Wilde, "Speranza")	The Itinerant Singing Girl	*Nation* 7, no. 19 (Dublin, Dec. 29)	Ireland		Periodical
1849	Samuel Ferguson	Dublin: A Poem	*Dublin University Magazine* 34, no. 199 (Jul.)	Ireland		Periodical
1849	Samuel Ferguson	Inheritor and Economist	*Dublin University Review*	Ireland		Periodical
1849	John De Jean Frazer	The Lost Labour	*Irishman* 1, no. 24 (Jun. 16)	Ireland		Periodical
1849	J. (possibly John De Jean Frazer)	The Queen's Visit	*Irishman* 1, no. 31 (Aug. 4)	Ireland		Periodical
1849	J. Frazer	The Artisan's Apology for Emigrating	*Irishman* 1, no. 38 (Sep. 22)	Ireland		Periodical
1849	J. Frazer	Extermination	*Irishman* 1, no. 40 (Oct. 6)	Ireland		Periodical
1849	Matthew Magrath	One of Many	*Irishman* 1, no. 25 (Jun. 23)	Ireland		Periodical
1849	James Clarence Mangan	The Funerals	*Irishman* 1, no. 13 (Mar. 31)	Ireland		Periodical
1849	James Clarence Mangan	The Famine	*Irishman* 1, no. 23 (Jun. 9)	Ireland		Periodical
1849	James Clarence Mangan	Siberia	*Nation* 2 (Dublin, new series, Sep. 8)	Ireland	Republ.	Periodical
1849	James Clarence Mangan	The Warning Voice	*Nation* 2 (Dublin, new series, Sep. 8)	Ireland	Republ.	Periodical
1849	Miro	Pro and Con	*Irishman* 1, no. 32 (Aug. 11)	Ireland		Periodical
1849	Margaret Percival	***The Irish Dove; or, Faults on Both Sides: A Tale***	Dublin: John Robertson	Ireland		Book

(continued)

Chronological List of Creative Works That Contain Famine (*continued*)

Year of publica-tion	Author	Title	Publ. details	Publ. location	First publ. or republ.	Publ. in periodical or book	Comments
1849	Margaret Percival	***The Irish Dove; or, Faults on Both Sides: A Tale***	London: Simpkin, Marshall & Co.	England		Book	
1849	John Thomas Rowland	The Battle of Antioch	*Irishman* 2, no. 2 (Jan. 12)	Ireland		Periodical	
1849	John Thomas Rowland	Tis Evening Now	*Irishman* 1, no. 46 (Nov. 17)	Ireland		Periodical	
1849	John Thomas Rowland	The Leaves Are Blighted	*Irishman* 1, no. 38 (Oct. 2)	Ireland		Periodical	
1849	Aubrey de Vere	Irish Colonization: 1848	*Dublin University Magazine* 34, no. 199	Ireland		Periodical	
1849	Richard D'Alton Williams	Implore Pace for Clarence Mangan	*Irishman* 1, no. 27 (Jul. 7)	Ireland	First publ.	Periodical	Later republished as "Lament for Clarence Mangan."
1849	T. C. D.	The Last Appeal	*Irishman* 1, no. 34 (Aug. 15)	Ireland		Periodical	
1849	James Tighe	The Boreen Side	*Irishman* 1, no. 39 (Sep. 29)	Ireland		Periodical	
1849	An Ulsterman	Advice	*Irishman* 1, no. 29 (Jul. 21)	Ireland		Periodical	
1850	Anon.	The Wanderer	*Nation* 7, no. 24 (Dublin, Feb. 9)	Ireland		Periodical	
1850	William Allingham	The Poor Little Maiden	In *Poems*. London: Chapman and Hall	England		Book	
1850	William Allingham	The Young Street Singer	In *Poems*. London: Chapman and Hall	England		Book	
1850	Anon. / W. C. B. (possibly William Carr Boyd)	Lay of the Famine: The Irish Husband to His Wife	*Irishman* 2, no. 9 (Mar.)	Ireland		Periodical	

Year	Author	Title	Source	Country	Note	Type	Comment
1850	Harriet Vaughan Cheney	**The Emigrants**	*Literary Garland* 8, no. 2	Canada		Periodical	
1850	Mrs. (Mary Anne) Hoare	**Little Mary**	*Household Words*	England	First publ.	Periodical	
1850	K.	A Christmas Chime for 1849	*Dublin University Magazine* 35, no. 205 (Jan.)	Ireland		Periodical	
1850	M. R. Leyne	The Dawning of Morning	*Nation* 7, no. 26 (Dublin, Feb. 23)	Ireland		Periodical	
1850	James Clarence Mangan	When Hearts Were Trumps	*Irishman* 2, no. 4 (Jan. 26)	Ireland		Periodical	
1850	M. B.	**Rose McCarthy's Sorrow**	*Literary Garland* 8, no. 10 (Montreal)	Canada		Periodical	
1850	John Walsh	Lament of the Ejected Irish Peasant	*Dublin University Magazine* 35, no. 205 (Jan.)	Ireland		Periodical	
1850	Richard D'Alton Williams	The Praise of Michaël	*Nation* 7, no. 29 (Dublin, Mar. 16)	Ireland		Periodical	
1850	Richard D'Alton Williams	Hand in Hand	*Nation* 8, no. 9 (Dublin, Oct. 26)	Ireland		Periodical	
1851	Anon.	**The Emigrant Ship**	*Literary Garland* 8, no. 11 (Montreal)	Canada		Periodical	
1851	William Carleton	***The Black Prophet***	Montreal: D. J. Sadlier	Canada	Republ.	Book	Information from advertisement Sadlier in *True Witness and Catholic Chronicle.*
1851	John De Jean Frazer	The Spring Flowers	In *Poems.* Dublin: McGlashan	Ireland	Republ.	Book	
1851	Mrs. (Mary Anne) Hoare	**The Black Potatoes**	In *Shamrock Leaves; or, Tales and Sketches from Ireland.* Dublin and London: J. M'Glashan, Patrick, and Oakey	Ireland, England	First publ.	Book	

(continued)

Chronological List of Creative Works That Contain Famine (*continued*)

Year of publication	Author	Title	Publ. details	Publ. location	First publ. or republ.	Publ. in periodical or book	Comments
1851	Mrs. (Mary Anne) Hoare	**Little Mary: A Tale of the Black Year**	In *Shamrock Leaves; or, Tales and Sketches from Ireland*. Dublin and London: J. M'Glashan, Patrick, and Oakey	Ireland, England	Republ.	Book	
1851	Mrs. (Mary Anne) Hoare	**A Sketch of Famine**	In *Shamrock Leaves; or, Tales and Sketches from Ireland*. Dublin and London: J. M'Glashan, Patrick, and Oakey	Ireland, England	First publ.	Book	
1851	H. D.	The Spectre	In *The Spectre: Stanzas with Illustrations*. London: Thomas M'Lean	England		Book	
1851	William Pembroke Mulchinock	Song of the Ejected Tenant	In *Ballads and Songs of W. P. M.* New York: T. W. Strong	United States		Book	
1851	Elizabeth Willoughby (Varian, "Finola")	Our Welcome	In *Poems by 'Finola.'* Belfast: John Henderson	Ireland		Book	
1851	Elizabeth Willoughby (Varian, "Finola")	Proselytizing	In *Poems by 'Finola.'* Belfast: John Henderson	Ireland		Book	
1851	Elizabeth Willoughby (Varian, "Finola")	The Tabinet Weaver	In *Poems by 'Finola.'* Belfast: John Henderson	Ireland		Book	
1852	William Carleton	***The Squanders of Castle Squander*, 2 vols.**	London: Office of the Illustrated London Library	England		Book	

Year	Author	Title	Place: Publisher	Country	Status	Format	Notes
1852	Henry J. Monahan	*O'Ruark; or, The Chronicles of the Balliquin Family*	Dublin: James Duffy	Ireland		Book	
1852	Henry J. Monahan	*O'Ruark; or, The Chronicles of the Balliquin Family*	London: Unknown	England	Republ.	Book	Mentioned in *Guide to Irish Fiction*.
1853	An Irishman	*Poor Paddy's Cabin; or, Slavery in Ireland*	London: Wertheim and MacIntosh	England	First publ.	Book	
1853	An Irishman	*Poor Paddy's Cabin; or, Slavery in Ireland*	Dublin: M'Glashan	Ireland	First publ.	Book	
1853	Miss Mason	*Kate Gearey; or, Irish Life in London: A Tale of 1849*	London: Charles Dolman	England		Book	
1853	Paul Peppergrass (John Boyce)	*Shandy M'Guire; or, Tricks upon Travelers, Being a Story of the North of Ireland*	Boston: Patrick Donahoe	United States	Republ.	Book	
1853	Father Hugh Quigley	*The Cross and the Shamrock*	Boston: Patrick Donahoe	United States	First publ.	Book	
1853	Father Hugh Quigley	*The Cross and the Shamrock*	Boston: Thomas Noonan & Co.	United States	First publ.	Book	
1853	Mrs. (Mary Anne) Sadlier	*New Lights; or, Life in Galway*	New York, Boston, and Montreal: D. and J. Sadlier	United States, Canada	First publ.	Book	The book was reprinted repeatedly at least until 1903; *Guide to Irish Fiction* is not specific about its reprints.
1853	Mrs. (Mary Anne) Sadlier	*New Lights; or, Life in Galway*	New York, Boston, and Montreal: D. and J. Sadlier	United States, Canada	First publ.	Book	

(continued)

Chronological List of Creative Works That Contain Famine (*continued*)

Year of publica-tion	Author	Title	Publ. details	Publ. location	First publ. or republ.	Publ. in periodical or book	Comments
1854	An Irishman	***Poor Paddy's Cabin; or, Slavery in Ireland***	London: Wertheim and MacIntosh	England	Republ.	Book	
1854	An Irishman	***Poor Paddy's Cabin; or, Slavery in Ireland***	Dublin: M'Glashan	Ireland	Republ.	Book	
1855	Charles Cannon	***Bickerton; or, The Immigrant's Daughter***	New York: P. O'Shea	United States	First publ.	Book	
1855	An Irishman	***The Irish Widow; or, A Picture from Life of Erin and Her Children***	London: Wertheim and MacIntosh	England		Book	
1855	James Martin	The Mirror of Satire: A Rhapsody	In *John and Mary: A Modern Irish Tale, Etc.* Trim: Henderson Bros	Ireland		Book	
1855	Mrs. (Mary Anne) Sadlier	***The Blakes and Flanagans: A Tale Illustrative of Irish Life in the United States***	New York and Boston: D. and J. Sadlier	United States	First publ.	Book	
1855	Mrs. (Mary Anne) Sadlier	***The Blakes and Flanagans: A Tale Illustrative of Irish Life in the United States***	New York and Montreal: P. J. Kenedy	United States, Canada	First publ.	Book	
1855	Mrs. (Mary Anne) Sadlier	***The Blakes and Flanagans: A Tale Illustrative of Irish Life in the United States***	Dublin: James Duffy and Sons	Ireland	First publ.	Book	*Guide to Irish Fiction* indicates that this book was still in print in 1879.
1856	An Irishman	**De Hut van den Armen Paddy of Slavernij in Ierland**	Amsterdam: H. de Hoogh	Netherlands	Republ.	Book	Dutch translation based on the fourth edition of *Poor Paddy's Cabin.*

Year	Author	Title	Publisher	Country	Publication	Format	Notes
1856	William Carleton	**Fair Gurtha; or, The Hungry Grass: A Legend of the Dumb Hill**	*Dublin University Magazine, a Literary and Political Journal 47*, no. 280. Dublin: Hodges, Smith, and Co. (Jan.–Jun.)	Ireland	First publ.	Periodical	
1856	William Carleton	**Fair Gurtha; or, The Hungry Grass: A Legend of the Dumb Hill**	*Dublin University Magazine, a Literary and Political Journal 47*, no. 280. London: Hurst and Blackett (Jan.–Jun.)	England	First publ.	Periodical	
1856	Charles Lever	***The Martins of Cro' Martin***	London: Chapman and Hall	England	First publ.	Book	
1856	Charles Lever	***The Martins of Cro' Martin***	Leipzig: Bernard Tauchnitz	Germany	First publ.	Book	
1856	Charles Lever	***The Martins of Cro' Martin***	New York: Harper & Bros	United States	First publ.	Book	
1856	Richard Baptist O'Brien	***Ailey Moore: A Tale of the Times***	London: Charles Dolman	England	First publ.	Book	
1856	Richard Baptist O'Brien	***Ailey Moore: A Tale of the Times***	Baltimore, MD: J. Murphy & Co.	United States	First publ.	Book	
1856	Richard Baptist O'Brien	***Ailey Moore: A Tale of the Times***	New York: Edward Dunigan and Brother	United States	First publ.	Book	
1856	Reginald Tierney (Thomas O'Neill Russell)	***Dick Massey: An Irish Story***	New York: P. J. Kenedy	United States	First publ.	Book	
1857	William Carleton	***The Emigrants: A Tale of Irish Life***	London and New York: George Routledge & Co.	England, United States	Republ.	Book	Railroad Library, no. 141. Also known as *The Emigrants of Ahadarra: A Tale of Irish Life.*
1857	William Carleton	**Owen M'Carthy; or, The Landlord and Tenant**	In *Ally Sheridan, and Other Stories.* Dublin: P. Dixon Hardy and Sons	Ireland		Book	

(continued)

Chronological List of Creative Works That Contain Famine (*continued*)

Year of publication	Author	Title	Publ. details	Publ. location	First publ. or republ.	Publ. in periodical or book	Comments
1857	Carolan (J. T. Campion)	The Felons of '48	*Celt* (Dublin)	Ireland		Periodical	
1857	Mrs. Anna H. Dorsey	**Nora Brady's Vow**	*Pilot* (Boston, serialized between early Jan. and Mar. 21)	United States	First publ.	Periodical	The version in the *Pilot* indicates that the narrative was written for the newspaper.
1857	M'Carthy More	**A Story: By an Irish Wife; Byan**	*Celt* (Dublin)	Ireland		Periodical	
1857	R. N.	**The Bridal of Death**	*Celt* (Dublin)	Ireland	First publ.	Periodical	
1857	Mrs. (Mary Anne) Sadlier	**Elinor Preston; or, Scenes at Home and Abroad**	*New York Tablet*	United States	First publ.	Periodical	
1858	Ethne	Recruiting	*Celt* (Dublin)	Ireland		Periodical	
1858	Mrs. (Mary Anne) Sadlier	**The Blakes and Flanagans: A Tale Illustrative of Irish Life in the United States**	New York and Boston: D. and J. Sadlier	United States	Republ.	Book	
1859	Carolan (J. T. Campion)	The Poor Scholar	*Celt* (Dublin)	Ireland		Periodical	
1859	John Swanwick Drennan	And the Famine Was Sore in the Land: 1847	In William Drennan (ed.), *Glendalloch and Other Poems by the Late Dr. Drennan, with Additional Verse by His Sons.* Dublin: William Robertson	Ireland		Book	

1859	John Swanwick Drennan	A Wail: 1847	In William Drennan (ed.), *Glendalloch and Other Poems by the Late Dr. Drennan, with Additional Verse by His Sons*. Dublin: William Robertson	Ireland		Book	
1859	William Drennan Jr.	1848	In William Drennan (ed.), *Glendalloch and Other Poems by the Late Dr. Drennan, with Additional Verse by His Sons*. Dublin: William Robertson	Ireland		Book	
1859	Ulick Dunloe (Charles J. Kickham)	**Never Give Up**	*Celt* (Dublin)	Ireland	First publ.	Periodical	
1859	Charles Lever	***The Martins of Cro' Martin***	London: Chapman and Hall	England	Republ.	Book	
1859	Miss Mason	***Catherine Geary ou les Irlandais à Londres***	Paris: Putois-Cretté	France	Republ.	Book	Originally published as *Kate Gearey*, translated by William O'Gorman.
1859	Richard Baptist O'Brien	***Ailey Moore, Scènes Irelandaises Contemporaines***	Paris: P. Lethielleux	France	Republ.	Book	French translation by Joseph Chantrel.
1859	R. O. J.	**A True Emigration Story**	*Celt* (Dublin)	Ireland		Periodical	
1859	Mrs. (Mary Anne) Sadlier	***New Lights; or, Life in Galway***	New York	United States	Republ.	Book	

(continued)

Chronological List of Creative Works That Contain Famine (*continued*)

Year of publication	Author	Title	Publ. details	Publ. location	First publ. or republ.	Publ. in periodical or book	Comments
1860	Reginald Tierney (Thomas O'Neill Russell)	***The Struggles of Dick Massey; or, The Battles of a Boy***	Dublin: James Duffy	Ireland	Republ.	Book	
1860	T. L. N.	**Captain Patrick Malony; or, The Irishman in Alabama**	*Pilot* (Boston, Jun. 2–23)	United States		Periodical	
1860	Anthony Trollope	***Castle Richmond: A Novel***	London: Chapman and Hall	England	First publ.	Book	
1860	Anthony Trollope	***Castle Richmond: A Novel***	Leipzig: Bernhard Tauchnitz	Germany	First publ.	Book	
1860	Anthony Trollope	***Castle Richmond: A Novel***	New York: Harper & Bros	United States	First publ.	Book	
1861	Allen H. Clington (Major David Power Conyngham)	***Frank O'Donnell: A Tale of Irish Life***	Dublin and London: James Duffy	Ireland, England	Republ.	Book	
1861	Robert Curtis	**McCormack's Grudge**	In *The Irish Police Officer: Comprising the Identification, and Other Tales, Founded upon Remarkable Trials in Ireland.* London: Ward and Lock	England	First publ.	Book	
1861	Darby Ryan (Jeremiah O'Ryan)	Ireland's Lament	In *The Tipperary Minstrel.* Dublin: Marcus Maddigan	Ireland		Book	
1861	Mrs. (Mary Anne) Sadlier	***Elinor Preston; or, Scenes at Home and Abroad***	New York: D. and J. Sadlier	United States	Republ.	Book	
1861	Mrs. (Mary Anne) Sadlier	***Bessy Conway; or, The Irish Girl in America***	*New York Tablet*	United States	First publ.	Periodical	

1861	Reginald Tierney (Thomas O'Neill Russell)	*The Adventures of Dick Massey: A Tale of Irish Life*	Dublin and London: James Duffy	Ireland, England	Republ.	Book	
1861 (?)	Reginald Tierney (Thomas O'Neill Russell)	*Dick Massey: A Tale of the Irish Evictions*	Dublin: M. H. Gill	Ireland	Republ.	Book	Found in *Guide to Irish Fiction*, no date.
1861	Anthony Trollope	*Het Kasteel Richmond: een Verhaal tijdens de Hongersnood in Ierland*	Emmerick: Binger	Netherlands	Republ.	Book	Dutch translation of *Castle Richmond*.
1862	Anon. (Robert Curtis)	*McCormack's Grudge; or, A Tale of the Famine Year*	*Irish-American* (New York, serial starts on Sep. 20)	United States	Republ.	Periodical	
1862	Izzie	A True Story	*Pilot* (Boston)	United States		Periodical	
1862	Mrs. (Mary Anne) Sadlier	*Bessy Conway; or, The Irish Girl in America*	New York: D. and J. Sadlier	United States	Republ.	Book	
1863	Anon.	*The Farmer of Inniscreen: A Tale of the Irish Famine in Verse*	London: Jarrold and Sons	England		Book	
1863	F. L. Boston	The Piercing Wail of Famine Comes	*Pilot* (Boston)	United States		Periodical	
1863	Allen H. Clington (Major David Power Conyngham)	*Frank O'Donnell: A Tale of Irish Life*	*Pilot* (Boston)	United States	Republ.	Periodical	
1863	Ellen Fitzsimon	Sonnet: 1849	In *Darrynane in Eighteen Hundred and Thirty-Two and Other Poems*. Dublin: W. B. Kelley	Ireland		Book	
1863	Mrs. (Mary Anne) Sadlier	*Con O'Regan; or, Emigrant Life in the New World*	*New York Tablet*	United States	First publ.	Periodical	
1863	Robert Young	Stanzas on the Death of Daniel O'Connell, Esq., M.P.	In *Poetical Works*. Derry: Derry Standard Office	Ireland		Book	

(*continued*)

Chronological List of Creative Works That Contain Famine (*continued*)

Year of publica-tion	Author	Title	Publ. details	Publ. location	First publ. or republ.	Publ. in periodical or book	Comments
1864	Emily Bowles	***Irish Diamonds; or, The Chronicles of Peterstown***	London: Thomas Richardson and Son	England		Book	
1864	Jane Elgee (Lady Jane Francesca Agnes Wilde, "Speranza")	The Exodus	In *Poems by Speranza*. London: Duffy	England	Republ.	Book	
1864	Jane Elgee (Lady Jane Francesca Agnes Wilde, "Speranza")	The Exodus	In *Poems by Speranza*. Dublin and London: Duffy	Ireland	Republ.	Book	
1864	Jane Elgee (Lady Jane Francesca Agnes Wilde, "Speranza")	The Famine Year	In *Poems by Speranza*. Dublin and London: Duffy	England, Ireland	Republ.	Book	Originally published as "The Stricken Land."
1864	Jane Elgee (Lady Jane Francesca Agnes Wilde, "Speranza")	A Lament for the Potato	In *Poems by Speranza*. Dublin and London: Duffy	England, Ireland		Book	
1864	Charles Joseph Kickham	***Sally Cavanagh; or, The Untenanted Graves: A Tale of Tipperary***	*Duffy's Hibernian Magazine*	Ireland	First publ.	Periodical	
1864	Mrs. (Mary Anne) Sadlier	***Con O'Regan; or, Emigrant Life in the New World***	New York, Boston, and Montreal: D. and J. Sadlier	United States, Canada	Republ.	Book	
1864	Mrs. (Mary Anne) Sadlier	***Con O'Regan; or, Emigrant Life in the New World***	New York: P. J. Kenedy	United States	Republ.	Book	

Year	Author	Title	Publication	Country		Type	Notes
1865	Robert Curtis	McCormack's Grudge	*Dublin Saturday Magazine*	Ireland	Republ.	Periodical	
1865	Mrs. Meredith	Ellen Harrington	In *The Lacemakers*. London: Jackson, Walford, and Hodder	England		Book	
1865	Elizabeth Hely Walshe	*Golden Hills: A Tale of the Irish Famine*	London: Religious Tract Society	England	First publ.	Book	
1866	Dillon O'Brien	*The Dalys of Dalystown*	Saint Paul, MN: Pioneer	United States		Book	
1866	Anon.	The Outlawed Chief; or, The Great Earl of Wicklow	*Shamrock* (Dublin)	Ireland	Republ.	Periodical	Translated from French.
1867	Mason T. Jones	*Old Trinity: A Story of Real Life*	London: Richard Bentley	England	First publ.	Book	
1867	Richard Baptist O'Brien	*Ailey Moore: A Tale of the Times*	Dublin: James Duffy	Ireland	Republ.	Book	
1867	D. O'C. Townley	The Tale of a Tombstone	*Catholic World* 24, no. 4	United States		Periodical	
1867	William Gorman Wills	*The Love That Kills: A Novel*	London: Tinsley	England		Book	
1867	Anon.	The Outlawed Chief; or, The Great Earl of Wicklow	*Shamrock* (Dublin)	Ireland	Republ.	Periodical	Translated from French.
1867	E. E. Callanan	Nora Arundel: A Tale of Roscaberry Bay	*Shamrock* (Dublin)	Ireland		Periodical	
1867	Desmond	The Maniac's Revenge: In Two Chapters	*Shamrock* (Dublin)	Ireland		Periodical	
1867	J. M.	Death of the Pauper Child	*Shamrock* (Dublin)	Ireland		Periodical	
1867	John Augustus O'Shea	Tried in the Crucible	*Shamrock* (Dublin)	Ireland		Periodical	
1868	Alice Nolan	*The Byrnes of Glengoulah: A True Tale*	*Irish Citizen* (New York)	United States	First publ.	Periodical	Indicates that it was written for the newspaper.
1868	Tupto	Unwilling Proselytes: A Story of the Famine Year	*Shamrock* (Dublin)	Ireland		Periodical	

(continued)

Chronological List of Creative Works That Contain Famine (*continued*)

Year of publication	Author	Title	Publ. details	Publ. location	First publ. or republ.	Publ. in periodical or book	Comments
1869	Anna Dorsey	***Nora Brady's Vow and Mona the Vestal***	Boston: Patrick Donahoe	United States	First publ.	Book	
1869	Anna Dorsey	***Nora Brady's Vow and Mona the Vestal***	Philadelphia: J. B. Lippincott	United States	First publ.	Book	
1869	Jane Chaplin Dunbar	***Gems of the Bog: A Tale of the Irish Peasantry***	Boston: American Tract Society	United States		Book	
1869	Jane Chaplin Dunbar	***Gems of the Bog: A Tale of the Irish Peasantry***	New York: Hurd & Haughton	United States		Book	
1869	Charles Joseph Kickham	***Sally Cavanagh; or, The Untenanted Graves: A Tale of Tipperary***	Dublin: J. J. Lalor	Ireland	Republ.	Book	
1869	Charles Joseph Kickham	***Sally Cavanagh; or, The Untenanted Graves: A Tale of Tipperary***	Dublin: W. B. Kelly	Ireland	Republ.	Book	
1869	Charles Joseph Kickham	***Sally Cavanagh; or, The Untenanted Graves: A Tale of Tipperary***	London: Simpkin, Marshall & Co.	England	Republ.	Book	
1869	Charles Joseph Kickham	***Sally Cavanagh; or, The Untenanted Graves: A Tale of Tipperary***	Dublin: James Duffy	Ireland	Republ.	Book	
1869	Thomas D'Arcy McGee	The Famine in the Land	In *The Poems of Thomas D'Arcy McGee*. London: D. & J. Sadlier	England	Republ.	Book	
1869	Thomas D'Arcy McGee	The Three Dreams	In *The Poems of Thomas D'Arcy McGee*. London: D. & J. Sadlier	England		Book	
1869	Thomas D'Arcy McGee	The Woeful Winter	In *The Poems of Thomas D'Arcy McGee*. London: D. & J. Sadlier	England		Book	
1869	Alice Nolan	***The Byrnes of Glengoulah: A True Tale***	New York: P. O'Shea	United States	Republ.	Book	

1869	Mrs. Lorenzo Nunn	*Heirs of the Soil: A Tale*	Unknown	Unknown	First publ.	Book	Mentioned in *Guide to Irish Fiction*.
1869	Aubrey de Vere	The Desolation of the West	In *Irish Odes*. New York: Catholic Publication Society	United States		Book	
1869	Aubrey de Vere	Ireland: 1851	In *Irish Odes*. New York: Catholic Publication Society	United States		Book	
1869	Aubrey de Vere	Ode: After One of the Famine Years	In *Irish Odes*. New York: Catholic Publication Society	United States		Book	
1869	Aubrey de Vere	The Sisters; or, Weal in Woe	In *Irish Odes*. New York: Catholic Publication Society	United States		Book	
1869	Aubrey de Vere	Widowhood: 1848	In *Irish Odes*. New York: Catholic Publication Society	United States		Book	
1869	Aubrey de Vere	The Year of Sorrow: Ireland—1849	In *Irish Odes*. New York: Catholic Publication Society	United States		Book	
1869	Canada West (William Anderson Cawthorne)	*Tim Doolan; or, The Irish Emigrant*	London: Partridge	England		Book	
1870	Anon.	The Emigrant	*Catholic World* 11, no. 66	United States		Periodical	
1870	Erigena (J. G. Barrett)	*Evelyn Clare; or, The Wrecked Homesteads: An Irish Story of Love and Landlordism*	London: Thomas Richardson	England	Republ.	Book	*Guide to Irish Fiction* refers to a publication in the 1850s.
1870	Charles J. Kickham	*Knocknagow; or, The Homes of Tipperary*	*American Celt* (New York)	United States	Republ.	Periodical	

(continued)

Chronological List of Creative Works That Contain Famine (*continued*)

Year of publication	Author	Title	Publ. details	Publ. location	First publ. or republ.	Publ. in periodical or book	Comments
1870	Charles J. Kickham	***Knocknagow; or, The Homes of Tipperary***	*Emerald* (New York)	United States	Republ.	Periodical	
1870	Charles J. Kickham	***Knocknagow; or, The Homes of Tipperary***	*Shamrock* (Dublin)	Ireland	Republ.	Periodical	
1870	Charles Joseph Kickham	***Sally Cavanagh; or, The Untenanted Graves: A Tale of Tipperary***	Boston: Patrick Donahoe	United States	Republ.	Book	
1870	Peter McCorry	***The Lost Rosary***	Boston: Patrick Donahoe	United States		Book	
1870	Alice Nolan	***The Byrnes of Glengoulah: A True Tale***	Unknown	Unknown	Republ.	Book	Mentioned in *Guide to Irish Fiction.*
1870	Mrs. Lorenzo Nunn	***Heirs of the Soil: A Tale***	Dublin and London: Moffat	Ireland, England	Republ.	Book	
1870	Julia and Edmund O'Ryan	***In Re Garland: A Tale of a Transition Time***	London, Derby, and Dublin: Thomas Richardson and Son	England, Ireland	First publ.	Book	
1870	Julia and Edmund O'Ryan	***In Re Garland: A Tale of a Transition Time***	New York: Henry H. Richardson	United States	First publ.	Book	
1871	David Power Conyngham	***The O'Donnells of Glen Cottage***	New York: P. J. Kenedy	United States	Republ.	Book	Also published as *Frank O'Donnell.*
1871	Jane Elgee (Lady Jane Francesca Agnes Wilde, "Speranza")	Attendite Popule	In *Poems*. Glasgow: Cameron & Ferguson	Scotland	Republ.	Book	Originally published as "Attendite Populæ."

1871	Jane Elgee (Lady Jane Francesca Agnes Wilde, "Speranza")	The Enigma	In *Poems*. Glasgow: Cameron & Ferguson	Scotland	Republ.	Book
1871	Jane Elgee (Lady Jane Francesca Agnes Wilde, "Speranza")	The Exodus	In *Poems*. Glasgow: Cameron & Ferguson	Scotland	Republ.	Book
1871	Jane Elgee (Lady Jane Francesca Agnes Wilde, "Speranza")	The Famine Year	In *Poems*. Glasgow: Cameron & Ferguson	Scotland	Republ.	Book
1871	Jane Elgee (Lady Jane Francesca Agnes Wilde, "Speranza")	Foreshadowings	In *Poems*. Glasgow: Cameron & Ferguson	Scotland	Republ.	Book
1871	Jane Elgee (Lady Jane Francesca Agnes Wilde, "Speranza")	France in '93	In *Poems*. Glasgow: Cameron & Ferguson	Scotland	Republ.	Book
1871	Jane Elgee (Lady Jane Francesca Agnes Wilde, "Speranza")	A Lament for the Potato	In *Poems*. Glasgow: Cameron & Ferguson	Scotland	Republ.	Book
1871	Jane Elgee (Lady Jane Francesca Agnes Wilde, "Speranza")	A Supplication	In *Poems*. Glasgow: Cameron & Ferguson	Scotland	Republ.	Book

(continued)

Chronological List of Creative Works That Contain Famine (*continued*)

Year of publication	Author	Title	Publ. details	Publ. location	First publ. or republ.	Publ. in periodical or book	Comments
1871	Jane Elgee (Lady Jane Francesca Agnes Wilde, "Speranza")	The Voice of the Poor	In *Poems*. Glasgow: Cameron & Ferguson	Scotland	Republ.	Book	
1871	Jane Elgee (Lady Jane Francesca Agnes Wilde, "Speranza")	Work While It Is Called Today	In *Poems*. Glasgow: Cameron & Ferguson	Scotland	Republ. (?)	Book	
1871	Ireland	***Forlorn but not Forsaken: A Story of (the Famine of 1848) the "Bad Times" in Ireland***	Dublin: George Herbert	Ireland		Book	
1871	M. F. Munroe	**How the Croziers Came to Canada**	*Canadian Literary Journal: Devoted to Select Original Literature and the Interests of Canadian Literary Societies* 1, no. 7 (Toronto, Jan.)	Canada		Periodical	
1871	Reginald Tierney (Thomas O'Neill Russell)	***Dick Massey: A Tale of the Irish Evictions***	Glasgow and London: Cameron & Ferguson	England, Scotland	First publ. (?)	Book	
1871	Reginald Tierney (Thomas O'Neill Russell)	***Dick Massey: A Tale of the Irish Evictions***	New York: P. M. Haverty	United States	First publ. (?)	Book	*Guide to Irish Fiction* suggests there might be an earlier version.
1873	Charles Joseph Kickham	***Knocknagow; or, The Homes of Tipperary***	Dublin: A. M. Sullivan	Ireland	Republ.	Book	

1873	Charles Lever	*The Martins of Cro' Martin*	Unknown	Unknown	Republ.	Book	Mentioned in *Guide to Irish Fiction.*
1873	Father Hugh Quigley	*Profit and Loss: A Story of the Life of a Genteel Irish-American, Illustrative of a Godless Education*	New York: T. O'Kane	United States		Book	
1874	Allen H. Clington (Major David Power Conyngham)	*The O'Donnells of Glen Cottage: A Tale of the Famine Years in Ireland*	New York and Montreal: D. & J. Sadlier & Co.	United States, Canada	Republ.	Book	
1874	Annie Keary	*Castle Daly; or, The Story of an Irish Home Thirty Years Ago*	*Macmillan's Magazine*	England	First publ.	Periodical	
1875	Annie Keary	*Castle Daly; or, The Story of an Irish Home Thirty Years Ago*	*Macmillan's Magazine*	England	First publ.	Periodical	
1875	Annie Keary	*Castle Daly; or, The Story of an Irish Home Thirty Years Ago*, 3 vols.	London: Macmillan	England	Republ.	Book	
1875	Annie Keary	*Castle Daly; or, The Story of an Irish Home Thirty Years Ago*, 2 vols.	London: Macmillan	England	Republ.	Book	
1875	Annie Keary	*Castle Daly; or, The Story of an Irish Home Thirty Years Ago*, 2 vols.	Leipzig: Bernard Tauchnitz	Germany	Republ.	Book	
1875	Annie Keary	*Castle Daly; or, The Story of an Irish Home Thirty Years Ago*, 2 vols.	Philadelphia: Porter and Coates	United States	Republ.	Book	
1875	Annie Keary	*Castle Daly; or, The Story of an Irish Home Thirty Years Ago*	*Nation* (Dublin)	Ireland	Republ.	Periodical	Excerpts from the novel used in a review.
1875	Charles J. Kickham	**The Home by Slievenamon**	*Young Ireland* 1, no. 34 (Dublin, Nov. 13)	Ireland	Republ.	Periodical	First published as "Never Give Up."
1876	William Carleton	**Fair Gurtha; or, The Hungry Grass**	*Irish-American* 28, no. 3–28, no. 38 (New York, Sep. 2–16)	United States	Republ.	Periodical	

(continued)

Chronological List of Creative Works That Contain Famine (*continued*)

Year of publication	Author	Title	Publ. details	Publ. location	First publ. or republ.	Publ. in periodical or book	Comments
1876	Edward Forbes	The Potato Commission	In *The Bentley Ballads; Comprising the Tipperary Hall Ballads*. London: R. Bentley	England		Book	
1876	Nannie H. H.	*Dick O'Dell: A Story of '48*	*Young Ireland* 2, no. 36 (Dublin, Sep. 2, 1876)–3, no. 6 (Feb. 10, 1877)	Ireland	First publ.	Periodical	
1876	Nannie H. H.	*Dick O'Dell: A Story of '48*	*Irish-American* (New York)	United States	Republ.	Periodical	
1876	Annie Keary	*Castle Daly; or, The Story of an Irish Home Thirty Years Ago*, 2 vols.	Dublin: M. H. Gill and Son	Ireland	Republ.	Book	
1877	Anon.	*The Zozimus Papers ('Jimmy Hoy')*	*McGee's Illustrated Weekly* 1, no. 10 (New York, Jan. 27)	United States	Republ.	Periodical	
1877	Anon.	*An English Christmas Story*	*McGee's Illustrated Weekly* 3, no. 6 (New York, Dec. 29)	United States		Periodical	
1877	M. M. Armstrong	*The Piper's Gift: A Tale of the Irish Famine*	*McGee's Illustrated Weekly* 1, no. 17 (New York, Mar. 17)	United States	First publ.	Periodical	
1877	William Carleton	*The Black Prophet*	*Weekly Freeman's Journal* (serialization starts on Jun. 23)	Ireland	Republ.	Periodical	
1877	Sister Mary Frances Clare (Margaret Anna Cusack)	*From Killarney to New York; or, How Thade Became a Banker*	*McGee's Illustrated Weekly* 2 (New York, May–Nov.)	United States	First publ.	Periodical	
1877	Sister Mary Frances Clare (Margaret Anna Cusack)	*From Killarney to New York; or, How Thade Became a Banker*	*Universe* (London)	England	Republ.	Periodical	*McGee's* complains that the London magazine pirated the narrative.

Year	Author	Title	Publication	Country		Type
1877	Nannie H. H.	*Dick O'Dell: A Story of '48*	*Young Ireland* 2, no. 36 (Dublin, Sep. 2, 1876)–3, no. 6 (Feb. 10, 1877)	Ireland	First publ.	Periodical
1877	Nannie H. H.	*Dick O'Dell: A Story of '48*	*Irish-American* (New York)	United States	Republ.	Periodical
1877	Annie Keary	*Castle Daly; or, The Story of an Irish Home Thirty Years Ago*	*Young Ireland* 3 (Dublin)	Ireland	Republ.	Periodical
1877	P. MacMahon	*The Fairy Dyke*	*Young Ireland* 3, no. 8 (Dublin)	Ireland		Periodical
1877	Lalla McDowell	*The Earl of Effingham*	London: Samuel Tinsley	England		Book
1877	Michael Segrave	The Eviction	In Ralph Varian (ed.), *Ballads, Popular Poetry and Household Songs of Ireland*. Dublin: M. H. Gill & Sons	Ireland		Book
1878	Anon.	The Cot in the Corner: Lament of the Evicted	*McGee's Illustrated Weekly* 4, no. 1 (New York, May 25)	United States		Periodical
1878	Anon.	The Exiles of Erin	*Young Ireland* 4 (Dublin)	Ireland		Periodical
1878	William Carleton	*The Black Prophet*	*Weekly Freeman's Journal* (serialization starts on Jun. 23, 1877)	Ireland	Republ.	Periodical
1878	Sister Mary Frances Clare (Margaret Anna Cusack, "the Nun of Kenmare")	*From Killarney to New York; or, How Thade Became a Banker: A Story of Real Life*	New York: J. A. McGee	United States	Republ.	Book
1878	Francis Davis	A Song of Ulster	In *Earlier and Later Leaves*. Belfast: Patrick Mallon	Ireland		Book
1878	Annie Keary	*Castle Daly; or, The Story of an Irish Home Thirty Years Ago*	*Young Ireland* 4 (Dublin)	Ireland	Republ.	Periodical

(continued)

Chronological List of Creative Works That Contain Famine (*continued*)

Year of publication	Author	Title	Publ. details	Publ. location	First publ. or republ.	Publ. in periodical or book	Comments
1878	Thomas Kelly	**The O'Rourkes of Goragh**	*Young Ireland* 4–5 (Dublin)	Ireland		Periodical	
1878	Charles J. Kickham	**Sally Cavanagh; or, The Untenanted Graves of Tipperary**	*Young Ireland* 4 (Dublin)	Ireland	Republ.	Periodical	
1878	Charlotte O'Brien	**Light and Shade, 2 vols.**	London: Kegan Paul	England	First publ.	Book	
1878	Charlotte O'Brien	**Light and Shade, 2 vols.**	New York: Harper & Bros	United States	First publ.	Book	
1878	Kathleen O'Meara	**The Battle of Connemara**	London: Burns, Oates and Washbourne	England		Book	
1879	Anon.	**The Gombeen's Ghost**	*Nation* (Dublin)	Ireland		Periodical	
1879	Mrs. (Mary Anne) Hoare	**The Blakes and Flanagans: A Tale Illustrative of Irish Life in the United States**	New York: Unknown	United States	Republ.	Book	Mentioned in *Guide to Irish Fiction.*
1879	Thomas Kelly	**The O'Rourkes of Goragh**	*Young Ireland* 4–5 (Dublin)	Ireland		Periodical	
1879	William Baptist O'Brien, DD	**The D'Altons of Crag: An Irish Story of '48 and '49**	*Harp: A Magazine of General Literature* 5, no. 1 (Hamilton/ Montreal, Nov. 1879)–5, no. 9 (Jul. 1880)	Canada	First publ.	Periodical	
1879	Charlotte O'Brien	**Light and Shade, 2 vols.**	*Illustrated Celtic Monthly* (New York)	United States	Republ.	Periodical	
1880	Anon.	**A Wild-Goose Chase**	*Celtic Monthly* 3, no. 2 (New York, Feb.)	United States		Periodical	
1880	Anon.	**Thade M'Sweeney; or, A Tenant Famer's Trials: A Story of the Great Famine**	*Irish-American* 32, no. 15 (New York, Apr. 10)	United States		Periodical	
1880	Louise Berens	**Steadfast unto Death: A Tale of the Irish Famine of To-Day**	London: Remington and Co.	England		Book	

1880	B. P. H.	Ireland	*Celtic Monthly* 4, no. 6 (New York, Dec.)	United States		Periodical	
1880	William Carleton	***The Black Prophet; or, The Grave by the Grey Stone: A Story of Irish Famine and Landlordism***	*Munster Express*	Ireland	Republ.	Periodical	
1880	Carmine	The Cause	*Young Ireland* 6, no. 17 (Dublin, Apr. 24)	Ireland		Periodical	
1880	Patrick Sarsfield Cassidy	Rathmullan Castle, Co. Donegal: A Reverie	*Celtic Monthly* 5, no. 1 (New York, Dec.)	United States		Periodical	
1880	Michael Cavanagh (translator)	A Song for Today	*Celtic Monthly* 3, no. 1 (New York, Jan.)	United States	Republ.	Periodical	Translated from Irish.
1880	Clareman	A Reproach	*Young Ireland* 4, no. 9 (Dublin, Feb. 28)	Ireland		Periodical	
1880	Clontarf	All Hail, Parnell!	*Young Ireland* 6, no. 27 (Dublin, Jul. 3)	Ireland		Periodical	
1880	Jane Elgee (Lady Jane Francesca Agnes Wilde, "Speranza")	The Famine Year	In C. A. Read (ed.), *The Cabinet of Irish Literature*. London: Blackie & Son	England	Republ.	Book	Originally published as "The Stricken Land."
1880	Gael	Little Deny	*Celtic Monthly* 4, no. 5 (New York, Nov.)	United States		Periodical	
1880	J. Harrington	The Legal Rights of Social Wrongs	*Celtic Monthly* 4, no. 1 (New York, Jul.)	United States		Periodical	
1880	Edward N. Hoare	***Mike: A Tale of the Great Irish Famine***	London: Society for Promoting Christian Knowledge	England		Book	
1880	Edward N. Hoare	***Mike: A Tale of the Great Irish Famine***	New York: Pott, Young & Co.	United States		Book	
1880	Miss M. Howitt (translator)	Ireland	*Celtic Monthly* 3, no. 1 (New York, Jan.)	United States	Republ.	Periodical	Translated from German.

(continued)

Chronological List of Creative Works That Contain Famine (*continued*)

Year of publication	Author	Title	Publ. details	Publ. location	First publ. or republ.	Publ. in periodical or book	Comments
1880	Edited by C. M. O'Donovan, written by Craoibin Aoibin (Douglas Hyde), translated by Michael Cavanagh	1879: November	*Celtic Monthly* 4, no. 5 (New York, Nov.)	United States		Periodical	Bilingual.
1880	Annie Keary	***Castle Daly; or, The Story of an Irish Home Thirty Years Ago***	*Daily Witness* (Montreal)	Canada	Republ.	Periodical	
1880	Annie Keary	***Castle Daly; or, The Story of an Irish Home Thirty Years Ago*, 3 vols.**	New York: G. Munro	United States	Republ.	Book	
1880	William D. Kelly	Boycotting	*Celtic Monthly* 4, no. 6 (New York, Dec.)	United States		Periodical	
1880	William D. Kelly	The Irish Peasant to Mr. Vere Foster	*Celtic Monthly* 4, no. 6 (New York, Dec.)	United States		Periodical	
1880	Toler King (Emily Fox)	***Rose O'Connor: A Story of the Day***	Chicago, IL: Chicago Legal News Company (printer)	United States		Book	
1880	John Locke	Ireland's Miserere: Dedicated to Charles Stewart Parnell	*Celtic Monthly* 3, no. 4 (New York, Apr.)	United States		Periodical	
1880	Mac	**Tiumpeen, the Fairy Queen: A Legend of '47**	*Young Ireland* 6, no. 21 (Dublin, May 22)	Ireland		Periodical	
1880	M. M'G.	We've Nothing to Eat or to Sow	*Young Ireland* 4, no. 19 (Dublin, May 8)	Ireland		Periodical	

Year	Author	Title	Source	Country		Type	Notes
1880	Rosa Mulholland	**The Hungry Death**	*All the Year Round* (new series) 25 (London, May 15, 1880–Oct. 16, 1880), extra summer issue (Jul. 1)	England	First publ.	Periodical	
1880	J. Murdock	Kyrei Eleison!	*Young Ireland* 6, no. 29 (Dublin, Jul. 17)	Ireland		Periodical	
1880	William Baptist O'Brien, DD	***The D'Altons of Crag: An Irish Story of '48 and '49***	*Harp: A Magazine of General Literature* 5, no. 1 (Hamilton/ Montreal, Nov. 1879)–5, no. 9 (Jul. 1880)	Canada	First publ.	Periodical	
1880	Charlotte O'Brien	***Light and Shade***	*Young Ireland* (Dublin)	Ireland	Republ.	Periodical	
1880	Fanny Parnell	To the Land Leaguers	*Celtic Monthly* 4, no. 3 (New York, Sep.)	United States		Periodical	
1880	The Southern Gael	Ely Mulcahy	*Celtic Monthly* 3, no. 1 (New York, Jan.)	United States		Periodical	
1880	Mrs. Margaret F. Sullivan	The Irish Famine of 1880	*Celtic Monthly* 3, no. 4 (New York, Apr.)	United States		Periodical	"Written to be recited by Miss Emilie Gavin, at the Irish Relief Meeting in Chicago, February, 1880."
1880	T. W. Taylor	The Returned Exile	*Young Ireland* 6, no. 8 (Feb. 21)	Ireland		Periodical	
1880	A Young Irelander	The Birth of Young Ireland	*Young Ireland* 6, no. 47 (Dublin, Nov. 20)	Ireland		Periodical	
1881	William Carleton	***The Black Prophet; or, The Grave by the Grey Stone: A Story of Irish Famine and Landlordism***	*Munster Express*	Ireland	Republ.	Periodical	

(continued)

Chronological List of Creative Works That Contain Famine (*continued*)

Year of publication	Author	Title	Publ. details	Publ. location	First publ. or republ.	Publ. in periodical or book	Comments
1881	William Carleton	***The Black Prophet***	In *The Works of William Carleton*, volume III. New York: P. F. Collier	United States	Republ.	Book	
1881	William Carleton	***The Emigrants of Ahadarra***	In *The Works of William Carleton*, volume II. New York: P. F. Collier	United States	Republ.	Book	
1881	Patrick Sarsfield Cassidy	Make the Landlords Emigrate	*Celtic Monthly* 5, no. 2 (New York, Feb.)	United States		Periodical	
1881	Patrick Sarsfield Cassidy	The Sassenagh Priest	*Celtic Monthly* 4, no. 6 (New York, Dec.)	United States		Periodical	
1881	Bessie Ford Garland	***The Old Man's Darling***	Toronto: B. Garland	Canada		Book	
1881	Bard of Thomond (Michael Hogan)	The Evicted Tenant	*Celtic Monthly* 5, no. 5 (New York, May)	United States		Periodical	
1881	Annie Keary	***Castle Daly; or, The Story of an Irish Home Thirty Years Ago***	*Montreal Weekly Witness*	Canada	Republ.	Periodical	
1881	Annie Keary	***Castle Daly; or, The Story of an Irish Home Thirty Years Ago***	*Daily Witness* (Montreal)	Canada	Republ.	Periodical	
1881	M. Mackey	**His Honour's Word; or, A Victim of "Painful Duty": A Tale of the Times**	*Young Ireland* 7, no. 37 (Dublin, Sep. 10) 7, no. 38 (Sep. 17)	Ireland		Periodical	
1881	James Clarence Mangan	The Warning Voice	*Nation* 39, no. 43 (Dublin, Oct. 22)	Ireland	Republ.	Periodical	
1881	Thomas McMullin	An Irish Mother's Lament	*Celtic Monthly* 5, no. 2 (New York, Feb.)	United States		Periodical	

Year	Author	Title	Publication	Country		Type
1881	R. Nicoll	We Are Lowly	*Celtic Monthly* 5, no. 5 (New York, May)	United States		Periodical
1881	Attie O'Brien	The M'Donoughs of Grovelands	*Young Ireland* 7, no. 25 (Dublin, Jun. 18)	Ireland		Periodical
1881	Myles O'Regan	The Landlord's Lament	*Celtic Monthly* 5, no. 2 (New York, Feb.)	United States		Periodical
1881	Reginald Tierney (Thomas O'Neill Russell)	***Dick Massey: A Tale; The Irish Evictions***	New York: P. J. Kenedy and Sons	United States	Republ.	Book
1882	F. G.	**A True Story of "Black '47"**	*Young Ireland* 8, no. 9 (Dublin, Mar. 4)	Ireland		Periodical
1882	Denis Florence MacCarthy	A Mystery	In *Poems*. Dublin: M. H. Gill & Sons	Ireland	Republ.	Book
1882	William Baptist O'Brien, DD	***The D'Altons of Crag: An Irish Story of '48 and '49***	Dublin: James Duffy	Ireland	Republ.	Book
1882	William Baptist O'Brien, DD	***The D'Altons of Crag: An Irish Story of '48 and '49***	New York: Benziger	United States	Republ.	Book
1882	William C. Upton	***Uncle Pat's Cabin; or, Life among the Agricultural Labourers of Ireland***	Dublin: M. H. Gill	Ireland	First publ.	Book
1883	Maelmuire	A Vision	*Young Ireland* 9, no. 39 (Dublin, Sep. 22)	Ireland		Book
1883	Norah (Margaret Dixon McDougall)	***The Days of a Life***	Almonte, Ontario: W. Templeman	Canada	First publ.	Book	Reworking of the author's special correspondence.
1883	William Baptist O'Brien, DD	***The D'Altons of Crag: An Irish Story of '48 and '49***	*Donahoe's Magazine* (Boston)	United States	Republ.	Periodical
1883	Anthony Trollope	***The Landleaguers***	London: Chatto & Windus	England		Book
1883	Anthony Trollope	***The Landleaguers***	New York: Geo. Munro's Sons	United States		Book

(continued)

Chronological List of Creative Works That Contain Famine (*continued*)

Year of publication	Author	Title	Publ. details	Publ. location	First publ. or republ.	Publ. in periodical or book	Comments
1884	Margaret W. Brew	*The Chronicles of Castle Cloyne; or, Pictures of the Munster People,* 3 vols.	London: Chapman and Hall	England	First publ.	Book	
1884	An Irishman (Henry F. Clayton)	*Scenes and Incidents of Irish Life*	Montreal: John Lovell (printer)	Canada		Book	
1885	Margaret W. Brew	*The Chronicles of Castle Cloyne; or, Pictures of the Munster People,* 3 vols.	London: Chapman and Hall	England	Republ.	Book	
1885	Charles James Cannon	*Bickerton; or, The Immigrant's Daughter: A Tale by a Distinguished Writer*	New York: O'Shea	United States	Republ.	Book	
1885	Charles James Cannon	*Bickerton; or, The Immigrant's Daughter: A Tale of Irish-American Life*	London: Burns & Lambert	England	Republ.	Book	
1885	Annie Keary	*Castle Daly; or, The Story of an Irish Home Thirty Years Ago*	J. H. Black: GPO (Government Printing Office)	United States	Republ.	Book	
1885	T. B. Kilerook	The Men of '48	*Young Ireland* 11, no. 51 (Dublin, Dec. 19)	Ireland		Periodical	
1885	Mrs. (Mary Anne) Sadlier	*New Lights; or, Life in Galway*	New York: Unknown	United States	Republ.	Book	Mentioned in *Guide to Irish Fiction.*
1886	Margaret W. Brew	*The Chronicles of Castle Cloyne; or, Pictures of the Munster People,* 3 vols.	Unknown	Unknown	Republ.	Book	Mentioned in *Guide to Irish Fiction.*
1886	Emily Lawless	*Hurrish: A Study,* 2 vols.	Edinburgh and London: Blackwood	England, Scotland	First publ.	Book	
1886	Emily Lawless	*Hurrish: A Study,* 2 vols.	London: Methuen	England	First publ.	Book	
1886	Emily Lawless	*Hurrish: A Study,* 2 vols.	New York: Harper & Bros	United States	First publ.	Book	

Year	Author	Title	Publication	Country	Publ. status	Format	Notes
1886	Rosa Mulholland	*Marcella Grace*	London: Kegan Paul, Trench & Co.	England	First publ.	Book	
1886	Rosa Mulholland	*Marcella Grace*	New York: Harper & Bros	United States	First publ.	Book	
1886	Richard Baptist O'Brien	*The D'Altons of Crag: An Irish Story of '48 and '49*	Unknown	Unknown	Republ.	Book	Mentioned in *Writing the Irish Famine.*
1886	Father Hugh Quigley	*The Cross and the Shamrock*	Dublin: James Duffy	Ireland	Republ.	Book	
1887	Charles Joseph Kickham	*Sally Cavanagh; or, The Untenanted Graves: A Tale of Tipperary,* 2 vols.	New York: A. E. & R. E. Ford	United States	Republ.	Book	
1887	Emily Lawless	*Hurrish: A Study,* 2 vols.	Unknown	Unknown	Republ.	Book	Mentioned in *Guide to Irish Fiction.*
1888	Anon.	*The Bridal of Death; or, The Curse of Landlordism: A Story of '47*	*Irish-American* (New York)	United States	Republ.	Periodical	Author indicated as R. N. in Dublin *Celt.*
1888	Emily Lawless	*Hurrish: A Study,* 2 vols.	Leipzig: Bernard Tauchnitz	Germany	Republ.	Book	
1888	Murty Mullowney	*The Shadow of Death; or, The Story of the Old Larch Tree*	*Irish-American* (New York)	United States		Periodical	
1888	Olena	*The American Letter: A Tale of the Great Famine*	*Young Ireland* 14, no. 5 (Dublin, Feb.)–14, no. 7 (Feb. 18)	Ireland		Periodical	
1888	Hester Sigerson	*A Ruined Race; or, The Last MacManus of Drumroosk*	*Young Ireland* 1, no. 14 (Dublin, new series, Sep. 1)–1, no. 22 (Oct. 27)	Ireland	First publ.	Periodical	
1889	Annie M. Kenny	The Exile's Message	*Young Ireland* 2, no. 9 (Dublin, new series, Mar. 2)	Ireland		Periodical	
1889	Justin H. McCarthy	*Lily Lass: A Romance*	London: Chatto and Windus	England	First publ.	Book	

(continued)

Chronological List of Creative Works That Contain Famine (*continued*)

Year of publication	Author	Title	Publ. details	Publ. location	First publ. or republ.	Publ. in periodical or book	Comments
1889	Thomas Sherlock	***The Lord of Dundonald: An Irish Story of To-Day***	*Irish-American* 41, no. 46 (New York, Nov. 9)–42, no. 1 (Jan. 5, 1890)	United States		Periodical	
1889	Hester Sigerson	***A Ruined Race; or, The Last MacManus of Drumroosk***	London: Ward and Downey	England	Republ.	Book	
1890	Emily Lawless	***Hurrish: een Iersche Roman***	Arnhem: Gouda Quint	Netherlands	Republ.	Book	Dutch translation by Anna Bok.
1890	Justin H. McCarthy	***Lily Lass: A Romance***	New York: D. Appleton and Co.	United States	Republ.	Book	
1890	William O'Brien	***When We Were Boys***	London: Longmans, Green	England		Book	
1890	Thomas Sherlock	***The Lord of Dundonald: An Irish Story of To-Day***	*Irish-American* 41, no. 46 (New York, Nov. 9, 1889)–42, no. 1 (Jan. 5)	United States		Book	
1891	James Doran	***Zanthon: A Novel***	San Francisco, CA: Bancroft	United States		Book	
1891	Rosa Mulholland	**The Hungry Death**	In W. B. Yeats (ed.), *Representative Irish Tales.* London and New York: Putnam	England, United States	Republ.	Book	
1891	Rosa Mulholland	***Marcella Grace***	New York: Vatican Library	United States	Republ.	Book	
1891	Rosa Mulholland	***Marcella Grace***	Braunschweig: Grüneberg	Germany	Republ.	Book	German Translation.
1891	John Talbot Smith	**The Deacon of Lynn**	In *His Honor the Mayor: And Other Tales.* New York: Vatican Library	United States		Book	

1891	John Talbot Smith	**How the McGuinness Saved His Pride**	In *His Honor the Mayor: And Other Tales*. New York: Vatican Library	United States		Book	
1892	Jane Barlow	**Herself**	In *Irish Idylls*. London: Hodder & Stoughton	England	First publ.	Book	
1892	John Brennan	***Erin Mór: The Story of Irish Republicanism***	San Francisco: P. M. Diers	United States		Book	
1892	Hilary Deccan	***Light in the Offing*, 3 vols.**	London: Hurst and Blackett	England		Book	
1892	William Butler Yeats	*The Countess Kathleen [play]*	In *The Countess Kathleen and Various Legends and Lyrics*. Boston: Roberts	United States	First publ.	Book	
1892	William Butler Yeats	*The Countess Kathleen [play]*	In *The Countess Kathleen and Various Legends and Lyrics*. London: T. Fisher Unwin	England	First publ.	Book	
1893	Jane Barlow	**Herself**	In *Irish Idylls*. Leipzig: Heinemann & Balestier	Germany	Republ.	Book	
1893	Jane Barlow	**Herself**	In *Irish Idylls*. New York: Dodd, Mead and Co.	United States	Republ.	Book	
1894	Jane Barlow	***Kerrigan's Quality***	New York: Dodd, Mead and Co.	United States		Book	
1894	Jane Barlow	***Kerrigan's Quality***	London: Hodder & Stoughton	England		Book	
1894	Finley Peter Dunne	**Mr. Dooley Column**	*Chicago Evening Post*	United States	First publ.	Periodical	Mentioned in *Finley Peter Dunne*
1894	Jane Elgee (Lady Jane Francesca Agnes Wilde, "Speranza")	The Famine Year	In M. MacDermott (ed.), *The New Spirit of the Nation*. London: T. Fisher Unwin	England	Republ.	Book	Originally published as "The Stricken Land."

(continued)

Chronological List of Creative Works That Contain Famine (*continued*)

Year of publica-tion	Author	Title	Publ. details	Publ. location	First publ. or republ.	Publ. in periodical or book	Comments
1894	Jane Elgee (Lady Jane Francesca Agnes Wilde, "Speranza")	Work While It Is Called Today	In M. MacDermott (ed.), *The New Spirit of the Nation*. London: T. Fisher Unwin	England	Republ.	Book	
1894	William James Linton	Rhymes for the Landlorded	In M. MacDermott (ed.), *The New Spirit of the Nation*. London: T. Fisher Unwin	England	Republ.	Book	
1894	Mrs. Charlotte Riddle	So Near; or, The Pity of It	In *The Banshee's Warning and Other Tales*. London: Remington and Co.	England		Book	
1894	Lady Dufferin (Helena Selina Sheridan)	Lament of the Irish Emigrant	In *Songs, Poems and Verses*. London: John Murray	England		Book	
1894	Katharine Tynan	**A Village Priest**	In *A Cluster of Nuts: Being Sketches among My Own People*. London: Lawrence and Bullen	England		Book	
1895	Author of "The Heart of Erin," "A Woman Scourned," etc.	**The Wages of Sin; or, The Serfs of the Soil**	*Shamrock* (Dublin)	Ireland		Periodical	
1895	Jane Barlow	**Con the Quare One**	In *Strangers at Lisconnell*. London: Hodder & Stoughton	England	First publ.	Book	
1895	Jane Barlow	**Con the Quare One**	In *Strangers at Lisconnell*. New York: Dodd, Mead & Co.	United States	First publ.	Book	

1895	Jane Barlow	**Herself**	In *Irish Idylls* (?)	Unknown	Republ.	Book	Mentioned in *Guide to Irish Fiction.*
1895	Rev. J. B. Dollard	The Carrick Piper	*Shamrock* (Dublin)	Ireland		Periodical	
1895	L.	**The Secret of Kilbawn Wood; or, The Story of an Agrarian Murder**	*Shamrock* (Dublin)	Ireland		Periodical	
1895	M. J. Murphy	**The Free-Fairy**	*Shamrock* (Dublin)	Ireland		Periodical	
1895	Ned of the Hill	**The Banshee's Call: An Episode of '48**	*Shamrock* (Dublin)	Ireland		Periodical	
1895	Nemo	A Song for the New Year	*Irish Emerald* (Dublin)	Ireland		Periodical	
1895	James Parton	**The Martins of Connemara**	*Shamrock* (Dublin)	Ireland		Periodical	
1895	Paul Peppergrass (John Boyce)	***Shandy M'Guire; or, Tricks upon Travelers, Being a Story of the North of Ireland***	Dublin: P. C. D.	Ireland	Republ.	Book	
1895	Robert Sellar	***Gleaner Tales***	Huntingdon, QC: Unknown	Canada		Book	
1895	William Butler Yeats	*The Countess Cathleen [play]*	In *Poems by W. B. Yeats.* London: T. Fisher Unwin	UK	Republ.	Book	
1896	Jane Barlow	**Con the Quare One**	In *Strangers at Lisconnell* (?)	Unknown	Republ.	Book	Mentioned in *Guide to Irish Fiction.*
1896	Daniel Crilly, MP	**A Christmas Exile; or, The Soil and the Serf**	*Irish Emerald* (Dublin)	Ireland		Periodical	
1896	Anna Dorsey	***Nora Brady's Vow and Mona the Vestal***	New York: Christian Press Association Publishing	United States	Republ.	Book	
1896	Mrs. E. M. Field	***Denis: A Study in Black and White***	London and New York: Macmillan	England, United States	First publ.	Book	
1896	Ethel Greene	**Sown in Tears; or, The Secret Chamber in the Devil's-Hoof: A Tale of Ireland in the Days of the Famine**	*Irish Emerald* (Dublin)	Ireland		Periodical	

(continued)

Chronological List of Creative Works That Contain Famine (*continued*)

Year of publication	Author	Title	Publ. details	Publ. location	First publ. or republ.	Publ. in periodical or book	Comments
1896	K. O'L. G.	**Jimmy Hackett's Temptation: A St. Patrick's Day Story of Uskamore**	*Irish Emerald* (Dublin)	Ireland		Periodical	
1896	John O'Hagan	Famine and Exportation	In *Songs and Ballads of Young Ireland*. London: Downey	England		Book	
1896	S. J. Stafford	In Exile	*Irish Emerald*	Ireland		Book	
1897	Jane Barlow	**Herself**	In *Irish Idylls* (?)	Unknown	Republ.	Book	Mentioned in *Guide to Irish Fiction*.
1897	Jane Barlow	**The Keys of the Chest**	In *A Creel of Irish Stories*. London: Methuen and Co.	England	First publ.	Book	
1897	Finley Peter Dunne	**Mr. Dooley Column**	*Chicago Evening Post*	United States	First publ.	Periodical	
1897	Marcella Fitzpatrick	**Desecrated**	*Irish Rosary* (Dublin)	Ireland		Periodical	
1897	James Clarence Mangan	Siberia	In Louise Imogen Guiney (ed.), *James Clarence Mangan: His Selected Poems*. Norwood, MA: Norwood Press, J. S. Cushing & Co.—Berwick and Smith	United States	Republ.	Book	
1897	Thomas O'Hanlon	Grosse Isle	*Shamrock* (Dublin)	Ireland		Periodical	
1897	William M. Wise	Columbia and the Irish Exile	*Shamrock* (Dublin)	Ireland		Periodical	
1898	W. B.	**A Pathetic Incident**	*Irish Rosary* (Dublin)	Ireland		Periodical	
1898	Jane Barlow	**Herself**	In *Irish Idylls* (?)	Unknown	Republ.	Unknown	Mentioned in *Guide to Irish Fiction*.

Year	Author	Title	Publication	Country		Type	Notes
1898	Jane Barlow	**The Keys of the Chest**	In *A Creel of Irish Stories.* New York: Dodd, Mead & Co.	United States	Republ.	Book	
1898	Emily Lawless	**After the Famine**	In *Traits and Confidences.* London: Methuen	England	First publ.	Book	
1898	Emily Lawless	**Famine Roads and Memories**	In *Traits and Confidences.* London: Methuen	England	First publ.	Book	
1898	Rosa Mulholland	*Marcella Grace*	Unknown	Unknown	Republ.	Book	Mentioned in *Guide to Irish Fiction.*
1898	Sarah Parker	The Mother's Grave	*Irish Emerald* (Dublin)	Ireland		Periodical	
1898	Fanny Parnell	To the Men of England	*Worker's Republic* (Dublin)	Ireland		Periodical	
1899	William Carleton	*The Black Prophet: A Tale of Irish Famine*	London: Lawrence & Bullen	England	Republ.	Book	
1899	Finley Peter Dunne	*Mr. Dooley in the Hearts of His Countrymen*	Boston: Small, Maynard and Co.	United States	Republ.	Book	Originally published in periodical.
1899	Finley Peter Dunne	*Mr. Dooley in the Hearts of His Countrymen*	Toronto: George N. Morang	Canada	Republ.	Book	Originally published in periodical.
1899	Finley Peter Dunne	*Mr. Dooley in the Hearts of His Countrymen*	London: Grant Richards	England	Republ.	Book	Originally published in periodical.
1899	William Butler Yeats	*The Countess Cathleen [play]*	In *Poems.* London: T. Fisher Unwin	England	Republ.	Book	
1900	Anon.	A Lay of the Famine	In S. A. Brooke and T. W. Rolleston (eds.), *A Treasury of Irish Poetry in the English Tongue.* London: Smith, Elder & Co.	England		Book	
1900	William Barry	*The Wizard's Knot*	London: T. Fisher Unwin	England	First publ.	Book	

(continued)

Chronological List of Creative Works That Contain Famine (*continued*)

Year of publication	Author	Title	Publ. details	Publ. location	First publ. or republ.	Publ. in periodical or book	Comments
1900	Jane Elgee (Lady Jane Francesca Agnes Wilde, "Speranza")	The Famine Year	In S. A. Brooke and T. W. Rolleston (eds.), *A Treasury of Irish Poetry in the English Tongue*. London: Smith, Elder & Co.	England	Republ.	Book	Originally published as "The Stricken Land."
1900	Mrs. Nellie Fitzgerald	**Frank O'Connor: A Story of Darkest Ireland**	*Rosary Magazine* 16, no. 4 (Apr.)	United States		Periodical	
1900	John A. Foote	**The Honor of Shaun Malia**	*Catholic World* (Oct.)	United States		Periodical	
1900	John Walsh	Drimin Donn Dilis	In S. A. Brooke and T. W. Rolleston (eds.), *A Treasury of Irish Poetry in the English Tongue*. London: Smith, Elder & Co.	England		Book	
1901	Jane Barlow	**The Keys of the Chest**	In *A Creel of Irish Stories* (?)	Unknown	Republ.	Book	Mentioned in *Guide to Irish Fiction*.
1901	William Francis Barry	***The Wizard's Knot***	London: T. Fisher Unwin	England	Republ.	Book	
1901	William Francis Barry	***The Wizard's Knot***	New York: Century Co.	United States	Republ.	Book	
1901	William Francis Barry	***The Wizard's Knot***	Toronto: Publishers' Syndicate	Canada	Republ.	Book	
1901	M. Cole	One Hundred Years	*Irish Emerald* (Dublin)	Ireland		Periodical	
1901	Kate McPhelim Cleary	**The Mission of Kitty Malone**	*McClure's* 18	United States		Periodical	

1901	Daniel Crilly	**A Christmas Exile; or, The Soil and the Serf**	*Irish-American* (New York)	United States	Republ.	Periodical	
1901	Shiela Mahon	**Little Nora's Christmas**	*Rosary Magazine* 19, no. 6 (Dec.)	United States		Periodical	
1901	Justin McCarthy	***Mononia: A Love Story of 'Forty-Eight***	London: Chatto and Windus	England		Book	
1901	Justin McCarthy	***Mononia: A Love Story of 'Forty-Eight***	Boston: Small, Maynard and Co.	United States		Book	
1901	Richard D'Alton Williams	The Extermination	In *The Poems of Richard D'Alton Williams*. Dublin: Duffy	Ireland		Book	
1901	Richard D'Alton Williams	Kyrie Eleison	In *The Poems of Richard D'Alton Williams*. Dublin: Duffy	Ireland	Republ.	Book	
1901	Richard D'Alton Williams	Vesper Hymn to the Guardian Angels of Ireland	In *The Poems of Richard D'Alton Williams*. Dublin: Duffy	Ireland		Book	
1901	William Butler Yeats	*The Countess Cathleen* [play]	In *Poems*. London: T. Fisher Unwin	England	Republ.	Book	
1902	M. M. Armstrong	**A Friend in Need; or, The Piper's Gift: A Tale of the Irish Famine**	*Irish-American* (New York)	United States	Republ.	Periodical	
1902	Charles Kennett Burrow	***Patricia of the Hills***	London: Lawrence & Bullen	England		Book	
1902	P. J. Coleman	**O'Carroll's Quest**	*Messenger* 37, no. 3 (Mar.)	United States		Periodical	
1902	Mrs. E. M. Field	***Denis: A Study in Black and White***	Unknown	Unknown	Republ.	Book	Mentioned in *Guide to Irish Fiction.*
1903	William Boyle	**The Rise and Fall of Rafferty O'Reilly**	*Irish Packet* 1, no. 10 (Dublin, Dec. 5)	Ireland		Periodical	
1903	David Power Conyngham	***The O'Donnells of Glen Cottage: A Tale of the Famine Years in Ireland***	New York: Unknown	United States	Republ.	Book	Mentioned in *Writing the Irish Famine.*

(continued)

Chronological List of Creative Works That Contain Famine (*continued*)

Year of publication	Author	Title	Publ. details	Publ. location	First publ. or republ.	Publ. in periodical or book	Comments
1903	Charles J. Kickham	***Knocknagow; or, The Homes of Tipperary***	*Gaelic American* (New York)	United States	Republ.	Periodical	
1903	Miriam Williams	**Home to Her Mother**	*Irish Packet* 1, no. 11 (Dublin, Dec. 12)	Ireland		Periodical	
1904	Anon.	**The Little Boy of the Powers (The Returned American's Story)**	*Irish Packet* 1, no. 25 (Dublin, Mar. 19)	Ireland		Periodical	
1904	Harry Allen	**The Frenzy of Famine: A Tale of '47**	*Irish Packet* 1, no. 24 (Dublin, Mar. 12)	Ireland		Periodical	
1904	William Carleton	***The Black Prophet: Thrilling Story of the Famine Days***	*Anglo-Celt*	Ireland	Republ.	Periodical	
1904	William Carleton	***The Black Prophet***	Distributed through the offices of the *Irish Standard* (Minneapolis, MN)	United States	Republ.	Book	
1904	Maud Gonne	***Dawn [play]***	*United Irishman* (Dublin, Oct. 29)	Ireland		Periodical	
1904	Charles J. Kickham	**Scenes and Characters from Famous Irish authors: The Homecoming of Connor Shea**	*Irish Packet* 3, no. 56 (Dublin, Oct. 22)	Ireland	Republ.	Periodical	Excerpt.
1904	Charles J. Kickham	***Knocknagow; or, The Homes of Tipperary***	*Gaelic American* (New York)	United States	Republ.	Periodical	
1904	Michael MacNamara	**Irish Paddy**	*Irish Packet* 3 (Dec.)	Ireland		Periodical	
1904	Matthew M'Donnell Bodkin	**The Holy Well**	*Irish Packet* 3, no. 62 (Dec. 24)	Ireland		Periodical	

Year	Author	Title	Publication	Country		Format	Note
1904	Patrick Sheehan	*Glenanaar*	*Dolphin*	United States	First publ.	Periodical	Mentioned in *Guide to Irish Fiction.*
1905	Jane Barlow	**Con the Quare One**	*Irish Packet* 4, no. 91 (Dublin, Jun. 24)	Ireland	Republ.	Periodical	
1905	Jane Barlow	**Herself**	*Irish Packet* 4, no. 80 (Dublin, Apr. 8)–4, no. 81 (Apr. 15)	Ireland	Republ.	Periodical	
1905	William Carleton	***The Black Prophet: Thrilling Story of the Famine Days***	*Anglo-Celt*	Ireland	Republ.	Periodical	
1905	William Carleton	***The Black Prophet***	Distributed through the offices of the *Irish Standard*	United States	Republ.	Book	
1905	P. J. Coleman	**Outrooted**	*Rosary Magazine* 26, no. 6 (Jun.)	United States		Periodical	
1905	Charles J. Kickham	***Knocknagow; or, The Homes of Tipperary***	*Gaelic American* (New York)	United States	Republ.	Periodical	
1905	Anna Parnell	To the Memory of Commandant Scheepers	In *Old Tales and New.* Dublin and London: Unknown	Ireland, England		Book	Mentioned in *Feminization of Famine.*
1905	Mollie Paterson	**Told on a Jaunting-Car**	*Rosary Magazine* 27, no. 1	United States		Periodical	
1905	Patrick Sheehan	*Glenanaar*	*Dolphin*	United States	First publ.	Periodical	Mentioned in *Guide to Irish Fiction.*
1905	Patrick Sheehan	*Glenanaar*	London, New York, and Bombay: Longmans, Green and Co.	England, United States, India	Republ.	Book	
1906	William Carleton	***The Black Prophet***	Distributed through the offices of the *Gaelic American* (New York)	United States	Republ.	Book	

(continued)

Chronological List of Creative Works That Contain Famine (*continued*)

Year of publication	Author	Title	Publ. details	Publ. location	First publ. or republ.	Publ. in periodical or book	Comments
1906	William Carleton	***The Black Prophet***	Distributed through the offices of the Standard Catholic Book Store/*Irish Standard* offices	United States	Republ.	Book	
1906	John H. Edge	***An Irish Utopia***	Dublin: Hodges, Figgis and Co.	Ireland		Book	
1906	Patrick Sheehan	***Das Christtagskind: Eine Erzählung aus Irland***	Steyl: Missionsdruckerei	Germany	Republ.	Book	German translation of *Glenanaar* by Oskar Jacob.
1907	John Keegan	The Dying Mother's Lament	In *Legends and Poems*. Dublin: Seely, Byrne & Walker	Ireland		Book	
1907	M. Lenahan	**Dark Mary's Sorrow**	*Irish Packet* 9, no. 211 (Dublin, Oct. 12)	Ireland		Periodical	
1907	Patrick Sheehan	***Ange Égaré d'un Paradis Ruiné***	Paris: Lethielleux	France	Republ.	Book	French translation of *Glenanaar*.
1907	William Butler Yeats	*The Countess Cathleen* [play]	In *The Poetical Works of William B. Yeats: Vol. II Dramatic Poems*. London and New York: Macmillan	England, United States	Republ.	Book	
1908	Joseph Guinan	***The Moores of Glynn***	London: R. and T. Washbourne	England		Book	
1908	Rosa Mulholland	***The Return of Mary O'Murrough***	London and Edinburgh: Sands and Co.	England, Scotland	First publ.	Book	
1908 (?)	Rosa Mulholland	***The Return of Mary O'Murrough***	Dublin: Phoenix	Ireland	First publ.	Book	Mentioned in *Guide to Irish Fiction*.

Year	Author	Title	Publication	Country		Format	Notes
1909	Eva of the *Nation* (Mary Kelly)	Home Again	In *Poems by 'Eva' of the Nation.* Dublin: M. H. Gill & Son	Ireland	Republ.	Book	
1909	Eva of the *Nation* (Mary Kelly)	A Scene for Ireland	In *Poems by 'Eva' of the Nation.* Dublin: M. H. Gill & Son	Ireland	Republ.	Book	
1909	James Clarence Mangan	Siberia	*Cork County Eagle and Munster Advertiser* (Jan. 16)	Ireland	Republ	Periodical	Excerpt.
1909	James Clarence Mangan	Siberia	*Southern Star* (Jan. 16)	Ireland	Republ.	Periodical	Excerpt.
1909	L. T. Meade	**The Stormy Petrel**	London: Hurst and Blackett	England		Book	
1910	James Berry	**Tales of the West: Recollections of My Early Boyhood**	*Mayo News*	Ireland		Periodical	
1910	Andrew Merry (Mildred Darby)	**The Hunger**	London: Melrose	England		Book	
1910	Rosa Mulholland	**The Return of Marry O'Murrough**	Unknown	Unknown	Republ.	Book	Mentioned in *Guide to Irish Fiction.*
1911	James Berry	**Tales of the West: Recollections of My Early Boyhood**	*Mayo News*	Ireland		Periodical	
1911	William Butler Yeats	The Countess Cathleen [play]	In *The Poetical Works of William B. Yeats: Vol. II Dramatical Poems.* London and New York: Macmillan	England, United States	Republ.	Book	
1912	Slieve Foy	**Attie and His Father: A Tale of the Poor**	In *Stories of Irish Life, Past and Present.* London: Lynwood	England		Book	
1912	Ruth Sawyer	**The Tinker's Meg**	*Outlook* (Feb. 24)	United States		Periodical	

(continued)

Chronological List of Creative Works That Contain Famine (*continued*)

Year of publica-tion	Author	Title	Publ. details	Publ. location	First publ. or republ.	Publ. in periodical or book	Comments
1912	William Butler Yeats	*The Countess Cathleen* [play]	In *The Poetical Works of William B. Yeats: Vol. II Dramatical Poems.* London and New York: Macmillan	England, United States	Republ.	Book	
1913	James Berry	**Tales of the West: Recollections of My Early Boyhood**	*Mayo News*	Ireland		Periodical	
1913	Alexander Irvine	**My Lady of the Chimney-Corner**	London: Eveleigh Nash	England		Book	
1914	William C. Upton	**Uncle Pat's Cabin: A Story of Irish Life**	New York: printed for the author by P. J. Kenedy and Sons	United States	Republ.	Book	
1915	G. A. Birmingham (James Owen Hannay)	**Minnie's Bishop and Other Stories**	New York: Hodder and Stoughton	United States		Book	
1915	Eugene Clancy	The Cleansing Tears	*Harper's Magazine* 130 (Feb.)	United States		Periodical	
1915	Patrick Sheehan	**The Graves at Kilmorna: A Story of '67**	New York, London, Bombay, Calcutta, and Madras: Longmans, Green and Co.	United States, England, India	First publ.	Book	
1916	Mary Synon	**My Grandmother and Myself**	*Scribner's Magazine* (Aug.)	United States		Periodical	
1917	Elizabeth Hely Walshe	**Kingston's Revenge: A Story of Bravery**	London: Religious Tract Society	England	Republ.	Book	First published as *Golden Hills* in 1865.

1918	Patrick Sheehan	*The Graves at Kilmorna: A Story of '67*	New York, London, Bombay, Calcutta, and Madras: Longmans, Green and Co.	United States, England, India	Republ.	Book	
1918	James Stephens	*Hunger: A Dublin Story*	Dublin: Candle Press	Ireland		Book	
1919	Louis J. Walsh	*The Next Time: A Story of 'Forty-Eight*	Dublin: M. H. Gill and Son	Ireland		Book	
1920	Aodh De Blácam	*Holy Romans: A Young Irishman's Story*	Dublin: Maunsel and Co.	Ireland		Book	
1926	Charles J. Kickham	**Never Give Up**	In *Tales of Tipperary*. Dublin: Talbot Press	Ireland	Republ.	Book	
1929	Jane Elgee (Lady Jane Francesca Agnes Wilde, "Speranza")	The Famine Year	In *Ballads of Irish History for Schools*. Dublin	Ireland	Republ.	Book	Originally published as "The Stricken Land."
1937	Liam O'Flaherty	*Famine*	New York: Random House	United States	First publ.	Book	
1937	Liam O'Flaherty	*Famine*	London: Gollancz	England	First publ.	Book	

BIBLIOGRAPHY

Periodicals

"Agitate! Agitate!" *McGee's Illustrated Weekly: Devoted to Catholic Art, Literature and Education* 3, no. 5, December 22, 1877, 67.

Allen, Harry. "The Frenzy of Famine: A Tale of '47." *Irish Packet* 1, no. 24, March 12, 1904, 567.

"All the Correspondents . . ." *McGee's Illustrated Weekly: Devoted to Catholic Art, Literature and Education* 5, no. 13, February 15, 1879, 194.

"The Announcement That Capt. Boycott . . ." *Daily Witness*, July 27, 1881, 4.

"Are the Irish a Reading People?" *Gaelic American: A Journal Devoted to the Cause of Irish Independence, Irish Literature, and the Interests of the Irish Race* 3, no. 51, December 22, 1906, 7.

Armstrong, M. M. "A Friend in Need; or, The Piper's Gift: A Story of the Irish Famine." *Irish-American* 54, no. 16, April 16, 1902, 1, 4.

———. "The Piper's Gift: A Tale of the Irish Famine." *McGee's Illustrated Weekly: Devoted to Catholic Art, Literature and Education* 1, no. 17, March 17, 1877, 262–63.

"Audacious English Lying." *Irish World and American Industrial Liberator* 33, no. 1793, April 18, 1903, 1.

"Banished for £5 a Head." *Wexford People* 30, November 29, 1882, 3.

Barlow, Jane. "Con the Quare One." *Irish Packet* 4, no. 91, June 24, 1905, 298.

———. "Herself." *Irish Packet* 4, no. 80, April 8, 1905, 25–27; 4, no. 81, April 15, 1905, 49–51.

Bodkin, Matthias McDonnell. "The Holy Well." *Irish Packet* 3, no. 62, December 3, 1904, 224–27.

"Book Notices." *True Witness and Catholic Chronicle*, February 10, 1886, 8.

"Books and Bookmen, a Weekly Review Column." *Irish Independent*, August 18, 1913, 9.

"A Candid Answer" [response to]. *McGee's Illustrated Weekly: Devoted to Catholic Art, Literature and Education* 3, no. 5, December 22, 1877, 67.

Carleton, William. "Fair Gurtha; or, The Hungry Grass: A Legend of the Dumb Hill." *Dublin University Magazine: A Literary and Political Journal* 47, January–June 1856, 414–35.

———. "Fair Gurtha; or, The Hungry Grass: A Legend of the Dumb Hill." *Irish-American* 28, no. 35, August 26, 1876–no. 38, September 16, 1876.

Carpenter, P. "To C. S. Parnell, M.P., on His Visit to the United States." *Young Ireland: An Illustrated Irish Magazine of Entertainment and Instruction* 6, no. 6, February 7, 1880, 95.

"A Case in Point" (editorial response to letter by D. D.). *McGee's Illustrated Weekly: Devoted to Catholic Art, Literature and Education* 2, no. 20, October 6, 1877, 306.

"Catholic Colonization." *McGee's Illustrated Weekly: Devoted to Catholic Art, Literature and Education* 6, no. 12, August 9, 1879, 595.

"The Christmas Number of 'Young Ireland.'" *Nation*, December 25, 1875, 12; December 20, 1884, 2.

"Circulation of THE WITNESS . . ." *Daily Witness*, April 14, 1881, 4.

A Clareman [pseud.]. "A Reproach." *Young Ireland: An Illustrated Irish Magazine of Entertainment and Instruction* 6, no. 9, February 28, 1880, 139.

Cole, M. "One Hundred Years." *Irish Emerald* 10, no. 15, April 13, 1901, 236.

"Correspondence." *Gael: A Monthly Journal Devoted to the Preservation and Cultivation of the Irish Language and the Autonomy of the Irish Nation*, November 1900, 325.

C. P. M. "A Chapter of Irish History: The Famine of 1846–1850." *Celtic Monthly: An Illustrated Irish-American Magazine; Devoted to Literature, Music, the Drama, and the Arts and Current Events* 3, no. 3, March 1880, 251–57; 3, no. 4, April 1880, 350–58; 3, no. 5, May 1880, 426–34.

Croghan [pseud.]. "Evicted!" *Young Ireland: An Irish Magazine of Entertainment and Instruction* 13, no. 24, June 11, 1887, 375.

Cruise, F. R. "The Emigrant Question." *Freeman's Journal* 114, July 3, 1880, 3.

Cusack, Margaret Anna (Sister Mary Francis Clare, "the Nun of Kenmare"). *From Killarney to New York; or, How Thade Became a Banker. McGee's Illustrated Weekly: Devoted to Catholic Art, Literature and Education* 2, no. 12, August 11, 1877–no. 22, October 20, 1877.

Davis, Thomas. "A Song for the Irish Militia." *Irish Packet* 1, no. 10, December 5, 1903, 233.

Davitt, Michael. "Davitt's Answer on Coercion." *Irish World and American Industrial Liberator* 28, no. 1472, November 12, 1898, 1, 9.

———. "The Distressed Districts of Ireland." *Irish World and American Industrial Liberator* 28, no. 1451, June 18, 1898, 5.

———. "Objections and Principles Good." *Irish World and American Industrial Liberator* 28, no. 1472, November 12, 1898, 4.

"Davitt on the Land Bill." *Irish World and American Industrial Liberator* 33, no. 1704, April 25, 1903, 6.

De. Grey [pseud.]. "An American Letter." *United Irishman: A National Weekly Review* 3, no. 58, April 7, 1900, 3.

Depasse, Hector. "Europe, England and the Transvaal." *United Irishman: A National Weekly Review* 2, no. 28, September 9, 1899, 4.

Devoy, John, Joseph I. C. Clarke, William Carroll, M. Kerwin, and Robert Ellis Thompson. "Irish Comments on an English Text." *North American Review* 147, no. 382, September 1888, 281–301.

"The Distress in Ireland." *Harp: A Magazine of General Literature* 5, no. 3, January 1880, 123–24.

"The Distress in Ireland." *Irish World and American Industrial Liberator* 28, no. 1440, April 2, 1898, 4.

Dougall, John. "Prospectus of the Montreal Witness, Weekly Review, and Family Newspaper." *Montreal Witness, Weekly Review and Family Newspaper* 1, no. 1, December 15, 1845, 1.

Editorial. *McGee's Illustrated Weekly: Devoted to Catholic Art, Literature and Education* 4, no. 21, October 12, 1878, 322.

"Editorial Department: Mr. Dillon O'Brien . . ." *Celtic Monthly: An Illustrated Irish-American Magazine; Devoted to Literature, Music, the Drama, and the Arts and Current Events* 4, no. 4, October 1880, 378.

"Emigration and Colonization." *McGee's Illustrated Weekly: Devoted to Catholic Art, Literature and Education* 1, no. 26, May 19, 1877, 402–403.

"De Engelsche Koningin . . ." *Soerabaiasch Handelsblad: Staat- en Letterkundig Dagblad van Nederlands-Indië* 48, no. 113, May 15, 1900, 1.

"England and India." *Irish World and American Industrial Liberator* 28, no. 1410, September 4, 1897, 5.

"England and Young Africa." Boston *Pilot* 11, no. 31, July 29, 1848, 6.

"England Wants the Earth." *Irish World and American Industrial Liberator* 26, no. 1323, January 4, 1896, 5.

"An English Christmas Story." *McGee's Illustrated Weekly: Devoted to Catholic Art, Literature and Education* 3, no. 6, December 29, 1877, 90–91.

"English Novels for English Ladies." *Hawaiian Gazette*, May 6, 1885, supplement.

Ether [pseud.]. "Recruiting." *United Irishman: A National Weekly Review* 3, no. 58, April 7, 1900, 6.

"Famine in India." *True Witness and Catholic Chronicle* 27, no. 28, February 23, 1877, 1.

"Famine in India and Ireland." *Nation*, February 23, 1867, 12.

"Famine, or Farms." *McGee's Illustrated Weekly: Devoted to Catholic Art, Literature and Education* 2, no. 16, September 8, 1877, 242.

F. G. [pseud.]. "A True Story of Black '47." *Young Ireland: An Illustrated Magazine of Entertainment and Instruction* 8, no. 9, March 4, 1882, 143.

"Fireside Gossip and General Notes." *Irish Fireside* 6, no. 146, April 3, 1886, 240.

"The Following Brief Item . . ." *Celtic Monthly: An Illustrated Irish-American Magazine; Devoted to Literature, Music, the Drama, and the Arts and Current Events* 2, no. 1, July 1879, 90.

"For a Free Ireland: Monster Meeting at the Academy of Music; Cheers for Boers—Hisses for English." *Irish-American* 53, no. 8, February 23, 1901, 4.

"Foreign Notes: England Starving the Boer Women and Children." *United Irishman: A National Weekly Review* 3, no. 46, January 13, 1900, 1.

Foreign Secretary [pseud.]. "Foreign Notes: Piracy in Africa and Famine in India." *United Irishman: A National Weekly Review* 3, no. 45, January 6, 1900, 1.

Gonne, Maud. "Appeal to the Women of America! Miss Maud Gonne, Writing on the Spot, Describes the Horrors Her Eyes Behold: English Government Wages Ten Cents a Day." *Irish World and American Industrial Liberator* 28, no. 1440, April 2, 1898, 1.

———. "The Boer Women." *United Irishman: A National Weekly Review*, March 17, 1900. In *Maud Gonne's Irish Nationalist Writings, 1895–1946*, edited by Karen Steele, 164–66. Dublin: Irish Academic Press, 2004.

———. *Dawn. United Irishman: A National Weekly Review*, October 29, 1904, 204–12.

———. "The Famine Queen." *United Irishman: A National Weekly Review* 3, no. 58, April 7, 1900, 5.

———. "Her Subjects." *United Irishman: A National Weekly Review* 3, no. 60, April 21, 1900, 5.

———. "Her Subjects" (part 2). *United Irishman: A National Weekly Review* 3, no. 61, April 28, 1900, 5.

———. "India." *United Irishman: A National Weekly Review* 3, no. 63, May 12, 1900, 5.

———. "In the Event of War." *United Irishman: A National Weekly Review*, December 22, 1900, 4.

———. "Ireland and Her Foreign Relations." *United Irishman: A National Weekly Review*, December 22, 1900. In *Maud Gonne's Irish Nationalist Writings, 1895–1946*, edited by Karen Steele, 177–81. Dublin: Irish Academic Press, 2004.

———. "Ireland and the Children." *United Irishman: A National Weekly Review*, June 7, 1902. In *Maud Gonne's Irish Nationalist Writings, 1895–1946*, edited by Karen Steele, 135–37. Dublin: Irish Academic Press, 2004.

———. "Ireland To-Day." *United Irishman: A National Weekly Review* 6, no. 135, September 28, 1901, 2–3.

———. "Irishman and the British Army." *Worker's Republic*, September 24, 1898. In *Maud Gonne's Irish Nationalist Writings, 1895–1946*, edited by Karen Steele, 47–49. Dublin: Irish Academic Press, 2004.

———. "Irishmen and the English Army." *United Irishman: A National Weekly Review* 4, no. 86, October 20, 1900, 5.

———. "Letter from Maud Gonne." *Irish World and American Industrial Liberator* 28, no. 1441, April 9, 1898, 5.

———. "Letter from Maud Gonne: We Live under a Hard Government Which Understands How to Make Poverty Not How to Soften or End It." *Irish World and American Industrial Liberator* 28, no. 1455, July 16, 1898, 5.

———. "Relief Work in Erris." *Freeman's Journal*, March 9, 1898. In *Maud Gonne's Irish Nationalist Writings, 1895–1946*, edited by Karen Steele, 122–25. Dublin: Irish Academic Press, 2004.

———. "The Reward of Serving England." *United Irishman: A National Weekly Review* 2, no. 34, October 21, 1899, 5.

———. "Signs of Hope." *United Irishman: A National Weekly Review*, January 13, 1900. In *Maud Gonne's Nationalist Writings, 1895–1946*, edited by Karen Steele, 162–63. Dublin: Irish Academic Press, 2004.

———. "The Situation Is Horrible! The Suffering of the People—In the Famine Districts—Is Beyond Description." *Irish World and American Industrial Liberator* 28, no. 1441, April 9, 1898, 1.

———. "Toleration." *United Irishman: A National Weekly Review* 5, no. 123, July 6, 1901, 6.

———. "The World's Justice." *United Irishman: A National Weekly Review*, August 25, 1900. In *Maud Gonne's Irish Nationalist Writings, 1895–1946*, edited by Karen Steele, 172–76. Dublin: Irish Academic Press, 2004.

"Good Books for the Holidays." *Irish Standard*, December 17, 1904, 2.

"Good Books for the Home and Fireside." *Irish Standard*, March 11, 1905, 2.

Greene, Ethel. "Sown in Tears; or, The Secret Chamber in the Devil's-Hoof: A Tale of Ireland in the Days of the Famine." *Irish Emerald* 5, no. 1, January 4, 1896–5, no. 8, February 22, 1896.

Gwynn, Stephen. "Looking at Ireland: I—Miss Jane Barlow." *Irish Times*, September 14, 1946.

"Haagsch Nieuws: Maud Gonne, de Schoone Iersche." *Java-Bode: Nieuws, Handels- en Advertentieblad voor Nederlandsch-Indië* 42, no. 286, December 11, 1893, 2.

Harriman, Alice. "Thomas Francis Meagher 1823–1867." *Irish Packet* 5, no. 107, October 14, 1905, 68.

H. H., Nannie. *Dick O'Dell: A Story of '48. Young Ireland: An Illustrated Magazine of Entertainment and Instruction* 2, no. 36, September 2, 1876–3, no. 6, February 10, 1877.

"Hibernians: What They Have Been Doing the Past Week—General News Notes." *Kentucky Irish American* 4, no. 19, May 12, 1900, 4.

"Home Rule for Ireland: Boer War Will Help It; Michael Davitt Now Claims Independence." *Irish-American* 53, no. 36, September 7, 1901, 4.

Ier [pseud.]. "Blackguarding the Boer." *United Irishman: A National Weekly Review* 2, no. 33, October 14, 1899, 5.

———. "Civilising the Kafir." *United Irishman: A National Weekly Review* 2, no. 41, December 9, 1899, 3.

———. "Slim Piet." *United Irishman: A National Weekly Review* 3, no. 58, April 7, 1900, 5.

"The Indian Famine." *True Witness and Catholic Chronicle* 28, no. 1, October 3, 1877, 1.

"India's Awful Visitation." *Irish World and American Industrial Liberator* 28, no. 1382, February 20, 1897, 5.

"International Unfairness." *McGee's Illustrated Weekly: Devoted to Catholic Art, Literature and Education* 2, no. 19, September 29, 1877, 290.

"Ireland and the Indian Famine." *True Witness and Catholic Chronicle* 28, no. 1, October 3, 1877, 1.

"Ireland in 1877." *McGee's Illustrated Weekly: Devoted to Catholic Art, Literature and Education* 3, no. 10, January 26, 1878, 146.

"Ireland's Continued Decay: Results of Eviction and Misgovernment; A Startling Picture." *Irish-American* 53, no. 21, May 25, 1901, 1, 5.

"The Irish Agitation." *Daily Witness*, April 12, 1881, 2.

"An Irish Boer Alliance." *Irish-American* 54, no. 38, September 30, 1902, 4.

"The Irish Industries Depot." *Gaelic American: A Journal Devoted to the Cause of Irish Independence, Irish Literature, and the Interests of the Irish Race*, July 29, 1916, 5.

"The Irish Land Bill." *Irish World and American Industrial Liberator* 33, no. 1701, April 4, 1903, 1, 2.

"Irish National Library." *Nation*, February 3, 1877, 17.

"Irish Nation Speaks Out." *Irish World and American Industrial Liberator* 33, no. 1704, April 25, 1903, 1, 2.

"Irish Store of New York." *Irish Press: A Journal of Irish News, Irish Opinion and Irish Literature, Published in the Interest of the Republic of Ireland*, June 26, 1920, 8.

"L'Irlande Libre." *United Irishman: A National Weekly Review* 3, no. 58, April 7, 1900, 4.

Isidore [pseud.]. "The Evicted Tenant's Ruined Home." *Young Ireland: An Irish Magazine of Entertainment and Instruction* 13, no. 3, January 15, 1887, 36.

———. "Old Times." *Young Ireland: A Literary Magazine for the Irish Race* 1 (new series), no. 16, September 15, 1888, 255.

"The 'Jail Journal' of John Mitchel." *Evening Herald* (Dublin), August 23, 1913, 5.

J. G. [pseud.]. "'Young Ireland'—A Retrospect." *Young Ireland: An Irish Magazine of Entertainment and Instruction*, February 5, 1887, 87–88.

"John Mitchel Centenary: Father Finlay Delivers Interesting Lecture on Irish Leader—Says 'Jail Journal' Is Literary Masterpiece." *Gaelic American: A Journal Devoted to the Cause of Irish Independence, Irish Literature, and the Interests of the Irish Race*, December 18, 1915, 2.

"John Mitchel's Jail Journal." *Freeman's Journal and Catholic Register*, September 10, 1863, 2.

"John Mitchel: The Dead Patriot; His Labours and Struggles for Ireland." *Irish-American* 27, no. 13, March 28, 1875, 2.

J. P. G. [pseud.]. "Ireland and 'The Tour in Ireland.'" *Daily Witness*, August 4, 1881, 2.

Justitia [pseud.]. "Ireland and the 'Witness' Correspondent." *Daily Witness*, October 26, 1881, 2.

Kavanagh, Henry J. "Is a Change Necessary in the Present System of Land Tenure in Ireland?" *Harp: A Magazine of General Literature* 5, no. 5, March 1880, 213–17.

Keary, Annie. *Castle Daly: The Story of and Irish Home Thirty Years Ago. Daily Witness*, November 17, 1880–May 17, 1881.

Kenny, Annie M. "The Exile's Message." *Young Ireland: A Literary Magazine for the Irish Race* 2 (new series), no. 9, March 2, 1889, 134.

Kickham, Charles. *Knocknagow; or, The Homes of Tipperary. American Celt* 1, 1870.

———. "Scenes and Characters from Famous Irish Authors: The Homecoming of Connor Shea." *Irish Packet* 3, no. 56, October 22, 1904, 83.

K. O'L. G. [pseud.]. "Jimmy Hackett's Temptation: A St. Patrick's Day Story of Uskamore." *Irish Emerald* 5, no. 12, March 21, 1896, 177–78.

"The Labor Movement." Boston *Pilot* 29, no. 46, November 17, 1867, 1.

"The Labour Question." *American Celt* 1, no. 10, October 22, 1870, 145.

"The Land League." *Daily Witness*, February 15, 1881, 4.

"The Land Purchase Act: Details of the Way It Works Described by Secretary O'Callaghan." *Irish World and American Industrial Liberator* 34, no. 1791, December 24, 1904, 1–2.

"Land Purchase Finance." *Freeman's Journal*, January 12, 1904, 5.

"Legalised Murder." *Connaught Telegraph*, April 4, 1885, 4.

"A Letter of Introduction." *McGee's Illustrated Weekly: Devoted to Catholic Art, Literature and Education* 1, no. 1, November 11, 1876, 2.

"Literature." *Leinster Express*, November 14, 1846, 3.

"The Little Boy of the Powers (The Returned American's Story)." *Irish Packet* 1, no. 25, March 19, 1903, 588–89.

Mackey, M. "Con Driscoll; or, The Hatchet the Smith Made." *Young Ireland: An Illustrated Magazine of Entertainment and Instruction* 7, no. 43, October 22, 1881, 673–76; 7, no. 44, October 29, 1881, 689–92; 7, no. 45, November 5, 1881, 705–708.

———. "His Honour's Word; or, A Victim of 'Painful Duty': A Tale of the Times." *Young Ireland: An Illustrated Magazine of Entertainment and Instruction* 7, no. 37, September 10, 1881, 577–80; 7, no. 38, September 17, 1881, 593–96.

MacNamara, Michael. "Irish Paddy." *Irish Packet* 3, no. 62, December 3, 1904, 238–40.

"Maud Gonne's Famine Queen." *Indianapolis Journal* 1, no. 98, April 8, 1900, 1.

"Maud Gonne's Roast." *Wichita Daily Eagle* 33, no. 124, April 10, 1900, 8.

Mayer, Denis L. "The Murder Famine of '48: But This Sort of Thing Is Sure to Last While English Rule in Ireland Lasts." *Irish World and American Industrial Liberator* 28, no. 1442, April 16, 1898, n.p.

McClure, J. "The Irish of Ulster." *Celtic Monthly: An Illustrated Irish-American Magazine; Devoted to Literature, Music, the Drama, and the Arts and Current Events* 4, no. 5, November 1880, 439–40.

McDougall, Margaret Dixon. "Belfast—Temperance—'The Eve of a Great Rebellion'—The Poor-House—County Down—Making Ends Meet—Waiting for Something to Turn Up." *Almonte Gazette*, March 25, 1881, 1. https://gazette.mvtm.ca/display-pdf?ref =1881-03-25-01. Accessed January 30, 2024.

———. "A Tour through Ireland." *Daily Witness*, March 15, 1881, 2. https://numerique.banq .qc.ca/patrimoine/details/52327/3625829. Accessed January 30, 2024.

———. "A Tour through Ireland." *Daily Witness*, March 24, 1881, 2. https://numerique.banq .qc.ca/patrimoine/details/52327/3625837. Accessed January 30, 2024.

———. "A Tour through Ireland." *Daily Witness*, April 12, 1881, 2. https://numerique.banq .qc.ca/patrimoine/details/52327/3625853. Accessed January 30, 2024.

———. "A Tour through Ireland." *Daily Witness*, April 16, 1881, 2. https://numerique.banq .qc.ca/patrimoine/details/52327/3625856. Accessed January 30, 2024.

———. "A Tour through Ireland." *Daily Witness*, April 27, 1881, 2. https://numerique.banq .qc.ca/patrimoine/details/52327/3625865. Accessed January 30, 2024.

———. "A Tour through Ireland." *Daily Witness*, May 14, 1881, 2. https://numerique.banq .qc.ca/patrimoine/details/52327/3625880. Accessed January 30, 2024.

———. "A Tour through Ireland." *Daily Witness*, May 16, 1881, 2. https://numerique.banq .qc.ca/patrimoine/details/52327/3625881. Accessed January 30, 2024.

———. "A Tour through Ireland." *Daily Witness*, June 8, 1881, 2. https://numerique.banq.qc.ca /patrimoine/details/52327/3625900. Accessed January 30, 2024.

———. "A Tour through Ireland." *Daily Witness*, July 13, 1881, 2. https://numerique.banq .qc.ca/patrimoine/details/52327/3625929. Accessed January 30, 2024.

———. "A Tour through Ireland." *Daily Witness*, July 27, 1881, 2. https://numerique.banq .qc.ca/patrimoine/details/52327/3625941. Accessed January 30, 2024.

———. "A Tour through Ireland." *Daily Witness*, September 29, 1881, 2. https://numerique .banq.qc.ca/patrimoine/details/52327/3625996. Accessed January 30, 2024.

———. "A Tour through Ireland." *Daily Witness*, October 19, 1881, 2. https://numerique.banq .qc.ca/patrimoine/details/52327/3626013. Accessed January 30, 2024.

McGee, James E. "The Immigrants." *McGee's Illustrated Weekly: Devoted to Catholic Art, Literature and Education* 1, no. 1, November 25, 1876, 10.

"McGee's Illustrated Weekly." *McGee's Illustrated Weekly: Devoted to Catholic Art, Literature and Education* 1, no. 8, January 13, 1877, 114.

Millevoye, Lucien. "From Pretoria to Pekin." *United Irishman: A National Weekly Review* 4, no. 85, October 13, 1900, 4.

"The Miners of Pennsylvania." Boston *Pilot* 26, no. 12, March 21, 1863, 4.

Mitchel, John. [installment of] *John Mitchel's Jail Journal. Kerryman*, November 16, 1907, 9.

———. "Leaves from John Mitchel's 'Jail Journal.'" *Nation*, April 24, 1875, 6.

Montreal [pseud.]. "The Irish Land Question." *Daily Witness*, February 9, 1881, 2.

"Mr. Parnell, Not Content . . ." *Daily Witness*, February 12, 1881, 4.

"Mr. T. O'Neill Russell . . ." *Celtic Monthly: An Illustrated Irish-American Magazine; Devoted to Literature, Music, the Drama, and the Arts and Current Events* 2, no. 1, July 1879, 91.

Mulholland, Rosa. "Recent Irish Novelists." *Charlottetown Herald* 19, no. 21, March 19, 1890, 1.

Mullowney, Murty [pseud.]. "The Shadow of Death; or, The Story of the Old Larch Tree." *Irish-American* 40, no. 17, May 5, 1888, 5.

"Murderous British Rule in India." *Gaelic American: A Journal Devoted to the Cause of Irish Independence, Irish Literature, and the Interests of the Irish Race* 2, no. 31, August 5, 1905, 4.

"National Works." *Nation*, January 17, 1901, 19.

"The New Land Policy." *Irish-American*, February 21, 1903, 4.

O'Brien, Charlotte Grace. *Light and Shade. Young Ireland: An Illustrated Irish Magazine of Entertainment and Instruction* 6, no. 6, February 7, 1880–6, no. 36, September 4, 1880.

O'Brien, Dillon. "To the Editors of the Irish-American Press." *McGee's Illustrated Weekly: Devoted to Catholic Art, Literature and Education* 3, no. 18, March 23, 1878, 295.

O'Brien, Richard Baptist. *The D'Altons of Crag: An Irish Story of '48 and '49. Harp: A Magazine of General Literature* 5, no. 1, November 1879–5, no. 9, July 1880.

O'Brien, Thomas [Clontarf, pseud.]. "Work for Ireland." *Young Ireland: An Illustrated Irish Magazine of Entertainment and Instruction* 6, no. 49, December 4, 1880, 780.

O'Brien, William Smith. "Never Despair." *Irish Packet* 1, no. 10, December 5, 1903, 220.

O'Horahan, M. J. "To Irish Slavery." *Young Ireland: An Irish Magazine of Entertainment and Instruction* 13, no. 36, September 3, 1887, 564.

Olena [pseud.]. "The American Letter: A Tale of the Great Famine." *Young Ireland: An Irish Magazine of Entertainment and Instruction* 14, no. 5, February 4, 1888–14, no. 7, February 18, 1888.

"One of the Resolutions . . ." *Freeman's Journal*, December 16, 1904, 7.

"The Only Possible Remedy." *Irish World and American Industrial Liberator* 34, no. 1747, February 20, 1904, 1, 2.

"On the Rock of Cashel." *Irish World and American Industrial Liberator* 29, no. 1484, February 4, 1899, 1, 6.

"Our Correspondent in Ireland." *Daily Witness*, March 9, 1881, 4.

"Our Illustrations: On a Farm and on the Docks." *McGee's Illustrated Weekly: Devoted to Catholic Art, Literature and Education* 6, no. 12, August 9, 1879, 595, 598.

"Our New Story." *McGee's Illustrated Weekly: Devoted to Catholic Art, Literature and Education* 2, no. 7, July 7, 1877, 98.

"The People of Ireland Demand Unity." *Irish World and American Industrial Liberator* 29, no. 1481, January 14, 1899, 1.

"Perpetuating 'Irish Famine': 'Unproductive Public Works' versus Seeding the Lands." *Irish-American* 32, no. 9, February 28, 1880.

"The Profit and Loss of Strikes." Boston *Pilot* 26, no. 52, December 26, 1863, 4.

"Rays of Hope." *McGee's Illustrated Weekly: Devoted to Catholic Art, Literature and Education* 2, no. 18, September 22, 1877, 274.

"Redpath Becomes Again Vituperative." *Daily Witness*, July 27, 1881, 3.

Redpath, James. "Famine Scenes in Ireland." *Harp: A Magazine of General Literature* 5, no. 9, July 1880, 435–39.

"Remember the Poor." *McGee's Illustrated Weekly: Devoted to Catholic Art, Literature and Education* 1, no. 6, December 30, 1876, 82.

"Republican Revolt against Imperialism." *Irish World and American Industrial Liberator* 29, no. 1484, February 4, 1899, 1, 6.

"Reviews: Ireland Thirty Years Ago." *Nation*, September 4, 1875, 10.

Reville, John. "The Great Irish Famine." *Irish-American* 27, no. 10, March 6, 1875, 5.

Roach, John, Robert Ellis Thompson, and Nelson Dingley Jr. "Benefits of the Tariff System." *North American Review* 139, no. 335, October 1884, 372–403.

"Seized by Police." *Kentucky Irish American* 4, no. 24, June 16, 1900, 1.

"Seizure of a Newspaper." *Irish Standard* 15, no. 32, June 16, 1900, 1.

Sigerson, Hester. *A Ruined Race; or, The Last MacManus of Drumroosk. Young Ireland: A Literary Magazine for the Irish Race* 1 (new series), no. 14, September 1, 1888–1, no. 22, October 27, 1888.

"Sister Mary Francis Clare, the Nun of Kenmare." *McGee's Illustrated Weekly: Devoted to Catholic Art, Literature and Education* 2, no. 12, August 11, 1877, 180.

"Sound Sense on Irish Politics." *McGee's Illustrated Weekly: Devoted to Catholic Art, Literature and Education* 2, no. 11, August 4, 1877, 166.

"South Africa Another Ireland." *Irish World and American Industrial Liberator* 33, no. 1710, June 6, 1903, 6.

"Strikes—Difficulty among the Coal Miners." Boston *Pilot* 28, no. 38, September 23, 1865, 4.

"Subscribe for McGee's Illustrated Weekly." *McGee's Illustrated Weekly: Devoted to Catholic Art, Literature and Education* 5, no. 13, February 15, 1879, 208.

Sullivan, Timothy D. "The Friends and Foes of Ireland" (serial). *Young Ireland: An Illustrated Magazine of Entertainment and Instruction* 1, 1875.

———. "The Story of England" (serial). *Young Ireland: An Irish Magazine of Entertainment and Instruction* 2, 1876.

Sweeny, John. "Letter of Rt. Rev. Dr. Sweeny on Emigration and Colonization in New Brunswick." *New York Tablet: A Family Journal* 4, no. 37, February 9, 1861, 10.

Templeman, William. "A Misapprehension." *Almonte Gazette*, July 13, 1883, 3.

"The Ten Hour Movement." Boston *Pilot* 29, no. 46, November 17, 1866, 1.

"Thade M'Sweeney; or, A Tenant Farmer's Trials: A Story of the Great Famine." *Irish-American* 32, no. 15, April 10, 1880, 3.

Thompson, Robert Ellis. "Free Trade Slays Millions." *Irish World and American Industrial Liberator* 28, no. 1382, February 20, 1897, 5.

———. "The Irish Dispersion." *Irish World and American Industrial Liberator* 33, no. 1727, October 3, 1903, 5.

———. "Modern Cannibalism." *Irish World and American Industrial Liberator* 28, no. 1459, August 13, 1898, 4.

———. "The Most Distressful Country." *Irish World and American Industrial Liberator* 34, no. 1791, December 24, 1904, 5.

Three Rivers [pseud.]. "The Irish Land Question: A Reply to 'Montreal' of February 9th." *Daily Witness*, March 5, 1881, 2.

"The Tide of Emigration to This Country Is Again upon the Flood." *McGee's Illustrated Weekly: Devoted to Catholic Art, Literature and Education* 6, no. 22, October 18, 1879, 754.
"Today's Telegraphs: The Irish Land Bill" (via Dominion Line). *Daily Witness*, July 27, 1881, 1.
"The Transvaal Irish Brigade." *United Irishman: A National Weekly Review* 3, no. 58, April 7, 1900, 2.
"Under the Union Jack." *United Irishman: A National Weekly Review* 3, no. 58, April 7, 1900, 5.
"The University Magazine." *Freeman's Journal*, June 4, 1846, 3.
"We Reproduce Today." *True Witness and Catholic Chronicle*. August 16, 1850, 5–6.
"A Western Landlady: Extraordinary Scene in Ballina." *Nation*, December 11, 1880, 12.
"The West's Awake!" *Irish World and American Industrial Liberator* 29, no. 1484, February 4, 1899, 1.
"What One Man Has Done for Catholic Literature" (reprinted from *Irish Canadian*). *McGee's Illustrated Weekly: Devoted to Catholic Art, Literature and Education*, December 2, 1876, 27.
"Who Will Help the Poor?" *McGee's Illustrated Weekly: Devoted to Catholic Art, Literature and Education* 1, no. 5, December 23, 1876, 66.
Williams, Miriam. "Home to Her Mother." *Irish Packet* 1, no. 11, December 12, 1903, 269–70.
"With Whom Shall We Sympathize?" *McGee's Illustrated Weekly: Devoted to Catholic Art, Literature and Education* 2, no. 10, July 28, 1877, 146.
W. M. C. [pseud.]. "A Compromise with the Landlords." *Irish World and American Industrial Liberator* 33, no. 1705, May 2, 1903, 6.
"Working of the Land Act: Opinion of Cork Evicted Tenants." *Freeman's Journal*, May 1, 1905, 11.
Yeats, William Butler. "Carleton as an Irish Historian." *Nation*, January 11, 1890, 9.

Other Sources

Akenson, Donald Harman. *Ireland, Sweden and the Great European Migration 1815–1914*. Liverpool: Liverpool University Press, 2011.
Alexander, Jeffrey C. "On the Social Construction of Moral Universals: The 'Holocaust' from War Crime to Trauma Drama." In *Cultural Trauma and Collective Identity*, by Jeffrey C. Alexander, Ron Eyerman, Bernhard Giesen, Neil J. Smelser, and Piotr Sztompka, 196–263. Berkeley: University of California Press, 2004.
———. "Toward a Theory of Cultural Trauma." In *Cultural Trauma and Collective Identity*, by Jeffrey C. Alexander, Ron Eyerman, Bernhard Giesen, Neil J. Smelser, and Piotr Sztompka, 1–30. Berkeley: University of California Press 2004.
———. *Trauma: A Social Theory*. Cambridge: Polity Press, 2012.
Allen, Rob. "'Pause You Who Read This': Disruption and the Victorian Serial Novel." In *Serialization in Popular Culture*, edited by Rob Allen and Thijs van den Berg, 33–46. Abingdon: Routledge, 2014.
Alphen, Ernst van. "Second-Generation Testimony, Transmission of Trauma, and Postmemory." *Poetics Today* 27, no. 2 (Summer 2006): 473–88. https://doi.org/10.1215/03335372-2005-015.
Anderson, Benedict. *Imagined Communities: Reflections on the Origin and Spread of Nationalism*. London: Verso Books, 1983.
Arnold, Bruce. "Yeats, Jack Butler." In *Dictionary of Irish Biography*, edited by James McGuire and James Quinn. Cambridge: Cambridge University Press, 2009. https://doi.org/10.3318/dib.009157.v1.
Assmann, Aleida. "Transnational Memories." *European Review* 22, no. 4 (2014): 546–56.

Assmann, Aleida, and Ines Detmers. "Introduction." In *Empathy and Its Limits*, edited by Aleida Assmann and Ines Detmers, 1–17. Basingstoke: Palgrave Macmillan, 2016.

Austin, William L. "Address by the Presiding Officer Mr. William L. Austin (55th Class)." *Barnwell Bulletin: Memorial Meeting in Honor of Robert Ellis Thompson* 2, no. 10 (February 1925): 4–5.

Bal, Mieke. "The Laughing Mice; or, On Focalisation." *Poetics Today* 2, no. 2 (Winter 1981): 202–10.

Balch, William S. *Ireland, as I Saw It: The Character, Condition, and Prospects of the People.* New York: Henry Lyon, 1852.

Barr, Colin. "The Devotional Revolution in Greater Ireland." *New Hibernia Review* 24, no. 4 (Winter/Geimhreadh 2020): 79–97.

———. *Ireland's Empire: The Roman Catholic Church in the English-Speaking World, 1829–1914.* Cambridge: Cambridge University Press, 2020.

Beetham, Margaret. "Periodicals and the Time of the Now." *Victorian Periodicals Review* 48, no. 3 (2015): 323–42.

Beiner, Guy. "Probing the Boundaries of Irish Memory: From Postmemory to Prememory and Back." *Irish Historical Studies* 39, no. 154 (November 2014): 296–307.

———. *Remembering the Year of the French: Irish Folk History and Social Memory.* Madison: University of Wisconsin Press, 2007.

Bhattacharya, Sourit. "Writing Famine, Writing Empire: Food Crisis and Anticolonial Aesthetics in Liam O'Flaherty's *Famine* and Bhabani Bhattacharya's *So Many Hungers!*" *Irish University Review* 49, no. 1 (May 1, 2019): 54–73.

Bigelow, Gordon. *Fiction, Famine, and the Rise of Economics in Victorian Britain and Ireland.* Cambridge: Cambridge University Press, 2003.

Bode, Katherine. *A World of Fiction: Digital Collections and the Future of Literary History.* Ann Arbor, MI: University of Michigan Press, 2018.

Bodkin, Matthias McDonnell. *Recollections of an Irish Judge: Press, Bar and Parliament.* New York: Dodd, Mead, 1915.

Bond, Lucy. "Types of Transculturality: Narrative Frameworks and the Commemoration of 9/11." In *The Transcultural Turn: Interrogating Memory between and beyond Borders*, edited by Lucy Bond and Jessica Rapson, 61–80. Berlin: de Gruyter, 2014.

Bond, Lucy, and Jessica Rapson. "Introduction." In *The Transcultural Turn: Interrogating Memory between and beyond Borders*, edited by Lucy Bond and Jessica Rapson, 1–26. Berlin: de Gruyter, 2014.

Bossard, James H. S. "Robert Ellis Thompson—Pioneer Professor in Social Science." *American Journal of Sociology* 35, no. 2 (September 1929): 239–49.

Boylan, Thomas A., and Timothy P. Foley. *Political Economy and Colonial Ireland: The Propagation and Ideological Function of Economic Discourse in the Nineteenth Century.* New ed., 1992. London: Routledge, 2005.

Brah, Avtar. *Cartographies of Diasporas: Contesting Identities.* 3rd ed., 1996. London: Routledge, 2002.

Brake, Laurel. "'Time's Turbulence': Mapping Journalism Networks." *Victorian Periodicals Review* 44, no. 2 (2011): 115–27.

Brake, Laurel, and Maryssa Demoor, eds. *Dictionary of Nineteenth-Century Journalism.* Gent: Academia Press, 2009.

Brand, Roy. "Trauma Witnessing in Film." In *Media Witnessing: Testimony in the Age of Mass Communication*, edited by Paul Frosh and Amit Pinchevski, 198–215. Basingstoke: Palgrave Macmillan, 2009.

Brew, Margaret. *The Chronicles of Castle Cloyne; or, Pictures of the Munster People.* 3 vols. London: Chapman and Hall, 1885.

Brewis, Georgina. "'Fill Full the Mouth of Famine': Voluntary Action in Famine Relief in India 1896–1901." *Modern Asia Studies* 44, no. 4 (July 2010): 887–918.

Brooker, Peter, and Andrew Thacker. "General Introduction." In *The Oxford Critical and Cultural History of Modernist Magazines.* Vol. 1, *Britain and Ireland 1880–1955,* edited by Peter Brooker and Andrew Thacker, 1–26. Oxford: Oxford University Press, 2009.

Bruna, Giulia. "Travel Journalism: Reporting from the Fringes of Revival Ireland." In *Global Literary Journalism: Exploring the Journalistic Imagination,* edited by Richard Lance Keeble and John Tulloch, 347–61. New York: Peter Lang, 2012.

Bruner, Jerome. "The Narrative Construction of Reality." In *Narrative Theory: Critical Concepts in Literary and Cultural Studies.* Vol. IV, *Interdisciplinarity,* edited by Mieke Bal, 213–32. London: Routledge, 2004.

Burge McAlpin, Michelle. *Subject to Famine: Food Crisis and Economic Change in Western India, 1860–1920.* Princeton, NJ: Princeton University Press, 1983.

Butcher, W. W. *W. W. Butcher's Canadian Newspaper Directory.* London: "Speaker," 1886.

Campbell, Fergus. "Irish Popular Politics and the Making of the Wyndham Land Act, 1901–1903." *Historical Journal* 45, no. 4 (2002): 755–73.

Carleton, William. *The Black Prophet: A Tale of Irish Famine.* London: Simms and M'Intyre, 1847.

———. *De zwarte profeet: Een verhaal uit den tijd van den Ierschen hongersnood.* Nieuwe Diep: C. Bakker, 1847.

Carleton, William, and Friedrich Gerstäcker, trans. *Der schwarze Prophet: Aus den Zeiten irischer Hungersnoth.* Dresden: Arnoldische Buchhandlung, 1848.

Carr, David. *Time, Narrative and History.* Bloomington: Indiana University Press, 1986.

Caruth, Cathy. "Unclaimed Experience: Trauma and the Possibility of History." *Yale French Studies* 79 (1991): 181–92.

Cawthorne, William Anderson. *Tim Doolan: The Irish Emigrant.* London: S. W. Partridge, 1869.

Clark, Samuel. *Social Origins of the Land War.* Princeton, NJ: Princeton University Press, 1979.

Clarke, Frances. "Barlow, Jane." In *Dictionary of Irish Biography,* edited by James McGuire and James Quinn. Cambridge: Cambridge University Press, 2009. https://doi.org/10.3318/dib.000374.v2.

Clayton, F. H. [An Irishman, pseud.]. *Scenes and Incidents in Irish Life.* Montreal: John Lovell, 1884.

Cleary, Joe. *Outrageous Fortune: Capital and Culture in Modern Ireland.* 2nd ed. Dublin: Field Day, 2007.

Clyde, Tom. *Irish Literary Magazines: An Outline History and Descriptive Bibliography.* Dublin: Irish Academic Press, 2003.

Collet, Dominik, and Daniel Krämer. "Germany, Switzerland and Austria." In *Famine in European History,* edited by Guido Alfani and Cormac Ó Gráda, 101–18. Cambridge: Cambridge University Press, 2017.

Collombier-Lakeman, Pauline. "The Canadian Press and the Great Irish Famine: The Famine as an Irish, Canadian & Imperial, Global Issue." *Mémoire(s), identité(s), marginalité(s) dans le monde occidental contemporain: Cahiers du MIMMOC* 12 (2015). https://doi.org/10.4000/mimmoc.1787.

Commons, John Rogers. *History of Labour in the United States.* New York: Macmillan, 1918–25.

Coogan, Tim Pat. *The Famine Plot: England's Role in Ireland's Greatest Tragedy.* Basingstoke: Palgrave Macmillan, 2012.

Cordell, Ryan. "'Q i-jtb the Raven': Taking Dirty OCR Seriously." *Book History* 20 (2017): 188–225.
———. "Reprinting, Circulation, and the Network Author in Antebellum Newspapers."
    American Literary History 27, no. 3 (2015): 417–45.
———. "What Has the Digital Meant to American Periodicals Scholarship?" *American Periodicals: A Journal of History & Criticism* 26, no. 1 (2016): 2–7.
Corporaal, Marguérite. "Black Patches and Rotting Weeds: The Great Famine as a Transcultural Figure of Memory in Irish (Diaspora) Fiction, 1855–1885." In *The Transcultural Turn: Interrogating Memory between and beyond Borders*, edited by Lucy Bond and Jessica Rapson, 247–66. Berlin: Walter de Gruyter, 2014.
———. "Political Economy? The Economics and Sociology of Famine." In *Irish Literature in Transition 1830–1880*, edited by Matthew Campbell, 78–91. Cambridge: Cambridge University Press, 2020.
———. *Relocated Memories of the Great Famine in Irish and Diaspora Fiction, 1847–70*. Syracuse, NY: Syracuse University Press, 2017.
———. "Relocating Regionalism: The Fin-de-Siècle Irish Local Colour Tale in Transnational Contexts." *Irish Studies Review* 28, no. 2 (2020): 155–70.
Corporaal, Marguérite, Christopher Cusack, and Lindsay Janssen. "Reimagining Rural Ireland: Famine, Migration, and Feudalism in Irish and Irish North American Fiction, 1860–1895." *Breac: A Digital Journal of Irish Studies*, January 28, 2018. https://breac .nd.edu/articles/reimagining-rural-ireland-famine-migration-and-feudalism-in-irish -and-irish-north-american-fiction-18601895/. Accessed 12 June 2020.
Craps, Stef, and Michael Rothberg. "Introduction: Transcultural Negotiations of Holocaust Memory." *Criticism* 53, no, 4 (2011): 517–21.
Cronin, Maura. "Sullivan, Timothy Daniel." In *Dictionary of Irish Biography*, edited by James McGuire and James Quinn. Cambridge: Cambridge University Press, 2009. https://doi .org/10.3318/dib.008386.v1.
Cronin, Mike. *A History of Ireland*. Basingstoke: Palgrave, 2001.
Crosbie, Barrie. "Networks of Empire: Linkage and Reciprocity in Nineteenth-Century Irish and Indian History." *History Compass* 7, no. 3 (2009): 993–1007.
Curtis, Daniel, Jessica Dijkman, Thijs Lambrecht, and Eric Vanhaute. "Low Countries." In *Famine in European History*, edited by Guido Alfani and Cormac Ó Gráda, 119–140. Cambridge: Cambridge University Press, 2017.
Curtis, L. Perry, Jr. *The Depiction of Eviction in Ireland 1845–1910*. Dublin: University College Dublin Press, 2011.
Cusack, Christopher. "Memory, History, and Identity in Irish and Irish-Diasporic Famine Fiction, 1892–1921." PhD diss., Radboud University, Nijmegen, 2018.
———. "'Seanachie to the New World': Seumas MacManus and the Transatlantic Appeal of Irish Local Colour." *Open Library of Humanities* 8, no. 2 (2022): 1–26.
Cusack, Christopher, and Lindsay Janssen. "Famine, Home, and Transatlantic Politics in Two Late Nineteenth-Century Irish-American Novels." *Atlantic Studies* 11, no. 3 (2014): 403–18.
Cusack, Margaret Anna (Sister Mary Francis Clare, "the Nun of Kenmare"). *From Killarney to New York; or, How Thade Became a Banker: A Story of Real Life*. New York: J. A. McGee, 1878.
CWRC. "Margaret Dixon McDougall." *Canadian Writing Research Collaboratory* (CWRC). https://cwrc.ca/islandora/object/ceww%3A689b2853-f4f2-4d0f-93b4-90898e0504bd. Accessed January 2, 2023.
Daly, Mary E. *Social and Economic History of Ireland since 1800*. Dublin: Educational Company of Ireland, 1981.

———. "Something Old and Something New: Recent Research on the Great Irish Famine." In *When the Potato Failed: Causes and Effects of the 'Last' European Subsistence Crisis, 1845–1850*, edited by Cormac Ó Gráda, Richard Paping, and Eric Vanhaute, 59–79. Turnhout: Brepols, 2010.

Davin, Nicholas Flood. *The Irishman in Canada.* Toronto: Maclear, 1877.

Davis, Thomas. *The Poems of Thomas Davis: Now First Collected; With Notes and Historical Illustrations.* Dublin: James Duffy, 1846.

Davitt, Michael. *The Fall of Feudalism; or, The Story of the Irish Land League.* London: Harper, 1904.

De Cesari, Chiara, and Ann Rigney. "Introduction." In *Transnational Memory: Circulation, Articulation, Scales,* edited by Chiara De Cesari and Ann Rigney, 1–25. Berlin: Walter de Gruyter, 2014.

Denness, Zoë. "Women and Warfare at the Start of the Twentieth Century: The Racialization of the 'Enemy' during the South African War (1899–1902)." *Patterns of Prejudice* 46, no. 3–4 (2012): 255–76. https://doi.org/10.1080/0031322X.2012.701497.

DeSpain, Jessica. *Nineteenth-Century Transatlantic Reprinting and the Embodied Book.* New ed., 2014. London: Routledge, 2016. Kindle version.

De Vere, Aubrey. *Irish Odes.* New York: Catholic Publication Society, 1869.

D'hoker, Elke. "Introduction to Special Section: The Short Story in Context." *Journal of the Short Story in English* (online) 71 (Autumn 2018). http://journals.openedition.org/jsse/2138. Accessed June 10, 2021.

———. *Irish Women Writers and the Modern Short Story.* Basingstoke: Palgrave Macmillan, 2016.

D'hoker, Elke, and Chris Mourant. "Introduction." In *The Modern Short Story and Magazine Culture, 1880–1950,* edited by Elke D'hoker and Chris Mourant, 1–24. Edinburgh: Edinburgh University Press, 2021.

Distad, N. Merrill, and Linda M. Distad. "Canada." In *Periodicals of Queen Victoria's Empire: An Exploration,* edited by Rosemary VanArsdel and Don J. Vann, 61–174. Toronto: University of Toronto Press, 1996.

DoCEWW. "MacDougall (or McDougall), Margaret Dixon." *Database of Canada's Early Women Writers* (DoCEWW), Simon Fraser University. https://dhil.lib.sfu.ca/doceww/person/2724. Accessed January 2, 2023.

Donovan, Josephine. "Local-Colour Literature and Cultural Nations." In *Other Capitals of the Nineteenth Century: An Alternative Mapping of Literary and Cultural Space,* edited by Richard Hibbit, 33–50. Basingstoke: Palgrave Macmillan, 2017.

Dooley, Terence. "The Big House." In *The Cambridge Social History of Modern Ireland,* edited by Eugenio F. Biagini and Mary E. Daly, 161–76. Cambridge: Cambridge University Press, 2017.

Easley, Alexis. "Authorship, Gender and Power in Victorian Culture: Harriet Martineau and the Periodical Press." In *Nineteenth-Century Media and the Construction of Identities,* edited by Laurel Brake, Bill Bell, and David Finkelstein, 154–64. Basingstoke: Palgrave, 2020.

Edkins, Jenny. *Whose Hunger: Concepts of Famine, Practices of Aid.* Minneapolis: University of Minnesota Press, 2000.

Egan, Maurice Francis. *Recollections of a Happy Life.* New York: George H. Doran, 1924.

Erll, Astrid. "Narratology and Cultural Memory Studies." In *Narratology in the Age of Cross-Disciplinary Narrative Research,* edited by Sandra Heinen and Roy Sommer, 212–27. Berlin: Walter de Gruyter, 2009.

———. "Remembering across Time, Space, and Cultures: Premediation, Remediation and the 'Indian Mutiny.'" In *Mediation, Remediation and the Dynamics of Cultural Memory*, edited by Astrid Erll and Ann Rigney, 109–38. New York: Walter de Gruyter, 2009.

———. "Travelling Memory." *Parallax* 17, no. 4 (2011): 4–18.

Fanning, Charles. *The Exiles of Erin: Nineteenth-Century Irish-American Fiction*. New ed., 1987. Chester Springs, PA: Dufour, 1997.

———. *Finley Peter Dunne and Mr. Dooley: The Chicago Years*. Lexington: University Press of Kentucky, 1978.

———. *The Irish Voice in America: 250 Years of Irish-American Fiction*. New ed., 1990. Lexington: University Press of Kentucky, 2000.

Feely, Catherine Clare. "Scissors and Paste Journalism." In *Dictionary of Nineteenth-Century Journalism in Great Britain and Ireland*, edited by Laurel Brake and Marysa Demoor, 561. Gent: Academia Press, 2009.

Fegan, Melissa. *Literature and the Irish Famine 1845–1919*. Oxford: Oxford University Press, 2002.

Ferguson, Trish. *Maud Gonne*. Dublin: University College Dublin Press, 2019.

Foucault, Michel, and Alan Sheridan, trans. *Discipline and Punish: The Birth of the Prison*. 2nd ed. New York: Vintage Books, 1991.

Fox, Emily [Toler King, pseud]. *Rose O'Connor: A Story of the Day*. Chicago, IL: Chicago Legal News, 1880.

Frawley, Oona. "Introduction: Cruxes in Irish Cultural Memory: The Famine and the Troubles." In *Memory Ireland*. Vol. 3, *The Famine and the Troubles*, edited by Oona Frawley, 1–14. Syracuse, NY: Syracuse University Press, 2014.

———. *Irish Pastoral: Nostalgia and Twentieth-Century Irish Literature*. Dublin: Irish Academic Press, 2005.

Frosh, Paul, and Amit Pinchevski. "Introduction: Why Media Witnessing? Why Now?" In *Media Witnessing: Testimony in the Age of Mass Communication*, edited by Paul Frosh, 1–19. Basingstoke: Palgrave Macmillan, 2009.

Ganguly, Keya. "Temporality and Postcolonial Critique." In *The Cambridge Companion to Postcolonial Literary Studies*, edited by Neil Lazarus, 162–79. Cambridge: Cambridge University Press, 2004.

Gantt, Jonathan. *Irish Terrorism in the Atlantic Community, 1865–1922*. New York: Palgrave Macmillan, 2010.

Geary, Laurence M. *The Land War in Ireland: Famine, Philanthropy and Moonlighting*. Cork: Cork University Press, 2023.

Goldberg, Amos. "Empathy, Ethics, and Politics in Holocaust Historiography." In *Empathy and Its Limits*, edited by Aleida Assmann and Ines Detmers, 52–76. Basingstoke: Palgrave Macmillan, 2016.

Gonne, Maud. *A Servant of the Queen: Reminiscences by Maud Gonne MacBride*. Paulton, Somerset: Purnell, 1938.

Gould, Warwick. "'Playing at Treason with Miss Maud Gonne': Yeats and His Publishers in 1900." In *Modernist Writers and the Marketplace*, edited by Ian Wilson, Warwick Gould, and Warren Chernaik, 36–80. Basingstoke: MacMillan, 1996.

Gray, Peter. "Famine and Land in Ireland and India, 1845–1880: James Caird and the Political Economy of Hunger." *Historical Journal* 49, no. 1 (March 2006): 193–215.

———. "Irish Social Thought and the Relief of Poverty, 1847–1880." *Transactions of the RHS* 20 (2010): 141–56. https://doi.org/10.1017/S0080440110000095.

Griffiths, Andrew. *The New Journalism, the New Imperialism and the Fiction of Empire, 1870–1900*. Basingstoke: Palgrave Macmillan, 2015.

Gwynn, Stephen. "Introductory Memoir." In *Charlotte Grace O'Brien: Selections from her Writings and Correspondence with a Memoir by Stephen Gwynn*, edited by Stephen Gwynn, 3–138. Dublin: Maunsel, 1909.

Hansson, Heidi. "Our Village: Linguistic Negotiation in Jane Barlow's Fiction." *Nordic Irish Studies* 7 (2008): 57–70.

Hartsock, John C. *Literary Journalism and the Aesthetics of Experience*. Amherst: University of Massachusetts Press, 2014.

Hepburn, Joseph S. "Robert Ellis Thompson, A.M., Ph.D., S.T.D., LL.D: A Biographical Sketch." *Barnwell Bulletin: Memorial Meeting in Honor of Robert Ellis Thompson* 2, no. 10 (February 1925): 22–23.

Heyningen, Elizabeth van. "A Tool for Modernisation? The Boer Concentration Camps of the South African War, 1900–1902." *South African Journal of Science* 106, no. 5–6 (2010): 1–10. https://doi.org/10.4102/sajs.v106i5/6.242.

Higgins, Michael D. "Speech at the National Famine Commemoration 2021." Glasnevin Cemetery, March 16, 2021. https://president.ie/en/media-library/speeches/speech-at-the-national-famine-commemoration-2021. Accessed February 20, 2024.

Hirsch, Marianne. "Surviving Images: Holocaust Photographs and the Work of Postmemory." *Yale Journal of Criticism* 14, no. 1 (Spring 2001): 5–37.

Hoare, Edward N. *Mike: A Tale of the Great Irish Famine*. London: Society for the Promoting of Christian Knowledge, 1880.

Hobhouse, Emily. *The Brunt of the War and Where It Fell*. London: Methuen, 1902.

Hooper, Glenn. *The Tourist's Gaze: Travellers to Ireland 1800–2000*. Cork: Cork University Press, 2001.

Howsam, Leslie. "Mediated Histories: How Did Victorian Periodicals Parse the Past?" *Victorian Periodicals Review* 50, no. 4 (Winter 2017): 802–24. https://doi.org/10.1353/vpr.2017.0057.

Huculak, Matthew J. "Reading Forensically: Modernist Paper, Newfoundland, and Transatlantic Materiality." *Journal of Modern Periodical Studies* 6, no. 2 (2015): 161–90.

Hughes, Linda K. "SIDEWAYS!: Navigating the Material(ity) of Print Culture." *Victorian Periodicals Review* 47, no. 1 (2014): 1–30.

Ireland, John. *Catholic Colonization in Minnesota*. Revised ed. St. Paul, MN: Catholic Colonization Bureau of Minnesota, 1879.

"Irish Famine: Refugee Crisis Similar to 19th [*sic*] Famine 'Rhetoric.'" *BBC News*, September 12, 2016. https://www.bbc.com/news/world-europe-37337878. Accessed May 22, 2019.

Jacobson, Matthew Frye. *Special Sorrows: The Diasporic Imagination of Irish, Polish, and Jewish Immigrants in the United States*. Berkeley: University of California Press, 2002.

Janis, Ely M. *A Greater Ireland: The Land League and Transatlantic Nationalism in Gilded Age America*. Madison: University of Wisconsin Press, 2015.

Janssen, Lindsay. "Diasporic Identifications: Exile, Nostalgia and the Famine Past in Irish and Irish North-American Popular Fiction, 1871–1891." *Irish Studies Review* 26, no. 2 (March 2018): 199–216. https://doi.org/10.1080/09670882.2018.1446401.

———. "Famine Traces: Memory, Landscape, History and Identity in Irish and Irish-Diasporic Famine Fiction, 1871–91." PhD diss., Radboud University, Nijmegen, 2016.

———. "From Silence to Plenty: The Famine in Early Twentieth-Century Periodical Fiction." *Éire-Ireland* 54, no. 3–4 (2019): 123–41.

———. "From Special Correspondence to Fiction: Memory and Veracity in Margaret McDougall's Writings on Ireland." In *Irish Women's Writing at the Turn of the Twentieth Century: Alternative Histories, New Narratives*, edited by Kathryn Laing and Sinéad Mooney, 179–92. Brighton: Edward Everett Root, 2020.

———. "Margaret Dixon McDougall's *The Days of a Life* (1883): An Irish-Canadian Perspective of the Repetitive Nature of Irish History." In *The Famine Diaspora and Irish-American Women's Writing*, edited by Marguérite Corporaal, Jason King, and Peter D. O'Neill, 209–35. London: Palgrave Macmillan, 2024.

———. "(Re)building Self and Country: Rebels, Landlords, and Landladies in Famine Fiction of the 1870s and 1880s." In *The Irish Bildungsroman*, edited by Matthew Reznicek, Sarah Townsend, and Gregory Castle. Syracuse, NY: Syracuse University Press, forthcoming.

Jordan, Donald. "The Irish National League and the 'Unwritten Law': Rural Protest and Nation-Building in Ireland 1882–1890." *Past & Present* 158 (February 1998): 146–71.

Judd, Denis, and Keith Surridge. *The Boer War: A History.* New ed., 2002. New York: I. B. Tauris, 2013. E-book version.

Kansteiner, Wulf. "Genealogy of a Category Mistake: A Critical Intellectual History of the Cultural Trauma Metaphor." *Rethinking History* 8, no. 2 (2004): 193–221. https://doi.org/10.1080/13642520410001683905.

Keary, Annie. *Castle Daly: The Story of an Irish Home Thirty Years Ago; In Two Volumes.* Leipzig: Bernhard Tauchnitz, 1875.

———. *Castle Daly: The Story of an Irish Home Thirty Years Ago; In Two Volumes.* Leipzig: Bernhard Tauchnitz, 1905.

Keene, Suzanne. "Introduction: Narrative and the Emotions." *Poetics Today* 32, no. 1 (Spring 2011): 1–53.

Kelleher, Margaret. "The 'Affective Gap' and Recent Histories of Ireland's Great Famine." In *Global Legacies of the Great Irish Famine: Transnational and Interdisciplinary Perspectives*, edited by Marguérite Corporaal, Christopher Cusack, Lindsay Janssen, and Ruud van der Beuken, 19–31. Oxford: Peter Lang, 2014.

———. *The Feminization of Famine: Expressions of the Inexpressible?* Cork: Cork University Press, 1997.

———. "Hunger and History: Monuments to the Great Irish Famine." *Textual Practice* 16, no. 2 (2010): 249–76.

———. "The Irish Famine: History and Representation." In *Palgrave Advances in Irish History*, edited by Katherine O'Donnell, Leeann Lane, and Mary McAuliffe, 84–99. London: Palgrave Macmillan, 2009.

Kennedy, Liam. *Unhappy the Land: The Most Oppressed People Ever, the Irish?* Dublin: Merrion Press, 2015.

Kenny, Kevin. *The American Irish: A History.* New York: Longman, 2000.

———. *Making Sense of the Molly Maguires.* Oxford: Oxford University Press, 1998.

Ketchum-Glass, Susannah. "Witnessing the Witness: Narrative Slippage in Art Spiegelman's *Maus.*" *Life Writing* 3, no. 2 (2006): 3–24.

Kickham, Charles. *Sally Cavanagh; or, The Untenanted Graves: A Tale of Tipperary.* Dublin: J. J. Lalor, 1869.

King, Andrew, Alexis Easley, and John Morton. "Introduction: Researching the Nineteenth-Century Periodical Press: Case Studies." In *The Routledge Handbook to Nineteenth-Century British Periodicals and Newspapers*, edited by Andrew King, Alexis Easley, and John Morton, 1–13. London: Routledge, 2016.

King, David Bennett. *The Irish Question.* New York: Charles Scribner's, 1882.

Kreilkamp, Vera. *The Anglo-Irish Novel and the Big House.* Syracuse, NY: Syracuse University Press, 1998.

LaCapra, Dominick. *Writing History, Writing Trauma.* Baltimore, MD: Johns Hopkins University Press, 2014.

Lanzendörfer, Tim. "Periodicals and Journalism in Nineteenth-Century America." In *The Handbook of Transatlantic North American Studies*, edited by Julia Straub, 316–33. Berlin: de Gruyter, 2016.

Larkin, Felix M. "'Green Shoots' of the New Journalism in the *Freeman's Journal*, 1877–1890." In *Ireland and the New Journalism*, edited by Karen Steele and Michael de Nie, 35–55. Basingstoke: Palgrave Macmillan, 2014.

———. "McDonnell Bodkin, Matthias." In *Dictionary of Irish Biography*, edited by James McGuire and James Quinn. Cambridge: Cambridge University Press, 2009. https://doi .org/10.3318/dib.000755.v1.

Law, Graham. "Copyright." In *Dictionary of Nineteenth-Century Journalism in Great Britain and Ireland*, edited by Laurel Brake and Marysa Demoor, 143. Gent: Academia Press, 2009.

———. *Serializing Fiction in the Victorian Press*. Basingstoke: Palgrave, 2000.

Law, Graham, and Robert L. Patten. "The Serial Revolution." In *The Cambridge History of the Book in Britain*. Vol. 6, *1830–1914*, edited by David McKitterick, 145–71. Cambridge: Cambridge University Press, 2014.

Lawless, Emily. *Traits and Confidences*. London: Methuen, 1898.

Lawless, Emily, and Anna Bok, trans. *Hurrish: een Ierse Roman*. Arnhem: Gouda Quint, 1890.

Lechner, Doris. *Histories for the Many: The Victorian Family Magazine and Popular Representations of the Past; The Leisure Hour, 1852–1870*. Bielefeld: Transcript, 2017.

Leerssen, Joep. "The Rhetoric of National Character: A Programmatic Survey." *Poetics Today* 21, no. 2 (Summer 2000): 267–92.

Legg, Mary-Louise. "Ford, Patrick (1837–1913), Journalist and Politician." In *Oxford Dictionary of National Biography*. Oxford: Oxford University Press, 2004. http://doi.org/10.1093 /ref:odnb/33198.

Levine, Caroline. *Forms: Whole, Rhythm, Hierarchy, Network*. Princeton, NJ: Princeton University Press, 2017.

Levine, Philippa. *The British Empire: Sunrise to Sunset*. 2nd ed. New York: Routledge, 2013.

Levy, Daniel. "Changing Temporalities and the Internationalization of Memory Cultures." In *Memory and the Future, Transnational Politics, Ethics and Society*, edited by Yfat Gutman, Adam D. Brown, and Amy Sodaro, 15–30. Basingstoke: Palgrave Macmillan, 2010.

Levy, Daniel, and Nathan Sznaider. *Human Rights and Memory*. University Park: Pennsylvania University Press, 2010.

Lloyd, David. "Colonial Trauma/Postcolonial Recovery?" *Interventions* 2, no. 2 (2000): 212–28. https://doi.org/10.1080/136980100427324.

———. "The Indigent Sublime: Spectres of Irish Hunger." *Representations* 92, no. 1 (Fall 2005): 152–85.

———. *Irish Times: Temporalities of Modernity*. Dublin: Field Day, 2008.

Loeber, Rolf, and Magda Loeber, with Ann Mullin Burnham. *A Guide to Irish Fiction 1650–1900*. Dublin: Four Courts Press, 2006.

Luddy, Maria. "Jane Barlow." In *Oxford Dictionary of National Biography*. Oxford: Oxford University Press, 2004. https://doi.org/10.1093/ref:odnb/46314.

MacRaild, Donald M. "Crossing Migrant Frontiers: Comparative Reflections on Irish Migrants in Britain and the United States during the Nineteenth Century." In *The Great Famine and Beyond: Irish Migrants in Britain in the Nineteenth and Twentieth Centuries*, edited by Donald M. MacRaild, 40–70. Dublin: Irish Academic Press, 2010.

———. *Irish Migrants in Modern Britain, 1750–1922*. New York: St. Martin's Press, 1999.

Madigan, Josepha. "Minister Josepha Madigan's Full Address for the National Famine Commemoration Day Ceremony, May 17th, 2020." *Great Famine Voices.* http:// greatfaminevoices.ie/minister-josepha-madigans-full-address-for-the-national-famine -commemoration-day-ceremony-may-17th-2020/. Accessed July 26, 2024.

Malcolm, Cheryl Alexander, and David Malcolm. "The British and Irish Short Story to 1945." In *A Companion to the British and Irish Short Story,* edited by Cheryl Alexander Malcolm and David Malcolm, 1–15. Oxford: Wiley-Blackwell, 2008.

Margalit, Avishai. *The Ethics of Memory.* Cambridge, MA: Harvard University Press, 2002.

Mark-FitzGerald, Emily. *Commemorating the Irish Famine: Memory and the Monument.* Liverpool: Liverpool University Press, 2013.

Martin, Amy E. *Alter-Nations: Nationalisms, Terror, and the State in Nineteenth-Century Britain and Ireland.* Columbus: Ohio State University, 2012.

———. "Representing the 'Indian Revolution' of 1857: Towards a Genealogy of Irish Internationalist Anticolonialism." *Field Day Review* 8 (2012): 126–47.

Maume, Patrick. "Cusack, Margaret Anna ('The Nun of Kenmare')." In *Dictionary of Irish Biography,* edited by James McGuire and James Quinn. Cambridge: Cambridge University Press, 2009. https://doi.org/10.3318/dib.002345.v1.

———. "Sullivan, Alexander Martin." In *Dictionary of Irish Biography,* edited by James McGuire and James Quinn. Cambridge: Cambridge University Press, 2009. https://doi .org/10.3318/dib.008376.v1.

McBride, Ian. "Introduction: Memory and National Identity in Modern Ireland." In *History and Memory in Modern Ireland,* edited by Ian McBride, 1–42. Cambridge: Cambridge University Press, 2001.

McCarthy, Justin Huntly. *Lily Lass.* London: Chatto and Windus, 1889.

McCarthy, Tara M. *Respectability & Reform: Irish American Women's Activism, 1880–1920.* Syracuse, NY: Syracuse University Press, 2018.

McClintock, Anne. *Imperial Leather: Race, Gender and Sexuality in the Colonial Contest.* New York: Routledge, 1995.

———. "'No Longer a Future in Heaven': Women and Nationalism in South Africa." *Transition* 51 (1991): 104–23.

McCormack, W. J. "'Never Put Your Name to an Anonymous Letter': Serial Reading and the 'Dublin University Magazine,' 1861 to 1869." *Yearbook of English Studies* 26 (1996): 100–15.

McDevitt, Harry S. "Address by Honorable Harry S. McDevitt, Judge Court of Common Pleas, Philadelphia." *Barnwell Bulletin: Memorial Meeting in Honor of Robert Ellis Thompson* 2, no. 10 (February 1925): 11–14.

McDougall, Margaret Dixon [Norah, pseud.]. *The Days of a Life.* Almonte: Templeman, 1883.

———. *The Letters of "Norah," on Her Tour through Ireland, Being a Series of Letters to the Montreal "Witness" as a Special Correspondent to Ireland.* Montreal: Montreal Witness Offices, 1882.

McDowell, Lalla. *The Earl of Effingham.* London: Samuel Tinsley, 1877.

McGann, Jerome J. *The Textual Condition.* Princeton, NJ: Princeton University Press, 1991.

McGee, Thomas D'Arcy. *The Poems of Thomas D'Arcy McGee.* London: D. and J. Sadlier, 1869.

McGill, Meredith L. *American Literature and the Culture of Reprinting 1834–1853.* Philadelphia: University of Philadelphia Press, 2003.

McGovern, Bryan P. *John Mitchel: Irish Nationalist, Southern Secessionist.* Knoxville: University of Tennessee Press, 2009.

McGreal, Edwin. "The Terrible Reign of Two Female Landlords." *Mayo News,* May 21, 2013. https://www.mayonews.ie/news/living/1099486/culture-the-terrible-reign-of-two -female-landlords.html. Accessed July 26, 2024.

McKivigan, John. *Forgotten Firebrand: James Redpath and the Making of Nineteenth-Century America*. Ithaca, NY: Cornell University Press, 2008.

McMahon, Cian T. *The Global Dimensions of Irish Identity: Race, Nation, and the Popular Press, 1840–1880*. Chapel Hill: University of North Carolina Press, 2015.

Mishra, Vimal, Amar Deep Tiwari, Saran Aadhar, Reepal Shah, Mu Xiao, D. S. Pai, and Dennis Lettenmaier. "Drought and Famine in India, 1870–2016." *Geophysical Research Letters* 46 (2019): 2075–83. https://doi.org/10.1029/2018GL081477.

Mitchel, John. *Ireland since '98: Daniel O'Connell; The Repeal Agitation; The Miseries of the Famine; The Young Ireland Party, Etc.* Glasgow: Cameron and Ferguson, 1871.

———. *Jail Journal; or, Five Years in British Prisons*. New York: Office of the *Citizen*, 1854.

Mohanty, Bidyut. "Orissa Famine of 1866." *Economic and Political Weekly* 28, no. 1/2 (January 2–9, 1993): 55–57, 59–66.

Montgomery, Richard. "Address by Reverend Dr. Richard Montgomery." *Barnwell Bulletin: Memorial Meeting in Honor of Robert Ellis Thompson* 2, no. 10 (February 1925): 6–8.

"The Montreal Witness" (Information Detaillée). *Bibliothèque et Archives nationales du Québec; BAnQ Numérique*. https://numerique.banq.qc.ca/patrimoine/details/52327/4182660. Accessed May 6, 2021.

Moran, Gerard. "'In Search of the Promised Land': The Connemara Colonization Scheme to Minnesota, 1880." *Éire-Ireland* 31, no. 3–4 (1996): 130–49.

Morash, Christopher. "An Afterword on Silence." In *Hungry Words: Images of Famine in the Irish Canon*, edited by George Cusack and Sarah Goss, 300–308. Dublin: Irish Academic Press, 2006.

———. "Famine/Holocaust: Fragmented Bodies." *Éire-Ireland* 32, no. 1 (1997): 136–50.

———. "Ghosts and Wires, the Telegraph and Irish Space." In *Ireland and the New Journalism*, edited by Karen Steele and Michael de Nie, 21–33. Basingstoke: Palgrave Macmillan, 2014.

———. *A History of the Media in Ireland*. Cambridge: Cambridge University Press, 2010.

———. *The Hungry Voice: The Poetry of the Irish Famine*. New ed., 1989. Dublin: Irish Academic Press, 2009.

———. "Spectres of the Famine." *Irish Review* 17/18 (1995): 74–79.

———. *Writing the Irish Famine*. New ed., 1995. Oxford: Oxford University Press, 2003.

Morgan, Cecilia. *A Happy Holiday: English-Canadians and Transatlantic Tourism, 1870–1930*. Toronto: University of Toronto Press, 2008.

Morgan, Kenneth O. "The Boer War and the Media (1899–1902)." *Twentieth Century British History* 13, no. 1 (2002): 1–16.

Moses, A. Dirk, and Michael Rothberg. "A Dialogue on the Ethics and Politics of Transcultural Memory." In *The Transcultural Turn: Interrogating Memory between and beyond Borders*, edited by Lucy Bond and Jessica Rapson, 29–38. Berlin: de Gruyter, 2014.

Mulholland, Rosa. *Marcella Grace*. New York: Vatican Library, 1891.

Mullen, Mary L. *Novel Institutions: Anachronisms, Irish Novels and Nineteenth-Century Realism*. Edinburgh: Edinburgh University Press, 2019.

Murphy, James H. "Rosa Mulholland, W. P. Ryan and Irish Catholic Fiction at the Time of the Anglo-Irish Revival." In *Forging in the Smithy: National Identity and Representation in Anglo-Irish Literary History*, edited by Joep Leerssen, A. H. Van der Weel, and Bart Westerweel, 219–28. Amsterdam: Rodopi, 1995.

Murphy, Maureen. "Ford, Patrick." In *Dictionary of Irish Biography*, edited by James McGuire and James Quinn. Cambridge: Cambridge University Press, 2009. https://doi.org/10.3318/dib.003328.v1.

Mussell, James. "Cohering Knowledge in the Nineteenth Century: Form, Genre, and Periodical Studies." *Victorian Periodicals Review* 42, no. 1 (2009): 93–103.

———. "Repetition; or, 'In Our Last.'" *Victorian Periodicals Review* 48, no. 3 (2015): 343–58.

Nally, David. "'That Coming Storm': The Irish Poor Law, Colonial Biopolitics, and the Great Famine." *Annals of the Association of American Geographers* 98, no. 3 (2008): 714–41.

"Nation, The." *The Waterloo Directory of English Newspapers & Periodicals: 1800–1900*. North Waterloo Academic Press. https://www.victorianperiodicals.com/series3/single_sample .asp?id=125157. Accessed January 25, 2024.

Ní Bhroiméil, Una. "Presidents, Protection, and Politics: Political Cartoons in the *Irish World and American Industrial Liberator*, 1890–1913." In *Politics, Culture, and the Irish-American Press, 1784–1963*, edited by Debra Reddin van Tuyll, Mark O'Brien, and Marcel Broersma, 154–81. Syracuse, NY: Syracuse University Press, 2021.

Nic Congáil, Ríona. "Young Ireland and *The Nation*: Nationalist Children's Literature in the Late Nineteenth Century." *Éire-Ireland* 46, no. 3–4 (Fall/Winter 2011): 37–62.

Nicholson, Asenath. *Annals of the Famine in Ireland, in 1847, 1848, and 1849*. New York: E. French, 1851.

Nicholson, Bob. "Transatlantic Connections." In *The Routledge Handbook to Nineteenth Century British Periodicals and Newspapers*, edited by Andrew King, Alexis Easley, and John Morton, 163–74. London: Routledge, 2016.

Nourie, Alan, and Barbara Nourie, eds. *American Mass-Market Magazines*. Westport, CT: Greenwood, 1990.

Nunn, Mrs. Lorenzo. *Heirs of the Soil*. London: Moffat, 1870.

Nussbaum, Martha. *Upheavals of Thought: The Intelligence of Emotions*. Cambridge: Cambridge University Press, 2001.

O'Brien, Charlotte Grace. *Charlotte Grace O'Brien: Selections from Her Writings and Correspondence with a Memoir by Stephen Gwynn*, edited by Stephen Gwynn. Dublin: Maunsel, 1909.

O'Brien, Dillon. *The Dalys of Dalystown*. St. Paul, MN: Pioneer Printing, 1866.

O'Brien, Richard Baptist. *The D'Altons of Crag: A Story of '48 & '49*. Dublin: James Duffy, 1882.

O'Callaghan, Margaret, and Caoimhe Nic Dháibhéid. "MacBride, (Edith) Maud Gonne." In *Dictionary of Irish Biography*, edited by James McGuire and James Quinn. Cambridge: Cambridge University Press, 2009. https://doi.org/10.3318/dib.005110.v1.

Ó Ciosáin, Niall. "Approaching a Folklore Archive: The Irish Folklore Commission and the Memory of the Great Famine." *Folklore* 115, no. 2 (August 2004): 222–32.

———. "Famine Memory and the Popular Representation of Scarcity." In *History and Memory in Modern Ireland*, edited by Ian McBride, 95–117. Cambridge: Cambridge University Press, 2001.

———. "Was There Silence about the Famine?" *Irish Studies Review* 4, no. 13 (1995): 7–10.

O'Connell, Marvin R. *John Ireland and the American Catholic Church*. St. Paul, MN: Minnesota Historical Society, 1988.

O'Donnell, Edward T. "'Though Not an Irishman': Henry George and the American Irish." *American Journal of Economics and Sociology* 56, no. 4 (October 1997): 407–19.

O'Donoghue, David J. *The Poets of Ireland: A Biographical Dictionary with Bibliographical Particulars*. London: published by the author, 1892.

Ó Gráda, Cormac. *Black '47 and Beyond: The Great Irish Famine in History, Economy, and Memory*. Princeton, NJ: Princeton University Press, 1999.

———. *Eating People Is Wrong, and Other Essays on Famine, Its Past, and Its Future*. Princeton, NJ: Princeton University Press, 2015.

———. "Famine, Trauma, and Memory." *Bealoideas* 69 (2001): 121–43.

———. "Ireland." In *Famine in European History*, edited by Guido Alfani and Cormac Ó Gráda, 166–84. Cambridge: Cambridge University Press, 2017.

———. *Ireland's Great Famine: Interdisciplinary Perspectives*. Dublin: University College Dublin Press, 2006.

O'Malley, Kate. *Ireland, India and Empire: Indo-Irish Radical Connections 1919–64*. Manchester: Manchester University Press, 2009.

O'Neill, Peter D. *Famine Irish and the American Racial State*. New York: Routledge, 2017.

O'Toole, Tina, ed. *Dictionary of Munster Women Writers*. Cork: Cork University Press, 2005.

Parfitt, Steven. *Knights across the Atlantic: The Knights of Labor in Britain and Ireland*. Liverpool: Liverpool University Press, 2016.

Pašeta, Senia. "Nationalist Responses to Two Royal Visits to Ireland, 1900 and 1903." *Irish Historical Studies* 31, no. 124 (November 1999): 488–504.

Phegley, Jennifer. "Family Magazines." In *The Routledge Handbook to Nineteenth-Century British Periodicals and Newspapers*, edited by Andrew King, Alexis Easley, and John Morton, 276–92. London: Routledge, 2016.

Pickering, Michael, and Emily Keightley. "Communities of Memory and the Problem of Transmission." *European Journal of Cultural Studies* 16, no. 1 (2012): 115–31.

Pine, Emilie. *The Politics of Irish Memory: Performing Remembrance in Contemporary Irish Culture*. Basingstoke: Palgrave Macmillan, 2011.

Póirtéir, Cathal. *Famine Echoes*. Dublin: Gill and Macmillan, 1995.

Pusapati, Teja Varma. "Going Places: Harriet Martineau's 'Letters from Ireland' and the Rise of the Female Correspondent." *Women's Writing* 24, no. 2 (2017): 207–26.

Quinn, James E. *Young Ireland and the Writing of Irish History*. Dublin: University College Dublin Press, 2015.

Rains, Stephanie. "City Streets and the City Edition: Newsboys and Newspapers in Early Twentieth-Century Ireland." *Irish Studies Review* 24, no. 2 (2016): 142–58.

———. "'Do You Ring? Or Are You Being Rung For?': Mass Media, Class, and Social Aspiration in Edwardian Ireland." *New Hibernia Review* 18, no. 4 (Winter 2014): 17–35.

———. "Going in for Competitions: Active Readers and Magazine Culture, 1900–1910." *Media History* 21, no. 2 (2015): 138–49. https://doi.org/10.1080/13688804.2014.995611.

———. "*Irish Packet*, 1903–1910." *Irish Media History*, November 12, 2015. https://irishmedia history.com/2015/11/12/irish-packet-1903-1910/. Accessed July 26, 2024.

Read, C. A., and K. T. Hinkson, eds. *The Cabinet of Irish Literature: Selections from the Works of the Chief Poets, Orators, and Prose Writers of Ireland*. Vol. 4. London: Blackie, 1903.

Ricoeur, Paul, and Kathleen Blamey and David Pellauer, trans. *Time and Narrative*. Vol. 3. New ed., 1985. Chicago, IL: University of Chicago Press, 1988.

Rigney, Ann. "Plenitude, Scarcity and the Circulation of Cultural Memory." *Journal of European Studies* 35, no. 1 (2005): 11–28.

———. "Remembering Hope: Transnational Activism beyond the Traumatic." *Memory Studies* 11, no. 3 (2018): 368–80.

"Robert Ellis Thompson, 1844–1924." *Penn University Archives & Records Center*. https://archives.upenn.edu/exhibits/penn-people/biography/robert-ellis-thompson. Accessed June 3, 2021.

Roddy, Sarah. *Population, Providence and Empire: The Churches and Emigration from Nineteenth-Century Ireland*. Manchester: Manchester University Press, 2014.

Rodechko, James Paul. *Patrick Ford and His Search for America: A Case Study of Irish-American Journalism, 1870–1913*. New York: Arno Press, 1976.

Rothberg, Michael. "From Gaza to Warsaw: Mapping Multidirectional Memory." *Criticism* 53, no. 4 (2011): 523–48.

———. *The Implicated Subject: Beyond Victims and Perpetrators*. Stanford, CA: Stanford University Press, 2019.

———. "Multidirectional Memory in Migratory Settings: The Case of Post-Holocaust Germany." In *Transnational Memory: Circulation, Articulation, Scales*, edited by Chiara De Cesari and Ann Rigney, 123–43. Berlin: Walter de Gruyter, 2014.

———. *Multidirectional Memory: Remembering the Holocaust in the Age of Decolonization*. Stanford, CA: Stanford University Press, 2009.

Rouse, John. "Donahoe, Patrick." In *Dictionary of Irish Biography*, edited by James Maguire and James Quinn. Cambridge: Cambridge University Press, 2009. https://doi.org/10.3318/dib.002681.v1.

Rynne, Frank. "The Great Famine in Nationalist and Land League Propaganda, 1879–1882." *Mémoire(s), identité(s), marginalité(s) dans le monde occidental contemporain* 12 (2015). https://doi.org/10.4000/mimmoc.1864.

———. "Young Ireland and Irish Revolutions." *Revue Française de Civilisation Britannique* 19, no. 2 (2014): 105–24.

Sadlier, J. (Mary Anne). *Bessy Conway; or, The Irish Girl in America*. New York: D. and J. Sadlier, 1861.

Saglia, Diego. "From Gothic Italy to Italy as Gothic Archive: Italian Narratives and the Late Romantic Metrical Tale." *Gothic Studies* 8, no. 1 (May 2006): 73–90.

Said, Edward W. *The World, the Text, and the Critic*. Cambridge, MA: Harvard University Press, 1983.

Sen, Amartya. "The Political Economy of Hunger: On Reasoning and Participation." *Common Knowledge* 25, no. 1–3 (April 2019): 348–56.

———. *Poverty and Famines: An Essay on Entitlement and Deprivation*. Oxford: Clarendon Press, 1981.

Shannon, James P. *Catholic Colonization on the Western Frontier*. New Haven, CT: Yale University Press, 1957.

Shrout, Anelise Hanson. *Aiding Ireland: The Great Famine and the Rise of Transnational Philanthropy*. New York: New York University, 2024.

Sigerson, Hester. *A Ruined Race; or, The Last MacManus of Drumroosk*. London: Ward and Downey, 1889.

Silvestri, Michael. *Ireland and India: Nationalism, Empire and Memory*. Basingstoke: Palgrave Macmillan, 2009.

Sims, Norman. "The Problem and the Promise of Literary Journalism Studies." *Literary Journalism Studies* 1, no. 1 (Spring 2009): 7–17.

Smith, David A., Ryan Cordell, and Elizabeth Maddock Dillon. "Infectious Texts: Modeling Text Reuse in Nineteenth-Century Newspapers." *2013 IEEE International Conference on Big Data* (2013): 86–94.

Snell, J. G. "Dougall, John." In *Dictionary of Canadian Bibliography*. Vol. 11. Toronto: University of Toronto/Université Laval, 2003. http://www.biographi.ca/en/bio/dougall_john_11E.html. Accessed January 3, 2023.

Steele, Karen, ed. *Maud Gonne's Irish Nationalist Writings 1895–1946*. Dublin: Irish Academic Press, 2004.

Sullivan, Alexander Martin. *New Ireland*. 3rd ed. New York: Peter F. Collier, 1878.

Sullivan, Eileen. "Community in Print: Irish-American Publishers and Readers." *American Journal of Irish Studies* 8 (2011): 41–76.

Sullivan, Thomas D. *Recollections of Troubled Times in Irish Politics*. Dublin: Sealy, Bryers and Walker, 1905.

Sumner, David E. *The Magazine Century: American Magazines since 1900*. New York: Peter Lang, 2010.

Sutherland, John. "Keary, Annie [Anna Maria]." In *The Longman Companion to Victorian Fiction*, edited by John Sutherland, 346–47. Harlow: Longman, 1988.

Terdiman, Richard. *Present Past: Modernity and the Memory Crisis*. Ithaca, NY: Cornell University Press, 1993.

Thompson, Robert Ellis. *Social Science and National Economy*. Philadelphia, PA: Porter and Coates, 1875.

Thompson, Spurgeon. "Famine Travel: Irish Tourism from the Great Famine to Decolonization." In *Travel Writing and Tourism in Britain and Ireland*, edited by Benjamin Colbert, 164–80. Basingstoke: Palgrave Macmillan, 2012.

Tilley, Elizabeth. *The Periodical Press in Nineteenth-Century Ireland*. Cham: Switzerland, 2020.

———. "Periodicals in Ireland." In *The Routledge Handbook to Nineteenth-Century British Periodicals and Newspapers*, edited by Andrew King, Alexis Easley, and John Morton, 208–20. Abingdon: Routledge, 2016.

"Todd-Bowden Collection of Tauchnitz Editions." *British Library*. http://vll-minos.bl.uk /reshelp/findhelprestype/prbooks/tauchnitz/index.html. Accessed December 11, 2022.

Trevelyan, Charles. *The Irish Crisis*. Reprinted from the *Edinburgh Review*, January 1848. London: Longman, Brown, Green and Longmans, 1848.

———. "Letter of Charles Edward Trevelyan to Thomas Spring-Rice, Lord Mounteagle." *Treasury*, October 9, 1846.

Tulloch, John, and Richard Lance Keeble. "Mind the Gaps: On the Fuzzy Boundaries between the Literary and the Journalistic." In *Global Literary Journalism: Exploring the Journalistic Imagination*, edited by Richard Lance Keeble and John Tulloch, 1–19. New York: Peter Lang, 2012.

Turner, Mark W. "Periodical Time in the Nineteenth Century." *Media History* 8, no. 2 (2002): 183–96.

———. "The Unruliness of Serials in the Nineteenth Century (and in the Digital Age)." In *Serialization in Popular Culture*, edited by Rob Allen and Thijs van den Berg, 11–32. Abingdon: Routledge, 2014.

Tuyll, Debra Reddin van. "John Mitchel: Transnational Journalist." In *Politics, Culture, and the Irish American Press, 1784–1963*, edited by Debra Reddin van Tuyll, Mark O'Brien, and Marcel Broersma, 117–31. Syracuse, NY: Syracuse University Press, 2021.

Tuyll, Debra Reddin van, Mark O'Brien, and Marcel Broersma, eds. *Politics, Culture, and the Irish American Press, 1784–1963*. Syracuse, NY: Syracuse University Press, 2021.

Upton, William C. *Uncle Pat's Cabin; or, Life among the Agricultural Labourers of Ireland*. Dublin: M. H. Gill, 1882.

———. *Uncle Pat's Cabin: A Story of Irish Life*. New York: Upton, 1914.

Walsh, Tom. "The National System of Education, 1831–2000." In *Essays in the History of Irish Education*, edited by Brendan Walsh, 7–43. London: Palgrave Macmillan, 2016.

Ward, Margaret. *Maud Gonne: A Life*. New ed., 1990. San Francisco, CA: Pandora, 1993.

———. *Unmanageable Revolutionaries: Women and Irish Nationalism*. New ed., 1983. London: Pluto Press, 1989.

Wertsch, James W. "The Narrative Organization of Collective Memory." *ETHOS* 36, no. 1 (2008): 120–35.

———. *Voices of Collective Remembering*. Cambridge: Cambridge University Press, 2002.

Whately, Richard. *Introductory Lectures on Political Economy, Being Part of a Course Delivered in Easter Term, MDCCCXXXI*. London: B. Fellowes, 1831.

White, Hayden. "The History Fiction Divide." *Holocaust Studies* 20, no. 1–2 (2014): 17–34.

———. *Metahistory: The Historical Imagination in Nineteenth-Century Europe*. New ed., 1975. Baltimore, MD: Johns Hopkins University Press, 1973.

Wiener, Joel H. *The Americanization of the British Press, 1830s–1914: Speed in the Age of Transatlantic Journalism*. Basingstoke: Palgrave Macmillan, 2011.

Wills, William Gorman. *The Love That Kills*. London: Tinsley, 1867.

Wood, T. F. *T. F. Wood & Co's Canadian Newspaper Directory*. Montreal: T. F. Wood, 1876.

Zeitlin, Froma I. "The Vicarious Witness: Belated Memory and Authorial Presence in Recent Holocaust Literature." *History & Memory* 10, no. 2 (Fall 1998): 5–42.

INDEX

Lindsay Janssen is Assistant Professor at the Department of Modern Languages and Cultures at Radboud University. She is editor with Marguérite Corporaal, Christopher Cusack, and Ruud van den Beuken of *Global Legacies of the Great Irish Famine: Transnational and Interdisciplinary Perspectives* (2014); with Christian Noack and Vincent Comerford of *Holodomor and Gorta Mór: Histories, Memories and Representations of Famine in Ukraine and Ireland* (2012); and with Marguérite Corporaal and Christopher Cusack of *Recollecting Hunger: An Anthology* (2012).

FOR INDIANA UNIVERSITY PRESS

Anna Garnai, *Editorial Assistant*

Sophia Hebert, *Assistant Acquisitions Editor*

Samantha Heffner, *Marketing and Publicity Manager*

Brenna Hosman, *Production Coordinator*

Katie Huggins, *Production Manager*

Alyssa Lucas, *Social Media Manager*

Darja Malcolm-Clarke, *Project Manager/Editor*

Bethany Mowry, *Acquisitions Editor*

Dan Pyle, *Online Publishing Manager*

Michael Regoli, *Director of Publishing Operations*

Leyla Salamova, *Artist and Book Designer*